NORDIC EXPLORATIONS:
FILM BEFORE 1930

NORDIC EXPLORATIONS: FILM BEFORE 1930

Edited by John Fullerton and Jan Olsson

John Libbey

JL

LONDON · PARIS · ROME · SYDNEY

Aura

Cataloguing in Publication Data

Nordic Explorations: Film Before 1930 (Stockholm studies in cinema)

1. Motion picture industry – Scandinavia – History
2. Motion pictures – Scandinavia – History
I. Fullerton, John   II. Olsson, Jan

791.4'3'0948

ISBN: 1 86462 055 2 (Hardback)

Published by

John Libbey & Company Pty Ltd, Level 10, 15–17 Young Street, Sydney, NSW 2000, Australia.
Telephone: +61 (0)2 9251 4099 Fax: +61 (0)2 9251 4428
e-mail: jlsydney@mpx.com.au

This volume constitutes volume 5, numbers 1/2 of *Aura. Film Studies Journal.*

Printed in Malaysia by KumVivar Printing Sdn Bhd, 48000 Rawang, Selangor Darul Ehsan.

Contents

Foreword

The cities that the silent-film community have come to regard as shrines – Brighton and Pordenone – were far from obvious candidates to be placed on the historiographical map. In retrospect, Brighton embodies the divide, a set of differences in terms of 'before' and 'after' a paramount FIAF event. If the advent of cinema blew asunder the old prison world (as Walter Benjamin eloquently puts it), then Brighton shattered the fortress model of archivism, to paraphrase Penelope Houston, by configuring a point of no return *vis-à-vis* the scholarly world. From a modest beginning (attendance-wise only, that is), Pordenone, by the sheer drawing-power of unrivalled retrospectives, has turned into an annual pilgrimage, attracting a colourful mix of communities devoted to the diversity of visual pleasures offered in Cinema Verdi. On a global map, Sacile is virtually indistinguishable from Pordenone. Hence, our friends behind Le Giornate del Cinema Muto will continue to explore silent cinema with the same burning passion and intellectual playfulness as always. When Nordic cinema, once showcased in Pordenone, returns to Le Giornate, Sacile is base camp for the exploration. This volume, and its mapping of the Nordic cinemas, is dedicated to the indispensable project of Le Giornate – irrespective of zip code.

Jan Olsson

Acknowledgements

Nordic Explorations: Film before 1930 is a joint publication between John Libbey & Company and *Aura*, with financial support from Humanistisk-samhällsveten-skapliga forskningsrådet (The Swedish Council for Research in the Humanities and Social Sciences), and has been prepared for the *Nordic Explorations – Into the Twenties* retrospective organised by the 1999 Giornate del Cinema Muto. We gratefully acknowledge the support of the Danish Film Institute, the Finnish Film Archive, the Norwegian Film Institute, The National Library of Norway, the Stills Archive, Swedish Film Institute, Svensk Filmindustri, the Storm P. Museum, Copenhagen, Biologiska Museet, Stockholm, and the National Library of Russia, St. Petersburg for assistance in providing illustrations. We thank Elaine King for her work as editorial assistant and for preparing the Index, and Bart van der Gaag for technical assistance digitising some of the illustrations.

John Fullerton and Jan Olsson

Notes on the Contributors

Antti Alanen has been film programmer at the Finnish Film Archive since 1985. He is author of *Marilyn – alaston naamio* (Marilyn: A Naked Mask, 1985), *Sähköiset unet – musiikkivideo eli miten taiteesta tuli pop* (Electric Dreams: The Music Video, or, How Art Became Pop, 1992), *MMM elokuvaopas* (MMM Film Guide, 1995), and co-author with Asko Alanen of *Musta peili – kauhuelokuvan kehitys Prahan ylioppilaasta Poltergeistiin* (Dark Mirror: The Development of the Horror Film from *The Student of Prague* to *Poltergeist*, 1986). He is currently working on *Pop Eye: Music Video and the Post-Modern Condition*.

Peter von Bagh is a film director working mainly for television (with a special interest in compilation). He is author of over twenty books including his dissertation *Vertigo* (1968), a history of Finnish cinema, and a history of world cinema, a new edition of which was published in 1998. He was Director of the Finnish Film Archive (1967–70), Program Director (1970–84), editor-in-chief of *Filmihullu* (1971), and since 1986 has been Artistic Director of the Midnight Sun Film Festival.

Bo Berglund is a film historian and researcher. As a freelance writer he has contributed more than twenty essays on early film to *Classic Images*, *Griffithiana*, *Sight and Sound*, *Cinegrafie*, and *Aura: Filmvetenskaplig tidskrift*.

Mats Björkin received his doctorate from Stockholm University in 1998 with a dissertation on Americanism and film culture in Sweden during the 1920s, *Amerikanism, bolsjevism och korta kjolar: Filmen och dess publik i Sverige under 1920-talet*. He is currently involved in a project to create a new archive of non-fiction film in Sweden, and teaches film and television in the Department of Cinema Studies, Stockholm University.

Thomas C. Christensen is Curator at the Danish Film Archive. He has contributed essays to *Sekvens* (1995/96 and 1997), and is currently researching the Danish silent film industry and film restoration.

Marina Dahlquist is a doctoral candidate in the Department of Cinema Studies, Stockholm University, researching images of invisibility in silent film. She has published in *Chaplin* (1996), and *Aura: Filmvetenskaplig tidskrift* (1997, 1998).

Marguerite Engberg is Professor Emerita of the Department of Cinema Studies, Copenhagen University, and is the author of *Dansk stumfilm: de store år* (2 vols, 1977) and *Registrant over danske film 1896–1930* (5 vols, 1977 and 1982). Her study of Asta Nielsen, *Filmstjernen Asta Nielsen* has recently been published, and she is currently working on a tinted reconstruction of Carl Th. Dreyer's film *Blade af Satans Bog*.

Bo Florin is a Research Fellow at Stockholm University working on a project dealing with Victor Sjöström's Hollywood years. He is author of *Den nationella stilen: studier i den filmens guldålder* (1997), and has contributed to the *Encyclopedia of European Cinema* (1995), *Lähikuva* (1995), *Aura: Filmvetenskaplig tidskrift* (1995, and as guest editor 1998), and *Film History* (1999).

John Fullerton is Associate Professor in the Department of Cinema Studies, Stockholm University. He has published many essays on early Swedish film, and edited *Celebrating 1895: The Centenary of Cinema* (1998). As Series Editor with Jan Olsson of Stockholm Studies in Cinema for John Libbey, he co-edited *Moving Images: From Edison to Webcam* (1999), and is a contributor to *Allegories of Communication: Intermedial Concerns from Cinema to the Digital* (forthcoming).

Tom Gunning is a Professor in the Department of Art History and the Committee on Cinema and Media at the University of Chicago. He is the author of *D.W. Griffith and the Origins of American Narrative Cinema: The Early Years at Biograph* (1991), and a forthcoming study of the films of Fritz Lang for the BFI. He has written over one hundred articles on early cinema, film genres, and avant-garde cin-

ema. He was a founding member of Domitor, the international association for the study of early film.

Gunnar Iversen is Associate Professor in Film Studies at the University of Trondheim – NTNU. He is co-author with Hans Fredrik Dahl, Jostein Gripsrud, Kathrine Skretting, and Bjørn Sørenssen of *Kinoens mørke, fjernsynets lys: Levende bilder i Norge gjennom hundre år* (1996), a social history of the moving image in Norway, edited *Nærbilder* (1997), an anthology of close readings of Norwegian feature films, and contributed to *Nordic National Cinemas* (1998).

Åsa Jernudd is a doctoral candidate in the Department of Cinema Studies, Stockholm University where she is researching a dissertation on film as educational practice. She teaches at Örebro University where she is co-ordinator of Film Studies. She recently published *Oscar Olsson's African Films: Examples of Touristic Edutainment* (1999).

Ib Monty was Head of The Danish Film Museum 1961–97, and editor-in-chief of *Kosmorama* 1960–67. He has published *Notes of Leonardo da Vinci* (1954), a three volume anthology of film essays (1964–66), and *The Letters of Asta Nielsen 1911–72* (1998). He has recently completed *Benjamin Christensen in Hollywood*.

Jan Nielsen is a musical consultant and researcher working for the Danish Radio Corporation. He has contributed to a variety of musical works and encyclopedias including *Rock nu* (1983), *Verdensrock* (1986), *Politikens Jazzleksikon* (1987), *Politikens Folkleksikon* (1989), *Politikens Rockleksikon* (1992, 1995), and has contributed essays on Danish film to *Aura: Filmvetenskaplig tidskrift* (1998) and *iichiko intercultural* (1999). He is currently researching the history and production of SRH/Filmfabriken Danmark.

Jan Olsson is a Professor of Cinema Studies at Stockholm University. He has published extensively on Scandinavian silent cinema, and is currently working on a cross-cultural reception project focusing on Los Angeles and Stockholm.

Astrid Söderbergh Widding is Associate Professor in Cinema Studies at Stockholm University. Her publications include *Gränsbilder* (1992), *Sätt att se*

(1994), *Flyktigheten fångad* (1996), *Blick och blindhet* (1997), and *Stumfilm i brytningstid* (1998).

Bjørn Sørenssen is Professor in Film Studies at the University of Trondheim – NTNU. His main research areas are in film history, documentary history and theory, and new media technology. He is co-author with Hans Fredrik Dahl, Jostein Gripsrud, Gunnar Iversen, and Kathrine Skretting of *Kinoens mørke, fjernsynets lys: Levende bilder i Norge gjennom hundre år* (1996), a social history of the moving image in Norway. He has written textbooks on film and television, and has contributed to a number of English, Swedish, and French anthologies on documentary, film history, and new media.

Gunnar Strøm is Associate Professor in Film and Television at Volda College, Norway. He has published books and articles on animation, documentary, and music video, and is currently researching animation in Norway before 1940. He is Vice President and former Secretary General of the international animation association, ASIFA.

Casper Tybjerg is Assistant Professor in the Department of Film and Media Studies, University of Copenhagen. He has written a number of essays on Danish silent cinema including contributions to *Schwarzer Traum und weisse Sklavin: Deutschdänische Filmbeziehungen 1910–1930* (1994), *A Second Life: German Cinema's First Decades* (1996), and *Celebrating 1895* (1998). He is currently researching a study of Carl Th. Dreyer and problems in the writing of film history.

Gösta Werner is Professor Emeritus of the Department of Cinema Studies, Stockholm University. He has directed seven feature films and about sixty short films, and has written several books and essays on film history, especially the Swedish silent period. He has also published studies of the Swedish writers Stig Dagerman and Hjalmar Bergman, and has written on James Joyce, Marcel Proust and Hugo von Hofmannsthal. His latest book is *Viking Eggeling, Diagonalsymfonin: spjutspets i återvändsgränd* (1997), with a key to the unsolved mystery of this film.

Introduction

John Fullerton

In 1986, Le Giornate del Cinema Muto organised a major respective of Danish and Swedish cinema before 1919. *Nordic Explorations: Film before 1930* is both a successor to the publication which accompanied the 1986 retrospective (in that some of the essays presented here explore terrain that was first mapped in the earlier retrospective), and an example of the ways in which the study of the medium has changed since the mid-1980s.

Although the time-frame of this anthology reaches back to some of the earliest years of cinema, the research presented here concentrates on the period from 1906 to 1930. The anthology is organised more or less chronologically by way of national production: Denmark, Finland, Norway and Sweden. One central organising principle, however, is common to the essays in the collection: they represent the best of current research which is being conducted, in most cases, in Nordic countries. Rather than present a group of essays which mark completed research (if such a point can ever be attained), this collection brings together material that is innovative and exploratory, representing a field of study that is becoming ever more broad in its concerns.

In the first part of the collection, Jan Nielsen examines the opportunities the Russian market offered Filmfabriken Danmark in the mid-1910s. The ways in which the company secured development in the Russian market, responded to different national tastes and cultural preferences, and responded to the impact of the First World War and the February and October revolutions on trade with Russia are assessed. The international focus for historical investigation is also considered by Thomas C. Christensen in his study of the decline of Nordisk Films Kompagni in the latter part of the 1910s. Arguing that earlier historiographies which privileged an artistic explanation for the decline of Nordisk failed to take account of the financial imperative, Christensen demonstrates that the company, in attempting to develop a vertically integrated industry in Germany, suffered a dramatic reversal of fortune in the period after 1917 when the company's international prospects were challenged by the formation of Ufa. Consideration of the international arena also provides the background for Casper Tybjerg's discussion of *Blade af Satans Bog*, a film in which Carl Theodor Dreyer has often been accused of being politically conservative. With a detailed exposition of the background to the production, Tybjerg argues that in the context of post-war Europe and the October Revolution, Dreyer sought to displace the moral imperative from one of class to one of conscience. The international context of reception forms the central concern of Ib Monty's examination of the work of Benjamin Christensen in Germany during the 1910s and 1920s. Through examining trade papers and national newspapers, Monty tracks the critical success that attended Christensen's work both as an actor and director. In a study of the

comic couple, Long and Short, Marguerite Engberg provides an overview of the comedies Lau Lauritzen directed for Palladium in the 1920s. Particular attention is given to the context of reception in the US and in Spain. In the last essay in this part of the collection, Bo Berglund discusses the rich findings that he and Jan Olsson recently made in the Norwegian Film Institute and the National Library of Norway. Berglund also identifies some hitherto 'lost' Danish films in the collection of the National Film and Television Archive, London.

Finland and Norway, who received no attention in the 1986 retrospective, are considered in the following two sections of the anthology. Arguing that silent cinema in Finland owes its inspiration to the work of Mauritz Stiller, Antti Alanen argues that *Sången om den eldröda blomman* provided Finnish cinema in the 1920s with a rich iconography that not only thematised the 'national project', but also demonstrated that the Nordic landscape was the nation's supreme production value. Developing this argument, Peter von Bagh examines the ways in which images of the Finnish landscape promoted a spontaneous if not atavistic response in the historical spectator, one which remained an emblem of Finnish cinema for much of the silent era. In this respect, Bagh argues, Finnish cinema tapped a profound sense of the archaic, an aspect of Nordic culture which may also be observed in some of the films by Dreyer.

Three quite different considerations inform the discussion of Norwegian cinema in the third part of the collection. Attentive to the ways in which the Film Theatres Act of 1913 gradually promoted the municipalisation of cinema ownership in Norway which, it is argued, generated insufficient production capital for sustained national production, Gunnar Iversen examines the careers of the three Egede-Nissen sisters who worked as actors, producers, and directors in Germany in the late 1910s. In the context of a male dominated industry, Iversen argues that Aud, Gerd, and Ada established a considerable track record not only as female pioneers but as artists and producers. Developing Tom Gunning's notion of the 'view' aesthetic, Bjørn Sørenssen examines the Norwegian travel

film genre in the 1920s. Relating the development of the genre to the growth of tourism in the latter part of the nineteenth century, Sørenssen argues that the Norwegian landscape powerfully evoked an iconography that helped construct a sense of national identity for the newly independent country. Such images not only fuelled the sense of national pride that attended Norwegian polar exploration, but helped reconcile the development of a modern industrial state with more traditional views of its national culture. In the final essay in this part of the collection, Gunnar Strøm provides a comprehensive overview of the development of the animated film – from caricature and cartoon to paper, cel, and live-action animation – and gives a detailed account of the development of Danish and Norwegian animation in film advertisements in the 1920s.

In the final part of the book, Swedish film provides the focus for discussion. In an essay on the Swedish Pathé subsidiary, Pathé filial, Jan Olsson maps the complex pattern of film exhibition, exchange and sales that typifies early permanent-site exhibition in Sweden in the period from the mid-1900s to the mid-1910s. Drawing upon the pedagogic notion of cinema as 'object lesson', Åsa Jernudd discusses the close relation between the development of non-fiction cinema in the mid-1910s with the cinematic reform movement in Sweden, censorship, and the establishing of a School Film Department by Svensk Filmindustri in 1921. Jernudd's essay closes with a case study of the exhibition and reception of *Among Wild Men and Beasts* shot by a Swedish expedition to British East Africa in 1919–20. The discussion of non-fiction film is also considered in the following essay where John Fullerton investigates the ways in which fiction and non-fiction film drew upon a popular fascination in earlier entertainment forms to promote multimedial visuality. Fullerton goes on to argue that interest in the ways in which optical technologies mediated the world was taken up by a later generation of avant-garde practitioners who began to theorise in what ways optical technologies could envision the world differently. Some of the ways in which Swedish film departed from the example of American cinema are

assessed in Astrid Söderbergh Widding's study of four films by Georg af Klercker in the mid-1910s. Arguing that Klercker's films not only adopted a variety of practices, Söderbergh Widding demonstrates that Klercker adopted quite complex formal solutions for films which, in narrative terms, were relatively unsophisticated. Stylistic concerns in the films of Sjöström are central to Tom Gunning's discussion of *Mästerman*. Attentive to the ways in which characterisation and interiority stage a drama of deferred desire, Gunning offers a highly nuanced reading of a film which, he argues, is a neglected masterpiece of world cinema. Gösta Werner's analysis, undertaken with Bengt Edlund, of Viking Eggeling's *Diagonal Symphony* proposes that the film's structuring principle accords with that of classical sonata form in music. Perhaps, Werner speculates, the film was planned as the first movement of a symphony? In the following essay, the concept of abstract form is further pursued by Marina Dahlquist in her discussion of the motif of snow in Swedish film in the 1920s. In a wide ranging discussion of little-known films, Dahlquist explores the ways in which snow was used as a symbol for a national landscape, and argues that snow also thematised the elemental relation of man to landscape and purification. The concern with national identity and the ways in which identity may be read as culturally specific is considered in Bo Florin's essay on Sjöström's career in Hollywood during the 1920s. Examining Swedish trade papers and privileging a close reading of *The New York Times*, Florin analyses the shifting discourse that attended Sjöström's career in the US, and evaluates responses to his films on either side of the Atlantic. In the final essay of the collection, Mats Björkin examines a film produced by the Tullberg Film company in Sweden in the early 1920s which was introduced by the young Greta Garbo. Björkin, noting that much non-fiction film still awaits restoration, argues the centrality of industrial film in promoting a highly ideological view of Sweden to an international audience in the 1920s.

In their engagement with issues at the forefront of film scholarship, the essays brought together for *Nordic Explorations: Film before 1930* make a timely contribution to the more general study of cinema, and offer insight into the research agendas of universities in the Nordic countries. The essays also collectively challenge many of the assumptions that characterised film historiography 'before Brighton', opening up territory ripe for investigation not only in the Nordic countries but farther afield. 'Before Brighton', after Sacile: who can tell what new vistas will open up, what new fields await exploration? Here's to Le Giornate del Cinema Muto – long may it continue to define and explore new boundaries!

1
Denmark

A Small Danish Player in a Big Market: A/S Filmfabriken Danmark's Output in Russia, 1913–1917

Jan Nielsen

Danish Radio Corporation, Rosenoernsallé 22, 1999 Frederiksberg C, Denmark

The mere fact that Filmfabriken Danmark *did* operate in Russia has been known for years, established in Marguerite Engberg's taped interview (24 May 1955, The Danish Film Museum) with the founder of the company, Johan Christensen. Although Christensen's various statements about the company and its activities are extremely detailed and generally well structured, the overall value of this interview lies in the way in which it has opened up avenues for further investigation. Such opportunities prompted me some years ago to embark on research into Det Skandinavisk-Russiske Handelshus/Filmfabriken Danmark.[1]

In the interview Christensen remarks that the company had sales in Russia, yet no details are given. Still, I found it important to include Russia among the foreign markets on which my investigations of the company's sales and distribution are focused. The fact that the company originally began producing films as Det Skandinavisk-Russiske Handelshus (The Scandinavian-Russian Trading Company – hereafter SRH) is not directly linked to the company's activities in Russia but, as shown below, this origin was nonetheless important. As the company's archives seem to be lost to posterity, an account of the company's production output in the Russian market is drawn principally from Russian trade journals.

Filmfabriken Danmark's first-hand access to the Russian film market was a sort of 'christening gift'. Prior to the SRH years, the company's business-manager-to-be, Johan Christensen (Fig. 1), was at the age of eighteen stationed in Siberia by his then employer, E.F. Esmann (later known as the Siberian Trade Co.). Christensen operated from a base in Kurgan in 1903–04, and in Omsk in 1904–06 as a salesman in butter and agricultural machinery. During these apprentice years he not only learned Russian, but gained insight into the Russian mentality and, of utmost importance, insight into the ways of commerce and negotiation in this foreign market. His private letters leave us with the impression of a shrewd and tough negotiator. Thus equipped, Johan Christensen founded SRH in Copenhagen in October 1908, a trading company that imported various articles including hides and

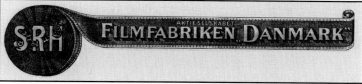

co-managers, Vilhelm Glückstadt and Kay van der Aa Kühle (both of whom were also directors), decided to reorganise and extend the company's operation, and on 14 March 1913 A/S Filmfabriken Danmark was formed (Fig. 2). Operating as a limited company, copying facilities were added, and the company was ready to add an important link to its production chain: the world-wide exploitation of the company's negatives, a task that was to be conducted by a network of well-chosen agents, the Russian agent being no exception.

Studying the European and American trade journals from the 1910s, several articles point to trade persons with insight in describing the Russian market, in providing statistics, and in giving details relating to Russian film production, the film trade, and cinemas in Russia. Over the years several writers made an effort to persuade native companies to try their luck in Russia, to open a branch or at least have their production distributed through traders in the major Russian cities.[2] The articles made no attempt to conceal the difficulties, and reading about the various obstacles that would have to be confronted for those working to extend into the Russian market, especially during the First World War, was sufficient to keep many companies away. The Russian market might be tempting, but it also entailed many risks.

Pathé Frères, never reluctant to capitalise on opportunities, had opened a branch, which example was soon followed by Itala, Gaumont and Cines. Thiemann and Reinhardt, former representatives of Gaumont and Cines, respectively, soon established their own film trade. These companies began producing films in Russia as well, using the resources offered by Russian actors, and thus limiting the expenses and difficulties of importing productions from their native countries. Those not daring to open a branch were left with a number of obstacles. First and foremost there was the problem of coping with Russian business methods and the Russian language. Later, the War added new obstacles for those both inside and outside Russia. Still, some foreign production companies and owners of world rights managed to have selected films circulated in Russia by local traders during

other goods from Russia. With this commercial focus, SRH was the only early Danish film company established with concerns other than those of film. However, in 1909 SRH turned its attention towards the film industry when it began to act as an exclusive agent for several major foreign film companies before venturing into film production. By 1911, SRH had released its first production, opened a studio, and controlled a major Copenhagen cinema, Victoriateatret.

Caution and circumspection were central to Johan Christensen's business philosophy during his years with SRH and with Filmfabriken Danmark. Every expansion of the company's activities was followed by retraction in other fields. Every risk of loss was to be shunned. Accordingly, mass copying and further exploitation of SRH's negatives was considered too risky. After the films had been shown in Victoriateatret, the company sold the negatives and the world rights, excluding those in Scandinavia. Noticing the success of these films in foreign markets, Christensen and his

the 1910s, e.g. Nordisk Films Kompagni until this company opened a Russian branch in 1915.

Compared with companies like Pathé Frères, Itala, Gaumont and Cines, Filmfabriken Danmark was in every respect a small company. However, the company was to play an impressive role in the Russian market in 1913, the year in which it began operating in Russia. Given that Filmfabriken Danmark never opened a branch in Russia yet managed to circulate almost all its production output from 1913 and 1914 of films produced outside Russia, Filmfabriken Danmark's business record in Russia was unprecedented.

Filmfabriken Danmark enters the Russian market

SRH/Filmfabriken Danmark produced a total of ninety-six dramatic films that were released between 1911 and 1919.[3] The first twenty-five of these (1911–13) were SRH productions of which SRH sold the negatives and the world rights excluding Scandinavia. With the exception of the final five titles, the circulation of any SRH film in Russia (and elsewhere) was outside the scope of SRH's operations, and therefore not in the market due to Filmfabriken Danmark's strategies.[4] Of the following seventy-one Filmfabriken Danmark productions, the company managed to market thirty-two in Russia, a rather good percentage considering that Russia introduced a blockade of foreign films in 1916 and became progressively less stable from 1917. Where other companies either refrained from attempting, or suffered in trying to make a breakthrough, every step towards entering the Russian market seems to have run smoothly for Filmfabriken Danmark, that is, from preparing material and transporting it, to negotiating and making deals. Though the actual number of copies sold in any of Filmfabriken Danmark's markets is generally unclear (since the company archives are apparently lost), we may presume that the Russian market was one in which Filmfabriken Danmark felt especially comfortable, and was one which they monitored at close range.

Whereas individual buyers only managed to bring a handful of the SRH films into the Russian market,[5] Filmfabriken Danmark's appearance was a *tour de force*. In the trade journal, *Cine-Fono* (17 August 1913), the following notice appeared:

Danmark.
The company produces films in Copenhagen.
Branch in Moscow.
Telegram address: Cine-Fono
2–3 box office smash hits pr. month.

Likewise in Russia, Filmfabriken Danmark had managed to find an agent with impact: the editor of *Cine-Fono*, S.V. Lure. This alliance was brilliant to say the least. Not only did Lure possess insight into the Russian industry and trade, he also edited one of the leading Russian trade journals. Lure was mainly occupied with editing, and since his film trade was almost exclusively limited to Filmfabriken Danmark's films, his advertising for the company's films shows a high degree of attention and dedication.

The advertisement cited above claims that Filmfabriken Danmark operated from a branch in Moscow, but according to my research into Filmfabriken Danmark's distribution in other markets, branches abroad seem to have been outside the company's business practice. It is unlikely, therefore, that, working from *Cine-Fono*'s address, the company operated a branch *per se* with staff and office financed by Filmfabriken Danmark. However, as cooperation with Lure seemed so focused on circulating Filmfabriken Danmark's production, a mild exaggeration of this kind, perhaps aiming to boost the impact of the company, is quite understandable. The advertisement promised the coming release of *Krigskorrespondenter* (War Correspondents, 1913)[6] and *Haanden, der griber* (The Hand Which Grasps, 1913), titled *Vojénnyje korrespondénty* (War Correspondents) and *Svétskij vor* (The Gentleman Thief) in Russia. From then on any coverage of Filmfabriken Danmark's films (advertisements, synopses, etc.) was presented under the names of 'Danmark', 'Lure' or 'Danmark/Lure'.

Fitting in

Once they had gained entry into the Russian market, the success of Filmfabriken Danmark's films was a question of whether these met the taste and preferences of the Russian cinema audience. Contemporary sources concerning this phenomenon are found in a variety of statements given by Russian intellectuals as well as Western trade persons reporting from Russia. In his book, *Early Cinema in Russia and its Cultural Reception*, Yuri Tsivian offers examples from Gurevich's 'Theatre Essays' in *Slovo* (6 November 1907) and 'Flanyor's' 'Cinematography' in *Zhizn'* (5 January 1909) describing Russian (urban) taste and preferences as well as the different repertoires of city-centre and outer city cinemas.[7] Later reports describing Russian (urban) taste are offered by foreign trade persons such as W. Whattam Ward in 1915. In this instance, however, no distiction is made between central and outer city cinema preferences:

> It is essential for manufacturers and producers to realise that the average Russian taste is ultra refined, which is accounted for by the fact that the average cinemagoer has been in the predominating percentage, a member of the educated class. Dramas depicting life in high society, and combining elegance in dresses and settings find a ready market. The same applies to detective, sensational and spectacular dramas. War dramas are also greatly in demand, but these must possess

the hallmark of originality, and must in no event be stage screened.[8]

Interviewed in 1916, W. Whattam Ward offered the following description of Russian taste:

> The Russian taste is ultra refined, and only first-class foreign productions can hope to do anything at all. Dramas must not be less than 5–6 reels, and must be distinguished by superb acting and settings. Russia is the market for super-films – i.e. films exhibiting colossal technical scenes in which branch the Russian producer is only in the elementary stage. Such films must, however, not be faked, or this would immediately spell failure.[9]

Though Gurevich's and 'Flanyor's' statements are given, respectively, in 1907 and 1909 there are several overall similarities to Whattam Ward's description. However, the different nature of the statements is to be noted. Gurevich and 'Flanyor' are intellectuals, critics, reviewers, but still *viewers*, members of the Russian cinema audience, and their statements are deductions based upon the reception of what was shown and to whom. Statements from the trade like Whattam Ward's, on the other hand, are filtered somewhat differently, focusing on the technical aspects, the making and designing of films, in order to adapt these as mere commodities to Russian consumers.

Filmfabriken Danmark, however, did not produce any 'super-films', since the films offered by the company were mostly 3- or 4-reelers. The company's 1914 production offered a vast array of genres, i.e. detective stories, westerns, sensation dramas, delicate social dramas, comedies and farces (Fig. 3). The occurrence of the *complete* 1914-production (eighteen films) thus also indicates that Filmfabriken Danmark's productions were of a broad competitive nature also in the Russian market. With the insight of S.V. Lure as guarantor for the exploitation of the films offered to the Russian market, it is obvious that Filmfabriken Danmark's production suited the parameters of taste of the Russian cinema audience. Entry into the Russian market included, among other things, the technical problem of producing intertitles in Russian.

As the Russian industrial apparatus for this process was strained and only worsened during the First World War, it is very likely that Johan Christensen's mastery of the Russian language came in handy. No sources reveal this as a fact, but several things make it an apt deduction. Firstly, Filmfabriken Danmark had the means of translating all written material, including titles and intertitles, and printing the latter in the company's laboratory. Such a procedure would help to advance the availability of the films in Russia. Secondly, relations with S.V. Lure would hardly have been so easy if he had been left with the task of preparing intertitles. Thirdly, the majority of the main titles of the films were directly translated from the Danish main titles.

From studying Filmfabriken Danmark's synopses in the Russian trade papers it becomes evident that no special measures were taken by Filmfabriken Danmark to alter or adapt the content of an individual film to the Russian market. The synopses are more or less translations of the original Danish programme texts, even with the Danish or English character names unchanged (the appearance of somewhat awkward versions of these names is mainly due to problems of transliteration). The so-called Russian *un*happy endings, in some cases especially shot for the Russian market by companies such as Nordisk Films Kompagni, were not, according to the synopses, considered necessary for marketing Filmfabriken Danmark's films in Russia.

One film, however, was presented differently in Russia. The film *Letsind* (Carelessness, 1914), which in Russia was titled *Sjértva sjenikhá* (The Lover's Sacrifice), proves interesting for several reasons. The film recounts how a young painter, Knud Juel, is engaged to a younger country girl, Johanne whom he brings to his home in the big city. City life is a new, but amazing experience for Johanne. Visiting a café, Knud notices a pale but elegant gentleman who seems to follow their every move. When leaving the café, the man, Rudolf Edwards, secretly follows the couple to their home. He writes down their address in his notebook. He is a white slave trader. During the next few days he keeps Johanne under surveillance and registers at the same Berlitz language class which she is attending. He soon wins her confidence, and persuades her to leave Knud to go with him to his mother in a foreign city where she is to marry Rudolf. Johanne writes a letter to Knud and leaves with Rudolf.

Shortly after her arrival, she finds out that Rudolf's mother leads a criminal organisation. Johanne attempts to escape but is held prisoner. Some months later she is forced to help the gang commit a theft, for which she is rewarded. She manages to send a letter to her mother. Knud reads the letter and notices the post stamp. Immediately he leaves by ocean liner to find Johanne. On board the liner he recognises Rudolf among the passengers. He decides to follow him. Thus he locates Mrs. Rudolf's apartment, enters in disguise, and is reunited with Johanne. He calls the police, and the gang is arrested, but Rudolf manages to escape onto the roof of the building, followed by Knud. Rudolf makes his escape from the roof by walking along the telephone wires connecting to the next building. He loses his balance and falls into the street far below. Knud who has followed Rudolf onto the wires is likewise in danger, but is saved.

For its release in Russia, the film was given an alternative title, *Nad bésdnoj* (Over the Abyss), and in *Cine-Fono* (1 March 1914) an advertisement announced: 'Anyone remembering the success of *The Abyss* should order …'. SRH had earlier bought the negative of *Afgrunden* (The Abyss, Kosmorama, 1910) after the film had been released in Denmark,[10] and in the *Cine-Fono* advertisement, Filmfabriken Danmark directly attempted to be associated with the masterpiece, though the plot of *Letsind* bears no resemblance to that of *Afgrunden*.[11] Napoleon [Moscow] (an associate of Lure's) chose to go all the way and market the film specifically under the alternative title of *Nad bésdnoj*, as reported in *Vestnik Kinematografii* (7 May 1914). According to a review in the Danish newspaper, *Politiken* (14 February 1914), some scenes of *Letsind* were apparently shot in St. Petersburg. Whether these scenes were studio shots or outdoor shots cannot be judged since no copy of the film is known to exist. However, since the majority of the film's many actors are cast

in indoor scenes (Fig. 4), I presume that interiors were shot in the company's studio in Hellerup, Copenhagen, and cleverly blended with shots of outdoor St. Petersburg scenery.

Decline

According to the Russian trade journals, the business relation with S.V. Lure apparently came to an end in October 1915. No statement on this matter is given, but from November 1915 the company's films appeared in advertisements by RDK (Russko-Datskaja cinematografitjeskar kontora) based in St. Petersburg and Moscow.

The sudden decline in the company's output in Russia which may be observed during Lure's distribution in 1915 was to continue rapidly. By October 1915, Lure had promoted only the three first films produced that year. When RDK took over in November, three additional films from the 1915 production year were distributed, though they did not follow the Danish order of release.

Although Filmfabriken Danmark's output in 1915 (twenty-two films) was larger than in previous years, only six seem to have been released in the Russian market, and many of these releases were delayed. There are, no doubt, many reasons for the decline. With the relatively high output of 1915, the company was able to maintain supply in 1915 but, even with a good contact such as Lure, Film-

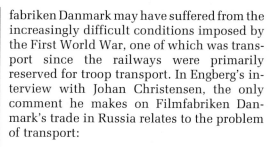

fabriken Danmark may have suffered from the increasingly difficult conditions imposed by the First World War, one of which was transport since the railways were primarily reserved for troop transport. In Engberg's interview with Johan Christensen, the only comment he makes on Filmfabriken Danmark's trade in Russia relates to the problem of transport:

> In 1914 during the War I travelled to Russia. This was the only way we could get in touch with them, going there with two big trunks full of films. ... So I travelled through Sweden, going through northern Sweden and Finland to Russia – St. Petersburg. I arrive in Karumbi, as the railway station is called, in pitch darkness. It was around Christmas, so there was practically no light except from the snow. As I arrive in Karumbi I find that my trunks are in Stockholm. I was very affected by this fact and telephoned Stockholm, to a good connection we had there, and he managed to have the trunks sent up. I had to spend two days waiting for this film material which I needed to bring across and sell in Russia. When I finally received it, I move on ... and arrive in St. Petersburg, as the calendar turns 'red' – so it is called over there, when it is a national holiday – turned red for thirteen days. So I had a fourteen day involuntary stay in St. Petersburg. Then it took a month and a half to sell these trunks of films, but I succeeded; that was the only way to do it. And what was sold there was actually mainly the sensation-films, because sensationfilms were what they wanted to see over there. Absolutely![12]

As sending films by mail had been prohibited in Russia from early spring 1914, and transport problems in Russia only worsened during the First World War, courier transport was considered to be one of the better ways of getting films into Russia, however inconvenient. According to the dates of the advertisements in the Russian trade journals, Lure apparently received the bulk of films in December 1914. RDK probably received the three films from the 1915 production year in December 1915.

As stated above, Christensen's recollections about SRH and Filmfabriken Danmark are, in general, very detailed. However, my research into other fields of the company's activities proves that Christensen, in recalling incidents forty years earlier, can be slightly inaccurate when it comes to stating the exact year in which an incident occurred. In this case I am inclined to believe that Christensen's trip to Russia took place close to Christmas 1915 and not 1914. Lure was the company's agent in 1914 and in the light of the successful distribution of films in 1914 and his business relation with Lure, it was hardly necessary for Christensen to spend a month and a half negotiating a bargain with him. With RDK, however, this may have been necessary. Unlike Lure, RDK (formed in 1915) was a fully fledged film trading company, distributing films from companies such as B. & C. (British & Colonial), Selig, Pasquali, Kinografen, and others, thus devoting no special attention to the promotion of Filmfabriken Danmark's production. Whether RDK was willing to take the complete 1915 cycle of production or not, it was still up to Filmfabriken Danmark to make decisions and estimate the gains from this export. In addition to losses in exchange, the Russian government took several measures which also affected the foreign film trade in Russia, no doubt making the Russian market less attractive to Filmfabriken Danmark. During the First World War it became increasingly more difficult to remit foreign currency from Russia, and bargaining on long-term credits became standard.[13] Both Filmfabriken Danmark as well as RDK would likely have selected the individual films carefully.

The three films from the 1915 cycle of production appear in RDK's advertisements as late as February 1916, during which year no further promotion for Filmfabriken Danmark is seen. Other obstacles aside, this no doubt arises from the ban on Danish films that the Russian Government introduced in March 1916 after disclosure that several Danish films were apparently of German origin.[14]

After the ban was lifted, RDK promoted one last series produced by Filmfabriken Danmark: *Nattens Datter II* (Daughter of the Night, 1916) and *Nattens Datter III* (1917), these appearing in almost identical advertisements in *Cine-Fono* (January and February 1917) titled *V víkhre prestuplénij (I-ja sérija)* and *V víkhre prestuplénij (II-ja sérija)* (In the Vortex of Crime I–II).[15] The two advertisements mark the end of Filmfabriken Danmark's distribution in the Russian market. By the end of December 1916 and through early January 1917, economic strikes hit district after district, famine swept, and Russia soon found herself collapsing into the turmoil of the February Revolution (23–28 February 1917) leading to the October Revolution and the Bolshevik take-over of power.

Hoping for a break

In spite of the increasingly chaotic state of things, Western trade refused to give up the idea of breaking into the Russian market. In 1917, on the brink of the Revolutions, a hope was fostered. In an essay, 'The World's Film Markets',[16] in *The Bioscope* (11 January 1917), 'H.N.' predicted improved trade in Russia after the War:

> So far none of us know exactly what terms of peace will be, but in the last few weeks one important fact has been allowed to emerge. By common agreement among the Allies, Russia is to have Constantinople.

In the essay, 'H.N.' saw in Constantinople a natural gateway to Southern Russia, and further predicted that a firm based in Constantinople would dominate the Balkans and thus break the Austro-Hungarian control of the film trade in the Balkans as well. Alas, none of the above was ever to happen. Russia did not get Constantinople, and by the end of the First World War she suffered losses of territory. To Filmfabriken Danmark, the outcome of the War for Russia made no difference. The company was faced with growing economic problems, and was forced to cut its production plans drastically. Filmfabriken Danmark produced six films in 1917, five in 1918, and only two films in 1919. With low production output, Filmfabriken Danmark concentrated mainly on the markets of Central Europe, Spain, and Japan, and left the bigger and more productive companies to

struggle with the diminishing business opportunities in Russia.

After the October Revolution and at the end of the First World War, Russia was thrown into civil war (1918–20), although the period of New Economic Policy made foreign film trade possible in the years 1921–28, during which period ideological control was relatively lax. However, in 1922, Lenin required that strict supervision be exercised over the character of the films exhibited throughout Russia and that films should be registered. The large number of foreign films imported during these years (especially by the Leningrad organisation, Sevzapkino) were therefore neutralised of their bourgeois ideology and re-edited. In November 1927, Sovkino (the department which had taken over the monopoly of film distribution throughout the Union from Goskino in 1922) was criticised by the Soviet leaders for showing foreign films. By March 1928, N.E.P. was terminated during the first Five Year Plan (of 1925), and ideological control was increased. Film production and the film trade in Russia was about to enter a different stage, one that would last for a lifetime.

Notes

1. My research into the history and production of Det Skandinavisk-Russiske Handelshus/Filmfabriken Danmark aims to uncover the company's enterprises and personnel in detail. As the aim of this essay is to focus on Filmfabriken Danmark's activities in the Russian market, I have chosen to omit all facts and details that do not advance the principal concerns of this essay. Thus the general chronology of the company is only sketched here.

2. A major problem for British and American companies during the 1910s seems to have been that the majority of foreign films entering the Russian market came via Scandinavia, primarily through Copenhagen and Stockholm, from whence few British and American films were offered to Russian agents. This issue is considered in Leonard Donaldson, 'Our Allies and the Cinema. A General Survey of Trade Conditions in the Countries at War with Germany', *The Bioscope* (11 November 1915): 637.

3. In referring to SRH/Filmfabriken Danmark productions in this essay, I present the original Danish release title, the Russian release title, and both titles translated into English. For the sake of clarity, I do not include English release titles.

4. From my research into other foreign markets in which Filmfabriken Danmark operated, it seems probable, yet not proveable, that SRH made a sort of 'trial run' with copy sales through agents some months before forming Filmfabriken Danmark. Thus it is possible that SRH exported two late examples of their production to Russia in early 1913: *Skibsrotten* (The Ship Rat, 1912) titled *Po kanátu nad morskími bojámi* (On Tightrope over the Naval Action), and *Den sorte Varieté* (The Black Variety, 1913) titled *Tjórnoje varjeté* (The Black Variety). The former was circulated by a major Russian trader/manufacturer, Tanagra (St. Petersburg), the latter by S. Mintus (Riga).

5. Among the SRH films distributed in Russia was *Den flyvende Cirkus* (The Flying Circus, 1912). This negative was bought by Nordisk Films Kompagni, and the film, titled *Smejá i sjénsjtjina* (The Snake and the Woman), was circulated by associates of Nordisk's agent, Thiemann & Reinhardt, from April 1912.

6. *Krigskorrespondenter* was the first of the company's films to be released and distributed as a Filmfabriken Danmark film.

7. As Yuri Tsivian observes: 'As early as 1907 the theatre critic Lyubov Gurevich drew attention to the difference between cinemas "intended for the intelligent classes" and "the whole net of small cinemas serving the general public, which were scattered throughout the streets and alleys of the outer city districts" '. According to Gurevich, the latter were 'particularly interesting as far as their selection of pictures was concerned'. They showed sentimental melodramas and, generally speaking, 'anything with a touching or moving content'. At the beginning of 1909 another observer, a reviewer for the newspaper *Life* writing under the pen-name *Flanyor* [Flâneur], provided a more detailed picture of the specific repertoires of the central and outer city cinemas. Audiences outside the centre preferred 'predominantly realistic films, whether dramatic or comic; they didn't like anything to do with fairy tales, witches, magical transformations, etc.' Newsreels, on the other hand, were widely

shown. The same author reported the details of the repertoires of the central Moscow luxury cinemas: 'If it's a drama, then it's got to be a particularly bloody one. If it's a comic picture, it's caricatured to the *n*th degree. The public enjoys the depiction of horrors, catastrophes, and of course anything even remotely to do with sex.' ... [A]mong Russian intellectuals of the 1910s it was a matter of good taste to prefer the outer city districts to the centre.', Yuri Tsivian, *Early Cinema in Russia and its Cultural Reception*, trans. Alan Bodger (London, New York: Routledge, 1994), 26–27.

8. W. Whattam Ward, 'Some Opinions on the Film Industry', *The Bioscope* (25 November 1915): 870–871.

9. Unsigned interview with W.W. Ward, 'The Russian Market. Difficulties and Possibilities. A Critical Survey', *The Bioscope* (21 December 1916): 1159. A similar description is given in 'Russlands kinematographische Industrie', *Der Kinematograph* (3 April 1918).

10. SRH immediately sold the negative to Düsseldorfer Film-Manufaktur Ludwig Gottschalk who turned it into a gold mine.

11. In 1914 *Afgrunden* was again used by Filmfabriken Danmark in a bid to gain wider recognition, as the company's Italian agent, Mario Ferrari & C. (Milano), in *La Vita Cinematografica* (7 April 1914) mentions 'successi con L'ABISSO' in the context of promoting the Danish company.

12. 'I 1914 under krigen rejste jeg til Rusland. Det var den eneste måde, vi kunne komme i forbindelse med dem, det var ved selv at rejse derover med to store kufferter fyldte med film. ... Og jeg rejste jo gennem Sverige, skulle op gennem Nordsverige og Finland til Rusland, Skt. Petersborg. Jeg kommer jo til Karumbi, som jernbanestationen hedder, og der var jo bælgravende mørkt. Det var jo ved juletid, så der var stort set ikke andet lys, end det der kom fra sneen. Da jeg kommer til Karumbi, så står mine kufferter i Stockholm. Jeg var jo meget ubehageligt berørt og fik telefoneret ind til Stockholm til en god forbindelse vi havde derinde, og han sørgede så for, at kufferterne kom op. Så måtte jeg ligge to dage og vente på detteher filmsmateriale, som jeg absolut skulle have med over og sælge til Rusland. Da jeg så endelig fik det, rejser jeg videre ... og kommer til Skt. Petersborg, da kalenderen så bliver 'rød', som man siger derovre, når det er helligdag – blev rød i tretten dage. Så jeg fik fjorten dages ufrivilligt ophold i Skt. Petersborg.
   Så varede det halvanden måned for at få solgt de der kufferter med film, men det lykkedes jo altså, og det var altså den eneste måde. Og det der blev solgt der, det var i virkeligheden hovedsageligt sensationsfilmene, for det var sensationsfilm, de ville se derovre. Dét var det!', Johan Christensen interviewed by Marguerite Engberg, 24 May 1955, The Danish Film Museum.

13. Unsigned interview with W.W. Ward, 'The Russian Market. Difficulties and Possibilities. A Critical Survey', *The Bioscope* (21 December 1916): 1159. The difficulty of getting money out of Russia also affected the Russian film industry, as well as those foreign companies producing films in Russia, since this obstacle, together with the difficulties of transport, hindered the import of filmstock, items which the Russian government, according to W. Whattam Ward, had classified 'Unnecessary luxuries'.

14. Quoting the St. Petersburg newspaper *Birschevija Vjodomosti*, the ban on Danish films was described in the Danish newspaper *Politiken* (9 March 1916) and in *Lichtbild-Bühne* (18 March 1916).

15. *Nattens Datter* (I) titled *Dotj nótji* (Daughter of the Night) was produced in 1915 and was distributed by RDK in the same year. However, as Filmfabriken Danmark's idea of turning *Nattens Datter* into a series concept seems to have been initiated with the production of Part II in 1916, Part I had already passed into oblivion (also with the Danish cinema audience). Thus it was decided to leave out the *Dotj nótji*-concept in Russia, and present *Nattens Datter* Parts II and III as Parts I and II, and change the main title.

16. The full title of the article is 'The World's Film Markets. An Examination of Present Conditions & Future Prospects. Changes that Peace may bring. Constantinople the Market for Eastern Europe?', *The Bioscope Foreign and Export Supplement*, *The Bioscope* (11 January 1917): vi–ix.

Nordisk Films Kompagni and the First World War

Thomas C. Christensen

Danish Film Institute, Vognmagergade10, 1120 Copenhagen K, Denmark

In recent years, early Scandinavian film has attracted a number of scholars and researchers. Paradoxically, most of the published studies have been researched by academics from outside Scandinavia with little or no knowledge of the primary written documents. Thus the studies are based on extant films and an older canon of historical writing on Scandinavian cinema. A recent example is *World Cinema* from 1996, in which Paolo Cherchi Usai bases his description of the stylistics of the Scandinavian silent cinema on canonical films and only mentions two published sources: Marguerite Engberg's pioneering book, *Dansk stumfilm*,[1] and the aesthetically-focused anthology, *Schiave bianche allo specchio*.[2]

Though an aesthetic approach is valid when it comes to a description of the stylistic characteristics and developments of cinema, there is an unfortunate belief among some film historians that the aesthetic approach is primary in all aspects of film history. The goal of this essay is to describe the demise of the dominant Danish film company, Nordisk Films Kompagni, which took place during the First World War. In my opinion, most descriptions of the Danish silent film industry are inadequate, at least in regards to methodology and causal reasoning. My main criticism is that it is impossible to explain financial success or failure by aesthetic judgment of the films produced by a certain company. Certainly the number of films produced and the quality of these films in terms of artistic investment and production value may indicate the financial standing of a film company. However, of 496 films produced by Nordisk in the period 1914–16, only 51 survive.[3] Of these, 22 are actualities and 29 fictional films. The aesthetic judgements of these central years of Danish cinema are thus based on approximately 10 per cent of total production.

The focus of this essay is of an industrial and financial nature, as I believe this aspect of the period 1908–16, often referred to as the 'golden age' of Danish cinema, deserves a more thorough analysis. In the following, I will first chart earlier descriptions of the demise of Danish cinema during the First World War, and then survey the industrial and financial demise of Nordisk through the 1910s.

The fact remains that Nordisk in 1913 held a dominant position in the world film market, whereas the company's production was marginalised and decimated to less than five films annually in the last half of the 1920s. The still-dominant explanation of the demise of Nordisk, and thus the 'golden age' of Danish cinema,[4] is that Nordisk did not manage to shift its production schedule from popular melodramas to more high-brow films when American film companies changed cinema into an art form with the creation of films like

D.W. Griffith's *The Birth of a Nation* (1915). This shift in audience taste supplemented by the distribution problems in connection with the War comprise the main explanations for the end of the 'golden age' of Danish cinema.

Ebbe Neergaard's *Historien om dansk film*[5] describes most of the conditions regarding the demise of Nordisk, and Ebbe Neergaard bases his description of the financial dealings of Nordisk on the memoirs of Ole Olsen.[6] How Ufa took over the German interests of Nordisk in 1917 is accounted for in broad terms, and Ebbe Neergaard also, correctly, determines that the production of Nordisk did not peak until 1916 (see Table 1).

After spending three pages in which he describes the financial factors involved in the decline of Nordisk, Ebbe Neergaard changes course and states:

> But external influences as these [the Ufa takeover] are not sufficient to describe the crisis that arose. There must have been internal problems – it must have been in the films themselves. Maybe the audiences changed without Nordisk itself changing.[7]

Ebbe Neergaard then goes on to describe extant films from Nordisk, evaluating them with regard to his own subjective ideas of quality. His conclusion is that Nordisk and Ole Olsen as head of production did not manage to change the production schedule from 'technically virtuoso entertainment' to the grander artistic productions required.

Despite having described, first, the external financial and then the artistic conditions of Nordisk during the First World War, Ebbe Neergaard finally states:

> One may ask oneself, why it was to end this way with the Nordisk film adventure, but the answer is evasive. There probably is no other answer than that Ole Olsen was a strong and domineering man, who seemed inspiring and enterprising as long as the product involved was the primitive 'Social Melodrama', whereas he did not understand how to give the freedom and encouragement needed to create great artists. The ideas he himself produced in the period were not fruitful.[8]

One may ask why Ebbe Neergaard does not

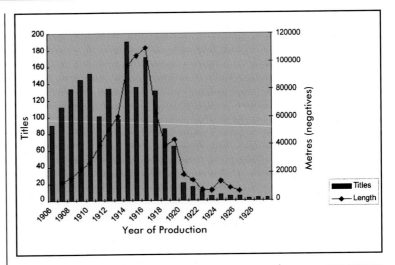

consider Olsen's own description of the period to be relevant. Maybe Ebbe Neergaard considers Ole Olsen's autobiography too self-promoting. However, in the end, Ebbe Neergaard chooses an aesthetic explanation for the financial downfall of a film company. The catastrophic decision here is that Ebbe Neergaard not only does not put Ole Olsen's financial description to the test, but that he prefers an aesthetic approach that cannot be given major significance due to the limited extant material.

Knud Rønn Sørensen's *Den danske filmindustri indtil tonefilmens gennembrud* is a marxist materialistic description of the Danish film industry in the silent period.[9] Knud Rønn Sørensen describes the corporate dispositions as they are reported by the trade paper, *Filmen*, and in the accounts of Ebbe Neergaard and Ole Olsen. Knud Rønn Sørensen regards Nordisk as an industrial enterprise striving for control and profit. This approach to Nordisk is probably the most relevant for finding the causes for the financial demise of Nordisk, and Knud Rønn Sørensen's conclusion as to why Nordisk after the War had lost its significance is clear and precise:

> After Ufa had taken over Nordisk Films Kompagni's distribution and theatre chains in Germany, the company had lost its international influence.[10]

It seems strange that Knud Rønn Sørensen's account of the period has not had greater influence on later film historians. His hand-

Table 1. Nordisk Films Kompagni: Production 1906–29.

ling of primary and secondary sources can seem a little problematic, but the methodological approach as to the business side of Nordisk and the following conclusions are precise. Maybe the answer is that the Marxist approach seemed repulsive to contemporary film historians and was therefore rejected.

The single most influential book on Danish silent cinema is Marguerite Engberg's two volume work, *Dansk stumfilm*. She states that Ole Olsen's poor artistic management 'more than the distribution difficulties caused by the world war … [was] the actual cause of the demise of Danish cinema'.[11] She thus chooses a thesis using an internal artistic explanation rather than an explanation incorporating external causes for the end of the 'golden age' of Danish cinema in 1914.

As with Ebbe Neergaard, Marguerite Engberg is of the opinion that Nordisk in 1914 lost its leading position in the world market due to Ole Olsen's lack of artistic savoir faire. Marguerite Engberg argues that Nordisk lost terrain because the company did not change its production from 'good craftmanship' to art at a point in film history when cinema established itself as an art form.[12] The influence of the War is included in Marguerite Engberg's account, but is intentionally marginalized in comparison with the criticism of Ole Olsen's poor artistic management. Marguerite Engberg's thesis is closely connected to the idea that cinema in the 1910s shifts from being commercial merchandise to works of art. Her objection towards Ole Olsen is underscored by the fact that she dates the beginning of the 'golden age' of Danish cinema with the shift to features. The feature film was innovated in Denmark by Fotorama with the production *Den hvide Slavehandel* (The White Slave Trade, 1910). Thus, according to Marguerite Engberg, it was not Nordisk, but a small innovative company that changed the history of cinema in Denmark. The 'golden age' was based on the swift transition to features, but ended with the artistic inflexibility of Ole Olsen, underscored by the artistic failure of *Atlantis* (1913).

A more current account of the Danish film industry in the 1910s is found in Niels Jørgen Dinnesen and Edvin Kau's *Filmen i Danmark*, in which they state:

The decline from the middle of the 1910s had … *both* financial *and* artistic causes. Nordisk could not compete with the Americans and Ufa since they, with a basis in large domestic markets, could invest more in their products. And should one succeed in selling a product, as Swedish cinema was able to at this point, one was relegated to the existing channels of distribution, which the major companies dominated.[13]

This seems to me to be a clear account of the workings of the film industry in the late 1910s and 1920s. However, since the scope of their history is the Danish cinema after the emergence of sound, Dinesen and Kau do not clarify what caused the market to take this turn, which would prove near fatal to the Danish silent film industry. The fact remains that Nordisk declined from a position as one of the world's largest film companies in 1913 to almost non-existence in the 1920s. The question to be answered is thus: what caused this massive decline?

I propose that the Danish film industry's decline was neither caused by artistic incapacities nor the War *per se*. Rather, I believe the actions of American producers, and German government intervention to secure control of their domestic markets, to be the main causes of the decline of the Danish film industry in the 1910s. I do not find that aesthetic reasons can be used as the main explanatory model. The artistic paths followed by the industry seem to be caused by financial decisions rather than the reverse.

In the United States the Motion Picture Patents Company (also known as the Trust) was founded in 1908 to standardise national distribution. One of the main achievements of the Trust was that it managed to put a cap on the number of European short subjects released in the United States. According to Robert Anderson: 'The Patents Company was responsible for ending the foreign domination of American screens'.[14] Though Nordisk had a weekly release schedule in the US of two shorts, and also supplied features to independent distributors in the 1910s, the scheme did not allow for expansion. I have, elsewhere, in a paper on the influence of European features in the United States, shown that

European features, contrary to common belief, were never allowed to dominate the American market.[15] With the creation of national feature distributors such as Paramount in 1914, the barriers to entry created by the American film companies were so restrictive that the American market no longer held much financial importance for European companies. Thus, there were already in the early 1910s strong efforts by American companies to gain control of their domestic market. This was of course an effort which affected all European producers, not just Nordisk.

The efforts by the Americans to gain control of their own market seem, I believe, to have spurred Ole Olsen of Nordisk to move towards vertical integration, even before the Americans did. In Denmark the formation of theatre chains was virtually impossible due to legislation. Small theatre chains did exist until 1922, but were of little financial importance. Also, Nordisk had relinquished its rights to the Scandinavian distribution of their films to Fotorama as a trade-off in connection with *The White Slave* (1910) copyright infringement.[16] Thus, Nordisk turned its efforts to the large German market.

Reading the Danish trade paper *Filmen*, little seems to indicate that Nordisk's efforts in Germany were hindered in any major way by the break out of the First World War in 1914. Also, the fact that Nordisk's production did not stagnate until 1916 seems to indicate a distinct optimism regarding the future. In the following, I will trace the efforts of Nordisk to create for itself a market in Germany, much like American companies were trying in the United States.

At the general assembly of Nordisk Films Kompagni on 26 May 1914, Ole Olsen stated: 'The company has, in order to maintain its leading position on the world market, been forced to spend much more money on artistic assistance and equipment than previously.'[17] In spite of the increased costs, a dividend of 33 per cent was granted to the stockholders. Not even a slight cue as to the War to come can be found in the minutes of this meeting which was dominated by continued optimism.

However, just a few months later, *Filmen* reported:

> The war that now rages over Europe has with one blow paralysed all business and with it, of course, also the film industry. … For the time being, almost all shipment is impossible, and the large film factories in Germany and France have had to cease production.[18]

Danish production companies were reported as continuing their production schedules, for the time being, shelving most of the prints to wait for better times.

Six months after the beginning of hostilities, on Monday 15 February 1915, *Filmen* took a retrospective overview:

> Immediately after the breakout of the war, all film trade practically stopped, but actually only a little time passed before even the warring parties got the film business back in some shape again and trading with bits and pieces started. The French factories received the hardest blow, and have not yet been capable of picking up even a semblance of their previous production.[19]

In the same issue of *Filmen*, it was reported that Nordisk was to expand its share capital from 2 million Danish kroner to 4 million Danish kroner. Ole Olsen declined from publicly announcing how the money was going to be used. Six months later, *Filmen* reported that:

> 'Nordisk' has recently reached an agreement with the two German factories known to produce the best living images, 'Projections Actien Gesellschaft Union' and 'Oliwer [sic] Film Gesellschaft m.b.H.', in order to jointly exploit film production.[20]

Filmen expands further on the arrangement, stating that since Nordisk runs offices all over Germany, the two factories mentioned in the article have seen the advantage of joining efforts. The distribution of all three companies would, through the established contract, be centralised in one distribution company in the German market. Since PAGU owned a large number of theatres in Germany, the arrangement caused quite a stir in German film circles.

At the general assembly in Nordisk in June 1915, the effects of the War can be traced through a declining surplus. In the fiscal year 1913/14 the surplus was 1,497,683.75 Danish kroner and in the year 1914/15 it had declined to 674,873.62 Danish kroner.[21] Despite the diminishing result, there was general optimism, and the rather large number of films awaiting distribution was expected to reap quite substantial profits 'when the times got better'.

In the autumn of 1916, Nordisk once again expanded its share capital. *Filmen* reported that the expansion from 4 to 8 million kroner in share capital had caused a great deal of concern, especially in Germany, and the trade paper, in an interview, allowed Ole Olsen to explain how the money was going to be used:

> What we intend to do with the new capital, and what we can tell the public, is to get film distribution, also in Germany, in our own hands, hereby establishing a direct link between the theatres and our company. This is what the American companies have already done, with the result that distribution and middle men have disappeared, but also with the result that the American market is closed to all foreign companies. The fear that the American system should also get the European market in its power after the war has preempted the Nordisk Films Co. to its actions. The United States now has a large number of finished negatives on hand, and will at the first opportunity throw these onto the European market at prices that exclude any European competition. This would mean the death of European film production, an agenda which we by our actions attempt to hinder.[22]

Though Ole Olsen in the interview denies that Nordisk is buying theatres on a grand scale in the autumn of 1916, *Filmen* could half a year later report that Nordisk acted wisely when it moved to buy German theatres. The conclusion *Filmen* drew in the summer of 1917 was that without the German theatres, and the creation of the German distribution scheme, Nordisk would have had major difficulties in getting through the last few years.[23]

The result for the fiscal year 1916/17 was 622,000.00 Danish kroner, slightly less than the previous year, but the poorer than expected result was mainly caused by losses in connection with receding foreign currencies.[24] At the general assembly the poor result was, apart from losses in foreign currencies, explained by the fact that Nordisk since 1 January 1917 had been almost totally unable to export films. For the first time in history the film production branch of the company had run in the red. When the result of the 1916/17 season was positive, it was due to Nordisk's interests in other companies, which had turned a profit of 989,218.00 Danish kroner.[25]

On 1 August 1917, *Filmen* stated that:

> Nordisk Films Co. has announced that, because of the international conditions that prevent the sale of films, it has decided to cease production and lay off personnel as the films currently in production are finished.[26]

A year later, at the general meeting, summer 1918, Nordisk presented its stockholders with a dividend of 8 per cent. The company announced that:

> Every film we shoot in reality brings us substantial losses. When the company nevertheless has brought in a surplus in 1917 ... it is only because of the sale of the German interests and the profit of these until the sale (on 1 December [1917]).[27]

Nordisk was in fact forced to give up its German interests, which were bought by the new German monopoly company Ufa in 1917. The fact that Nordisk received 10 million Reichsmark for their German interests (Ufa's stock capital was 30 million Reichsmark) is witness to the size of Nordisk's German empire.

With the loss of its German companies, Nordisk lost control over its international distribution and exhibition network. In Knud Rønn Sørensen's words: 'it was, as before the war, possible to distribute quality products ... *But it had to take place through already-established channels*, i.e. it had to take place through the major companies' distribution branches, meaning that the main profits went to the already-existing production companies.'[28] Nordisk could still distribute its best films internationally, but the 'standard product' was taken over by the large vertically integrated companies. Thus, Nordisk Films Kompani during the 1910s changed its position from a leading international film company to a marginal national film company. The background for this change is to be found in external forces stronger than the otherwise healthy and innovative company itself.

As American film companies formed monopolistic structures in their domestic market, Nordisk with Ole Olsen at the helm, sought to form similar structures in Europe, in particular in Germany. Around 1915 Nordisk's endeavour seemed successful, since the German market was large enough to support such a scheme. However, the German general staff resisted the Danish company and formed Ufa in 1917, through which Nordisk had to give up its control of the well-trimmed, vertically integrated company structure.

The conclusion is that Nordisk in 1916 had faced up to the expected pressure from American film companies which was bound to come with the War's end. Nordisk, together with Oliver and PAGU had created a tight monopolistic structure in Germany. However, it was not Nordisk, but Ufa, which was to enjoy the scheme engineered by Ole Olsen. Thus, it was not the War itself, but the German government in its efforts to protect national interests that brought Nordisk Films Kompagni, and thus the 'golden age' of Danish cinema, to an end.

Notes

1. Marguerite Engberg, *Dansk stumfilm: de store år* (Copenhagen: Rhodos, 1977), 2 volumes.
2. Paolo Cherchi Usai (ed.), *Schiave bianche allo specchio: Le origini del cinema in Scandinavia (1896-1918)* (Pordenone: Edizioni Studio Tesi, 1986).
3. Marguerite Engberg, *Registrant over danske film 1896-1930* (Copenhagen: Institut for filmvidenskab, 1977/82), 5 volumes.
4. Nordisk's production amounts to well over 70 per cent of the total Danish silent film production of approximately 2500 films.
5. Ebbe Neergaard, *Historien om dansk film* (Copenhagen: Gyldendal, 1960).
6. Ole Olsen, *Filmens Eventyr og mit eget* (Copenhagen: Jespersen og Pios Forlag, 1940).
7. Ebbe Neergaard, *Historien*, 75.
8. Ebbe Neergaard, *Historien*, 85.
9. Knud Rønn Sørensen, *Den danske filmindustri (prod., distr., konsumption) indtil tonefilmens gennembrud* (Copenhagen: Institut for filmvidenskab, Copenhagen University, 1976).
10. Knud Rønn Sørensen, *Den danske filmindustri*, 100.
11. Marguerite Engberg, *Dansk stumfilm*, 9.
12. Marguerite Engberg, *Dansk stumfilm*, 9.
13. Nils Jørgen Dinnesen and Edvin Kau, *Filmen i Danmark* (Copenhagen: Akademisk Forlag, 1983), 33.
14. Robert Anderson, 'The Motion Picture Patents Company: A Reevaluation', in Tino Balio (ed.), *The American Film Industry* (Madison: University of Wisconsin Press, 1985 [1976]), 133-152.
15. Thomas C. Christensen, 'The Influence of European Feature Films in the United States 1909-1914', in *A Century of Cinema. Sekvens* (1995/96), Department of Film & Media Studies, Copenhagen University.
16. Nordisk remade the film by Fotorama, whereafter Fotorama successfully sued Nordisk. Part of the ensuing agreement consisted in Fotorama taking over all distribution of Nordisk films in Scandinavia.
17. *Filmen* 2, 16 (1 June 1914): 250.
18. *Filmen* 2, 21 (15 August 1914): 319.
19. *Filmen* 3, 9 (15 February 1915): 75.
20. *Filmen* 3, 21 (15 August 1915): 181.
21. *Filmen* 4, 17 (15 June 1916): 142.
22. *Filmen* 5, 3 (15 November 1916): 25.
23. *Filmen* 5, 16 (1 June 1917): 166.

24.   *Filmen* 5, 17 (15 June 1917): 175.
25.   *Filmen* 5, 18 (1 July 1917): 184.
26.   *Filmen* 5, 20 (1 August 1917): 214.
27.   *Filmen* 6, 17 (15 June 1918): 165.
28.   Knud Rønn Sørensen, *Den danske filmindustri*, 100.

Red Satan: Carl Theodor Dreyer and the Bolshevik Threat

Casper Tybjerg

Department of Media Studies, University of Copenhagen, Njalsgade 80, 2300 Copenhagen S, Denmark

In the summer of 1919, the 30-year-old director Carl Theodor Dreyer made his second film, *Blade af Satans Bog* (Leaves from Satan's Book) at Nordisk Films Kompagni. It was an extremely ambitious work, explicitly intended to set new standards for the young art of the cinema. The film is divided into four segments; the only recurring character is Satan, the tempter of mankind, who appears in different times and places down the ages. The first segment concerns the betrayal of Jesus, the second the Spanish Inquisition. The third segment takes place during the French Revolution – here, the revolutionaries do Satan's work; and in the final, contemporary segment, set in 1918 during the Civil War in Finland, Satan takes on the guise of a Bolshevik, preaching a gospel of hatred and destruction. At the time the film was made, world revolution seemed a real possibility to many people, and *Blade af Satans Bog* thus addressed political issues of the greatest moment.

It is worth looking at the film in this historical context. Not only will it allow us to discover some interesting parallels with other contemporary films, it will help us get a more nuanced view of one of the most significant Danish silent films. The identification of revolutionism and devilry in *Blade af Satans Bog* has made some commentators on Dreyer's work uneasy. Some writers, like Tom Milne and Edvin Kau, dismiss this aspect of the story as 'absurdities';[1] the plot of the contemporary story is judged to be 'schematic and simple-minded'.[2] Others observe that the film appears to carry a conservative message, but warn against the hasty conclusion that Dreyer was himself a reactionary. Among those making this point is Jean-Louis Comolli:

> Two explanations may be put forward: the first, perhaps a little too simple, is that Dreyer always takes the side of the weak and the oppressed against the oppressors, no matter what camp they belong to. The second is that for Dreyer oppression, with its manifestations of intolerance or violence, is all the more to be condemned and the more strongly denounced in that it stems from those who are supposedly responsible for justice, in that it is a stigma besetting good causes, and here one is reminded of Paulhan's *Lettre aux Directeurs de la Resistance*: 'It is worse when Inquisition is carried out in the name of

Good, Terror in the name of Equity, Repression in the name of Revolution.'[3]

Maurice Drouzy quotes this passage with explicit approval in his biography of Dreyer.[4] David Bordwell presents a somewhat different argument in 'Dreyer's Uses', the concluding chapter of his 1981 book on Dreyer.[5] Bordwell adduces a number of indications that Dreyer was indeed a conservative (among them, the anti-communism of *Blade af Satans Bog*), yet seeks to defend him with reference to his unique style of filmmaking: Bordwell, too, refers to Jean-Louis Comolli, this time to 'Cinema/Ideology/Criticism', a programmatic article from *Cahiers du cinéma* co-written with Jean Narboni, which discusses 'the ways in which films may be related to the dominant political ideology'.[6] Bordwell aligns Dreyer's work with their description of a type of film which is 'riddled with cracks; it is splitting under an internal tension which is simply not there in an ideologically innocuous film'.[7] More recently, Bordwell has subjected this article and the propositions it advances to scathing criticism;[8] but in the Dreyer book, his reservations are muted.

The underlying assumption for all these writers would seem to be that 'a moral man can have "no enemies to the Left" ', as the historian Martin Malia has put it:[9] they feel a need to defend Dreyer from charges of being a reactionary; implicitly, that would be a very bad thing. No one, apparently, has really wanted to acknowledge the possibility that Dreyer

may have had legitimate reasons to oppose, not oppression in general, but communist oppression, specifically. As we shall see, there are good reasons why, among all the possible guises Satan could assume in a contemporary story, that of a Bolshevik would seem a logical choice.

Influences

From the start, nearly all discussions of *Blade af Satans Bog* have compared it with Griffith's *Intolerance* because both films have four episodes and both involve big ideas. In fact, on the day the film opened in Copenhagen, a newspaper report on the film began:

> A couple of years ago, an American film, 'Intolerance', played at Paladsteatret; in brief sections from all ages, it showed how horribly intolerance had everywhere intervened in the destinies of men and nations.

> Tonight, again at Paladsteatret, will be played a film developed according to the same principles, but this one has been written by a Danish author and is performed by Danish actors.[10]

It is likely that Dreyer's decision to choose this particular project for his second film may have been influenced by seeing *Intolerance*. Griffith's 1916 masterwork could not be seen in Europe before 1918; it had its Danish premiere in November, but Dreyer first saw it during the summer of 1918, at a special screening. In 1965, Dreyer said: 'It was only after seeing *Intolerance* that the idea came to me that I might, in fact, attempt to do something analogous'.[11] Drouzy goes somewhat further. He writes of Dreyer's viewing of *Intolerance* that Griffith 'struck the most secret chords in Dreyer's mind', even if he does not tell us how he came to know this. In fact, the four-part structure (in which the episodes are presented consecutively, not intertwined with each other in Griffith's manner), like the theme, owes little to Griffith.

As Drouzy himself notes,[12] the script, written by Edgard Høyer (Fig. 1), a solicitor and successful playwright, was submitted to Nordisk Films Kompagni in October 1913 at the latest. A film more likely to have inspired Høyer is Luigi Maggi's *Satana* (Ambrosio, 1912), which similarly follows Satan's activities down the ages in four episodes: the Garden of Eden, the betrayal of Jesus, the invention of strong liquor by a medieval monk, and a modern episode entitled 'The Red Demon, or Satan in Modern Life', where the disguised Satan instigates a violent clash between capitalists and workers. He corrupts an innocent girl, Maria, so that she becomes the mistress of the steel king. The latter entrusts the management of his factories to Satan, who soon provokes the workers to a strike, led by the girl's jilted lover, Furio. Satan, claiming to be on the side of the workers, incites them to violence, and Furio kills the capitalist. He barricades himself against the police, but Satan convinces Maria to betray him. As the police storm in, Furio ignites a powder-keg, blowing up both himself, Maria, and the policemen. Satan stands on the smoking ruins and smirkingly lights a cigarette. Alas, the film has been lost.[13]

Høyer's screenplay was initially rejected by Nordisk and returned with a brief covering letter (dated 30 October 1913) to the Danish Dramatists' Association.[14] Dreyer was working at Nordisk at the time as (among other things) a screenplay reader, so it is likely that he read the script either then or some months later, when Høyer resubmitted it after the distinguished actor Karl Mantzius had caused a minor sensation by signing on with Nordisk. A letter from Nordisk to Mantzius dated 1 May 1914 reads:

> Furthermore, we permit ourselves to send you a screenplay that Mr Edgar [*sic*] Høyer submitted to us some time ago, but which we did not accept at the time, especially because it was much too long, and because certain parts of it are unsuitable. Occasioned by your engagement, Mr Høyer has now once again submitted the screenplay with the comment that nothing, after all, stood in the way of shortening it according to our needs. The screenplay does not altogether appeal to us, on the other hand we would like to hear your opinion. The third and fourth scene should in our view be dropped in case we decide to acquire and stage the film.[15]

Included with the same letter was a copy of

the novel *Guldkuglen* by Viggo Cavling, which was proposed as an alternative to *The Scarlet Pimpernel* (Baroness Orczy having refused to sell Nordisk the film rights); this would soon be developed into the film *Pavillionens Hemmelighed* with Mantzius as director and star, working from a screenplay by – Dreyer. *Blade af Satans Bog*, on the other hand, was rejected once again and returned to the Danish Dramatists' Association on 27 May 1914.[16]

It is not clear what all the episodes were at this point, nor what was meant by the 'third and fourth scene' referred to in the letter to Mantzius. Obviously, the revolution in Finland still lay some years in the future, so the contemporary tale we now have could not have been part of the original concept. In the Dreyer collection at The Danish Film Institute (DFI),[17] a draft screenplay may be found which ends with the French Revolutionary episode; it is rather tattered, however, and it may well be that pages are missing at the end. There is also a carbon copy of the same draft which consists of loose leaves and has not been stapled together: it has a cover page indicating that it consists of a prologue, five scenes, and an epilogue (but is otherwise identical to the stapled script). The French Revolution episode is divided into two parts, so it is possible that it counted as two scenes. That still leaves one episode and the epilogue unaccounted for.

We know, however, that the last, modern-day episode was only written in late 1918 or early 1919. In a contract with Nordisk dated 21 November 1918, Edgard Høyer agrees 'as soon as possible and without further remuneration to prepare a further episode, a modern story, for the screenplay. This episode must be approved by N.F.Co [Nordisk] and revised by me until N.F.Co finds it satisfactory'. In an interview a few days before the film's premiere, Høyer said: 'But this one, by the way, I wrote back in 1913 – except of course the Finnish episode'.[18] Both in this interview and in an essay about the film he wrote around the same time,[19] Høyer makes no secret of his dislike for some of the changes made to his script, but there is no mention of any complete episodes cut from the script. His complaints mainly concern the removal of the trial of Marie Antoinette, one of the biggest scenes in

his original version (Høyer was a lawyer, after all); it seems to have been cut quite late in the process, as it appears in Dreyer's personal shooting script, where he has crossed it out and scribbled 'cancelled' in the margin.[20]

The new Finnish episode carries the heaviest political freight. Georges Sadoul blamed its 'violent spirit of propaganda' on a novel by the English writer Marie Corelli on which Høyer supposedly based his script, a novel into which she 'had been able to put certain notions brought back from her journeys, as she found herself in Russia during the Revolution and returned to her country through Finland'.[21] There is no evidence for this at all: Corelli was nowhere near Russia, and published no novels between 1911 and 1923. It is persistently maintained that the film was based on a Corelli novel, and the obvious candidate is *The Sorrows of Satan* from 1895.[22] Drouzy notes that this novel has 'practically nothing' to do with the script of the film,[23] and David Bordwell writes: 'Although the credits claim that the script was adapted from a Marie Corelli novel, there is no evidence for this in the film'.[24] In fact, the credits Bordwell is referring to were probably not originals; at Nordisk, the titles for each film were written down in large ledgers, which have been preserved at the DFI Archive. According to those, the original credits ran:

Title 2: Four Tales by **Edgard Høyer**
Adapted for film by Carl Th. Dreyer

Title 3: Directed by
Carl Th. Dreyer
photographed by George Schneevoigt

No mention of Corelli here, nor does her name feature anywhere in the Danish advertising, promotional material, or programme booklets for the film. Drouzy claims that Corelli's name was used to promote the film abroad, but I have not been able to find any evidence for this. He also points out that Dreyer crossed out the words 'based on a novel by Marie Corelli' in a handout written by Erik Ulrichsen for a Film Museum presentation of the film.[25]

When the film came out in 1921, a couple of newspaper reports mention Corelli. One remarks that Høyer had 'received the impulse' for the film from a book by Corelli.[26] Another wrote: 'At the centre is Satan, provided with

the same double nature as Marie Corelli has done in her hysterical book 'The Sorrows of Prince Lucio' [*The Sorrows of Satan*], devoured by tens of thousands'.[27] What Høyer may indeed have taken from Corelli is the peculiar theological conception of Satan as a sort of reluctant undercover agent for God, doomed as a punishment for his rebellion to wander the Earth and tempt mankind, hoping against hope to meet a human who will resist his temptations, for only thus will his torments be relieved. Corelli's novel is set against the background of the English publishing world of the 1890s, and it is shot through with vitriolic attacks against both publishers and critics, whose decadent and sensual ideals, and corrupt business practices prevent the communion between the author and the great mass of readers that should be the true goal of literature. Corelli's own massive popularity and clashes with publishers and (especially) critics come through very clearly; indeed, the one person who actually manages to resist Satan's wiles, the novelist Mavis Clare, is very evidently an idealised self-portrait of Marie Corelli herself. Apart from the conception of Satan's personality, however, there are no similarities between Corelli's novel and the film.

Revolutionary terror

In November 1918, when Edgard Høyer agreed to write an additional, contemporary episode, the fear of world revolution was at its height. The social fabric of many European states had been seriously weakened by the ravages of the Great War, presenting revolutionaries with extraordinary opportunities. Before the War, the socialist parties of Europe had pledged to halt any hostilities with mass strikes: proletarians everywhere were brothers and should not kill each other in the ruling classes' wars. Thus, international working-class solidarity would preserve peace. This hope was bitterly disappointed in August 1914, when socialist deputies in parliaments across Europe voted overwhelmingly for war credits. Denmark remained neutral throughout the War, but in August 1914, the Danish Social Democratic Party was confronted with the same dilemma that confronted the socialist parties of the belligerent nations: to defend

Danish neutrality, the government asked parliament to allow a massive increase in military spending and a great expansion of the armed forces. Like the German and French socialists, the Danish party put patriotism ahead of internationalist ideals and voted for the war budget. International socialism had been dealt a crippling blow.

As the War wore on, considerable friction arose within the socialist parties between minorities of revolutionary maximalists and the mainstream, who sought reforms through parliament and in many cases joined cross-party coalition governments of national solidarity. In Denmark, the energetic party leader Thorvald Stauning joined the cabinet in 1916 as an observer-minister. Moves of this sort were much criticised from the left, especially as the privations of war made themselves felt among the working classes. Besides the vast numbers of casualities of war, severe shortages of food and sharply rising prices without corresponding pay increases were experienced across Europe; international trade dropped sharply, and the non-belligerent nations (including all the Scandinavian countries) experienced severe unemployment.

When the Bolsheviks seized power in Russia on 7 November 1917, their attempts to end the War immediately strengthened their popular appeal, outside Russia as well as inside it. A Communist Europe, however, did not seem a very encouraging prospect to most people. In Denmark, this became especially true when accounts of Red atrocities in Finland began to appear in the first week of February. There had been expectations of a clash for some time. Finland had declared independence from Russia on 6 December 1917, after the fall of the Kerensky government; tensions were already running high between right and left in Finland over the independence declaration, over the widespread food shortages, and over the maintenance of law and order (the tsarist police had ceased to function after the February Revolution). One historian writes of the Finnish Revolution: 'no one date or single event marks its beginning. The country drifted into revolution, and from early November it became virtually impossible to

avert.'[28] On 28 January 1918, a full-scale civil war broke out.

Press coverage in Denmark and elsewhere was largely hostile to the socialist side, and stories of the brutal depredations of the Red Guard were common. Among the eyewitnesses was the celebrated Danish actor Adam Poulsen, who was the manager of the Swedish Theatre in Helsinki at the time. (He appeared in a few films around 1910, including *Balletdanserinden* with Asta Nielsen.) Poulsen fled on 3 February and reached Denmark six days later. He told an interviewer:

> … there isn't really anyone here who can comprehend how terrible it is to be staying in Helsinki. In the streets there is murder and looting everywhere, so that no one can feel safe.

They force their way into peoples' homes and drag young and old men out into the streets. And once they have come outside the house, they make short work of them. They are killed right away, and afterwards the bloody corpses are dragged onto the ice, where they are stuffed down the holes in the ice.[29]

In his autobiography, Poulsen convincingly describes two killings he witnessed in the streets of Helsinki, and gives a sense of the cheapening of human life brought about by the revolutionary turmoil. He also reports a number of horrible atrocity stories, including one of a minister being tortured and crucified on the altar of his church.[30] When interviewed in 1918, Poulsen, who was a friend of several prominent Danish Social Democrats, made a point of shielding their Finnish comrades from blame:

> I hasten to say, though, that the Social Democrats have no responsibility for the killing. It is the utterly ignorant Asiatics who are now terrorizing Finland like savage beasts. They have no idea why they kill. They have at one point been given the watchword *that the entire bourgeoisie must be exterminated*, and then they shoot or stab to death everyone they meet.[31]

This terrible rumour was widely repeated; the Danish newspaper *Politiken*, associated with the governing party, ran it as a front-page headline on 18 February 1918. Most modern histories, however, make clear that it was

quite unfounded. Nonetheless, the call to exterminate the bourgeoisie seems to have circulated widely, and ordinary working-class people sometimes took it up with approval. Poulsen writes that when he left Helsinki, his kindly old cleaning lady wished him a safe journey, but she did not think that he would be coming back soon. She let him in on a secret: Helsinki had been mined and would soon be blown up. Poulsen asked what was going to happen with the inhabitants:

> To this, she replied with shocking cynicism: 'Ah, you see, Sir ... we "Reds" will take care of our own, and we will also spare all children below the age of eight, because they can be raised like we want them to be – but the rest will have their heads chopped off!'[32]

The other claim in Poulsen's interview, that 'ignorant Asiatics' – i.e. Russians – were largely to blame for the excesses, was widely accepted at the time. In fact, those who fought on the Red side were largely Finnish workers. Pro-Bolshevik Russian military units did fight in Finland, however, and Lenin and his government were eager to aid the Finnish revolutionists, even if in practice their own position was too precarious to allow them to do much. Not only were many Finns given reason to fear for their lives and property, but their patriotic sentiments were outraged, because Red rule seemed to deliver Finland into the clutches of the Russians, against whom there was widespread ethnic prejudice in Finland. Anthony Upton writes of the Russian soldiers stationed in Finland:

> The Russians were racial untouchables, and the idea of sexual relations between the servicemen and Finnish women set off incredible hysteria among the Finns.
>
> The socialists were accused of joining with these animalistic violators against their own countrymen, the very worst of all possible combinations of political and racial treason.[33]

A striking example of anti-Russian prejudice is a letter written to a film magazine in Helsinki, protesting against the many inaccuracies in the depiction of Finnish life in *Blade af Satans Bog*:

> Siri [the heroine] was dressed in a typi-cally *Russian* costume. [Her husband] Paavo's cabin was constructed from round, unhewed timber, and both in its exteriors and interiors, it looked rather too much like a Russian cabin, with its crib suspended from the roof and so on. And further: before going to bed, Siri moves to a picture of a saint hung in a corner of the room and crosses herself totally in accordance with Russian custom!
>
> A few words to the film's director, Carl Th. Dreyer: my dearest wish is that you, should you again have the notion of filming a Finnish subject, should first take the trouble to find out whether our people consists of Europeans or Negroes, for it is an equal mistake to portray Finns as Russians.[34]

The Revolution in Finland was ferociously repressed; thousands were shot, and tens of thousands jailed. In the West, this was generally seen as healthy decisiveness that had averted a great danger, not only to Finland, but to the rest of Europe as well. The article on Finland (written in 1919) in the superb *Salmonsen* encyclopaedia described this danger: 'Riven by internal struggles, the [Finnish] Social Democratic Party slid further and further into anarchy and formed an alliance with Russian Bolshevism, the purpose of which was a possible Bolshevik conquest of the Scandinavian countries and later also Central and Western Europe'.[35]

This conquest would not be carried out with ordinary troops (who had their hands full with keeping the Bolsheviks in power) but with the ghostly force of ideas. In a proclamation from early February 1918, inspired by massive anti-war strikes in Germany, Zinoviev stated: 'The red spectre of Communism is flooding the whole of Europe. The general social revolution has come. The hour of midnight has struck. We must sacrifice everything for the great fortune of taking part in this decisive struggle.'[36] The historian Eric Hobsbawm has written:

> ... the October revolution saw itself less as a national than as an ecumenical event. It was made not to bring freedom and socialism to Russia, but to bring about the

world proletarian revolution. In the minds of Lenin and his comrades, the victory of Bolshevism in Russia was primarily a battle in the campaign to win the victory of Bolshevism on a wider global scale, and barely justifiable except as such.[37]

They therefore greeted the collapse of Imperial Germany with triumphant expectations. In late September 1918, the relentless allied advances made the German High Command, who had hitherto maintained that defeat was inconceivable, admit that it was inevitable. The state rapidly fell apart. In the early days of November 1918, revolution spread across Germany; princes, kings, and the Kaiser himself were deposed. The old imperial authorities handed power to the Social Democrats in the hope that they could prevent Germany from sliding into complete revolutionary chaos, where all established institutions would be swept away, as they were in Bolshevik Russia.

In Denmark, the revolutionary Left was not a numerous group, but the actions of the syndicalists, as they were generally known, attracted much attention and concern. In February 1918, they led a group of demonstrators in a storm on the Copenhagen stock exchange, and in November, they stirred up substantial riots, even if these fell very far short of the revolutionary general strike they dreamed about. The schoolteacher Marie Nielsen, one of their leaders, wrote a euphoric article called 'The Revolution in Denmark':

> The horizon shines a fiery red, lit up by the blaze of the revolution. It will be but a moment, and – the flames will have engulfed us too.

> But from this conflagration, a new world shall rise, where justice dwells, a society in which exploiters and exploited have disappeared, and only human beings live.[38]

Having urged soldiers to mutiny, her agitation earned her a year and a half in jail. The other members of the syndicalist leadership were given similar sentences.

In Germany, there were many more serious disturbances and much harsher repression (Fig. 2). On 6 January 1919, the ultra-leftist

Fig. 2. German anti-Bolshevik propaganda poster, 'Germany's Ideal Future under Bolshevik Rule', reproduced in Ekstrabladet, *19 April 1919.*

Spartacists staged an uprising in Berlin, attempting to bring down the state. The uprising was quashed in a few days, and the Spartacist leaders Karl Liebknecht and Rosa Luxemburg were brutally killed. Over the next months, other uprisings followed in various places across Germany, culminating in the proclamation of a council (= Soviet) republic (i.e. a Communist government) in Bavaria in April. All failed dismally, but to restore order, the Social Democratic government was forced to call on militarist reactionaries; the result was artillery in the streets and hundreds of dead, many summarily executed.[39]

Across Europe, Communists inspired strikes, insurrections, and other forms of civil unrest.[40] In March 1919, they came to power in Hungary and established a council republic which lasted until August, when it was brought down by the Rumanian army. There were failed attempts to seize power in Vienna and in Switzerland during the summer of 1919. Even in Argentina, Bolsheviks took control of the capital Buenos Aires and held it for three days before being bloodily suppressed by the army.[41]

After these setbacks, Communist hopes seemed to revive in 1920, with widespread strikes in various Western countries, includ-

Fig. 3. Folkets Ven, *German poster, 1918.*

ing France, England, and especially Italy, where many factories were occupied. There were renewed risings in Germany, provoked by the militarist Kapp putsch in March, but they were ruthlessly suppressed. In Russia, after having come very close to defeat in the Civil War, the Bolsheviks finally overcame the White armies. The Red Army marched westwards, pushing back the Poles who had advanced into Russia earlier in the year. Its objective was not only to defeat Poland, but to carry the revolution into Central Europe and beyond. On 2 July 1920 the Red commander, Tukhachévskii, issued a famous order of the day, 'To the West!':

> Over the dead body of White Poland shines the road to world-wide conflagration. On our bayonets we shall bring happiness and peace to toiling humanity. To the West![42]

On 15–16 August, at the very gates of Warsaw, the Red Army was stopped; it was soon forced back by decisive defeats, dashing Lenin's fondest hopes. By the end of the year, the likelihood of a world revolution, whether brought about by revolt or invasion, seemed much diminished.

Flickers from the world-wide conflagration

In the revolutionary years, a number of films were made that warned or agitated against the menace of the Bolsheviks in various ways. A number of American examples are discussed in detail in Kevin Brownlow's book about films of social consciousness, *Behind the Mask of Innocence*;[43] some of these, as well as examples from various European countries, are described in a highly useful article by Roger Icart.[44] There are some additional German films worth mentioning. One is *Sturmzeichen*, a 1918 short about the need to defend Germany's Eastern borders from Bolshevik marauders from the East. It emphasises the threat to German women from Russo-Polish rapists.

Another is Robert Reinert's *Nerven* (Nerves, 1919), wherein 'two politicians – one a conservative, one a leftist radical – use all legal and illegal means to combat each other, leading them to suffer mental breakdowns'.[45] Family conflict is as important as Red Revolution, but there is an early scene where one of the main characters is almost summarily executed – for no apparent reason – by a band of paramilitaries with armbands and guns: it gives a vivid impression of the way terror reigned in the streets of German cities in 1919–20. Further German films touching on revolutionary themes are Ludwig Beck's *INRI – die Katastrophe eines Volkes* (1920) and Murnau's *Satanas* (1920), to which I shall return.

All these films, including those described by Brownlow and Icart, deal directly with the contemporary political scene. Of course, one might well take in the numerous films about the French Revolution made around this time (Lubitsch's *Madame Dubarry* and Griffith's *Orphans of the Storm* being the best-known), especially since *Blade af Satans Bog* also devotes an episode to the French Revolution. The whole issue of the way representations of the French Revolution were used to comment on contemporary politics, however, is too large a subject to broach here, and I will confine myself to films that were set in the present.

Icart does not mention any Scandinavian examples, but several interesting films apart from *Blade af Satans Bog* were made. The most significant, both artistically, financially, and in terms of impact, is undoubtedly *Folkets Ven* (Friend of the People) from 1918 (Fig. 3).

Produced by Nordisk Film, it had a script co-written by the well-known author Sophus Michaëlis and the general director of Nordisk, Ole Olsen himself. While Michaëlis may have done most of the writing, it was very rare for Olsen to attach his own name to films; only this one and two others were given this distinction. The film illustrates the central political conflicts of its time through the story of three brothers: Ernst, a natural leader, and convinced reformist and parliamentarian, rises swiftly to become the leader of a thinly disguised Social Democratic party; Waldo, a brawny metalworker, becomes the dupe of conniving revolutionist agitators; and Kurt, a crippled, highly-strung watchmaker, misguidedly attempts to assassinate the reactionary prime minister.

The film is a full-scale Nordisk production with the company's top male star, the Norwegian Gunnar Tolnœs, in the lead. It is arrestingly directed by Holger-Madsen (who also plays the role of the unbalanced Kurt), and is moving and powerful in its determined rejection of political violence. The horror of civil war is strikingly visualized in a few scenes shot literally next door to the Nordisk studio in Valby (Fig. 4): no distant threat, this. *Folkets Ven* also tries to show that there is a better way: late in the film, Ernst speaks to a large gathering of hostile workers, describing the benefits of a reformist policy (Fig. 5); these are shown as a series of then-and-now inserts, where deprivation is replaced with care: for instance, a thatched schoolhouse run by an unsmiling, birch-rod-wielding master is replaced by a large brick structure where teachers employ modern visual aids, displaying stuffed animals and picture placards to attentive pupils.

Fig. 4 (above). Folkets Ven, 1918. Production still, the horrors of civil war. The location is recognisably the Nordisk studio backlot in Valby.

Fig. 5 (left). Folkets Ven, 1918. Video print, Ernst speaking among the ruins of his house.

The impetus for writing the film would appear to have been the syndicalist riots in February 1918. The film was shot that summer and had its premiere in Berlin on 21 November 1918; it was first shown in Denmark a month later. The Social Democrats in both Denmark and Germany were enthusiastic about the film; the German Social Democrats would use it as a propaganda film for years.

In Norway, the producer-director-cameraman Ottar Gladtvet[46] made a film in 1918 called *Revolutionens Datter* (The Daughter of the Revolution), which was first shown in Oslo (then Kristiania) on 14 October 1918. During the War, Norway was hard hit by shortages and rising prices. In March 1918, the Norwegian Labour Party turned sharply to the left, with the radical Kyrre Grepp as new chairman, promulgating a statement in which 'the party was characterised as a 'party of revolutionary class struggle' that would not necessarily accept majority decisions in parliament, and reserved itself the right to carry out "revolutionary mass action"'.[47] In 1918 and 1919, there was considerable unrest; in April 1919, a Labour Party editor wrote hopefully that it would be only 'a question of months before the ill-treated Europe has been freed from the rusty fetters of capitalism and can enjoy her newfound freedom to the full'.[48] A full-scale confrontation, however, never came close.

Fig. 6.
Revolutionens
Datter, 1918. Video
print, the factory
burns.

Fig. 7.
Revolutionens
Datter, 1918. Video
print, marauding
Reds roam the
streets.

In Gladtvet's film, on the other hand, it does happen. Provoked by the hard-hearted factory owner Staalhammer ('Steel-hammer'), striking workers turn violent. A title states:

> A time of unrest. The class hatred that has smouldered for a long time has at last grown strong – and Staalhammer was not a man who understood how to calm the turbulent spirits. His hard treatment of the workers was well known, and it thus took only an insignificant incident to rouse the slumbering forces.

Soon, 'Anarchy triumphs'. The factory is burned down (Fig. 6), and marauding gangs of Reds roam the streets (Fig. 7). They attack Staalhammer's villa, killing him, but his daughter is saved by the hero, a worker named Albert Fjeld ('Rock') to whom she had earlier been kind. They escape to another country, where they fall in love; Fjeld wins her away from an aristocratic suitor by defeating him in a boxing match.

It is an unabashedly melodramatic film and indeed identifies itself as such at the begin-

ning. The first title calls it 'A *folkekomedie* in four acts'. *Folkekomedie* means 'popular comedy', but it is in fact the usual term for nineteenth-century melodramas of the sort with moustache-twirling aristocratic villains and young girls being chased out in snowstorms. *Revolutionens datter* is action-packed and contains quite a bit of rough-and-tumble humour: during a brawl, a blimp-like barmaid is hurled out by the Samson-like hero, and a title identifies her as 'Zepe Lina'. The film has clearly been made on the cheap (its total budget, 9000 kroner, was two-thirds of Dreyer's personal salary for directing *Blade af Satans Bog*), with flimsy sets illuminated by natural light; for the factory fire, there are just a few beams, some smoke, and a painted backdrop. On the other hand, there are some interesting real exteriors. This lively film was no success with the public, though, making only 2000 kroner for Gladtvet, who gave up making feature films.[49]

Soon after *Revolutionens datter* came another film dealing directly with the theme of political strikes and revolutionary disorder, *Vor tids helte* (Heroes of Our Time), directed by Peter Lykke-Seest, who worked as a screenwriter in Denmark and Sweden before becoming one of the most prolific of early Norwegian directors. The film opened on 13 December 1918. It has been lost, but in an interview the director spelled out its message:

> A film which events across the world have made very topical, as it refers to the syndicalist movement. It provides a foretaste in images of what we can expect if Bolshevism should prosper in a free, democratic society. The entire 'movement' [he is referring to the labour organisation] in a society like ours is an anachronism, it has no preconditions, it is without idea and cannot become anything other than mob-rule anarchy. We have treated the 'heroes' whimsically, but the jest can also carry a serious point.[50]

The film shows a violent strike provoked by a pair of brutish, shiftless rabble-rousers; after a hard struggle, the honest working-men reject the felonious agitators, who are brought to justice.

Sweden has long taken a particularl interest

in Finland; it used to be Swedish, and still has a substantial Swedish-speaking minority, who continued to occupy a dominant position in society when Finland was under Russian rule. During the Civil War, a full regiment of Swedish volunteers fought on the White side. It is evidently the revolution in Finland that furnishes the background for *Jefthas dotter* (Jeftha's Daughter, 1919); although the country appears not to have been identified (the film is lost), all the characters have Finnish names. It was produced by Skandinavisk Filmcentral, set up by the veteran Lars Björk; although the company and most of the actors were Swedish, the company's studio was in Hellerup, north of Copenhagen. The company's artistic director, Robert Dinesen, who had made a number of films at Nordisk and who directed *Jefthas dotter*, was a Dane, as was the prolific Laurids Skands, the film's screenwriter.

The film took its story from the tale of Jephthah in the Old Testament (Judges, Chapter 11), who promised the Lord to sacrifice the first creature he met upon his return home in return for victory in battle; this was his daughter, whom he indeed sacrificed. The film has a modern-day setting: 'Society is in turmoil after the great revolutionary events, and the classes stand with raised hands against each other', begins the synopsis in the film's programme booklet.[51] Jephthah has become Juhani Leno, a brilliant lawyer with a grudge against society, which he satisfies as a defence attorney, getting criminals acquitted. One of them, Aho, a murderer, stays at his castle. To quell the revolutionary unrest in the country, a strong leader is needed, and Juhani Leno is offered the job – if only he will distance himself from Aho. Instead, he decides to force society to accept Aho, and that Aho shall marry his daughter Maria. While Leno is away, Aho tries to rape her, but the man she loves saves her at the last minute; the murderer tumbles down a flight of stairs and is killed. Maria seeks out her father: 'I now know that Gustav Aho was a murderer; yet I would sacrifice myself, but God would not accept the sacrifice. Make now your own sacrifice and help your people, not in hatred and spite, but in humility!' 'And Leno under-

stands that it is the will of God' concludes the synopsis.

The film included a staging of the biblical story, with an Assyrian temple set said to be twenty-five metres high (though it does not look it in photographs), and the entire corps de ballet of the Royal Swedish Ballet performing a temple dance, led by the ballet star Ebon Strandin (who appeared as the heroine, Isabella, in the Spanish Inquisition episode in *Blade af Satans Bog*). The reviews were polite, but not enthusiastic, and the film rapidly became a notorious flop (it had apparently been very expensive to make). The critic August Brunius fired off an utterly devestating piece on the film in a theatrical magazine:

> It is in fact so perfectly wretched that one cannot help but feel oneself faced with a peculiar sort of harmony. There are probably idealistic people who, when they see such concentrated rubbish and think of all the money and all the labour of skilled and intelligent people that have gone into making it, feel a tweaking urge to go home and hang themselves. For my own part, I am deeply thankful to have seen the true … rubbish film in such a complete and opulent form. *Jefthas dotter* does not have one clever idea, not one really dramatic situation, not one spark of real acting art, not one well-photographed shot.[52]

It is difficult to say from the surviving material how much attention the film gave its revolutionary background. The programme booklet does include a still apparently showing Maria trying to make her way into parliament, her way blocked by guards with fixed bayonets; they wear armbands, one of the most characteristic features seen in pictures (both actual and fictional) of the revolutionary disturbances and civil war conditions following in the wake of the First World War.

In Germany, the Danish director Urban Gad made a two-part film called *Christian Wahnschaffe* (1921), based on a novel by Jakob Wassermann. The direction is uninspired, but the story is not without interest. The first part, *Weltbrand* (World Conflagration), takes place in 1905 and concerns Christian, the effete son of a wealthy industrialist (Conrad Veidt) who is bewitched by an exotic dancer and seduced

by the ideas she shares with her friend Ivan, a Russian revolutionary (Fritz Kortner). Ivan's bomb-throwing gets the dancer killed, and a failed uprising against Christian's father also results in misery. In part two, *Die Flucht aus dem Goldenen Kerker* (The Flight from the Golden Cage), Christian turns away from his gilded existence in disgust, and devotes himself to good works in the slums. When the selfless young woman who guided him is murdered by a brutal pimp (Werner Krauss), Christian has acquired the moral force to compel him to confess; but the resentment of the slum-dwellers against the man from the rich world wells up, and the mob tears Christian to pieces.

The red catechism: developing the screenplay

While anti-revolutionary films were quite numerous at the time, few approach the artistic importance of *Blade af Satans Bog*. Fortunately, a variety of materials have survived that reveal interesting details concerning the development of the Finnish story, which undoubtedly carries the greatest weight, both artistically and ideologically. The Dreyer Collection at the DFI Archive contains two different screenplay drafts of the Finnish episode, both entitled 'The Red Rose of Suomi [Finland]', as well as Dreyer's personal copy of the final screenplay (two other copies of the final screenplay also exist). Of the two drafts, one has numbered scenes, while the other is written in more or less continuous prose; the latter is probably the earlier of the two and will be referred to as draft I in the following – the other will be called draft II.

Draft I divides the story into two parts, the first part taking place at a factory in Helsinki in 1917; the second part still takes place at a rural station in 1918. The first part shows the outbreak of revolution and the disorder that follows:

> (Title: Turmoil in Helsinki) Picture: A gang consisting of some sailors and some Finns – all with red armbands and armed with rifles and sabres storms a shop, shoots the owner, who tries to resist, and begins looting.[53]

The Bolshevik monk, Ivan (actually Satan)

appears at the factory, inciting the workers to rebel with readings from 'The red catechism':

> The proletarian has only one God – his own will.
> The proletarian has only one Law: the one he writes himself with the capitalists' blood!
> The proletarian has only one Friend: himself. Only one enemy: all the others.[54]

Ivan then conjures up images of the revolution to come:

> Ivan points to the white wall. There, an image appears – with the title '<u>As it is</u>' – of a splendid restaurant, where roués are drinking, dancing, and eagerly flirting with dressed-up, décolleté ladies. The image changes. At the exit, freezing and ragged, stand proletarians, staring into the illuminated hall. The doorman chases them off. Then, a new image is seen with the title '<u>As it should be</u>'. In the splendid room, there are now proletarians with red armbands and heavily armed; now they are the ones to drink, dance, and 'flirt' in the most drastic way with the dressed-up demi-monde. The image changes and shows the roués from before in their very threadbare, once so elegant, outfits. One is shovelling snow – one is sitting on a waiting carriage as a coachman. One sells newspapers, etc. A couple of red guards keep them in line with their rifle butts. The image fades. – Loud cheering. Ivan is carried on the men's shoulders in acclaim. The workers rush off with him.[55]

The workers stand the factory inspector up against a wall and shoot him. Except for 'The red catechism', none of this reappears in the following versions of the script.

The second part of draft I is even more virulent in its anti-Bolshevism. Here, Ivan tries to threaten the heroine Elsa (Siri in the film) to send a telegram that will lure the Whites into an ambush:

> You too can operate the telegraph. So you will dispatch my telegram. If not, you will first see your child and your husband die. And then you will belong to Rauteniemi. Have you understood me?

She sends a warning message instead. When the Whites arrive, Rauteniemi (a Finn whose

lust for Siri drives him to join the Reds) stabs the husband to death and has another Bolshevik bayonet the infant in its crib. Elsa stabs herself just as the Whites arrive:

> Then Elsa suddenly sits up and in ecstasy seizes Finland's white flag, held by one of the White guards, presses it with her left hand to her bleeding chest, while she lifts her right hand heavenward – a fiery exhortation! Then she sinks down dead. (Intertitle) <u>The red rose of Suomi</u>. The image shows Finland's white flag imprinted with Elsa's red blood-rose.

Draft I ends with a church service; three coffins, containing Elsa, her husband, and her child are lined up, surrounded by White soldiers. The minister makes the sign of the cross, and Satan, who is present, shields his face with his hand.

Draft II jettisons the whole Helsinki section and concentrates on the events around the station. A new character appears here, Sahlstrøm, an aristocratic landowner (note the Swedish name) who is also the father of Naomi, a girl who joins the White army. He is captured by the Reds, and they conduct a trial of sorts before they shoot him. Ivan now reads from 'The red catechism' during this trial. Sahlstrøm displays aristocratic bravery of the expected sort: when he is to be shot, he 'calls out "Fire!" himself and proudly receives the deadly volley'.

While Satan again threatens Else (as she is called here) with the same words as in draft I, in this version neither husband nor child are injured. What is more, she herself survives and recovers from her wound. Naomi announces her engagement to a White guard officer, and the whole thing ends idyllically. The final scene is this:

> 66. At the end: again the image of the red rose of Suomi, worn by Satanas with an expression of peace and gratitude.

In Dreyer's final version, there are a number of differences. Dreyer ends with the death of Siri (as Elsa is now called), but her husband and child are allowed to survive. (A happy ending, where Siri survives and Naomi is united with the officer, was also made and is still extant. In the assembly list for the film, it is headlined 'Extra ending – England'.) The

Fig. 8. Blade af Satans Bog, *1921. Video print, the cross on the cover of* The red catechism.

Fig. 9. Blade af Satans Bog, *1921. Video print, Satan (Helge Nissen) orders the death of Naomi's father.*

Red Catechism is still there, and carries considerable emphasis (Fig. 8), even if there are now only two commandments; in a close-up, Satan's little prayer-book is opened, so that we can read the words printed there:

> You need fear only one God – your own will.
> You need only obey one Law: The one you make yourself with the blood of the rich.

This is the original English-language text; Dreyer also filmed Danish, Swedish, French and German versions of the little book.

Dreyer removed Sahlstrøm and his exaggerated heroics; Naomi's father is now just an ordinary peasant, and his execution takes place off-screen (Fig. 9), allowing Dreyer to emphasise Naomi's grief rather than her father's death (Fig. 10). He also got rid of all the 'Red Rose of Suomi' stuff. Though Siri still declares that she has died for her country, the literally blood-drenched nationalism of her final gesture has been removed. For that reason also, it is misleading when Drouzy (along with Comolli) use the title 'The Red Rose of

Fig. 10. Blade af Satans Bog, *1921. Video print, Naomi (Katarina Bell) embraces her father as the Reds lead him away.*

Suomi' for the Finnish episode. In his discussion of the film, he indicates that the 'Red Rose' is a poetic way of referring to Siri, but the material does not bear this out: the only 'Red Rose' is the bloodstain in Høyer's draft scripts. Neither the intertitle list, nor the programme booklet, nor the distributor's publicity folder, nor any of the other printed materials use the title 'The Red Rose of Suomi' for the last episode. The intertitle list does not give the episode a specific name; the programme booklet and the publicity folder both refer to it as 'The Red Guard'. This is certainly a more logical title, because 'Red' and 'White' have very specific connotations in this civil-war context, and 'Red Rose of Suomi' goes completely against them.

The most important change also has to do with the way Siri's death is handled. Both drafts stress Rauteniemi's eagerness to rape her, and in both cases, Satan adds the threat of rape to that of having her husband and children killed. When the Reds, having learned of the imminent arrival of the Whites, begin to panic, Rauteniemi declares that Ivan's sentence must be carried out – in other words, Elsa must be his. He takes hold of her, dislodging her clothes, so that 'her hair cascades down over her shoulders like a river of gold'. This phrase, with its unmistakable sexual connotations, appears in both drafts, but not in Dreyer's final version. In the ensuing struggle, Elsa manages to get hold of Rauteniemi's knife, and she immediately plunges it into her chest. One gets the sense that she kills herself to escape violation, the way 'white women' in imperialist fictions charac-

teristically choose death rather than be defiled by savages.

Dreyer changes this completely. The threat of rape is shifted to the background, and Satan does not use it to force Siri to send the fatal telegram. The hair that Høyer used to emphasise the sexual nature of Siri's plight was deliberately played down by Dreyer; he convinced Clara Pontoppidan, who played Siri, *not* to wear the blond wig she usually wore in movies.[56]

The lives of the children are only threatened after the husband has been led away to be shot, building suspense more gradually. Crucially, rather than stab herself in the heat of a violent fight with an attacker, Siri is now given the time and opportunity to think about whether or not to kill herself: she struggles with herself, rather than any outside assailant, and her suicide becomes a deliberate choice, rather than a panic reaction.

All in all, Dreyer's telling of the story is less blatant in its glorification of the cause of Finnish nationalism than the original drafts. It is also somewhat more compact: no Helsinki episode (budget restrictions may also have played a part here), fewer subsidiary characters. On the other hand, the message that Bolshevism is the gospel of Satan is expressed with undiminished force; and to a much greater extent than any of the drafts, Dreyer's film presents resistance to Satan as a moral triumph.

The Antichrist unbound

The authenticity of the depiction of Finland in *Blade af Satans Bog* was, as previously mentioned, attacked in a Finnish film journal. Dreyer replied to the charges with a letter of his own, where he writes that he had intended to travel to Finland in the autumn of 1918, to get at least some first-hand knowledge of conditions there, but was denied permission to enter Finland at the time, 'when I did not have other, more important reasons' to go there. He had to fall back on printed sources, as well as interviews with two Danish officers who had fought as volunteers with the White army; they also provided Dreyer with photographs:

I report this to show that I have not lacked

the inclination or the will to acquaint myself as best I could with the conditions that provided the framework for the most important section of my film. But I must honestly confess that I do not myself attach that much weight to the *outward* scenery. Film is for me like any other art the means to portray human beings. … [My film] does not pretend to be either a course in Finnish architecture or an authentic segment of Finland's war of independence. It is quite simply a universal tale of a woman who dies for a sacred cause. It could take place in Finland – or anywhere else in the world.[57]

David Bordwell cites this passage and takes it as indicating how Dreyer would have answered the attacks on the political message of *Blade af Satans Bog*. To Bordwell, Dreyer's claim of universality is 'ingenuous', considering the film's fervent support of the Finnish nationalists: 'Despite the universalizing impulse of *Leaves*, and despite Dreyer's insistence upon it as a timeless human document, the film takes a stand on issues of mass action and revolution that arose in Denmark at the time', Bordwell writes.[58]

I think, however, that there are some important distinctions to be made here. Let us first examine the attacks to which Bordwell refers. They were fired off by the newspapers of the revolutionary left, *Arbejdet* and *Solidaritet*. Both papers were small: *Arbejdet*, the Communist Party daily, had a circulation of two to three thousand; *Solidaritet*, published by a Syndicalist trade union association, was somewhat larger, with a circulation of six to seven thousand in early 1921. In May 1921, they were merged as *Arbejderbladet*, the official paper of the Danish Communist Party, partly financed by Moscow.[59] Both newspapers published two different items attacking Dreyer's film. *Arbejdet* published an 'Open Letter' to Dreyer from one V. Lundbjerg on 5 February 1921, and a review by A.D. Henriksen entitled 'Danish Upper-Class Propaganda' on 8 February. *Solidaritet* printed a review signed 'N-s.' on 5 February and, the following day, an article called 'Danmarks Hansen' by Christian Christensen, the editor, writing under his usual pseudonym Den Ensomme ('The Lonely One').

The 'Open Letter' mainly complains that the title-page of the book Marie Antoinette reads in prison was printed in Danish – she did not know the language, after all. This literalist complaint seems all the more silly when one knows that Dreyer did in fact shoot versions of this title-page in four different languages, as mentioned above. The letter also insinuates – on the sole basis of the art title 'Pro Finlandia' at the beginning of the last episode – that some of the profits from the film would be sent to the Whites in Finland. If Dreyer bothered to make a reply, it was not published.

Arbejdet's review calls Edgard Høyer a 'mental degenerate'; *Blade af Satans Bog* is nothing but 'one big scream against the hated "Reds"' that compares unfavourably with Griffith's *Intolerance*:

> [In *Intolerance*] the animus was turned against society and sympathy lay with the oppressed.
>
> That is how large-minded the great capitalist American film company can afford to be, whereas the Danish film as so often before sets the record for baseness, mental myopia, and poisonous hatred of the workers.[60]

The review in *Solidaritet* labels *Blade af Satans Bog* 'an extremely obscene agitational film'. The somewhat clumsily written piece describes the film in some detail, if always in a truculent manner: the reviewer assumes that the Jesus episode is 'mainly intended to beguile the female, impulsive part of the audience, intended to arouse the hatred of the devil that was planted in their souls in infancy'. The review concludes: 'This film has from the outset been assured of easily passing the bourgeois censorship. It serves, after all, as a welcome screen for the fainéants who fear the coming reckoning before the rightfully cleansing tribunal of the revolution.'[61]

Even more shrill in tone, and repeating the threats against the indolent bourgoisie, is the piece *Solidaritet*'s editor wrote the next day, attacking a stage comedy about a working man, various magazines and newspapers, and especially the Social Democrats, in addition to *Blade af Satans Bog*:

> Through its depiction of the workers as brutish bandits, this film is a preparation

to murdering them if they should rise up to fight for just social conditions and force those idlers – including the contrivers of the film – who are now living it up on the toil and misery of the workers, to do useful work.

Yet there has not even been a hint of a disruptive protest against this 'loathsome, treacherous smearing and taunting of the working class', and the writer has to conclude that the workers of Denmark are 'sluggish and mentally dead'.[62] This sort of bloody-minded rhetoric shows that the depiction of Ivan's rabble-rousing in draft I of the script for the Finnish episode ('As it is' – 'As it should be') is not, in fact, a caricature at all, but reflects the tenor of real-life communist agitation.

However, it was not only these relatively marginal papers that voiced the complaint that the film was, as *Solidaritet*'s reviewer had it, 'from one end to the other the most insolent imputation against the working class we have seen here in a long time: the revolution as the work of the Devil'.[63] The moderately socialist party paper *Social-Demokraten* (which had a circulation of 49,000)[64] wrote of Edgard Høyer:

> In the last pages of his (so to say) Satanic book he doesn't really stand on the same side as the good Lord, who after all let his son appear as the spokesman of the proletariat against the rich of his day and age, and who, if he himself were to put in place his Judas, surely would have had him betray, not the cause of the rich, but that of the poor, during both the French revolution and the Finnish.[65]

It is the film's diabolization of the revolutionaries far more than its support for Finnish nationalism that offended leftists at the time and continues to trouble many commentators.

Going back to Dreyer's claim of universality, it can only be seen as evasive if the cause of the White Finns had been his central concern. But the comparison with Høyer's drafts clearly showed that Dreyer in fact toned down that very aspect in the final film, particularly by removing the heroine's dying exhortation and the blood-rose business. When Dreyer states that the story could have happened anywhere, this does not mean that he is trying

to hoodwink anybody about the film's political tendencies. The Finnish Civil War is an appropriate, but not a necessary background for what is clearly a central idea of the film (and nothing suggests that Dreyer wanted to explain it away): that revolutionism is diabolical and that resisting it is a sacred cause.

This idea is far from being exclusive to Dreyer. Indeed, the 'Open Letter' to Dreyer in *Arbejdet* points out to the film's writer that 'if he thinks it is an original idea that the Good Lord – and Satan – are *pro* the Whites and *contra* the Reds in Finland, this is a great blunder, for all the nation's newspapers of both right and left have for more than four years expounded this as a fact'.[66] It is important to remember that in society and in the life of many, if not most people, Christianity and the Church played a central role; and that the revolutionary left was, by and large, fiercely hostile to them. Richard Pipes, historian of the revolution in Russia, writes:

> The Communists attacked religious beliefs and practices with a vehemence not seen since the days of the Roman Empire. Their aggressive atheism affected the mass of citizens far more painfully than the suppression of political dissent or the imposition of censorship.[67]

In a headline in a Danish illustrated magazine from early 1919, Lenin is described as *'The man who has turned the Devil loose'*,[68] and the struggle against Communism was often described in religious terms: just before Christmas 1918, a right-wing Danish newspaper urged in an editorial that a 'crusade' against Bolshevism be launched.[69] When the Poles routed the Red Army before Warsaw in 1920, a British diplomat who had witnessed some of the fighting compared the battle to the Battle of Tours in 732, which decisively halted the advance of the armies of Islam:

> Had Piłsudski and Weygand failed to arrest the triumphant march of the Soviet Army at the Battle of Warsaw, not only would Christianity have experienced a dangerous reverse, but the very existence of Western civilisation would have been imperilled. The Battle of Tours saved our ancestors from the Yoke of the Koran; it is probable that the Battle of Warsaw

saved Central and parts of Western Europe from a more subversive danger – the fanatical tyranny of the Soviet.[70]

Many other examples of describing the Communist threat in religious terms could be given, including Churchill's famous 1946 'Iron Curtain' speech at Fulton, Missouri: 'Except in the British Commonwealth and in the United States, where communism is in its infancy, the communist parties or fifth columns constitute a growing challenge and peril to Christian civilization.'

The most interesting cinematic instance is obviously Friedrich Wilhelm Murnau's *Satanas* (1920), scripted by Robert Wiene and with Conrad Veidt in the title role, which has unfortunately been lost. It had three episodes: one set in ancient Egypt, one in Renaissance Italy, and one in contemporary Germany, torn by revolutionary strife. Apparently, there was also a prologue in Heaven, where God tells Satan that he is accursed until the time a single person does good out of evil, 'bis ein Einziger aus Bösem das Gute tut'.[71] Both the structure and the conception of Satan is thus quite similar to that found in Dreyer's film, but despite the many similarities, I have not come across any evidence that one of the films was an imitation of the other. They were shot more or less at the same time, Dreyer's in the summer of 1919 (some of the Finnish scenes may have been shot later in the year), Murnau's in September and October 1919.[72] It is more likely that they both derive from Luigi Maggi's previously mentioned *Satana* from 1912.

In the contemporary episode of Murnau's film, as in Dreyer's, Satan appears as a fanatical Russian Bolshevik. When a young student becomes the leader of a popular revolution in a small German city-state, Satan entices him to order atrocities against the counter-revolutionaries, resulting in the killing of both his parents and the girl he loves. Satan reveals himself to him, and he goes mad. Here, Satan the Bolshevik does not appear to have had the many religious trappings he has in Dreyer's film, where he is an ex-monk, resembling the notorious Rasputin, who preaches from a cathecism book. However, a still from the modern episode of *Satanas* reproduced in Luciano Berriatúa's book on Murnau (probably originally from *Illustrierter Film-Kurier*)

shows Veidt with chin-length hair parted down the middle, as Russian monks (including Rasputin) would typically wear theirs; on the other hand, Veidt does not have a beard.[73]

The soul in revolution

One may well think that identifying Bolshevism with Satan himself is somewhat heavy-handed, but in order to give *Blade af Satans Bog* its due, it is important to remember that interpretations of political events in terms of overt Christian symbolism were quite common at the time and widely accepted, however ham-fisted and naive they may appear to present-day viewers. One example is the American pacifist film *Civilization*, produced by Thomas Ince in 1916. It takes place in a mythical European kingdom, which could in principle be any of the belligerent powers (though it resembles Germany much more than France), and depicts the many horrors of war; finally, having assumed the guise of a gravely wounded officer, Christ himself returns to Earth to preach peace.

The Danish anti-war film *Pax Æterna* (Nordisk, 1917), directed by Holger-Madsen, resembles it in many ways, although it does not contain any scenes from Purgatory, as the American film does; nor does Jesus intervene personally. It does share the feature of an international league of women working for peace under the symbol of the cross, although the Danish film identifies it with the Interna-

Fig. 11. Pax Æterna, *1917. Production still, war and religious symbolism.*

tional Red Cross, giving it a little more credibility. *Pax Æterna* contains some rather striking symbolic tableaux of peace and war, one featuring a horseman of the apocalypse, another showing a ruined church with only the crucifix still standing, starkly outlined against the sky, with corpses strewn around it (Fig. 11). A very similar shot may be found in Cecil B. DeMille's *The Little American* (1917), although intended to carry an anti-German rather than an anti-war message. Other famous examples using this sort of visionary symbolisation of war and peace are of course *Intolerance* and *The Four Horsemen of the Apocalypse*.

Strong symbolic effects are used in a different context in Holger-Madsen's *Mod Lyset* (Nordisk, 1918). Here, Asta Nielsen falls in love with an evangelist and tempts him with the pleasures of the flesh; her temptation of him is intercut with shots showing Satan's temptation of Christ in the Desert. The evangelist reads out the biblical passage, and the words appear at the bottom of the frame; fortified, he resists her.

Returning to politics, it is worth mentioning Ludwig Beck's weird *INRI – die Katastrophe eines Volkes* (1920). Its hero is an idealistic young Russian student who writes a book of ideas that would allow the realisation of 'utopian hopes for peace and humanity'. The book is stolen by an evil rival, and a long struggle ensues. As the title suggests, the student is clearly a Christ figure.

In *Folkets Ven*, there is an image which suggests a similar commingling of politics and religion: at the end of the film, Ernst, the great leader, calls on all men of good will to work towards 'our great objective: the ideal society'. The intertitle is followed by a symbolic shot showing Ernst, dressed in a white cassock, leading a great procession through the darkness; the only light comes from the many torches they carry, providing an almost magical illumination.

This sacralisation of politics also helps to bring out that in a number of ways Christianity and Communism were competitors, contesting the same ground. It has many times been argued that Communism resembles a religious creed, with its promise of a paradise to

come, etc.; François Furet describes it as a 'psychological investment comparable to that of a religious faith, even if its object is historical', 'a way of reinvesting the ambitions of religion in politics, because the revolution too is a quest for salvation'.[74] A succinct presentation of the case may be found in Martin Malia's *The Soviet Tragedy*.[75] The cult of Lenin is another case in point; in fact, though they were committed atheists, his supporters would sometimes portray him as the Saviour himself. The German communist Clara Zetkin wrote of his reaction to the defeat in the war against Poland:

> While Lenin was speaking … an expression of unutterable suffering was on his face … In my mind, I saw the picture of the crucified Christ of the medieval master Grünewald … And as such 'a man of sorrows' Lenin appeared to me, burdened, pierced, oppressed with all the suffering of the Russian working people.[76]

In films, the missionaries of the two faiths often resemble each other; there are many links between the figure of the Bolshevik agitator and that of the evangelist. A striking example comes from *Civilization*. In the film, an important spokesman of the anti-war message is a minister named Luther Rolfe. In *The War, the West, and the Wilderness*, Kevin Brownlow recounts how *Civilization* was transformed into a piece of anti-German war propaganda for showing in England by identifying the mythical kingdom of the film as Germany: 'Luther Rolfe was spared any change of name – his own sounded German enough – but he was transformed into a socialist'.[77]

The call for peace was voiced by both Communists and Christians (though many of the latter instead sanctified the hosts of the nation). Even more important to both was the plight of the poor. The numerous preachers and evangelists that appear in Danish films in the 1910s are usually committed to work in the slums. Similarly, in *Behind the Mask of Innocence*, Kevin Brownlow mentions *The Lion's Den* (George D. Baker, 1919), which concerns the struggles of a pastor to raise money for a boy's club. He also describes *The One Woman* (1918), directed by Reginald Barker, written and produced by Thomas

Dixon, which concerns a pastor given to furious sermonising: 'You are driving the best people out of your church with your socialist rubbish', he is warned. Soon, he 'is engulfed "in a whirlpool of violent radicalism".'[78] He commits adultery and kills a man, is sentenced to death, but finally pardoned and returned to his loyal wife, renouncing all socialist iniquity.

The explicit opposition between Christianity and political radicalism also appears (though in a less strident form) in *Folkets Ven*. Kurt, the deluded hunchback brother, is imprisoned for attempting to assassinate the prime minister. In jail, he experiences a crisis which the parson helps him to resolve. He recalls his childhood and the simple Christian faith his mother taught him and his brothers. He cannot bear the weight of his reawakened conscience, but his suicide brings home to his impetuous brother Waldo that political violence is abhorrent, and Waldo is brought back on the right track.

A similar point is made in *Christian Wahnschaffe*: in part I, Christian lets himself be duped by the revolutionaries, while in part II he devotes himself to good works after the fashion of slum missionaries. The programme booklet for part I declares:

> We have lately seen the Russian revolutionary idea triumph – a pyrrhic victory which has so far only brought debasement and misery to millions of people without bringing humanity any closer to the ideal life – the distant utopian dream.

> This ideal life, these utopian dreams can *only* be reached through individual revolution within society's millions of single individuals, a revolution of the mind and reformation of thought ...[79]

Questions of conscience are even more important in *Blade af Satans Bog*. There is every reason to believe that Dreyer was very serious about the theological issues of the film.

In draft II of the screenplay, as previously noted, there appears a fearless aristocrat named Sahlstrøm who is shot by the Reds. The scene describing his final moments runs as follows:

> 20. In the forest. Rauteniemi commands.

The two [Red] guards are ready for the execution. Ivan approaches the condemned man with 'the comfort of religion'. Sahlstrøm crosses himself – 'Get thee hence, Satan'. And Ivan's face lights up.

The last sentence has been underlined in pencil, and a note (the only one in the entire draft) in what appears to be Dreyer's handwriting is scribbled beneath it: 'Why? There is no temptation here'. The point is that every time someone resists Satan, the length of his punishment is shortened by a thousand years; but this practically never happens. As Satan has in this case not tried to tempt Sahlstrøm, the latter's defiance does not give him any particular reason for joy. In the finished film, aspects of the scene have been retained, but it is now Paavo, Siri's husband, who rejects the 'comfort of religion' offered by Satan. Moreover, Paavo does not cross himself, but draws back in horror, and Satan does not smile, but only registers a certain surprise.

When the stereotypical bravado of Sahlstrøm brings relief to Satan, it diminishes the importance and moral gravity of Siri's self-sacrifice, and the removal of Sahlstrøm from the story is an important element in Dreyer's efforts to shift the focus of the story to Siri. The long scene where Siri sees a knife on the table, draws back, fearfully reaches out, hesitates, then snatches it up and finally stabs herself is far and away the most famous scene of the film. What is particularly important in this context is the way this scene makes Siri's courageous act an uncertain and difficult choice. In Høyer's script, on the other hand, both Elsa (= Siri) and Sahlstrøm go to their deaths without any hesitation at all, a fearlessness which is largely a function of their belonging to a better class of people than the rabble who act against them. Dreyer displaces the moral impulse from class to conscience.

The emphasis on the redemptive power of individual moral decisions again underscores that Dreyer was very much in earnest about the religious aspect of the story. From this perspective, the greatest danger that communism presented was not its threat to dispossess the bourgeoisie and punish them with forced labour (with which we have seen the syndicalist leader Christian Christensen threaten

Dreyer)[80] or worse. While the Bolsheviks in the eyes of some were the champions of the just cause of the have-nots, others less exclusively concerned with material things saw them as the enemies of religion and, therewith, the entire foundation of morality. In this light, it makes sense to let Satan assume the guise of a Communist. In doing so, Dreyer does not attack the cause of social justice, of the little people, the oppressed, as many commentators would claim. He signals that the rightfulness of society is less important than the rightfulness of the soul.

Acknowledgements

I should like to thank Stephan M. Schröder for guiding me through the Nordisk correspondence, and Lars Gaustad and Gunnar Iversen for their help with *Revolutionens datter*.

Notes

1. Edvin Kau, *Dreyers filmkunst* (Copenhagen: Akademisk forlag, 1989), 36.
2. Tom Milne, *The Cinema of Carl Dreyer* (London: A. Zwemmer, 1971), 45.
3. Jean-Louis Comolli, 'Filmographie commentée: *Les pages du livre de Satan*', *Cahiers du cinéma* no. 207 (December 1968): 67, as translated in Mark Nash, *Dreyer* (London: British Film Institute, 1977), 43.
4. Maurice Drouzy, *Carl Th. Dreyer, né Nilsson* (Paris: Editions du Cerf, 1982), 186.
5. David Bordwell, *The Films of Carl-Theodor Dreyer* (Berkeley, Los Angeles: University of California Press, 1981), 191–201.
6. Ibid., 193.
7. Jean-Louis Comolli and Jean Narboni, 'Cinema/Ideology/Criticism', in Bill Nichols (ed.), *Movies and Methods: An Anthology* (Berkeley, Los Angeles: University of California Press, 1976), 27.
8. See David Bordwell, *Making Meaning: Inference and Rhetoric in the Interpretation of Cinema* (Cambridge, Mass.: Harvard University Press, 1989), 84, where the same passage is cited.
9. Martin Malia, 'The Lesser Evil?', *Times Literary Supplement* (27 March 1998): 4.
10. 'Peter Vilh. 'paa Filmen'', *Aftenbladet*, 24 January 1921.
11. Michel Delahaye, 'Between Heaven and Hell: Interview with Carl Dreyer,' *Cahiers du cinéma in English* no. 4 (1966): 11. First published in French, *Cahiers du cinéma* no. 170 (September 1965).
12. Drouzy, *Carl Th. Dreyer, né Nilsson*, 180.
13. Based on a plot summary from contemporary publicity materials, reprinted in Aldo Bernadini and Vittorio Martinelli, *Il Cinema muto italiano, 1912* (Rome: Bianco e Nero/Centro Sperimentale di Cinematografia, 1995), II, 192–199, where excerpts from reviews and other interesting material may be found.
14. Copybook, 'Breve til Returmanuskript' [Returned script letters], vol. 1, letter no. 624.
15. Copybook, 'Breve' [Letters], vol. 31, letter 558.
16. Copybook, 'Breve' [Letters], vol. 31, letter 928.
17. The Danish Film Museum is now part of DFI: Danish Film Institute/Archive & Cinematheque.
18. 'Blade af Satans Bog: En ny stor dansk Film af Edgard Høyer', *København*, 23 January 1921.
19. Edgard Høyer, 'A propos *Blade af Satanas Bog*', *Politiken*, 9 January 1921.
20. In the Dreyer Collection, DFI.
21. Georges Sadoul, *Histoire Générale du Cinéma*, 2nd ed., IV: *Le Cinéma Devient un Art, 1909–1920: La première guerre mondiale* (Paris: Denoël, 1974), 450.
22. Recently reissued in an excellent new edition: Marie Corelli, *The Sorrows of Satan*, ed. Peter Keating (Oxford: Oxford University Press, 1998).
23. Maurice Drouzy, *Carl Th. Dreyer, né Nilsson*, 181.
24. David Bordwell, *The Films of Carl-Theodor Dreyer*, 206.
25. Maurice Drouzy, *Carl Th. Dreyer, né Nilsson*, 367.
26. 'Peter Vilh. 'paa Filmen'', *Aftenbladet*, 24 January 1921.
27. 'En dansk Film', *Dagbladet*, 26 January 1921.
28. Risto Alapuro, *State and Revolution in Finland* (Berkeley, Los Angeles: University of California Press, 1988), 167.

29. 'Borgerkrigen i Helsingfors', *Social-Demokraten*, 10 February 1919.

30. Adam Poulsen, *En Skuespillers Erindringer*, II: *Årene efter 1916* (Copenhagen: Hirschprung, 1962), 32, 44.

31. 'Tilstanden i Finland', *Social-Demokraten*, 12 February 1919; original emphasis.

32. Adam Poulsen, *En Skuespillers Erindringer*, II, 46.

33. Anthony F. Upton, *The Finnish Revolution 1917–1918* (Minneapolis: University of Minnesota Press, 1980), 16, 49.

34. Oski Talvio, 'Ett ord om den danska filmen med motiv ur vårt frihetskrig', *Filmrevyn* no. 2 (1922): 35.

35. Eva Moltesen, 'Finland: Historie', in *Salmonsens Konversationsleksikon* (Copenhagen: J. H. Schultz, 1919), 102.

36. Quoted in *Ekstrabladet*, 7 February 1918, evening edition.

37. Eric Hobsbawm, *Age of Extremes: The Short Twentieth Century 1914–1991* (London: Abacus, 1995), 56.

38. Printed in the newspaper *Klassekampen*, 10 November 1918; reprinted in Bent Jensen, *Købmænd og kommisærer: Oktoberrevolutionen og dansk Ruslandspolitik 1917–1924* (Copenhagen: Gyldendal, 1979), 90.

39. For details on the latter, see Richard J. Evans, *Rituals of Retribution: Capital Punishment in Germany, 1600–1987* (Harmondsworth: Penguin, 1997), 487–506.

40. Bernard Droz, 'Et l'Europe ne sera pas communiste ...', *L'Historie* no. 223 (July–August 1998) provides a convenient overview.

41. Martin Gilbert, *A History of the Twentieth Century* (London: HarperCollins, 1997), I, 573.

42. From the Red Army Gazette *Krasnoarmeets*, quoted in Norman Davies, *White Eagle, Red Star: The Polish-Soviet War, 1919–20* (London: Orbis Books, 1983), 145.

43. Kevin Brownlow, *Behind the Mask of Innocence: Sex, Violence, Prejudice, Crime: Films of Social Conscience in the Silent Era* (Berkeley, Los Angeles: University of California Press, 1990), 442–462.

44. Roger Icart, 'Le bolchevisme dénoncé par le cinéma des années 20', *Cahiers de la Cinémathèque* nos. 67–68 (December 1997): 35–41.

45. Jan-Christopher Horak, 'Robert Reinert: Film as Metaphor', *Griffithiana* nos. 60/61 (October 1997), 183.

46. See Gunnar Iversen, 'En norsk filmpionér: Ottar Gladtvet og filmen', *Z* (1988): 26–30.

47. Per Fuglum, *Norges Historie*, ed. Knut Mykland, XII: *Norge i støpeskjeen, 1884–1920* (Oslo: J. W. Cappelens Forlag, 1978), 511.

48. Quoted in Knut Kjeldstadli, *Aschehougs Norgeshistorie*, ed. Knut Helle, X: *Et splittet samfunn, 1905–35* (Oslo: Aschehoug, 1994), 89.

49. Gunnar Iversen, 'En norsk filmpionér': 28.

50. Quoted in Sigurd Evensmo, *Det store tivoli: Film og kino i Norge* (Oslo: Gyldendal Norsk Forlag, 1992), 119.

51. Danish programme booklet, DFI Archive folder: *Jeftas Datter*.

52. Quoted in Lars Åhlander (ed.), *Svensk filmografi*, I: *1897–1919* (Stockholm: Svenska filminstitutet, 1986), 410.

53. Draft I, p. 5.

54. Draft I, p. 5.

55. Draft I, p. 6.

56. Interview with Clara Pontoppidan, *Nationaltidende*, 23 January 1921.

57. Carl Th. Dreyer, 'Med anledning av filmen 'Blad ur Satans bok',' *Filmrevyn* no. 5 (1922): 92.

58. Bordwell, *The Films of Carl-Theodor Dreyer*, 191, 192.

59. Niels Thomsen, *Dagbladskonkurrencen 1870–1970: Politik, journalistik og økonomi i dansk dagspresses strukturudvikling* (Copenhagen: (Universitetsforlaget) G.E.C. Gads Forlag, 1972), 358–359; Morten Thing and Jørgen Bloch-Poulsen, *Danmarks Kommunistiske Parti 1918–1941* (Copenhagen: politisk revy, 1979), 37.

60. A. D. Henriksen, 'Dansk Overklasse-Propaganda', *Arbejdet*, 8 February 1921.

61. "Blade af Satans Bog'. En fræk Agitationsfilm i Paladsteatret', *Solidaritet*, 5 February 1921.

62. Christian ['Den Ensomme'] Christensen, 'Danmarks Hansen', *Solidaritet*, 6 February 1921.

63. "Blade af Satans Bog'. En fræk Agitationsfilm i Paladsteatret', *Solidaritet*, 5 February 1921.
64. Niels Thomsen, *Dagbladskonkurrencen 1870–1970*, 895.
65. "Blade af Satans Dagbog': Den nye Paladsteater-Film', *Social-Demokraten*, 26 January 1921.
66. V. Lundbjerg, 'Aabent Brev til Hr. Filminstruktør C.Th.Dreyer', *Arbejdet*, 5 February 1921.
67. Richard Pipes, *Russia under the Bolshevik Regime* (New York: Alfred E. Knopf, 1994), 337.
68. *Verden og Vi*, 10 January 1919; reprinted in Bent Jensen, *Købmænd og kommisærer*, 103.
69. 'På Korstog til Rusland', *Nationaltidende*, 23 December 1918.
70. Lord d'Abernon, *The Eighteenth Decisive Battle of World History* (1931), quoted in Norman Davies, *White Eagle*, 265.
71. Lotte Eisner, *Murnau* (Hannover: Friedrich Verlag, 1967), 66–68; see also Uli Jung and Walter Schatzberg, *Robert Wiene: Der Caligari-Regisseur* (Berlin: Henschel, 1995), 56.
72. Luciano Berriatúa, *Los proverbios chinos de F. W. Murnau* (Madrid: Filmoteca Española/Instituto de la Cinematografía y de las Artes Audiovisuales, 1990), I, 88.
73. Berriatúa, *Murnau*, I, 89.
74. François Furet, *Le passé d'une illusion: Essai sur l'idée communiste au XXe siècle* (Paris: Robert Laffont, 1995), 13–14, 46.
75. Martin Malia, *The Soviet Tragedy: A History of Socialism in Russia, 1917–1991* (New York: Free Press, 1994), especially Chap. 1.
76. Zetkin, *Reminiscences of Lenin*, quoted in Norman Davies, *White Eagle, Red Star*, 266–267.
77. Kevin Brownlow, *The War, the West, and the Wilderness* (New York: Knopf, 1979), 77.
78. Kevin Brownlow, *Behind the Mask of Innocence*, 402.
79. *Christian Wahnschaffe I: Weltbrand*, Danish programme booklet, DFI Archive folder: *Christian Wahnschaffe*.
80. Christian ['Den Ensomme'] Christensen, 'Danmarks Hansen', *Solidaritet*, 6 February 1921.

Benjamin Christensen in Germany: The Critical Reception of His Films in the 1910s and 1920s

Ib Monty

Vodroffslund 2, 1914 Frederiksberg C, Denmark

There are many connections between German and Danish cinema during the silent period. So far this chapter in European film history is rather unexplored. A first attempt to scratch the surface was made in Hamburg in November 1993 when CineGraph organised the symposium, 'Deutsch-dänische Filmbeziehungen 1910–1930'.[1]

The Danish influence on German cinema was much greater than the influence of German cinema of Danish film. A few German and Austrian actors such as Alwin Neuss, Ferdinand Bonn, Lilly Lamprecht, Rita Sacchetto and Ida Orloff appeared in Danish films, but this is nothing when compared with the Danish invasion of German films before 1930. Directors such as Urban Gad, Viggo Larsen, Stellan Rye, Alfred Lind, Robert Dinesen, Einar Zangenberg, Holger-Madsen, A.W. Sandberg, Svend Gade, Preben Rist, Alf Nielsen, Mogens Enger, Carl Th. Dreyer and Benjamin Christensen, and cameramen such as Axel Graatkjær, Frederik Fuglsang, Sofus Wangøe, Mads Anton Madsen, Christen Jørgensen, Carl Ferdinand Fischer and Marius Clausen contributed to shaping German cinema in the silent era. And to the German public in this period, actors such as Emilie Sannom, Frederik Buch, Olaf Fønss, Pat and Patachon (Long and Short), and above all, Asta Nielsen, were well-known and popular names. Some day the story of the Danish influence on German cinema may be written. Here I shall try to give an impression of Benjamin Christensen's rather modest efforts in Germany, where he directed two films in the 1920s, and played a major role in Carl Th. Dreyer's *Michael* (1924).

There are striking similarities in the careers of the two major Danish directors, Dreyer and Christensen (Fig. 1). They both directed fourteen features, and half of these films were produced outside Denmark. Of the seven films which Dreyer directed abroad, two were made in Germany, and of Christensen's eight foreign films, two were produced in Germany. But there are also obvious resemblances in the personalities of the two filmmakers. In an article about Benjamin Christensen and his ideas before the premiere of *Häxan* (Witchcraft Through the Ages, 1922),[2] Dreyer

Fig. 1. Benjamin
Christensen circa
1920 [Photographic
portrait courtesy of
The Danish Film
Museum.]

Fig. 2 (below).
Skæbnebæltet,
1913. [Production
still courtesy of The
Danish Film
Museum.]

described his colleague as 'a man who knew exactly what he wanted, and pursued his purpose with unyielding stubbornness, undeterred by obstacles of any kind'. These words were, of course, at the same time a characterisation of Dreyer himself, even if the differences between the two artists are, in the end, more conspicuous than the resemblances.

Both directors had an obvious talent for hand-ling actors even though Dreyer was never an actor himself. Christensen, however, was an actor. He attended the Royal Theatre's acting school and was trained both as an actor and an opera singer. He lost his voice, but he never lost his inclination for performing, and made his debut in films as an actor after having earned his living for a couple of years as the Copenhagen representative of the champagne firm, Lanson père et fils. Benjamin Christensen appeared in five films as an actor in 1913. Two of the films were probably never shown in Denmark. He made his debut in *Skæbnebæltet* (Fig. 2), written and directed by Svend Rindom and produced by Carl Rosenbaum (Gefion Film) who had been involved in the filming of Herman Bang's short story, *De fire Djævle* (The Four Devils, 1911). The European rights for this film were sold to the German firm Zimmelhag und Schmidt, and as it was a financial success, Zimmelhag und Schmidt put money at Rosenbaum's disposal to set up a film production company which would produce films for the German market.

Skæbnebæltet was Rosenbaum's first production, and from his and Svend Rindom's perspective, was conceived as the start of a major offensive directed at the German public. The film was shot in a studio at Taffelbays Allé 2 in Hellerup, a suburb of Copenhagen. It was shot in 1912, but the premiere in Copenhagen was not held until 13 November 1913 in Victoriateatret. The German censor viewed the film under the German title of *Der Schicksalgürtel* at the end of 1913, and according to the censorship lists,[3] the film, which was in two Akte, was cut.[4] After censorship, the film was 369.40 metres (I Akt) and 311.50 metres (II Akt), i.e. 680.90 metres in length, and was prohibited from exhibition to children. In 1916 it was submitted to the censor in Munich, and was banned outright. No prints have survived.

In the Danish programme for *Skæbnebæltet*, the film is described as 'a moving artist's drama from modern Paris', and the programme goes on to note that 'the arrangements are after Balestreri's world-famous studio paintings'. According to the programme, *Skæbnebæltet* is 'an Art film in a prologue, 4 days and an epilogue'. In the prologue, a young man and his girlfriend are sitting in a cosy corner, lost in their thoughts. She asks him to tell a story. 'A story about what?' he replies. She looks around the room and sees the painting *Beethoven* by Balestreri.[5] The young man looks at the picture and starts telling the story which, a love triangle, concerns a blind organist, Ravaud (Benjamin Christensen), his wife Jeanne (Karen Sandberg), and Jeanne's lover, the painter Léon. Jeanne has scruples about deceiving her blind husband, and she and Léon decide to part. But Ravaud finds out that his wife deceived him, and he kills himself. A 'destiny belt' which he once bought from an Arab peddler is the central narrative device. The peculiarity of the belt is that when it is touched by deceitful hands, it causes death. Ravaud has given the belt to his wife, and after his death, when the lovers try to get together again, Jeanne dies, maybe because of the belt.

This erotic melodrama, typical of its time, mixes the modern with the exotic and the irrational. We do not know how the film was received, and I have not come across any reviews or other references. Among the other actors in the film were Ellen Malberg, Albrecht Schmidt, Fritz Lamprecht, and Carl and Gunner Rosenbaum, all members of the stock company. Benjamin Christensen was not very satisfied with *Skæbnebæltet*, and he left Carl Rosenbaum's company which in the spring of 1913 changed its name to A/S Dansk Biografkompagni.

At the same time, another film production company was founded. Its name was Dania Biofilm, and the company had the ambition of establishing itself as an art film company. Behind it were the best names within Danish cultural life and art, an aspect which the company's press material promoted. Financially supported by Gyldendal, the biggest and most prestigious Danish publishing company, the head of Gyldendal, the writer Peter Nansen, was not only a member of the board of the new company, but also functioned as literary adviser. For Benjamin Christensen, it was flattering to be among the first to be contacted by Dania Biofilm. He signed a contract in April 1913, and played in four of the company's films shot from June to August/September 1913 in a new studio at

Hellerupvej 72, not far from the studio in which Christensen made his debut.

Dania Biofilm was very interested in producing films for export, and in 1913 had a representative in Berlin by the name of Otto Schmidt. Schmidt was very critical about the films he received from Copenhagen, and according to correspondance between Schmidt and the Copenhagen office,[6] was very pessimistic about the possibilities of selling the films to German customers. Concerning *Lille Claus og Store Claus*, the first of the Dania Biofilm productions in which Benjamin Christensen appeared, he wrote: 'I dare not go into business with the film in this condition'.[7]

Dania Biofilm was evidently not enthusiastic about an agent who did not like their films, and on 21 February 1914, signed a contract with the German company, Literaria Film GmbH. Literaria was founded in 1912 by Alfred Duskes who was financed by Pathé. In 1913, the company built a studio in Tempelhof next to the studio which PAGU built and which Asta Nielsen used. According to the contract, Dania Biofilm gave Literaria the right to print from the company's Danish negatives, to sell prints, and also to make changes or shorten films. Their films were traded under the name 'Literaria-Daniafilm' or 'Dania-Film'.[8] The collaboration was not very fruitful. When Dania Biofilm tried to persuade Literaria to sell the films produced in 1913 and sent them to Berlin, Literaria wrote in a letter dated 30 June 1914 that after having seen all of the prints, they were not interested in marketing them and would return them.[9]

It is, therefore, doubtful whether German film-going audiences saw any of the four films in which Benjamin Christensen acted in 1913. The first of them was *Lille Claus og Store Claus*, directed by Elith Reumert from The Royal Theatre and, with a script by Peter Nansen, based on H.C. Andersen's story of the same name. The film was shot in May–June 1913, and had its premiere on 20 December 1913 in Paladsteatret in the presence of the Empress of Russia, Maria Feodorovna.[10] The film was 845 metres in length, and besides Benjamin Christensen, included Henrik Malberg (Lille Klaus), Peter Malberg (the parish

clerk), Victor Neumann (the farmer), and Martha Hegner (the farmer's wife). The prominent premiere indicates that Dania Biofilm had acquired the status of a serious film producing company. The reception accorded the film by the Copenhagen press was also benevolent in its verdict, but one reviewer suggested that the projected print, which was too blurred, should be replaced. The technical standard of the prints from Dania Biofilm were considered to be poor. Otto Schmidt from Berlin complained constantly about the quality of the prints.

Twelve prints of the films were sold. One was sold to Germany and one to Austria, but there it was banned because of the scene in which Store Claus kills Little Claus' grandmother after Little Claus transports the body to an inn. The innkeeper gets mad at the silent old woman, strikes her with a mug, and thinks that he has killed her. This rough treatment of an elderly woman was too much for the Austrians. Otto Schmidt did not like the film. He was apparently not interested in selling the film in Germany, and it was probably never shown there.

Lillee Claus og Store Claus was the first film produced by Dania Biofilm, but it was the company's second film, *Scenens Børn*, that received the earlier premiere. *Scenens Børn* was shot between July and September 1913 and was 925 metres in length. It is a drama of

jealousy among actors, and Benjamin Christensen appeared in a small role as a doctor who is called when an actor shoots his wife. Christensen was not credited in the programme. The actors in the film were prominent stage actors, and included Bodil Ipsen and Adam Poulsen, and from Norway, Bjørnstjerne Bjørnsons's son, Bjørn Bjørnson. *Scenens Børn* was a prestige production, but it was not a success. Three prints were sent to Berlin under the title *Wenn die Liebe spricht*; two prints were prohibited from exhibition to children, and one print was completely banned. In Munich, three scenes were removed from a fourth print.[11] In *Der Kinematograph* no. 359 (1913), an advertisement appears giving extracts from the four Copenhagen newspapers: *Berlingske Tidende*, *Politiken*, *København*, and *Hovedstaden*. The advertisement, which is signed by Dania Biofilm's general agent, Otto Schmidt, says that *Wenn die Liebe spricht* and another Bjørn Bjørnson film, *Ein Kind der Sünde* (Danish title: *Syndens Barn*), will soon appear. I have not traced any reviews of the film. Benjamin Christensen appeared in two other films at Dania Biofilm: *Vingeskudt* (626 metres) shot in June–September 1913, and *Søstrene Corrodi* (also known as *Rumænsk Blod*, 585 metres) shot in August–September 1913. None of the films were shown in Denmark. Two prints of the first film were sent to Berlin, and one print of the second, but it has not been possible to find any trace of the films in the German censorship lists or any reviews.

Benjamin Christensen was not very satisfied with his acting at Dania Biofilm, and when he got an offer from A/S Dansk Biografkompagni to become managing director, he accepted and started shooting *Det hemmelighedsfulde X* (The Mysterious X) in August 1913. But Benjamin Christensen took his time, and the premiere was not held until 23 March 1914. *Det hemmelighedsfulde X* was immediately recognised as an exciting film, both by the reviewers and the public. It is possibly the most remarkable directorial debut in Danish cinema. It was a spy story, and spies were an interesting subject in the period before the Great War. The film was first and foremost praised for its style, technique and visual inventiveness (Fig. 3). Several of the

Danish reviewers claimed that with this film, Danish film had a world success and that it was already being shown in Europe and in the United States. Before its premiere in Denmark, Benjamin Christensen went on a business trip in order to sell his first film. Contrary to Dreyer, Christensen was always both an artist and a businessman. He visited London, Paris and Berlin, and three or four months later, Russia.

Concerning his visit to Berlin, Benjamin Christensen recounted:

> The most powerful man in Germany in the field of cinema was standing in front of me, asking for some information about the film, before he would waste some of his precious time on viewing it. 'Well,' I started, 'it's a film in a popular style, 2000 metres, and I have tried to attach the greatest importance to the exciting and …' '2000?' he exclaimed, as if it was the most insane length a film might have at all.'

Somehow Benjamin Christensen got the great man to look at the film, but after a short while he turned to Christensen and said:

> 'Excuse me, but one of the main characters, this count – isn't he … a spy?' I answered, 'Yes, I thought so'. 'You might have told me at once. Spy films were forbidden in Germany and Austria-Hungary a fortnight ago.'

According to Benjamin Christensen, the case ended in the Prussian Ministry of War, and after many negotiations it was decided that the film might be shown with some minor alterations; some scenes which were considered threatening to the security of the state were removed. Maybe it is one of Benjamin Christensen's imaginative interpretations of reality which we so often meet in interviews with him. In the short story, 'Film and Reality', for example, which was published on 19 April 1942 in the supplement *Magasinet* to the daily newspaper, *Politiken*,[12] Christensen tells a story about how he involuntarily became a courier for a spy while travelling in Europe in 1914 between Germany and France. It *is* a fact, however, that *Det hemmelighedsfulde X*, under the German title of *Das Geheimnisvolle X*, was cut by the censors. In 1914 in Berlin,

Fig. 4. Hævnens Nat, *1916. [Production still courtesy of The Danish Film Museum.]*

the censors removed the following scenes: 'In Act III, a scene following the tenth intertitle, Spinelli fastens a message under the wing of the carrier-pigeon (enlargement); furthermore, the scene in which Spinelli enters the cellar, takes a cage with carrier-pigeons, writes on paper: The second division shall attack at sunrise, and photographs this message. Length of the shortened film, Act III, 235 m. Also forbidden to children after censorship.'[13] The film was also prohibited from exhibition to children in Hamburg in 1915.[14]

Das Geheimnisvolle X was a success in Germany. *Der Kinematograph* no. 377 (18 March 1914) reported: 'Es präsentiert sich tätsächlich als ein hoch interessantes, kurzweiliges und dramatisch überaus rückbewegtes Stück … Das Milieu fesselt durch sein Vielseitigkeit, die Handlung bringt Momente höchster Spannung, die Szenerie Bilder von entzückendem landschaftlichen Reiz und das treffliche Spiel der Darsteller, die überaus geschickte Regie und die technische Vollendung des Films trugen das ihre zu einem schönen und ungeteilten Erfolge bei.'[15] And *Erste Internationale Film-Zeitung* no. 12 (21 March 1914) observed: 'Durch die sechs Akte dieses gewaltigen Films bewegt sich sichtbar die Kraft eines genialen, von allem Kleinlichen losgelösten Regisseurs. Er heisst Benjamin Christensen und spielt im Stück selbst den Marineleutnant van Houven. – Wenn es nicht

ein Drama wäre, möchte ich sagen: einfach pompös! Es entspringt dem Wesen des Films, ist echt empfunden, das heisst, man hat gewusst: *was man wollte und für was man seine Kraft ins Zeug legte.*'[16]

In August 1915 Benjamin Christensen started shooting his second film, *Hævnens Nat*. It was finished eight months later. The film received its premiere at Palads Teatret in Copenhagen on 25 September 1916. The reviews were very positive, and Benjamin Christensen's portrayal of the prisoner who returns, seeking revenge, was considered as his breakthrough as an actor (Fig. 4).

In Germany the film was censored in Berlin in 1916 and, prohibited from exhibition to children, was released under the titles of *Rache* or *Die Nacht der Rache*. The film was distributed in Germany by Nordische Film Ko. and was released in October 1916. It was well received. *Der Kinematograph* (1 November 1916) wrote: 'Benjamin Christensen ist ein Schauspieler von hervorragenden, dramatischen Ausdrucksmitteln. Die Durchführung des schwierigen Charakters in diesem Film kann geradezu als Lehrmittel dienen. Wenn ich nochmals an mir diese riesige Leistung herüberziehen lasse, dann kommen mir immer wieder jene Szenen in Erinnerung, in denen der weltfremde Mann endlich die Freiheit erhält und nun hinaus taumelt, ohne zu wissen, wohin. Aber sein erster Gedanke gilt seinem Kinnde [sic]. Und dann der Schmerz,

als er es nicht finden kann. Das waren erschütternde Momente, voll von Lebenswahrheit bis zum Aeussersten. Schon dieser einen Leistung wegen verdient dieser Film einen vollen Erfolg, der ihm auch das Publikum bereitete. Dazu kommt eine auffallend sauber gearbeitete Regie, die Christensen selbst besorgte und eine ausgezeichnete Photographie.'[17] And *Der Kinematograph* no. 514 (1 November 1916) was also laudatory: 'Benjamin Christensen hat zuerst ein Textbuch geschrieben, das eine interessante Handlung in einem noch interessanteren Milieu zeigt und da er auch gleichzeitig für die Regie verantwortlich zeichnet, so hatte er es in der Hand, alle technischen und szenischen Möglichkeiten restlos auswirken zu lassen. Photographie und Aufmachung sind vorzüglich ... und das gute Spiel der beliebten Nordisk-Künstler ist hier wieder so selbstverständlich wie sonst.'[18]

After having worked for nearly three years on the production, Benjamin Christensen's most famous film *Häxan* had its premiere in Stockholm on 18 September 1922, and was first shown in Denmark at Palads Teatret, Copenhagen on 7 November 1922 (Fig. 5). The film was shot in Copenhagen but produced by Svensk Filmindustri. The reception accorded the film was very positive, and the film had no problem with the Danish censors. Christensen called his grand experimental film 'a lecture on cultural history in moving pictures', and the film is an ambitious attempt to break down the barriers between art and science. It was also widely recognised as an important film and received a lot of discussion. This was also the case in Germany, but there *Häxan* (German title: *Die Hexe*) faced many problems with censors.

The film was shown at a closed performance on 15 October 1923 in a screening room at Decla-Bioscop in Berlin to an invited audience, but it may have been shown before. Anyhow, on 30 June 1924, Alfred Rosenthal,[19] writing under the pseudonym of 'AROS', claimed that he had seen it two years before in the company of Asta Nielsen. When he saw it a year later with a group of writers the censor had already softened it, he declared. According to Rosenthal, the censor was especially offended by the description of the hysterics of the modern woman. Rosenthal's assumption does not seem credible. According to the censorship lists, a print was first presented to the German censors, Filmprüfstelle Berlin, on 7 February 1924 when exhibition was completely prohibited. The print was then 3005 metres long. A new and shortened version was submitted to the censors on 16 April 1924. The seven reels were now 308, 315, 541, 381, 250, 331 and 487 metres in length, the total length of the film being 2613 metres. The film was now prohibited to children under 18, and the Berlin premiere took place on 30 June 1924 at Ufa-Palast am Zoo.

The film was well received by the Berlin press. Before the premiere there were several articles written about the film. On 16 October 1923, after the closed screening at Decla-Bioscop, *Film-Kurier* published a short description of the film and concluded: 'Der ganze Film ist das Muster einer Synthese zwischen Kultur- und Spielfilm, wie sie vor uns schon mehrfach gefordert worden ist.'[20] *Der Kinematograph* was also present at the special viewing, and on 21 October 1923, published a piece in which it called *Die Hexe* 'ein kulturfilmisches Experiment',[21] but it also wrote: 'Man befürchtet, vielleicht nicht mit Unrecht, dass diesem Film Zensurschwierigkeiten gemacht werden. Das wäre ausserordentlich zu bedauern.'[22] In *Montagspost* 23 June 1924, Eugen Tannenbaum wrote: 'Kultur- oder besser: Unkultur-Film … mehr aufrührend als das sommerliche Wochenprogramm sämtlicher Berliner-Kinos.'[23] And on 28 June 1924, *Film-Kurier* published an article on the coming film and on witchcraft. The same magazine published an extensive review two days later (30 June 1924) in which it said: 'So ist dieser Film nicht nur eine wissenschaftliche und künstlerische, sondern auch eine ethische Tat.'[24]

After the premiere, the reviews appeared. Most of them were positive. Among the reviews the day after the premiere (1 July 1924), '-or' in *Berliner Börsen-Courier* was much preoccupied with witch burnings, and '-nn' in *Germania* was also concerned about the horrors of witch-hunts. But the reviewer found that because of censorship, the film was only a 'torso'. 'Ejac' in *Berliner Zeitung* also found that the censor had changed the work into a pamphlet, *in usum delphini*. In *Berliner Tage-*

blatt, Maria Kamp was laudatory, but found that too many intertitles were tiresome. Two of the papers from 1 July 1924 were directly negative. 'M.S.' writing in *Deutsche Tageitung* was of the opinion that Ufa (the German distributor) might have spared us from the film, and in *National-Zeitung*, '-e' wrote: 'Der Film mit seinen prachtvollen Bildern, seinen interessanten Episoden verliert durch die allzu schwerfällige, pedantische und doktrinäre Art, mit der der deutsche Text das Bild begleitet. Man fühlt sich oft peinlich in die Schulstube zurückversetzt. Der Film wurde mit starken Beifall, in den sich aber auch Zischen mischte, aufgenommen.'[25] The next day (2 July 1924) more reviews followed. In *Der Tag*, Rudolf Arnheim ('Ar.- ') also found that the film was a 'torso', and thought that the parallels to the Great War should be removed in Germany. This is interesting because these scenes were specifically added to the German version; they do not appear in the Swedish original print. In *12 Uhr Blatt*, 'st.' mentioned that a knowledgeable introduction, which accompanied the programme, was written by Dr. Kurt Pinthus. And 'F.O.' in *Berliner Börsen-Zeitung* wrote that *Die Hexe* was a cultural and informative film in the best sense of the word. On 3 July 1924, there were positive reviews in *Die Zeit* where 'M.F.' found the film very lucid, although too pedagogical, and in *Berliner Lokal-Anzeiger*, 'f.' found the film visually very successful, although the censors had created some gaps in the film, and the review concluded: 'Auch die Schlussworte, dass eine spätere Zeit über die vielen Millionen Todesopfer des Weltkrieges ebenso urteilen werde wie wir heute über die Opfer des Herzensglaubens, waren recht unangebracht und weckten mit Recht Widerspruch'.[26] Finally 'F.G.' in *Vossische Zeitung* discussed *Kulturfilme* and was of the opinion that the film lacked psychological absorption and, therefore, did not touch us directly in a human way. And the review in *Vorwärts* on 6 July 1924, which was positive, read: 'Und das Schlusswort des Films, das einen Vergleich zwischen den Auswirkungen des Hexenwahns und dem Weltkrieg mit seinen 20 Millionen Toten andeutet, wird doch vielleicht manchen Vater und manche Mutter über die Notwendigkeit von Kriegen nachdenklich machen'.[27] After the premiere of *Die*

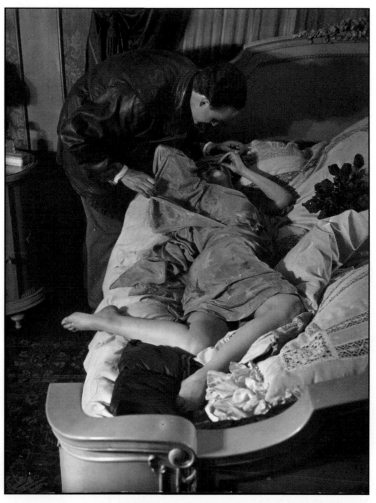

offensive. An imposing group of people, including a chaplain and a professor as experts, considered the case, and the outcome was a rejection of the application on 2 February 1925. It was another victory for Benjamin Christensen who could enjoy the fact that his film was not only recognised by most of the film reviewers in Germany, but also received support from the highest authority on the matters which he treated in his film. The detailed reasons for the rejection can be read in *Reichfilmsblatt* no. 7 (17 February 1925).[28]

Benjamin Christensen had a fine reputation in Germany after his first films, and Erich Pommer wanted him to come to Berlin in order to make films for Decla-Bioscop. A year before the first public exhibition of *Die Hexe*, German audiences had seen the first German film by Christensen, *Seine Frau die Unbekannte*. The film was approved by the censor on 1 October 1923 (6 Akte, 2232 metres) and was prohibited from exhibition to children. The premiere took place on 19 October 1923 at the Theater Ufa-Lichtspiele Tauntzien Palast. The film was shot from May to September at the Ufa-studio, Berlin-Tempelhof with a few exteriors in Neubabelsberg. According to Lil Dagover the film was forty days in production.[29] Originally titled *Wilbur Crawfords wundersames Abenteuer*, press material with this title was printed (in one case with an incorrect spelling: Crowford), but the final distribution title was *Seine Frau die Unbekannte*.

The film begins as a melodrama, evolves into a comedy, and ends as a farce. Benjamin Christensen wrote the bizarre script which had some interesting features in its *mise-en-scène*. The photography by the Dane, Frederik Fuglsang was up to Christensen's normal standard which, with strong contrast in the use of light, threw a glow over characters' faces (e.g. in the scene where the main actors stand in front of a fire-place). Hans Jacoby's sets also accurately reflected the upper-class milieu in which the film was set. The film starred Maria Reisenhofer, Lil Dagover, Jaro Fürth, Maria Wefers, and established Willy Fritsch as a major screen attraction.

Although the film's narrative is absolute nonsense, the German reviews were surprisingly friendly and praised Christensen for his hand-

Hexe, the film's problems were not over. On 19 January 1925, the Prussian Ministry of the Interior, in consent with the Ministry of Science, Art and General Education (Volksbildung), and in accordance with § 4 in Reichlichtspielgesetzes of 12 May 1920, made an application for the cancellation of the decision of the censor regarding the two last acts of *Die Hexe* to die Film-Oberprüfstelle. The reasons given for this application were that the film was calculated to offend religious feeling, threaten public order, and demoralise and brutalise. The application was sustained by a decision on 23 December 1924 from the head of Bildstelle der Zentralinstitut für Erziehung und Unterricht. The representations of the witch-trials, torture, and the Dominican monks who were members of the Inquisition courts were considered

ling of the story. 'M-s' in *Film-Kurier* (20 October 1923) called the film a capriccio, and found that the old theme about a husband who falls in love with his own wife without knowing that she is his wife was presented in a new and original variation. 'Christensen hat einen kultivierten Lustspielfilm geschaffen, von Feinheit in der Linienfürung, beseeltem Humor und jenem leisen Hauch von Sentiment der vom Wesen des Lustspiels unzertrennlich ist … Vor allem: dieser Film hat Atmosphäre, ein Milieu, durch das die Träger der Handlung bedingt sind … Christensen hat ein Zusammenspiel geschaffen, in dem alle Faktoren sich zu einem reizvollen Kammerorchester zusammenfinden.'[30] Also 'Th.' in *Der Film* (4 November 1923) found that 'In dem Film liegt eine hohe Kultur … Es ist eine Art filmischer Kammermusik'.[31] *Deutsche Allgemeine Zeitung* was also full of praise. Most of the reviewers praised Lil Dagover, and *Berliner Volks-Zeitung* (23 October 1923) remarked that the film was Lil Dagover's great success. She attended the premiere with Willy Fritsch who was also well received. *Vorwärts* (24 October 1923) wrote that the young, very talented Willy Fritsch 'ist bezaubernd in seiner Natürlichkeit'.[32] But there was, of course, also a negative review. *Roland* (1 November 1923) observed: 'Das ganze [ist] zu abgeschmackt, witzlos und langweilig … Willy Fritsch als Crawford oberflächlich und seelenlos. Lil Dagover als Eva schlank, graziös, ob in reichen Kostümen oder sehr unbekleidet, aber ohne Kraft der Charakteristik.'[33]

The role of Wilbur Crawford was not Willy Fritsch's first apperance in film, which is often claimed, but it was his first major role and proved an immediate breakthrough for him. In her memoirs, Lil Dagover relates how, at a screen test, the man with an irresistible laugh got the part. At the screen test Benjamin Christensen was not content with the actors. About one of them he remarked that he moved like a blind cow-actor in front of the camera. Fritsch heard this remark and began to laugh. Suddenly Christensen was interested and shouted: 'Keep on laughing, man'. He signalled to the cameraman that he should shoot, and the screen test was successful. Willy Fritsch was hired, and Benjamin Christensen

launched a star, as he did with Norma Shearer in Hollywood and, back in Denmark in 1939, with the young Grethe Holmer.[34]

On 17 March 1924 Benjamin Christensen left Berlin to take a vacation in Copenhagen. He stayed at Hotel Hafnia, and on 18 March 1924, *Berlingske Tidende* printed an interview with him. He said that he would go back to Berlin in May or, at the latest, in June, because he was due to direct two new films for Ufa. He praised German film which was having a renaissance. He had just seen Fritz Lang's *Siegfried* (premiere 14 February 1924), and he thought that it was a very important, even grandiose work; 'there are beautiful effects in the *mise-en-scène*', Christensen observed. He had seen very few Danish films in Germany, but he knew that the Pat and Patachon films from Palladium were very popular. He told the interviewer that he had long since signed a contract with the Germans and that – contrary to rumours – he had no contract with Nordisk Films Kompagni.

Back in Berlin, Benjamin Christensen used the summer to play one of the major roles in Carl Th. Dreyer's *Michael* adapted from Herman Bang's novel (Fig. 7). Benjamin Christensen's wife, Sigrid, attended the shooting of the film, and sat in the viewing room every night because her husband insisted on her presence. In a taped interview with Marguerite Engberg (18 November 1978), Sigrid

recounted her experiences in Berlin. She found Erich Pommer charming and Nora Gregor (the leading lady) beautiful and pleasant. She also thought that Dreyer was a kind and nice man, and that relations between the quiet and calm Dreyer, and the temperamental and often nervous Benjamin Christensen were good. Benjamin Christensen, on the other hand, has said that during the breaks the two friends quarrelled a great deal in Danish.[35] 'Listen', Dreyer said, and called Christensen to a corner, 'we must agree about one thing: not to use the word idiot, because this is understood by the others'. *Michael* was censored on 23 August 1924 (1966 metres) and was prohibited from exhibition to children. It had its premiere at Ufa Theater Kurfürstendamm on 26 September 1924 and was well received by the press.

The day before the premiere, *Film-Kurier* published a short article in which it noted that Der Meister was played by 'Benjamin Christensen, der bekannte dänische Regisseur' (Fig. 8).[36] The article went on to observe: 'Jahre hindurch hat Christensen nur als Regisseur, nicht aber als Darsteller gewirkt und unserem Berichterstatter gegenüber gab er seiner Befriedung darüber Ausdruck, dass es ihm gestattet sei, wieder einmal selbst tätig zu sein, und zwar in einer so schwierigen Rolle wie der des Meisters. Seine Arbeit für diesen Film war insofern besonders interessant, als

er ein vertrauter persönlicher Bekannter des dänischen Romanschriftstellers Hermann [sic] Bang war. Christensen selbst bezeichnet den Roman seines Freundes und Landsmannes Bang als eine Arbeit des gereiften Schriftstellers, eines Mannes, dessen Stern, wie der des Meisters in dem Roman "Michael" bereits im Zenith [i.e. Zenit] stand, und in der Tat dürfte Michael für Hermann [sic] Bang das bedeuten, was Faust für den gereiften Goethe bedeutet hat, sein Lebensbekenntnis, sein Testament.'[37] In a review in *Film-Kurier* two days later (27 September 1924), Heinz Michaels wrote: 'Über allen aber: Benjamin Christensen als Meister. Aus diesem durchgeistigten Leidensgesicht spricht das Martyrium des Mannes, der um der Kunst willen dem Leben abgeschworen hat. Um ihn ist die Abseitigkeit des grossen Schweigenden. Als ein abgeschiedener Geist blickt er auf die Menschen gleichsam durch eine gläserne Wand hindurch, durch die er die Menschen zwar erblickt, ihre Hand aber nicht zu ergreifen vermag.'[38] *Lichtbild-Bühne* (27 September 1924) noted: 'Abermals ist es die hohe Kultur der Dänen, die uns im Hauptdarsteller Benjamin Christensen, dem bekannten Regisseur und Autor des Hexenfilms, entgegentritt. Schauspieler wie er sind für den deutschen Film ein ganz hoher Gewinn.'[39] Dr. Roland Schacht writing on Christensen in *Berliner Zeitung am Mittag* (27 September 1924) observed: 'Er vereinigt Noblesse mit Wucht, äusserliche Ruhe mit tiefstem seelischem Ausdruck, seine Sterbeszene gehört zu den ganz wenigen grossen Meisterstücken filmischer Darstellungskunst.'[40] And Josef Melnik in *Berliner Börsen-Courier* (28 September 1924) wrote: 'Christensen spielt den Meister mit der grossen Selbstbeherrschung des einsamen und gepeinigten Künstlers, die im Roman lebt und für Bang selbst so bezeichnend war. Von Christensens Darstellung führt eine Brücke zum Roman, zu Bang.'[41]

Michael became Christensen's greatest triumph in German film but he, more than anyone else, would like to forget his last German film, *Die Frau mit dem schlechten Ruf*. In a letter dated 25 March 1939 to Ove Brusendorff, the later founder of The Danish Film Museum, Benjamin Christensen wrote:

During this year [1924] I wrote and directed my life's greatest and really brilliant failure, *The Woman Who Did*, the only one of my own films which I never dared to see after I shot it. Who edited this masterpiece I don't know, but it must have been a tough job. The whole business was what you in Hollywood call, 'Just one of those things', something Mr. Erich Pommer *should* have one of his men do. As I had to go to America I sacrificed myself. During the shooting of this film there was the charming fact, so to say, that none of the actors understood the same language. Russians, Germans, and Englishmen frisked about merrily, and after having interpreters during the first few days, I gave up, as the film had to be done in a hurry, and I let them say what they wanted. It was Babylon.

In this film I had the charming Russian actress, Madame Zorina, in the main role. In the male roles I had Mr. Lionel Barrymore and Mr. Henry Vibart from London.

We all had a glorious time, it appeared, [but] the film was forced through by some mad man in London who – for some unknown reason – wanted to get the film finished at any price, although I, from the first day, tried to dissuade him by telegram from going on with the project. Probably the man had something to do with the old English sentimental novel which lay behind my shooting script. The novel was about a young girl who wanted to have children out of wedlock. If she had a child, I don't remember any longer. At the outset I was told that he would be very grateful if I could read the novel and write the script in 48 hours.

In a letter of 20 March 1955 to the author of this essay, Benjamin Christensen told the same story, but added:

Before I started it [the project], I popped into London in order to dissuade the Englishman from putting money into it. His only answer to all my various 'reasons of common sense' was, with a big smile, to invite me to his lovely cottage a few miles outside London, where he presented me to his charming wife who suggested that the three of us – instead of discussing the film – should take a refreshing swim in the Thames, which so seductively wound through the rather big backgarden of the cottage.

As late as 1967, the film was believed not to have been finished and, therefore, never distributed.[42] But the film was both finished and distributed. The film was censored in Berlin on 31 July 1925 (1894 metres) and, on a second occasion, on 3 August 1925 (1608 metres). On both occasions the film was prohibited from exhibition to children. Ufa was not satisfied with the film, and removed almost 300 metres before the premiere which was held on 18 December 1925 in Ufa-Theater, Nollendorfplatz, Berlin. The film only ran for one week, even if it got pretty good reviews. There are no prints in existence. The film was based on the novel *The Woman Who Did* by Grant Allen. It was photographed by Carl Hoffmann, and the sets were designed by Hans Jacoby. The players included Alexandra Sorina, Lionel Barrymore, Gustav Frölich, Henry Vibart, Daisy Campbell, Herta Müller and Marian Alma.

The film is 'a tract on the marriage', as *Kinematograph* observed in December 1925, and gave a detailed description of the story: Herminia Barton, a young high society woman, has sworn never to marry because she sees marriage as an antiquated and unworthy form of cohabitation between man and woman. The young girl tries to live according to her theory. She leaves her parents' house and earns her living by giving music lessons. She meets Allan, who is the son of the famous children's doctor, Dr. Merrick. Allan wants to marry her, but Herminia wants a 'free marriage'. They have a child, Allan dies, and Herminia must fight her way through life with her child. The rich grandfather wants to adopt the child, but she refuses indignantly. In the course of her life, Herminia becomes an influential journalist. Her daughter, Dolores, grows up but does not like the bohemian way of life which her mother prefers. She is invited to a schoolfriend's house in the country where she suddenly feels an outcast when her background is revealed. Dolores lectures her mother about how weak her lifestyle and world views are. Herminia asks the grandfather to adopt Dolores. Dolores wins her loved

one, a young man whom she could not marry before because of her background. Herminia has to admit that 'marriage is still, in spite of its shortcomings, the most worthy form of cohabitation between man and woman'.

The film got mixed reviews. *Neue Berliner Zeitung* (19 December 1925) observed: 'Eine menschliche Tragödie, von dem Regisseur sicher gestaltet und mit vielen zarten Feinheiten durchsetzt. Christensens Stärke liegt im Bildhaften, hier weiss er die stärksten und überzeugendsten Wirkungen zu gewinnen. Alexandra Sorina bleibt zwar die Kämpferin schuldig, aber sie gibt mit tiefer Wärme die Leidende; diese Frau ist die grosse Darstellerin der Innigkeit und des Schmerzes, ihre Gestalten tragen stets den Hauch eines gewinnenden stillen Liebreizes. Eugenie Teichgräber gibt mit Anmut und Frische die Tochter.'[43] *Reichsfilmblatt* no. 45, 1925 reported: 'Der Film, den die bewährte Hand Benjamin Christensen schuf, ist eine feine künstlerische Arbeit, ein Werk, an dem man das ehrliche Streben nach künstlerischer Veredelung des Lichtspiels spürt und das uns das schon früher bewiesene Können Christensen im rechten Licht zeigt. Manches an dem Film wirkt freilich etwas langatmig, an anderen Stellen stören wieder die zahlreichen und reichlich langen Titel.'[44] And the review concluded: 'Ein Film weniger für das Provinzpublikum, als für die anspruchlosen Besucher der Grosstadt gemacht, die den Bildern mit Interesse folgen werden'.[45]

In *Reichsfilmblatt* nos. 51/52, 1925 one finds a rather contradictory review by 'Di' who observed: 'Eine derartige Behandlung des Eheproblems wird beim Gros des Publikums wenig Anklang finden. Man sollte dieses Thema bei der Herstellung von Filmen tunlichst vermeiden.'[46] The final lines of the review concluded: 'Ein Film, der vielleicht dem grossen Publikum, in Verkennung seiner eigentlichen Tendenz, gefallen wird'.[47] *Deutsche Filmwoche* (1 January 1926) found that the film's theme was, '[u]ebermässig originell und wirksam ... es wird aber durch die psychologische Note der Regie Benjamin Christensens so herausgebracht, dass man den Dingen mit Spannung folgt'.[48] *Der Kinematograph* (December 1925) concluded that 'Regie: Benjamin Christensen mit vielen feinen Zügen ... Das manchmal zu Konstruierte der Begegenheiten ist auch sie [Alexandra Sorina] natürlich nicht imstande, zu überbrücken'.[49]

It was not a film for a mass audience was the opinion of 'F.O.' in *Berliner Börsen Zeitung*, but went on to observe: 'der Filmkenner hat seine Freude an der Regie von Benjamin Christensen, ein stark ausgeprägtes Gefühl für sein differenzierte gesellschaftliche Atmosphäre ist das beste daran, dazu kommt eine sehr sorgsame Auswahl auch der scheinbar unwichtigsten Darstellertypen, so wurden z.B. einmal die bekanntesten Bohemetypen der Romanischen Cafés gezeigt; milieuvollendete Bauten und eine angenehme weiche Photographie unterstützen den günstigen Eindruck. Schade, dass das Sujet als solcher [sic] nicht eben packend wirkt.'[50]

Even if Christensen himself found *Die Frau mit dem schlechten Ruf* a disaster, it was not gunned down by the critical establishment. Christensen did not have to leave Germany as a fugitive. He simply got an offer from MGM like so many other European directors and in February 1925, he arrived in Hollywood. He would never return to Germany.

German reviews translated in the notes by Vreni Hockenjos.

Notes

1.   A collection of essays from the symposium was published in 1994, see Manfred Behn (ed.), *Schwarzer Traum und weisse Sklavin: Deutsche-dänische Filmbeziehungen 1910–1930* (Munich: edition text + kritik, 1994).

2.   *Politiken*, 1 January 1922.

3.   *Verbotene Kinematografien-Bilder.* Alphabetishes Verzeichnis verbotener Filme zum Gebrauch für die Polizei-Behörden und Kinematographen-Inhaber, 3 Jahrgang nr. 100 (Hauptausgabe). Güben den 30. Dezember, 116. The information was provided by Rolf Burgmer, Cologne, who claims to be the owner of the only existing copy of this publication.

4. Ausschitte [sic]: Akt I: Szene in welcher der blinde Organist durch die Luke auf dem Turm anlangt u. dann über die Brüstung steigt und abstürzt. (Cut: Act 1: Scene in which the blind organist reaches through the hatch a[nd] then climbs over the parapet and falls down the precipice.)

5. The painting *Beethoven* by the Italian painter, Lionello Balestreri (1872–1958), shows the interior of a painter's studio. In the background, two musicians are playing the violin and the piano. Three young artists and an elegant young woman – presumably the wife or mistress – are listening with enthusiasm to a piece by the great composer, whose portrait-mask is seen on the wall. The painting, which got a gold medal at the World Exhibition in Paris in 1900, was Balestreri's breakthrough. From 1901 it was exhibited in Venice and in the United States, and was often reproduced. The painting is now in the collection of the Galleria d'Arte Moderna, Trieste.

6. *Beretning om Dania Biofilm A/S*, 1915.

7. Ibid.

8. For details of the contract, see *Beretning om Dania Biofilm A/S*, 1915.

9. Ibid.

10. Known (from her maiden name) in Denmark as Empress Dagmar (1847–1928), Maria Feodorovna was a daughter of the Danish King, Christian IX.

11. 'II Akt 1. Der Anblick der bewusstlossen Leonie auf der Bühne in der Vergrösserung. 2. Die schwerverletzte Schauspielerin wird weggetragen u. auf die Sopha gelegt. 3. Das Abtupfen der Wunde in der Vergrösserung.', see Herbert Birett (ed.) *Verzeichnis in Deutschland gelaufener Film 1911–1920* (Berlin, Hamburg, Munich,Stuttgart: K.G. Saur, 1980). (II Act 1. Shot [view] of the unconscious Leonie on the stage in close-up. 2. The badly injured actress is carried away a[nd] placed on a couch. 3. The dabbing of the wound in close-up.)

12. The short story was also later included in *Hollywood Skæbner* (Copenhagen: Det Schønbergske Forlag, 1945).

13. Herbert Birett, *Verzeichnis in Deutschland gelaufene Filme 1911–1920* (Berlin, Hamburg, Munich,Stuttgart: K.G. Saur, 1980).

14. Ibid.

15. It [the film] presents, in point of fact, a highly interesting, entertaining, and exceedingly dramatic piece … The settings are arresting because of their variety, the action includes moments of high excitement, and the views of the provincial countryside transport the viewer with their charm. The exquisite acting of the performers, the exceedingly skilful direction, and the technical perfection of the film created this beautiful and perfect success.

16. The power of a director of genius, freed from all small-mindedness, can be felt throughout all of the six acts of this tremendous film. The director's name is Benjamin Christensen, and he plays the part of the naval lieutenant van Houven in the drama. If it had not been a drama, I would be tempted to call it simply grandiose. It accords with the nature of film, it is felt for real, that is, one simply knew: *what was wanted and for what goal one invested with energy*.

17. Benjamin Christensen is an actor with an outstanding range of dramatic expression. His way of portraying the difficult character of this film can really serve as an object lesson. When I once again recall this enormous achievement, the scenes come to my mind when the unworldly man finally receives his freedom and staggers out not knowing where to go. His first thought is for his child, but then comes the moment of pain when he cannot find the child. These were shattering moments, full of the utmost truth to life. For this achievement alone, the film deserves to be a big success, which it has indeed become in the eyes of the public. In addition to this, the directing which Christensen himself has undertaken achieves an exceptional accuracy, as too the camera work which is remarkable.

18. Benjamin Christensen first prepared a script which depicts an interesting plot with an interesting environment, and since, at the same time, he was responsible for the production of the film, it was in his hands to make extensive use of all the technical and dramaturgical resources. Photography and set design were excellent and the good acting of the popular Nordisk artists is as natural as ever.

19. Alfred Rosenthal, using the pseudonym 'AROS', wrote a book on Marlene Dietrich for Verlag Scherl. As a young man, Rosenthal accompanied Olaf Fønss during the presentation of *Atlantis* in Germany. In his memoirs, *Films-Erindringer gennem 20 Aar*, (Nutids Forlag, 1930), Fønss writes: 'The young poet is now the editor-in-chief Alfred Rosenthal, the feared film critic, who under the name AROS writes film reviews in *Berliner Lokalanzeiger*, who is president of the Film Press Association, and

within the big Scherlverlag is editor-in-chief of the magazines *Kinematograph*, *Film Echo*, and *Film Magazin*'.

20. The whole film is a perfect example of the synthesis between *kultur* film and the feature film, just as we have called for on many previous occasions.

21. A *kultur* film experiment.

22. One is afraid, possibly not without due reason, that the film may face problems over censorship. This would be very regretable.

23. *Kultur*, or rather, 'anti-*kultur*' film … more rebellious than all the weekly summer programmes of the Berlin cinemas put together.

24. The film is not just scientific and artistic, it is an ethical event.

25. The film with its magnificent images and interesting narrative episodes, loses something through the dull, pedantic, and doctrinal tone of the accompanying German titles. One often feels embarrassingly sent back to school again. The film was received with great applause, but some hissing could also be heard.

26. Also the final words, about which a later age will judge many of the million victims who died in the Great War in the very same way that we, today, judge victims for their inner beliefs, were quite inappropriate, and prompted a justified response.

27. And the film's final remark, hinting at a comparison between the mania of the witch hunt and the World War with its 20 million deaths, may have influenced some fathers and mothers to rethink the necessity of war.

28. Reprinted in *Geschichte des Films in 365 Filmen* (*So viele Filme wie das Jahr hat*) no. 19 (Berlin: Freunde der Deutschen Kinemathek).

29. Lil Dagover, *Ich war die Dame* (Moewig: Taschenausgabe 1980).

30. Christensen has created a sophisticated light comedy, sensitive in its style, inspired in its humour, and with that touch of sentiment that is so characteristic of light comedy. Above all, this film has atmosphere, an environment which conditions the formal devices of the plot. … Christensen has created an ensemble in which every element is brought together as in a charming chamber orchestra.

31. This film is of a high cultural standard … it is a sort of cinematic chamber music.

32. is enchanting in his naturalness.

33. The whole thing is too clichéd, without humour, and boring … Willy Fritsch as Crawford [is] superficial and without soul. Lil Dagover as Eva [is] slender, graceful, whether in rich costumes or in a state of undress, but lacks tha aura of character.

34. It has been claimed that Benjamin Christensen directed a film by the title *Unter Juden* in 1923. In the biography of Christensen by Bertil Hagman in *Enciclopedia dello Spettacolo* (Rome: Casa Editrice Le Maschera, 1954–68), this title is included as a directorial assignment and Charles Higham wrote, in a letter to the editor of *Sight and Sound* in Autumn 1966, that Christensen gave Willi Fritsch his first important role in *Unter Juden*. Although an Austrian film produced in 1924 with the title of *Die Stadt ohne Juden* was directed by H.K. Breslauer after a novel by Hugo Bettauer, Benjamin Christensen was not associated with the production, nor did he direct a film with the title *Unter Juden*.

35. See Tage Heft, 'Klip af en Livsfilm', *Politiken*, 26 March 1939.

36. Benjamin Christensen, the well-known Danish director.

37. For many years Christensen has only worked as a director and not as an actor, and he expressed to our reporter his satisfaction at finally having the opportunity to act himself, especially in such a demanding rôle as that of Meister. Working on the film was particularly interesting since he was an intimate [and] personal friend of the Danish novelist Hermann [sic] Bang. Christensen describes the novel by his friend and fellow countryman Bang as the work of a mature writer, of a man whose star was at its zenith just like that of Meister in the novel, *Michael*; and, indeed, Michael may have the same importance for Hermann [sic] Bang as Faust had for the mature Goethe – his life's confession, his legacy.

38. But most outstanding: Benjamin Christensen as Meister. Out of this spiritualised and suffering face speaks the martyrdom of a man who has abstained from life for the sake of art. He is surrounded by the sense of absence that is typical of a great man who does not need words. As a distanced spirit, he looks upon human beings as through a glass wall through which he can see people, but is unable to reach out to meet their hands.

39.   Once again it is the high culture of the Danes that we meet in the main actor Benjamin Christensen, the famous director and author of the witch-film. Actors like him are a great gain for German cinema.

40.   He unites noblesse with force, outer calm with deepest expressions from the soul; the scene in which he dies belongs to one of the few great masterpieces of cinematic acting.

41.   Christensen plays Meister with the great self-control of the lonely and tormented artist which was so manifest in the novel and so characteristic of Bang himself. Christensen's portrayal forms a bridge to the novel and to Bang.

42.   See John Ernst, *Benjamin Christensen* (Copenhagen: Det Danske Filmmuseum, Copenhagen, 1967).

43.   A human tragedy, convincingly shaped by the director and pervaded with numerous sensitive delicacies. Christensen's strength lies in the visual; it is here that he knows how to get the strongest and most convincing effects. Alexandra Sorina is not convincing as the struggling woman, but she gives you suffering with deep warmth; this woman is the great actress of intimacy and pain, her rôles are always characterised by this touch of silent winning charm. Eugenie Teichgräber plays the daughter with grace and freshness.

44.   The film, made by the experienced hand of Benjamin Christensen, is an elegant artistic work, a work in which one can feel the honest intention to refine film in an artistic manner. It also casts the right light on Christensen's talent as evidenced earlier. Some parts of the film seem, however, long-winded; at other times, the numerous and lengthy intertitles are distracting.

45.   It is a film which is not so much made for provincial audiences as for modest metropolitan spectators who will follow the picture with interest.

46.   Such treatment of a marital problem will not be received well by most of the audience. When producing films, we should take every means to avoid such a topic.

47.   A film which might be a success for the public that fails to recognise the film's actual meaning.

48.   original nor is it effective ... yet the psychological mood is formed in such a way under Benjamin Christensen's direction that it makes one follow the events with suspense.

49   Director: Benjamin Christensen with many elegant features ... But not even she [Alexandra Sorina] can bridge the sometimes too obviously constructed course of events.

50.   but a film expert will appreciate Benjamin Christensen's directing, a distinct feeling for social atmosphere full of subtle distinction are its highlights. Additionally, mention should be made of the care with which even the most seemingly unimportant actor is chosen as, for example, the well-known bohemians so perfectly demonstrate in the cafés of Rome. Buildings that perfectly echo their environmental atmosphere together with pleasantly soft photography support the favourable impression. It is a pity that the subject as such is not exactly thrilling.

Palladium and the Silent Films with 'Long and Short'

Marguerite Engberg

Hvidegårdsparken 39, 2800 Lyngby, Denmark

At the end of 1919, the Danish film director Lau (Lauritz) Lauritzen (1878–1938) was engaged by the Swedish company Skandinavisk Filmcentral. Lau Lauritzen had worked as a director for Nordisk Films Kompagni in Denmark since 1914, and during five seasons directed about two hundred short comic films. But at the end of 1919, when Nordisk Films Kompagni continued to reduce its staff, Lauritzen preferred to accept an offer from the new Swedish film company, Skandinavisk Filmcentral. This company was founded in 1919 by the film distributor, Lars Björck who owned several cinemas in Sweden including Palladium, the largest cinema in Stockholm. Most of the company's films were produced in Denmark, where Björck took advantage of the unfortunate situation in Danish film arising from film companies that had collapsed during the First World War. Björck bought two studios in Hellerup, on the outskirts of Copenhagen. The larger studio had belonged to Kinografen and, later, Dansk Astra Films. The major part of Björck's production was carried out in these two studios. The Danish branch was called Palladium, and Svend Nielsen was appointed as its administrative leader. The artistic leader for the production of film dramas was entrusted to Robert Dinesen, a Danish director who had worked since 1911 as an actor and

director in Danish cinema, and who had won international fame with *Maharadjahens Ynglingshustru* (A Prince of Bharata, 1917). To direct comic films, another Danish director was chosen, Hjalmar Davidsen, but he was no great success, and was dismissed in 1919 to be replaced by Lau Lauritzen. During his years at Nordisk Films Kompagni, Lauritzen had worked with a regular team of actors, many of whom he brought to Palladium. Among them were Olga Svendsen, Oscar Stribolt (two fat comic actors), Torben Meyer, Carl Schenstrøm and Aage Bendixen.

Skandinavisk Filmcentral produced its first feature film in 1919. Directed by Robert Dinesen and titled *Jefthas dotter* (Jeftha's Daughter), the film was a lavish costume drama in the style of *Maharadjahens Ynglingshustru*. The film was released in the autumn of 1919, but in no way fulfilled the expectations of the producer. The film was a flop. Dinesen directed one more film in 1919, *Ödets redskap* (The Instrument of Destiny), a film which fared even worse. Lars Björck found it so bad that he did not dare release it. Not until 1922, when Skandinavisk Filmcentral went into liquidation, did the premiere take place. On the whole, Björck had no success with his feature films, and therefore decided, in 1921, to stop producing films.

The Danish branch of Skandinavisk Filmcentral, Palladium, which, among other films,

had produced the comedies that Lau Lauritzen directed, had some minor successes in 1920. In 1921, *Landvägsriddare* (The Knights of the Road) became a success in Sweden and Denmark. Thus, when Björck gave up as producer, Svend Nielsen and Lau Lauritzen decided to take over the production of comedies. In 1921 they founded the Danish film company, Dansk Films-Industri Palladium, soon shortened to Palladium. They settled down in a small studio and office in Hellerup in the neighbourhood of Björck's largest studio. The following year they bought his studio where Palladium remained until 1970 when the company ceased production.

The production policy of Palladium

The basis for the new Danish production company was the production of feature length films with 'Fyrtaarnet' (Long) and 'Bivognen' (Short). During the first years of Palladium's existence, the company only produced films with Long and Short. Even when Lau Lauritzen worked at Nordisk Films Kompagni, he had been interested in the possibilities of a tall comic figure and a short one. He was not the first one to have this idea. In 1915 the American company Kalem had released some films with a comic couple called 'Ham' and 'Bud'. But they were no great success, so production soon ceased. The first comic couple to appear in one of Lau's films was in *Væddelöberen* (A Dead Cat), produced by Nordisk Films Kompagni in 1919, in which Carl Schenstrøm and Aage Bendixen played a couple of young men in love with the same girl. In the next film, *De keder sig paa Landet*, also produced by Nordisk in 1919, they appeared for the first time as tramps. But it was not until *Landvägsriddare* that they were called 'Fyrtaarnet og Bivognen' (Long and Short). That film was produced by Skandinavisk Filmcentral in 1920 with a Swedish comic actor, Axel Hultman, in the main part. But it was Carl Schenstrøm and Aage Bendixen who made the film a success, and attracted all the attention when it was released at the beginning of 1921. When starting the Danish film company, Lau Lauritzen wanted to replace Aage Bendixen with an actor who would be a better contrast to the long, lean Schenstrøm. Bendixen was a small, agile ac-

tor, not unlike the French comic actor André Deed or some of the early Italian film comics such as Polidor or Tontolini. After a long search, Lauritzen found the man he wanted. He was a circus actor by the name of Harald Madsen. He was just what Lau was looking for: a small, broad actor with a round face. He was a brilliant match for Schenstrøm. And for the next eighteen years, they worked as a couple in Danish films.

As soon as Lau had engaged Harald Madsen, film production began. Before the end of 1921 Palladium had made three films with 'Fyrtaarnet og Bivognen'. Svend Nielsen and Lau considered the third one to be the best, and therefore released *Film, Flirt og Forlovelse* (The Film and the Flirt) first on 17 October 1921. It was a scoop to introduce a comic film couple. France, Italy and the United States, in particular, had produced farces and comedies with great success for many years, but never before – apart from the films with 'Ham' and 'Bud' – had a director worked with a pair of comics. The advantage of a comic couple (compared with a single comedian) is that the director has more strings on which to play. Whereas a single comedian performs his gags direct to the audience, a couple may, besides this kind of acting, also exploit the opportunity for keeping a reciprocal gag or joke going. And Lau Lauritzen was skilled in knowing how to make the most of this extra possibility.

Film, Flirt og Forlovelse was a tremendous success at the world premiere in Copenhagen. *Dagens Nyheder*, one of the main Copenhagen papers, wrote on the following day: 'Now also we can make comedies which ought to be shown all over the world. The audience was unceasingly amused by the story which, in reality, was nothing but what the film title says: a film, a flirt and, at last, an engagement.' The critic of *Berlingske Tidende*, another leading paper, ended his review by saying: 'and then Lau Lauritzen's greatest discovery: the circus clown Harald Madsen. Sometime he acted like Chaplin, but also when he was himself, as we know him from the circus, he was quite simply priceless. ... Madsen had a thundering success whenever his shining, little philosopher's face appeared on the screen.' A fortnight after the Danish release of the film, *Film, Flirt og Forlovelse* had been

sold to the Netherlands, Belgium, England and Italy. Soon the film was also sold to Sweden, Norway and Germany. A sign of the popularity of the comic couple was that every country invented their own name for them. In France, they were initially called Triplesec et Rondouillard; later on they became known as Doublepatte et Patachon. In Italy their names were Y and X; in Hungary, Zoro és Huru; in England, Long and Short; in Turkey, Düztaban ve Bastibacak, and in the Netherlands, Watt en ½ Watt where they were often portrayed against the background of an electric light bulb so that the joke could not be missed. In Norway they were called Telegrafstolpen og Tilhængeren; in Sweden, Fyrtornet och Släpvagnen; in Finland, Majakka ja Perävaunu and in Arabia, Duz Tabanaje bazdi badjagh. But the most successful name was the one used in Germany: Pat und Patachon. This name was soon adopted by a great many countries, for instance, the USSR, Poland, Yugoslavia, Rumania, Spain, Portugal and, later on, also by France, Italy and, to some extent, England.

There was one country, however, to which Svend Nielsen had great difficulty in selling their films: the United States. Nielsen even travelled to New York in a vain attempt to introduce them. But at last, in 1926, a chance seemed to appear. A Mr. Kofeldt, an American distributor on the West Coast, bought one of the films with Ole and Axel as he named the comic couple. The film was *Takt, Tone og Tosser* (Misplaced Highbrows, 1924), perhaps one of the wittiest of their films. Kofeldt launched the film in San Francisco as the first feature-length European film comedy. It was shown at a private performance for film people on 13 August 1926, and on 16 August the film was mentioned in *The Pacific Coast Independent Exhibitor* under the headline: 'Danish Humour wins American Laughter'. Amongst other things, the critic wrote: 'That American audiences can and do appreciate the humour of foreign comedies was illustrated at the preview of the Walter W. Kofeldt importation 'Misplaced Highbrows', given recently at the Coliseum. The Coliseum audience was thoroughly responsive to the humour of the Danish production, which features the vicissitudes of two types, Ole and

Axel, in ludicrous situations much the same in Denmark as in this country.' Another newspaper, *The Pacific Coast* in Southern California wrote (1 October): 'At a preview showing held at the Highland Theater, Pasadena Avenue … the Danish comedians "Ole and Axel" proved a decided hit. The audience enjoyed the European feature comedy immensely – starting with titters and giggles, which soon swelled into laughs, roars and screams of delight.' After his success with *Misplaced Highbrows*, Kofeldt decided to import another film with Long and Short. He chose *Dödsbokseren* (The Demon Boxer, 1926). It was shown on 11 January 1927, and was well received. But shortly afterwards, on 13 March, an American comic film was released: *Duck Soup*, Stan Laurel and Oliver Hardy's first film. Thereafter no American distributor was interested in importing films with Long and Short.

A portrait of Fyrtaarnet (Long) and Bivognen (Short)

As early as *Film, Flirt og Forlovelse*, the parts of Fyrtaarnet and Bivognen were fully-fledged. Fyrtaarnet (Long) was a good-natured, fatherly person who took the initiative. Bivognen (Short) was a youthful, inexperienced, and naïve person sometimes also a little bold. Neither of them were particularly brainy, a fact that furthered their popularity among children, for every normal child of ten could feel superior to Fy og Bi (Fy and Bi), by which name they were mostly known in Denmark. Their popularity with Danish children remained undiluted until the advent of television around 1950, and Fy and Bi films were shown in many Danish cinemas at children's Sunday matinées.

As a rule, they played tramps or had some odd jobs as in *Film, Flirt og Forlovelse* where they were travelling knife-grinders or, in another film, *Blandt Byens Børn* (The Lodgers of the Seventh Heaven, 1923), where they worked as jumping-jack manufacturers. In almost all their films they were dressed as tramps. Long wore a ragged jacket, one size too small for him so that the sleeves were too short. His trousers were also ragged and too short so that they made him look taller than he really was. On his head he wore a crumpled

bowler hat. His hair was long and dishevelled, as too was his moustache. A big, broad snubnose completed his make-up. Contrary to Long, Short did not put on make-up; just a bit of powder on his face. His hair was close-cropped, and he, too, wore a small, shabby bowler, mostly tilted. His clothes did not fit well. His jacket was too tight and too short, his trousers too big at the waist, and too tight and short at the bottom. He wore boots similar to the ones worn by the Italian comic, Cretinetti. In the course of time their costumes became less shabby, but the style of their clothes remained the same. Their gestures were also repeated from film to film: Long had a shy, somewhat cautious gait, whereas Short was characterised by quick movements, and his swaying gait was seen in all his films and, in time, became even more pronounced.

The typical Fy and Bi film

Forty-six films were produced with Fyrtaarnet and Bivognen from 1921 to 1940. Lau Lauritzen was the director of the first fourteen of these films, and in all, he directed thirty films with the couple. All these films – apart from *Don Quixote* – have some characteristic traits in common:

Lau Lauritzen wrote the majority of the scripts sometimes assisted by A.V. Olsen;

The films were feature length, apart from the first two films from 1921, *Landligger-Idyl-Vandgang* and *Sol, Sommer og Studiner* (Sun, Summer and Students) which meant they could be shown as the main film in a cinema programme;

In most of the films, Fy and Bi are not the main characters of the plot, even if they play the main rôles in the film. The principal story is, as a rule, a love story between a young couple who for some reason or other meet obstacles on their way to happiness. Fyrtaarnet and Bivognen then come to their assistance. This happens, for instance, in *Film, Flirt og Forlovelse* and *Takt, Tone og Tosser*. Rarely do the films end with Fy and Bi marrying the young girls, but it does happen as, for instance, in *Kraft og Skønhed* (Strength and Beauty, 1928). Generally

the audiences thought the girls too charming and too good-looking for such tramps;

The story is set in the present among middle-class people;

The greater part of each film is shot on location, out of doors. Lau always chose a beautiful Scandinavian location for his films: in *Film, Flirt og Forlovelse*, much of the film takes place in Hornbæk, a well-known Danish seaside resort; in *Daarskab, Dyd og Driverter* (The Reformed Daughter, 1923), the location of Möens Klint, a beautiful chalk cliff area, something like the Cliffs of Dover, is used, and in *Vester Vov Vov* (People of the North Sea, 1927), the story is set on the west coast of Jutland;

The Danish title often uses alliteration as, for instance, *Film, Flirt og Forlovelse*, *Blandt Byens Børn*, and *Han, Hun og Hamlet* (He, She and Hamlet, 1922 and 1932);

The Lau-Girls. Inspired by Mack Sennett's Bathing Beauties, Lau Lauritzen introduced a series of young girls into his films. We encounter them first in *Film, Flirt og Forlovelse*, but as Lau said in an interview: 'I do not, as in the case in certain American films, use them all the time, and in more or less daring costumes ... I only place the little ladies in the situation where they are needed and where they can supply the film with a breath of youth and high spirits'. In other words, he tried to integrate the girls into the plot. Thus we meet them as bathing girls in *Film, Flirt og Forlovelse*, as skiing girls in Norway in *Vore Venners Vinter* (The Run-away Bride, 1923), as gym girls in *Kraft og Skønhed*, and as fisher girls in *Vester Vov Vov*;

Comic gags are employed in a way different to the films of, for instance, Stan Laurel and Oliver Hardy. In a Laurel and Hardy film, the entire plot is constructed around a few gags which constitute the climaxes of the films; if you enjoy seeing these films again and again, it is for the joy of seeing how the gag works, and how it develops towards the final climax. It is different with a Fy and Bi film. Here we have a more or less well-constructed story

which is now and then enlivened with a comic scene.

In 1925 Lau Lauritzen decided to fulfil a long-cherished wish to make a film based on Cervantes' *Don Quixote* with Long and Short in the two main parts. After preparatory work, he left for Spain with his whole team, and stayed in Toledo and the neighbouring area for about nine months. After returning to Denmark, the editing took several months. *Don Quixote* became the most ambitious work in Lau's career. During the fourteen months he spent on this film, all other work was put to one side. For a director who, between 1914 and 1919, had directed about forty two-reelers a year, and from 1921 to 1925 directed three or four feature films annually, *Don Quixote* changed the rhythm of his work completely. The film was released on 26 November 1926 in Berlin in a shortened version. The full version of 3829 metres, i.e. with a running time of about three hours, was premiered in Copenhagen on 30 November 1926.

Don Quixote was not well received in Denmark. Critics found that Lau's veneration for Cervantes' work had hampered him in making a great film. One of the critics tried to imagine what would have happened if Chaplin had directed the film and had played Sancho Panza: 'Then we would have spent an enjoyable evening in the cinema with tears in the eyes from laughter – instead we had tears from yawning now and then'.

In Spain, on the other hand, the critics were satisfied with *Don Quixote*. A journalist from Barcelona wrote in his review on 20 May 1927: 'To touch these figures without profaning them; to transfer their souls to the screen without the loss of their original and innate vigour, is a victorious exploit, and Palladium Film has, in our opinion, obtained it by means of their great and awe-inspiring work ... and Palladium was in luck when chosing Lau Lauritzen as a director and especially Long and Short in the parts of Don Quixote and Sancho Panza. These actors are already well-known to our audiences from some comic films in which they, however, have not reached the success they have in "The Ingenious Knight Don Quixote de la Mancha". The former of the above-mentioned actors is very convincing in the part of the good-natured

peasant who acts as armour-bearer for the ingenious knight, and the latter with typical Nordic head excellently expresses the hero from la Mancha.' The critic of *Correra Catalan* in Barcelona began his review of the same date with the following words: 'We must admit that disbelief disappeared at once when we saw that the greatest respect and most complete engagement with Cervantes' mind has been observed'.

Seeing the film today, it is difficult to agree with the two laudatory Spanish critics. Certainly, there are excellent scenes in the film, such as Don Quixote's fight with the windmills (even if this scene is too long), and both Fyrtaarnet and Bivognen have the right appearance for the two main parts. Harald Madsen is very good in the scenes where, as a governor, he tastes the pleasure of power. And Carl Schenstrøm is touching in the last scenes of the film where he returns to his home, ill and scorned. Here the tragedy comes to life. But Lau Lauritzen does not succeed in giving a convincing description of Spain. It is hard to believe that the film was shot on the Castillian plateau; it might easily have been the plains of Jutland.

The long production schedule for *Don Quixote* had consequences for Palladium. A contract had existed between the company and a German distributor, Lothar Starck since 1922. According to this contract, Starck had bought the sole distribution rights for Germany. Palladium, for their part, had promised to deliver four feature-length films annually with Long and Short. Until 1925 there had been no problems. But when Lau began working on *Don Quixote*, he could no longer keep to this agreement. As a result, other directors were engaged to direct films with Long and Short. The first new director was the Swede, Gustaf Molander, who in 1925 directed *Polis Paulus' påskasmäll* (The Smugglers). Molander had made his name as a director both of literary films and comedies. Among his comedies, the most well-known is *Thomas Graals myndling* (Thomas Graal's Ward, 1922). As this film had been a success, Molander was considered the right choice as director for a film with Long and Short. The result was a well-composed film, made in a lively style like American comedies. But Molander did not quite grasp

the specific humour of Long and Short. So this became his only film with the couple. Immediately after *Polis Paulus' påskasmäll*, Molander started on a Selma Lagerlöf film (*Ingmarsarvet*, Ingmar's Inheritance, 1925) based on her *Jerusalem*.

The first Dane to take over the direction of a film with Long and Short was Urban Gad. He had returned from Germany where he had worked as a director since 1911. During the period from 1911 to 1914, he directed thirty-two films with Asta Nielsen and contributed to her international success. Among the many Asta Nielsen films Gad had directed were comedies such as *Engelein* (The Little Angel, 1913) which many considered to be her best film in this genre. Gad directed *Lykkehjulet* (The Wheel of Fortune, 1925–26) at a time when Lau was busy editing *Don Quixote*. As a director, Gad usually wrote the script himself, as was the case with *Lykkehjulet*. Gad did not experiment with his Fy and Bi film, but shaped the characters in the same way as Lau. The film was released shortly after *Don Quixote*. The disappointed public wanted a film with Carl Schenstrøm and Harald Madsen in which the comic couple played their familiar rôles. And that was what they got. So Gad's film became a success which was well deserved, even if some of the critics thought the story too complicated.

Two Austrian directors also tried their hands with Long and Short. But only a fragment from one of these films has survived. The film was too compressed and somewhat inept. After the production of the two Austrian films, Schenstrøm and Madsen were sent to London where they were to act in a British film. Palladium had signed a co-production agreement with the English company, British International Pictures who had engaged an American actor, Sidney Scott. Unfortunately, Scott died on the day shooting was due to start. Within a few hours, he was replaced by another American actor who had just finished acting in a film in England. His name was Monty Banks. Banks was familiar with American film farces, especially the farces with Harold Lloyd. He gave the film the title *Cocktails* (1928). Fy and Bi again played a couple of tramps, and the story did not differ much from the ordinary Lau Lauritzen film. But the

speed of the film did. Never before had a film with Long and Short shown such rhythm and pace. This still makes the film worth seeing today.

The following year, Long and Short played in another English film, *Alf's Carpet*. Here we meet them as bus drivers of an old London bus. The film is, however, clumsy and heavy, and cannot stand comparison with Douglas Fairbanks' *The Thief of Bagdad* made some five years later. A disastrous thing happened, moreover, in the middle of shooting: the producer decided suddenly that the film should be a 'talkie', and as neither Schenstrøm nor Madsen had command of a cockney accent, two English actors had to replace them on the soundtrack. As an English critic wrote at the time of its release on 17 October 1929: 'The film is ruined by its attempt to be a sound film'.

After having played in several films abroad, Fy and Bi returned to Denmark where Lau directed them in *Vester Vov Vov*, his first film after *Don Quixote*. This was a typical Lau film with all the ingredients familiar from his earlier work. For setting, Lau chose the west coast of Jutland with dunes and roaring waves. It is a story about smugglers and greedy film dealers, where Fy and Bi once again help the young couple to find a happy ending. The film excels in comic scenes, the best one being perhaps the one where Fy and Bi demonstrate the secrets of the charleston to a group of shy, young fisher-girls.

During the five years between 1927 and the end of the silent period, Lau directed eleven films with Fy and Bi. Among these, *Højt paa en Kvist* (Long and Short as Mannequins, 1929) deserves special mention. For this film, Lau had found two young talented actresses to play the main female parts: Nina Kalckar and Marguerite Viby. They were very successful, and we encounter them in all of the next films with Long and Short. Marguerite Viby quickly developed into being the leading comedienne of Danish film (and partly also Danish theatre), a position she held for several generations.

Gradually Lau Lauritzen slowed down his rate of direction. In 1930 he only directed one film, in 1931 two films, and in 1932, he directed

his last film with Fyrtaarnet and Bivognen, the sound film, *Han, Hun og Hamlet*, a remake of the 1922 film.

Fyrtaarnet and Bivognen lived from 1921 to 1940 in Danish films. But they did not grow a day older during this period. They were static characters; that was their strength, but also their weakness. On the one hand, the audience loved to meet them again and again, and see that they had not changed. On the other hand, as they did not change, they did not develop with the century. They could not, therefore, avoid becoming old-fashioned; they no longer belonged to the time in which they lived. This is quite clear when you see their last film from 1940, *I de gode, gamle Dage* (In the Good Old Days) directed by a young Danish director, Johan Jacobsen.

Bibliography

Marguerite Engberg, *Fy & Bi* (Copenhagen: Gyldendal, 1980).

Hauke Lange-Fuchs, *Pat und Patachon: Eine Dokumentation unter Mitwirkung von Marguerite Engberg und mit einem Beitrag von Kaj Wickbom* (Schondorf: Roloff und Seesslen, 1979).

Jonathan Sanders, *Another Fine Dress* (London, New York: Cassell, 1995).

Carl Schenstrøm, *Fyrtaarnet fortæller* (Copenhagen: Hagerup, 1942).

Lars Åhlander (ed.), *Svensk filmografi*, II, *1920–1929* (Stockholm: Svenska Filminstitutet, 1982).

The archive at Palladium (which contains newspaper clippings for all the Fyrtaarnet og Bivognen films), Det Danske Filmmuseum.

À la recherche des films perdus: A Substantial Find of Early Danish Cinema

Bo Berglund

V. Ryttmästaregatan 19, 217 52 Malmö, Sweden

Lost films can be found everywhere: in attics, cellars, garages, mental hospitals;[1] yes, and even in film archives. Only a fraction of all the films produced during the silent period has survived. The paradoxical thing is that even this 'small' amount is too much for us to save in time. Ideally, everything should be saved, but films die in their cans every day. However reluctantly, we need to prioritise. But to be able to prioritise correctly, we must know exactly what we have got; otherwise it becomes impossible, and desultoriness reigns. All archives have got unidentified films. Formerly they would not readily admit it. Inertia plagues all bureaucratic organisations and they have a tendency to stay put like the dragon on the gold.[2] But things have changed and, in all fairness, there is much more openness now. An archive's first duty is to preserve domestic production; foreign films must come second, and this means they are often neglected. Unidentified films are not just the ones catalogued as such. A catalogue in the vernacular, with domestic distribution titles only, is neither sufficient nor satisfactory; thus you have a catalogue with many neat titles, but which films you actually hold you do not know. Every film must *de facto* be considered unidentified until you know the country of origin and the original title. Consequently, there are many films, primarily not thought of as unidentified, that need to be identified, and for this work you need a silent film expert. You cannot employ just anybody; a crash course will not do. Long experience, both practical and theoretical, is required to fulfil the task. Apart from all the obvious historical, geographical and cultural clues contained in the image, the filmstrip itself is also of use to us, and I do not mean a self-evident Kodak edge code: the shape of the frame, the shape of the camera gate, and the thickness of the frame-line may give a clue as to which company produced the film. To recognise as many actors as possible, even the more obscure ones, is of paramount importance.[3] The smallest detail may be decisive. Sometimes you have to muster ratiocinative powers of the highest order. Many archives, especially the small and understaffed ones, have not got the time, the resources, nor the expertise to make this kind of inventory, inspection and identification of their old silent foreign material. Therefore, there should be a permanent pool of various silent film experts from which the FIAF archives could draw when the need arises – and it always will. Otherwise the work

Fig. 1. Video print, Falliten, 1907.

Fig. 2. Video print, Rivalinder, 1906. The husband takes leave of his wife.

Convict (R.W. Paul, 1903). (For a more complete list of titles, see the Appendix at the end of this essay.) But now we are going to concentrate on the Scandinavian films, or rather the Danish ones.

If you see a sign saying Carlsberg Pilsner (Fig. 1), you need not possess extraordinary deductive faculties to conclude that the film is Danish, especially if the film is very old. (Carlsberg was not that international in those days.) That the film is old is obvious from the fact that everything is in Long Shot and there is strong sunlight in indoor scenes. There is no main title, and only one intertitle, a telegram. The story: a clerk courts a ship-owner's daughter but is rejected. She and her intended, an officer, laugh at the poor clerk. While ship-owner and clerk are working in an office, a telegram arrives:' "Capella" forlist. Alt tabt. Smith.' (*Capella* foundered. Everything lost. Smith.) The clerk tries to console the ship-owner who is in great despair. The officer, not wanting to marry a pauper, breaks off the engagement to the daughter. Suddenly the ship-owner pulls out a gun, but just as he is going to shoot himself through the head, the clerk grabs the gun and averts suicide. The ship-owner's wife and daughter thank the clerk for having saved the ship-owner's life. We then see a family idyll a year or two later: the clerk and the ship-owner are now the owners of a grocery store; the clerk and the daughter are married and they have a child. This must be *Falliten* (The Bankruptcy) produced by Nordisk Films Kompagni in 1906 and premiered in January 1907. In the collections of The Danish Film Museum in Copenhagen there is no material from this film to corroborate identification: no stills, not even a synopsis. But, even so, there can be no doubt. This is the only fitting title.

In April 1905 Ole Olsen, the founder of Nordisk Films Kompagni, opened a cinema in Copenhagen at Vimmelskaftet 47. Early in 1906 he began making films, scenics and actualities at first, but soon also short fictional films. This film is thus from his very first production year. He made 101 films in 1906, thirty-seven of which are fiction films. Of those thirty-seven, only three were known to have survived: *En ny Hat til Madammen* (A New Hat for Madame) – more about this film

will never be done properly. If there still are any skeletons in the cupboard or closet – and I am sure there must be many – now is the time to bring them out. Instead of rattling skeletons there might come some glittering nuggets of gold because 'there is gold in them thar hills'. Let's start digging – now!

It is always a special joy and satisfaction to find films long sought after and thought to be lost forever. This is exactly what happened – not once, but many times – in late April 1998 when Jan Olsson and I visited the Norwegian Film Institute in Oslo. During three busy but exciting days we inspected some 30,000 feet of nitrate; most of it was silent and in good condition, though shrunken and brittle. Two Roscoe 'Fatty' Arbuckle films were discovered: *The Cook* (1918), in which Fatty appears with Buster Keaton, and *A Reckless Romeo* (1916/17) which has been something of a mystery; some suppose it was never made, while others say there are two films by the same title. (More about those two films in another context.) We also found some early British films such as *The Polite Lunatic* (Williamson, 1905), and *Bloodhounds Tracking a*

Fig. 3 (top left). Video print, Rivalinder, 1906. The husband greet his mistress.

Fig. 4 (top right). Video print, Rivalinder, 1906. The gossip squeals to the wife.

Fig. 5 (middle left). Video print, Rivalinder, 1906. The duel. Mistress shoots ...

Fig. 6 (middle right). Video print, Rivalinder, 1906. ... wife.

Fig. 7 (bottom left). Video print, Rivalinder, 1906. The husband rejects his mistress.

Fig. 8 (bottom right). Video print, Rivalinder, 1906. Mistress shoots ...

later – *Anarkistens Svigermoder* (The Anarchist's Mother-in-Law), both comedies, and *Den hvide Slavinde* (The White Slave Girl), a drama. So *Falliten* is a welcome addition to that small number.

That there was another very early Danish film among all that footage was much harder to perceive. The story: a man meets his mistress (Fig. 2 and Fig. 3), and they are both observed by the gossip; she hurries to the man's wife and tells her what she has seen (Fig. 4). With the help of the gossip the wife challenges the mistress to a duel. The man is informed about the duel by a letter from his wife. When he arrives at the duel, the mistress has just killed his wife (Fig. 5 and Fig. 6). In despair he rejects his mistress (Fig. 7) who then shoots him down in cold blood (Fig. 8 and Fig. 9) before shooting herself (Fig. 10 and Fig. 11). Three deaths within a minute! Strong stuff indeed! Not surprisingly, there is no main title, and only one intertitle, a letter. To identify this film, there was absolutely nothing to go by

except the letter which was written in German. But, somehow, I did not think the film was German. The letter is signed 'Mary'. Could it be English? I scoured Gifford's *British Film Catalogue* to no avail.[4] Later, when I watched the film anew, it suddenly occurred to me that the entrance to the ship-owner's house in *Falliten* (Fig. 12) resembled a door in this film. What made it so difficult and not at all conspicuous was the fact that in *Falliten* the door is seen at rather close range, whereas in this film it is seen from afar, from outside a fence, and through some trees and bushes in the garden. But close scrutiny showed that it was indeed the same house and the same door. Now the problem was more or less solved: it could only be another early Nordisk production. The most appropriate title would be *Rivalinder* (Female Rivals). Once again, there are no stills nor any synopsis to confirm identification. In the Nordisk business records deposited at The Danish Film Museum, I found an alternative title not mentioned in the Danish filmography, 1896–1914, compiled by Marguerite Engberg (hereafter, Engberg's *Registrant*).[5] The reason why it is

not in the filmography may be the fact that still in the mid-1970s only part of this material had been deposited at the Museum; the rest came later. The alternative title is *En Kvindeduel* (A Duel Between Women), and there can be no mistake, for both titles have got the same production/negative number. At Det Kongelige Bibliotek (The Royal Library) there is a collection – incomplete, though – of printed programmes from Ole Olsen's own movie theatre, and among them I found a synopsis for *En Kvindeduel* which proves the identification to be accurate.

The study of these programmes and synopses clearly shows how prominent the use of firearms and violence is in the Nordisk films of 1906 and 1907; they abound in duels, violent killings, suicides, shoot-outs, and executions, so *Rivalinder* is far from the only instance. In *Røverens Brud* (The Robber's Bride) and *Røverhøvdingens Flugt og Død* (The Robber Chief's Flight and Death) there are long shoot-outs between robbers and the police/military. *Tro til Døden* or *Rosenborg Have* (True to Death/Rosenborg Garden): a costume drama of the love of a poor nobleman for a young girl and her father's objections to their alliance; in the end the father decides to let the girl witness her lover's execution, but just as the shots are fired the girl rushes to her lover and both are killed to the horror of her father. *Stenhuggerens Datter* (The Stone Cutter's Daughter): When a girl sees her former lover with a new mistress, she fetches her father's rifle and shoots him down. *Hævn* (Revenge): Marie, engaged to be married to Hammer, is violated by Lund. In great despair, unable to face such disgrace, she drowns herself. Hammer forces Lund to fight a duel. Lund manages to fire the first shot, but misses; then Hammer aims very carefully and, thinking of Marie's pale face, shoots Lund. The way the synopsis puts it – 'thinking of Marie's pale face' – makes one wonder if it really reflects what was seen on the screen, i.e. was there a superimposition of the girl's face, or some kind of mind screen? Impossible to tell; the film is not extant. *Blomsterpigen* (The Flower Girl) is yet another variation on the now almost hackneyed theme of revenge: a poor flower girl, seduced by a squire and then deserted when pregnant, is rescued from suicide by a poacher who helped her once before when she ran away from her brutal father. Eventually the poacher shoots the squire. *Anarkistens Svigermoder* is a comedy but no less violent. Irritated by his mother-in-law, a man takes some dynamite and blasts her into smithereens. He then expects his wife to be as happy as he is at the way he straightened out the problem.

At present *Rivalinder/En Kvindeduel* is the oldest surviving fiction film made by Nordisk. Wanting to give the impression that Nordisk was a well-established film production company and much older than it actually was, Ole Olsen gave the very first film he made production number 101. The production/negative numbers for the extant 1906 fiction films are: *Rivalinder* 154, *En ny Hat til Madammen* 164, *Anarkistens Svigermoder* 170, *Den hvide Slavinde* 173, and *Falliten* 177.

In 1995 Jan Olsson discovered a collection of early fiction films in the Television Archive of Sveriges Television and arranged a seminar at which all those films were screened. To identify some forty early Pathé films even before seeing them was no major problem

thanks to the excellency of the catalogue cards and their detailed synopses. Some films, however, remained unidentified even after the seminar. Later I came to realise that a film called *Gammeldags frieri* (Old-Fashioned Proposal of Marriage) was indeed a Danish film entitled *Rosen* or *Fra Rokokotiden* (The Rose/From the Rococo Times) shot in June 1907 and released early in 1908. According to Engberg's *Registrant*, a print of this film was preserved at The Danish Film Museum. I searched for it in vain; in fact, nobody could find it. Finally, I asked Marguerite Engberg who told me it was a mistake; she had been misinformed at the time. So this is indeed the only print known to exist. The film has got German flashtitles, but the main title and the first intertitle are missing. The intertitles of the film are not numbered, so the reason I can tell one is missing is that from 1908 onwards all intertitles are preserved in title books belonging to the collection of Nordisk business records.[6] The Danish Film Museum has also got six stills from the film. In October 1908, *Moving Picture World* commented on this picture, but started by saying that *Bear Hunting in Russia* was really excellent:

> It is not surprising that this subject won for the producers the gold medal at the Cinematographic Exposition at Hamburg. That it is not a single instance of the superior work of the company was shown by *In* [sic] *the Rococo Times*, a colored subject released a few weeks ago. The fine grounds of a castle in Denmark furnished the setting for a pretty story and the composition of the pictures showed that the photographer was also an artist, while the delicate coloring, to which the scenes were well adapted, stamped it as a production of equal merit.[7]

> …The old nobleman wants to give a banquet to a rich old man of noble family. But his young and pretty daughter wants to have a younger and handsomer bridegroom, and therefore … she refuses the old suitor when her father introduces him to her. In the moonlight the young people meet and talk over their future prospects … The two rivals quarrel about a rose and the old gentleman settles the quarrel by saying that his daughter is to throw the

rose into the water and the one who fetches it up again shall have not only the rose but also the hand of his beautiful daughter ... In a second the young man is in the water, and while the spectators are shouting with joy he reaches the rose, which he at once offers to the fair judge. The old suitor has to acknowledge his adversary's strength and courage, and congratulates the two young people and withdraws his suit in favor of his successful rival.[8]

One of the Pathé films screened at the seminar was called *Den lilla blinda*, which literally means *La petite aveugle* (The Little Blind Girl) and this is the title of a 1906 Pathé film. By comparing the Swedish synopsis with the French one, the identification was established: a little blind girl is snatched away by a gypsy woman, but she manages to escape and is finally brought back to her parents by a policeman. Only later when seeing the film at a subsequent screening, did I realise that the Stockholm print of *La petite aveugle* did not stop where the French synopsis concluded but went on to tell the story of how the girl, on another occasion, gets lost in the woods but is found in the nick of time just as she encounters a vicious-looking tramp. The parents track her down with the help of a psychic boy who is able to point out on a map exactly where she is. It does not take long before one realises, however, that this is not the same girl as in the earlier part of the story, and the same goes for the parents. Hence, this is quite another film that has been tacked on to the end. With regard to identification, though, there was not a clue. Later it occurred to me that there is a Danish film called *Drengen med den sjette Sans* or *Den sjette Sans* (The Boy with the Sixth Sense/The Sixth Sense, 1907). This title would fit the story. On the other hand, one must always be circumspect and ask oneself the question: Who is first? Who is plagiarising whom? Ideas are stolen all the time. There could be more than one film that told more or less the same story. Alas, there are no stills and no synopsis at The Danish Film Museum. What finally convinced me that the film is Danish was the set of the girl's home; there is a particular piece of scenery also seen in many other Nordisk

productions of 1906 and 1907. Unfortunately, the very beginning of the film is missing. So films *can* be found everywhere: even in the middle of another film, or as here, hidden at the end of it.

Since 1962 The Danish Film Museum has had in their collection a film catalogued as *Den glade Enke* (The Merry Widow). Nobody seems to have bothered about it and apparently nobody thought it was Danish, although two films by that title were made by Nordisk, one in 1906, the other in 1907. But is it really Danish? If so, which version is it? The film has Swedish intertitles, but that should not fool anybody. (Incidentally, a film was made in Sweden in 1907 in which Danilo and Hanna Glawari dance the famous Merry Widow Waltz: the film exists and looks quite different from *our* version.) In the stills department of the Museum there are three stills, but they are from the non-extant version. On the envelope containing the stills a date has been written (1906), but it has been crossed out and replaced by 1907. So, which is which? Stalemate. The film is in fact Danish because there is a backdrop which can be seen in many Nordisk films of the time: a backcloth with painted palms. But the stills? Also Danish and for the same reason: here the scenery is the same as in *Drengen med den sjette Sans* and many more films. There is no synopsis for either film. It is not known who acted in the 1906 version; but Oda Alstrup and Viggo Larsen are said to be in the 1907 film. Since there are no close-ups in these early films, it is hard to recognise actors and really tell who is who. I cannot be absolutely sure, but as far as I can see, we have Viggo Larsen as Danilo in the stills, but I do not think Hanna Glawari is played by Oda Alstrup. Larsen is not in the film, and to confuse the matter even more, nor is Oda Alstrup. Naturally the basis for the film is Lehár's famous operetta, *Die lustige Witwe*, but in this short film we get little more than the dances: The Merry Widow Waltz, Montenegrin folk-dances, some dancing by the 'grisettes' etc.

While looking at the cinema programmes at The Royal Library, I was happy to find a synopsis for the 1906 version, and this is something quite different from the 1907 film. This is a farce making fun of the Merry Widow

Craze that raged throughout the world during those years. The synopsis states:

> Our picture shows what the thousandth performance of The Merry Widow looks like. All of you who are suffering from the Merry Widow Craze do not despair. And those poor people, now obliged to perform The Merry Widow for the thousandth time, though they seem to be in a very bad state both as to mind and body, may recover some day after a long convalescence. Only the two leads will come to a sad end: the mentally deranged composer sweeps the pitiful remains of that valiantly dancing couple into a dustpan, and now we hope we have got rid of The Merry Widow, that European plague sent to us by the wrathful Gods.

One should always be cautious: is this really the Danish 1906 version, or could it be a foreign film? There are some Merry Widow films made by other companies: Kalem, Biograph, Lubin, Vitagraph, Edison and Pathé. But these films are all later. The Danish 1906 version was released in November 1906, and Kalem's *The Merry Widow*, which is the oldest of these films, was released more than a year later, in December 1907. So, in all probability, this synopsis is for the Nordisk 1906 film. The stills do not reveal the farcical nature of the film, alas, but only show people dancing. Very few prints of the film were sold, and only locally, except for two prints sent to Norway in May 1907. In any case, it seems to have been a popular film at Olsen's own cinema because it was screened there many times, as can be seen from the printed programmes. My conclusion is that the stills are the 1906 version and the preserved motion picture is the 1907 film. But who plays the two leads if not Larsen or Alstrup?

Arnold Hending has written many books on Danish silent cinema. None of these books is indexed, which makes them difficult to use. Recently, in a book from 1936, I found, by sheer serendipity, some pertinent information quite out of context.[9] Regarding the years 1916–17 and the Alhambra Film Co. whose director was Knud Gerner, Hending suddenly asks: 'Does anybody remember Knud Gerner as Danilo together with his wife Tilley Christiansen in a fragment of *The Merry Widow*

shown at the cinema in Vimmelskaftet [i.e. Ole Olsen's cinema]?' Having checked photographs of Knud and Tilley, I am inclined to think Hending is right. Here is probably the answer to our question.

As we have seen, there is a lot to gain from letting a silent film specialist inspect your collection. But, at the same time, there is a risk that we may lose some films, and by that I do not mean the expert will abscond with them, merely that the films may turn out to have been misidentified. Here are some examples.

In *Schiave bianche allo specchio*, published in connection with the Scandinavian retrospective at the Pordenone Festival in 1986, there is an article by Barry Salt in which he discusses *Opiumsdrømmen* (The Opium Dream), a 1914 comedy directed by Holger-Madsen, and there is also a frame enlargement from the film.[10] What Salt obviously never realised was the fact that he was seeing *not* a fragment of a Danish 1914 film but an American one-reel Joker comedy of 1916 called *The Harem Scarem Deacon* – complete but without titles – directed by Allen Curtis, with Gale Henry, William Franey, Lillian Peacock, Charles 'Heinie' Conklin and Milburn Moranti. Of course, the mistake is the archive's in the first place, and it is an old one; the film was acquired back in 1962. But a little prosopic knowledge would have helped reveal the mistake. How on earth can an American film called *The Harem Scarem Deacon* have been confused with the Danish *Opiumsdrømmen*, especially as the film is without titles? On the leader, however, *Opium Dreams* is handwritten in English. This was apparently the British distribution title of the film. When the archive received a lot of material from Nordisk in the 1960s, they took it for granted that everything would be Danish – Nordisk's own productions, not foreign films once distributed by them.

A film catalogued as *En Bortførelse* (An Elopement, Nordisk 1910) turned out on closer inspection to be *Love vs. Title, or An Up-to-Date Elopement* (Vitagraph, 1906). Another example of this kind is *Den Sømand han maa lide* (A Seaman Has to Suffer) which the archive received in 1967. The actual film is not the 1919 comedy directed by Lau Lauritzen, with

Oscar Stribolt and Laurits Olsen. In this case, however, somebody got suspicious, for at some juncture the handwritten words 'Engl. farce' were added to the typed card. Well, what English farce is it? It is not English but American: *Neptune's Naughty Daughter*, a 1917 two-reel comedy directed by J.G. Blystone, with the famous film comedienne Alice Howell. Not so many of her films have survived – and least of all her Century comedies made when she was in her prime – so this is a welcome addition.

As mentioned above, *En ny Hat til Madammen* (A New Hat for Madame, 1906) is one of only three films still extant from that production year – before the recent additions, that is. Ron Mottram describes the film thus:

> The third of the surviving 1906 films, *En ny Hat til Madammen*, exhibits an unusually absurd humor. The story involves a woman who buys a new hat that has such a large brim that the boy delivering the hat box cannot get it through the door of the woman's house. Instead, they hoist the box to the second floor where the husband breaks out the window frame to get it through. Later, the woman causes havoc with the brim while walking along the street. To contain the damage, her husband buys a little wagon in which he pulls his wife. Another man sees this, likes the idea, and buys a wagon for his wife. The two men get into a race with the wagons, and the wives fall out. Finally, the husband is injured in a duel over the hat, which is then used as a stretcher to carry him away.[11]

Apparently it has survived only as a 16mm print; otherwise The Danish Film Museum would have asked for a 35mm copy back in 1973 when they obtained the print from Stiftung Deutsche Kinematek, Berlin. As seen in the print, the German title of the film is *Ein Hut nach neuerster Mode* (A Hat of the Latest Fashion), a title not found in Engberg's *Registrant*; there the German title is said to be *Ein neuer Hut* (A New Hat). Among the old Nordisk business records there is a contemporary letter in which the film is listed as *Ein neuer Hut für Muttern* (A New Hat for Mother). In the collections of The Danish Film Museum no other material relating to this film exists:

no stills, no synopsis, in fact nothing to corroborate identification. The end title of the film shows the famous polar bear logo together with the two sides of a gold medal won at the Cinematographic Exposition in Hamburg, Germany. I smell a rat. Here we might have a case of mistaken identity. But why? What seems to be the trouble? Now, a film domestically released in November 1906 and then exported and shown abroad during 1907 could not possibly contain a reference to a gold medal won in June 1908. But the obvious explanation is, of course, that the film was later reissued under a new title. Recently, however (and this will drive the final nail into the coffin), I found a synopsis at The Royal Library amongst the printed programmes mentioned earlier:

> *En ny Hat til Madammen*
> It is Saturday. Father comes home with his weekly pay, and Mother persuades him to buy her a new hat. The whole family, with pram and all the trimmings, set out to buy a new hat for Madame. But Father prefers to leave this matter to Mother, and therefore suggests he take a walk with the children until she has decided which hat to buy. The walk turns out to be a long one, and he pays a visit to every pub in the neighbourhood. Finally, when Mother finds her dear old hubby, he is in a terrible state. Father exchanges places with Baby and is brought home in the pram.

We immediately notice that this differs from the existing film, and the discrepancies are not small; on the contrary, this is an entirely different story. So it could not be a reissue of the old film but another one altogether; it is not the 1906 film but some later Nordisk comedy. But which comedy? So far I have not found out. Herbert Birett confirms that the 1907 German distribution title for *En ny Hat til Madammen* is indeed *Ein neuer Hut für Muttern*. But what does he say about the other title? Birett writes: '*Ein Hut nach neuerster Mode*, 1911?, producer: not listed.'[12] So the year is uncertain, but why is the producer unknown? Does this mean that it is not a Nordisk film? No: the main title displays the polar bear logo. Have the main and end titles been tampered with by some film dealer sell-

ing 16mm prints to collectors? Right now I am at the end of my tether. More research is needed. So – at least for the time being – I rest my case.

Now we may have lost a 1906 film, but, incredibly enough, I will immediately be able to redress the balance and give you still another 1906 Nordisk production. John Fullerton is working on a project which involves watching all the early Danish films in the Copenhagen archive in chronological order; those prints I know fairly well. But Jan Olsson pointed out to me that John had also got some prints from the National Film and Television Archive in London. I asked John about it, and he kindly gave me a list of the titles. Most of these titles are not found in Magliozzi's *Treasures from the Film Archives* nor – and this is even more surprising – in the up-dated CD-ROM version of that book.[13] Most films had been identified and given their original Danish title, but some still lacked a Danish title. *Ohne Zahnartzt geht's auch* (No Need for a Dentist): this German title is not in Engberg's *Registrant*, but seeing the film convinced me that it is *Tandpinens Kvaler* (The Painful Toothache, 1906). The film starts with an emblematic close-up of a man having a bad toothache. He tries to kill the pain by drinking himself into a stupor. Eventually, he takes a piece of string, goes out into the street, and extracts the tooth with the help of a departing tram.

Another film is called 'Driven from Home' but this is no main title; as a matter of fact, it is the second intertitle in a film whose original title is *Magdalene* or *En uartig Pige* (Magdalene or A Bad Girl, 1908).

Ein Radfahrkursus is another unknown German title, but it was released in the US under its English equivalent *Lesson in Cycling*. The original Danish title is *Happy Bob som Cyklist* (Happy Bob as a Cyclist, 1907). Robert Storm Petersen, humourist, cartoonist, painter, actor, and author (a multi-talented man indeed, much admired and celebrated in Denmark), made a series of comedies in which he played a character called Happy Bob. It has been a much deplored 'fact' that no footage from any of the six comedies he made has survived. Now, however, we have got *Happy Bob som Cyklist*. But – drat! – there is only the first minute left of the film.

Revolutionsbryllup (A Wedding during the French Revolution, 1909) is the first of three film versions of the famous play by the well-known Danish playwright Sophus Michaëlis. The second version was directed in 1914 by August Blom, and among the leading actors were Betty Nansen and Valdemar Psilander. The third version was made in Germany in 1927 by the Danish director A.W. Sandberg, and the lead was played by the Swedish actor Gösta Ekman. The play was also made into an opera, *Revolutionshochzeit*, by Eugen d'Albert in 1919. The first 1909 one-reel version, directed by Viggo Larsen, is a true Film d'Art. Only seconds before the film ends there is a short reverse shot from outside the street just as our hero gets shot; otherwise we see one and the same room, in long shot, from the same angle all the time. And were it not for the twenty-four intertitles not much of the story would be understood. Nevertheless, it is nice to have it at long last; now we can compare all three versions. The London print has German flashtitles. Other films, lost and found, are:

> *Bomben* (The Shell, 1909);
>
> *Gar el Hamma III. Slangeøen* (The Abduction, 1914), first reel only;
>
> *Den forfaldne Husleje* (When the House Rent Was Due, 1907);
>
> *De forhexede Galoscher* (The Bewitched Rubber Shoes, 1912);
>
> *Privatopdageren* (The Private Detective, 1912), N.B.: made by Skandinavien, not Nordisk;
>
> *Den Kvindelige Dæmon* (Theresa, The Adventuress, 1913), incomplete;
>
> *Ruth* (A Girl's Crossroads, 1909);
>
> *Spionen* (The Spy, 1909);
>
> *Den stjaalne Politibetjent* (The Stolen Policeman, 1910);
>
> *De to Guldgravere* (Temptations of the Goldfields, 1909).

There are also several Danish non-fiction titles.

The American distribution of Nordisk films in 1907

Before Ole Olsen established a New York branch, known as The Great Northern Film Company, in early 1908, the distribution of Nordisk films in the US was handled by Miles Brothers. Ron Mottram has touched upon this subject in an article in *Film History* in 1988;[14] he mentions a couple of titles in passing, but he gives no complete list of the films exported to America. Miles Bros. advertised in *Moving Picture World* in April 1907 that they were distributing British, German, and Danish films. Only four Nordisk films are clearly marked as such in the advertisements: *Anarchist's Mother-in-Law* (= *Anarkistens Svigermor*); *Auntie's Birthday* (= *Tantes Fødselsdag*); *Polar Bear Hunt* (= *Isbjørnejagt*); *True until Death* (= *Tro til Døden/Rosenborg Have*). Most titles are without the name of the producer. As a consequence, *The American Film Institute Catalog: Film Beginnings, 1893–1910* has a special heading: Country of origin undetermined.[15] The Nordisk business records give detailed information concerning which films were exported to whom, exactly when, and how many prints. Therefore I can now reduce this list of films of unknown origin. The following titles, distributed by Miles Bros. of New York in 1907, are Nordisk productions: *A Disturbed Dinner* (= *Forstyrret Middag*); *The White Slave* (= *Den hvide Slavinde*); *A Woman's Duel* (= *Rivalinder/En Kvindeduel*); *Revenge* (= *Hævnet/Hævn/Den, der hævner*); *That Awful Tooth* (= *Tandpinens Kvaler*); *Because My Father's Dead* (= *Violinistindens Roman/Fordi min Fader døde*); *Female Wrestlers* (= *Kvindelige Brydere*, N.B.: not the same as *The Petticoat Regiment*); *Great Lion Hunt* (= *Løvejagten*), later relesed in 1908 as *Lion Hunting* by the Great Northern Company; *Happy Bob as a Boxer* (= *Happy Bob som Bokser*); *For a Woman's Sake* (= *For en Kvindes Skyld/Et Drama fra Riddertiden*); *Once Upon a Time There Was …* (= *Der var engang*).

Nordisk sent a few more films to Miles Bros., but I cannot find any American equivalents. For example, *En Foræring til min Kone* (A Present for My Wife) is about a man who has imbibed too much. To placate his wife, he buys a bottle of port of the brand she likes best. Despite his wobbly state, he manages to bring it home unscathed, but just as he is handing it over to her, he drops it, and then gets a sound thrashing from the wife. What title did it get in America? Could it possibly be *I Never Forget the Wife*? I looked it up and it turns out to be a British production by the Warwick Trading Co. I checked Gifford number 01587 and looked at the story: Drunkard's mishaps taking bottle of wine to wife. Now it is time once more to ask ourselves: Who is first? Who is plagiarising whom? But then I look at the adjacent numbers 01588 *True till Death*; same story as Nordisk's *True until Death*. And number 01589 *My Mother-in-Law's Visit* Comedy: Persecuted man blows up mother-in-law. But this is *Anarchist's Mother-in-Law*! It is not just the same story; even the lengths of the films are the same. And when we learn that before Nordisk set up their branch in London in October 1907 they were doing business with Warwick Trading Co., there can be no doubt whatsoever: these are Nordisk productions.[16] So Gifford has had the same trouble as the compilers of the *American Film Institute Catalog*: companies that handle many different film brands without distinguishing them in their advertising. This is conducive to mistakes.

Appendix

Films inspected and identified in Oslo, Norway in April 1998:

> *Say It With Babies* (Roach/Pathé, Fred Guiol, 1926), with Glenn Tryon, Blanche Mehaffy;
>
> *Hobbled Hearts* (Triangle, 1917);
>
> *The Hold-Up* (Cub/Mutual, 1915), with George Ovey;
>
> *Rigadin explorateur* (Pathé, Georges Monca, 1912), with Prince;
>
> *Jack Spratt's Parrott as the Artful Dodger* (Clarendon, 1916);
>
> *On est poivrot mais on a du cœur* (Gaumont, 1906);
>
> *A Gay Time in Atlantic City* (Lubin, 1911);[17]
>
> *La Fille du sonneur* (Pathé, 1906);

Hyménée tragique (Pathé, 1906);

The Master of His House (Vitagraph, 1915), with Billy Quirk, Constance Talmadge;

Bobby the Pacifist (Vitagraph, Wesley Ruggles, 1917), with Bobby Connelly;

Bébé protège sa sœur (Gaumont, Louis Feuillade, 1911), with Clément Mary;

Boireau, victime de sa probité (Pathé, 1913), with André Deed;

Le vieux comédien Charley veut un gendre à son gout (Eclair, 1911);

Dad's Girls (Selig, 1911), with Kathlyn Williams, Tom Mix;

When Tilly's Uncle Flirted (Hepworth, 1911), with Alma Taylor, Chrissie White;

Wanted – a Sister (Vitagraph, James Young, 1912), with George Cooper, James Young, Clara Kimball Young, Lillian Walker, Rosemary Theby;

Kvinden med de smukke Øjne (Nordisk, A. Christian, 1917), with Marie Dinesen, Robert Schmidt, one reel only.

In Mo i Rana, Norway, I found another Danish film: *Vikingeblod* (Nordisk, Robert Dinesen, 1916), one reel only. There I also found a very interesting, satirical German film: *Guido der Erste oder Der getäuschte Wurstfabrikant* (Guido the First or The Duped Sausage Maker, Oliver Film, Paul Otto, 1915) with the Berlin comedian Guido Thielscher. A parvenu sausage-maker builds a castle *ad majorem porci gloriam* (to the greater glory of the pig). All architectural embellishments consist of various parts of the pig's anatomy. I only found one reel of three. Let us hope that the other two reels will turn up somewhere.

Notes

1. In 1981 a print of Dreyer's *La Passion de Jeanne d'Arc* was found in a mental hospital in Norway. This print was made from the original negative which was destroyed in a fire in December 1928. Dreyer then had to assemble a new negative from out-takes; all other known prints come from this second negative. Nobody has ever been able to explain how or why this print ended up in the hospital.
2. As Fafner, the dragon, sings in Wagner's *Siegfried*: 'Ich liege und besitze. Lasst mich schlafen!' ('I lie and possess. Let me sleep!' In English, this becomes a bit ambiguous, or, perhaps I should say, even more to the point.)
3. I once found a film in a cellar here in Malmö. What did I see? Ancient Greece: a poet in bucolic surroundings, some scantily clad girls etc. ... This must be a French or Italian film, I thought. In the background I saw a man who resembled Wallace MacDonald, but I dismissed it from my mind; no American actor could be in this European film. Nevertheless I checked his filmography and it immediately hit me: of course, this is *Purity* (1916), a film that caused a scandal in America because of its many nude scenes. As far as I know, no prints exist. Alas, the footage found is only some 250 ft.
4. Denis Gifford, *The British Film Catalogue 1895–1985* (Newton Abbot, London: David & Charles, 1986).
5. Marguerite Engberg, *Registrant over danske film 1896–1914* (Copenhagen: Institut for Filmvidenskab, 1977), 3 volumes.
6. In one of the intertitles – both in the book and in the print – there is a linguistic error: 'Der, die Rose holt, bekommt meine Tochter.' Here is a case of haplography. The title should read: 'Der, der die Rose holt, bekommt meine Tochter.'
7. *Moving Picture World* (24 October 1908): 319.
8. *Moving Picture World* (3 October 1908): 263.
9. Arnold Hending, *Stjerner i Glashuse* (Valby, Copenhagen: Winkelmanns forlag, 1936), 161.
10. Barry Salt, ' Schiave bianche e tende a strisce. La ricerca del 'sensazionale'', in Paolo Cherchi Usai (ed.), *Schiave bianche allo specchio: Le origini del cinema in Scandinavia 1896–1918* (Pordenone: Edizioni Studio Tesi, 1986), 69–70, 76.

11. Ron Mottram, *The Danish Cinema Before Dreyer* (Metuchen, London: Scarecrow Press, 1988), 21–22.

12. Herbert Birett, *Das Filmangebot in Deutschland 1895–1911* (Munich: Filmbuchverlag Winterberg, 1991), 478, 299.

13. Ronald S. Magliozzi, *Treasures from the Film Archives: a catalog of short silent fiction film held by FIAF archives* (Metuchen, London: Scarecrow Press, 1988).

14. Ron Mottram, 'The Great Northern Film Company: Nordisk Film in the American Motion Picture Market', *Film History* 2, 1 (Winter 1988): 71–86.

15. *The American Film Institute Catalog: Film Beginnings 1893–1910* (Berkeley, Los Angeles, Oxford: University of California Press, 1995), 541, 196–197.

16. Marguerite Engberg, *Dansk Stumfilm* (Copenahgen: Rhodos, 1977), 88, 2 volumes.

17. Same story, more or less, as in *Sons of the Desert* with Laurel and Hardy.

2
Finland

Born Under the Sign of the Scarlet Flower: Pantheism in Finnish Silent Cinema

Antti Alanen

Finnish Film Archive, P. O. Box 177, 00151 Helsinki, Finland

If we want to sum up the inspiration to mainstream Finnish silent cinema in one word, that word is Stiller. In early writing on Finnish film,[1] two works are highlighted as inspiration for the development of Finnish film production of significance: *Sången om den eldröda blomman* (The Song of the Scarlet Flower, 1919) and *Johan* (1921), both directed by MauritzStiller, and both based on well-known Finnish novels by, respectively, Johannes Linnankoski and Juhani Aho.[2] Their impact was immediate, as the obituaries for Stiller confirmed a decade later when *The Song of the Scarlet Flower* and *Johan* were re-released. Their importance was once more confirmed in the first Finnish history of cinema[3] when Roland af Hällström, writing in 1936 on Stiller's filming of Aho and Linnankoski in Sweden, observed: 'He saw in the landscape what was common to both Nordic countries, not what was different and special'.[4] On *Sången om den eldröda blomman* (hereafter, *Sången*), Hällström noted: 'Finnish film production was born under the sign of this film and for many years followed its path'.[5] We might add that a part of it still does.

The predominance of rural subject matter in traditional Finnish cinema should not be exaggerated. Statistically, if non-fiction shorts are included, urban milieux dominated Finnish cinema from the earliest days. However, in the silent era the most enduring films were stories of the countryside and sea. Urban Finnish silents were poor cousins to the international models they copied. In the 1930s, Valentin Vaala and his colleagues put an original spin into urban Finnish cinema.

While Finnish film production of significance started in 1919, there had been several efforts by pioneer filmmakers as early as 1904.[6] In general these efforts were not well received, and as the films themselves soon vanished, 'only a collection of tragi-comical anecdotes and rumours remained'.[7] One of these anecdotes is about the film *Kesä* (Summer, 1915 – a lost film). Eino Leino, Finland's greatest poet and bohemian, needed money for train tickets for the following day. His friend, the theatre director Kaarlo Halme, commissioned an original screenplay from him. Fuelled by strong coffee, Leino wrote the script during the night, pocketed the fee, and everyone was happy. However, the photography turned into a disaster. The critics reported that what they saw appeared like ghosts running around in fog.[8] A tantalising exception to this general situation may have been the very first Finnish

Fig. 1 (top). Koskenlaskijan morsian *(The Logroller's Bride, 1923): location shooting on the great northern rivers. [Production still courtesy of the Finnish Film Archive.]*

Fig. 2 (bottom). Koskenlaskijan morsian *(The Logroller's Bride, Finland 1923): the survivors, Oiva Soini and Heidi Korhonen as the young couple, and Konrad Tallroth as the father of the bride. [Production still courtesy of the Finnish Film Archive.]*

fiction film, *Salaviinanpolttajat* (The Moonshiners, 1907 – a lost film), a comedy about the adventures of bootleggers in the forest depths. The film, produced by Atelier Apollo's talented team,[9] was well received. It was also, significantly, the first appearance on screen of what is called 'the mythical drunkenness of the Finnish male'.

We must question the validity of opinions stated in the 1920s and later regarding early

cinema. When Finnish film production started to hit a significant commercial stride in the early 1920s, it conformed to the modes of narration gaining dominance in Western cinema. The evidence from the preceding decades is too scarce to determine whether there had been original developments in pre-classical Finnish cinema.

Sången had its Finnish premiere in October 1919. Stiller had wanted to shoot the film in Finland, but the conditions in 1918 in the shattering aftermath of a bloody civil war made such a project impossible. The expectations of the film had been marked by scepticism and jealousy, but as soon as the film was actually seen, it turned out to be a revelation. The success of the film was instant: in the box office, in the reviews, and in the minds of film producers. And more than a matter of success, it was a matter of love and pride. The impact of *Sången* was not based on cinematic artifice but truth to life. The film gave Finnish cinema some basic situations for decades to come: the village dance by the river, the couple dreaming in the midsummer night, love-making in the haystack, and the climactic shooting of the rapids.

More importantly, *Sången* taught Finns that well-known national themes could be turned into electrifying popular cinema. In October 1919, as a new production company called Suomen Filmitaide was established, the founders declared that they planned to film the national classics from *Kalevala* to Juhani Aho. Another company established in December 1919, Suomen Filmikuvaamo (since 1921, Suomi-Filmi), would realise much of the national project during the century.[10]

The expression, 'national project', can be taken literally. Finnish national culture in the serious meaning of the word was only a few generations old. Sweden had conquered pagan Finland during the Crusades, and after seven hundred years as part of the Kingdom of Sweden, Finland was conquered by Russia during the Napoleonic Wars in 1809 and became an autonomous Duchy. During this period, Finnish culture started to flourish in the spirit of confidence that even a small nation was capable of heroic feats in the fields of culture. *Kalevala*, an epic in the league of the *Iliad* and the *Odyssey*, was received with enthusiasm all over the world. The development of Finnish culture was a conscious national project in the spirit of German idealism and National Romanticism. The first Finnish novel, Finnish drama, and the first Finnish comedy were all created during the latter half of the nineteenth century. Finnish music and fine arts rose to great heights of achievement – now called the 'golden age' – during the last decades of the nineteenth century and during the first decades of the twentieth century. Those same decades – which coincide with the silent era in cinema – were also a period which witnessed a flourishing tradition in Finnish literature. The Finns knew that a vital national culture was a decisive factor on the road to independence (Finland became an independent state in 1917, after the October Revolution). Culture had brought Finland self-confidence and international awareness. The declarations on cinema in 1919 were a part of this project.

The most demanding goals like *Kalevala* and *The Seven Brothers* were wisely postponed. But Aleksis Kivi's short comedy, *Kihlaus* (The Betrothal, 1922), was soon filmed with charming ambience and attention to detail. Based on this experience, Erkki Karu dared to tackle Kivi's bucolic masterpiece, *Nummisuutarit* (The Village Shoemakers, 1923, Fig. 3), and the gamble paid off, the result being the culminating effort of Finnish silent cinema. Although based on plays, both films have the freshness of the open air, and the characters really belong to the landscape, not to the stage.

Minna Canth was another founding figure of Finnish drama. Her last play, the tragic *Anna-Liisa* (1922) about a young woman who has murdered her illegitimate baby, was adapted so successfully by Suomi-Filmi that it became the first Finnish film to be exported. *Murtovarkaus* (The Burglary, 1926) was a more ambitious Canth project: the drama covers half a century of people's destinies, including a witch-doctor from Lapland, the devastating famine years of the 1870s, romance in the midsummer night sun, and a fatal theft of money. Minna Canth, a pioneer of women's rights,[11] provided strong, complex, and ambitious roles for women.

The province of Pohjanmaa held a dramatic attraction of its own, and again as an exercise,

Fig. 3 (top). Nummisuutarit *(The Village Shoemakers, Finland 1923): the failed suitors coming home to the tune of the March of Pori, with Axel Slangus, Martti Tuukka, Kaarlo Kari, Juho Puls, and Antero Suonio. There is no bride, all the money has been spent on drink, but they believe they have caught the big thief who is worth even more money than the bride. [Production still courtesy of the Finnish Film Archive.]*

Fig. 4 (bottom). Pohjalaisia *(Plainsmen, 1925): the opening scene shot on authentic locations with authentic people, for which some of the fighting was not simulated. [Production still courtesy of the Finnish Film Archive.]*

Suomi-Filmi produced an easy initial project. *Suursalon häät* (The Wedding at Suursalo, 1924) introduced to the screen a national stereotype well-known from songs and books: the *puukkojunkkari* (the knife-slinger) or the *häjy* (the badman or the tough guy) who loves to gatecrash weddings and turn them into

Fig. 5. Pohjalaisia *(Plainsmen, 1925): Oiva Soini broods in authentic Pohjanmaa wear, Einar Rinne stands proud in chains, Kaisa Leppänen says a prayer and dresses in grey, having become religious. [Production still courtesy of the Finnish Film Archive.]*

Fig. 6. Pohjalaisia *(Plainsmen, 1925): Oiva Soini confronts the sheriff (Thorild Bröderman). [Production still courtesy of the Finnish Film Archive.]*

achieve considerable authenticity (Fig. 4).[13] The landscape was shot with such loving care that the viewer understands the fugitive's decision to turn himself in because these plains are the only place in the world where he can live. The climax is the most electrifying instance of violence on the Finnish silent screen. This time, it is no longer the destructive outburst of a knife-slinger, but the defiant gesture of a freedom-loving Finn against oppression. People like these cannot be held in chains was Järviluoma's theme, which Suomi-Filmi conveyed with cinematic means (Fig. 5 and Fig. 6).

During the silent era, Finns, unlike the Swedes, did not have means for extravagant film projects. A seminal national classic was thus lavishly produced by the Swedes, although filmed largely in authentic locations in Finland. Based on the epic tales by Finland's national poet, Johan Ludvig Runeberg, *Fänrik Ståls sägner 1–2* (Ensign Stål's Tales, 1926) starts with Finland's national anthem and relates how the young poet encounters an old veteran whose stirring tales from the Finnish War of 1808–09 come alive on the screen. This film was successful for decades, and was re-released as late as 1939 in a sonorised version. It was popular in Swedish schools until well after the Second World War, but has largely been forgotten since, and would deserve 'rediscovering' in the same spirit as the French historical epics of the 1920s which Kevin Brownlow has uncovered and championed.

To return to *Sången*: from this film, the Finns learned that the Nordic landscape could itself be the supreme production value. The Finns could not compete with the Americans or the Germans in budgets, but nature itself was sublime, incomparable and majestic. There was the forest, of mythical significance to Finns; there were the rivers, the lakes and the sea. There was also the snow, impressive in black and white. Shooting on location became a virtue of Finnish cinema, which accordingly became less studio-bound than in most other countries. The beauty of leaves rippling in the wind and waving cornfields had been seen in D.W. Griffith's Biograph shorts,[14] but the Swedes discovered the grandeur of Nordic nature for cinema. Stiller was criticised for a

funerals.[12] The film was so successful that Suomi-Filmi immediately proceeded with a bigger production based on Artturi Järviluoma's highly successful play, *Pohjalaisia* (Plainsmen, 1925) which, during one decade, received two thousand performances, and which had even been turned into an opera the year before the film was produced. Järviluoma, himself, wrote the screenplay, and filming in the great plains was conducted to

certain superficiality and a tendency to pictorialism;[15] Victor Sjöström delved deeper into the mysteries of the landscape. Stiller was the extrovert, and Sjöström the introvert, but both played a part in the discovery of the Nordic landscape for cinema, and the Finns learned from them both.

The word, 'soul-scape' (*sielunmaisema* in Finnish), is a valid expression for the profundity of this discovery. The relationship to nature (*luonnonsuhde*) is an essential part of the identity of the Finnish and Nordic people. It is a vital source of energy and contemplation. Wild nature in Finland is benevolent. There are no twisters, volcanoes or earthquakes; even extreme circumstances can be turned to advantage. The beasts of the forest are as eager to avoid people as people are to avoid them. There are no ravishing mountains, but there is variety in a landscape of one hundred thousand lakes and the mosaic-like archipelago, and the seasons provide a familiar landscape with four different costumes. Wandering in the forest, the Finn may actually feel more at home than dwelling in the city. But, simultaneously, the relationship to nature has an element of the sacred: pantheism, nature worship, was a profound elemental current in the art of Sibelius, Kivi, Linnankoski, Aho and the Järnefelt family. It would be an exaggeration to characterise Finnish silent cinema as pantheistic, but its most sublime moments were certainly inspired by nature worship.

Sången gave the Finnish cinema one of its most popular characters, the lumberjack (*tukkijätkä, tukkipoika, tukkilainen*) who at his most heroic hour becomes the log-roller or the shooter of rapids (*koskenlaskija*). The significance of this character in Finnish cinema is comparable to that of the westerner in American film. He is the pioneer, the wanderer, the adventurer: he negotiates the frontier, he is an embodiment of the conflict between wilderness and civilisation. We meet this figure in *Koskenlaskijan morsian* (The Log-roller's Bride, 1922 – remade 1937), *Tukkijoella* (Log River, 1928, Fig. 7 – remade 1937 and 1951), and *Tukkipojan morsian* (The Lumberjack's Bride, 1931, Fig. 8). The figure of the lumberjack, who in the last act turns out to be the inheritor of a prosperous farm, had

Fig. 7. Tukkijoella *(Log River, 1928): the only Finnish film star of the silent era was Urho Somersalmi, discovered by Mauritz Stiller in* Johan. *In the Finnish National Theatre, Somersalmi played heroic leads; in the cinema, lumberjacks and tall men from Pohjanmaa. Popular magazine advertisement. [Courtesy of the Finnish Film Archive.]*

Fig. 8. Photographic portrait of Urho Somersalmi. [Courtesy of the Finnish Film Archive.]

some basis in reality. From the end of the nineteenth century, it was common that the oldest sons of the farm went to work in the forests until their father retired and it was time for the first-born to take over. It fits quite

Fig. 9. Suvinen satu *(A Summer Saga, 1925): the final scene on a moonlit pond, rippled by a sudden breath of wind, with Maire Heide and Sven Hildén. [Production still courtesy of the Finnish Film Archive.]*

Fig. 10. Meidän poikamme *(Our Sons, 1929), with Margit Tirkkonen and Helge Ranin. [Production still courtesy of the Finnish Film Archive.]*

well with the Finnish sense of humour that a lumberjack would pretend to be just a poor tramp in order to test one's true friends and lovers. The lumberjack's quest is about growing into manhood. His worth is not based on inherited wealth but on virility, of which taming the wild rapids on a rolling log is a powerful symbol.

Stiller's film had a personal dimension, too,

since the director could identify with Olavi Koskela, the hero. Stiller, himself, was a wanderer. Born in 1883, raised, and *barmitzvahed* in Helsinki, he carried a Russian passport, since Jews were not allowed Finnish citizenship during the Russian Empire. In order to escape being drafted into the Russian army, he moved to Sweden in 1904 although he did not take up Swedish citizenship until 1921. Until then, he was officially a Russian. Stiller, like Olavi, was also a well-known charmer, but Stiller seduced both women and men in an era when homosexuality was a criminal offence.

Then there was the miracle of the photography. The midsummer night views were a revelation to Stiller. *Sången*, Stiller's thirty-eighth film, was the first in which he displayed any real interest in location shooting.[16] But it grew into something bigger than just filming on location or even capturing the essence of the landscape. People had expressed doubts about cinema's ability to convey the poetry of Linnankoski's novel. Stiller rose to the challenge with his ability to handle light, and this miracle, carried out by Ragnar Westfelt and Henrik Jaenzon, became in turn a model for Finnish cinematography. The technical standards of Finnish cinematography had been high from the first efforts of Atelier Apollo. From the start, Finnish cinematographers knew where to place the camera; they had a sense of composition and could achieve a full range of tones in shooting and printing. But the Swedes taught Finns how to find cinematic poetry on one's doorstep. The magic of the summer night, the meadow in bloom, the forking road through the forest, the village dance by the river, the cumulus clouds on the wide open sky: these became the treasures to be sought by cinematographers.

Finally, *Sången* revealed the force of Finnish music when combined with moving images. *Sången om den eldröda blomman* by Armas Järnefelt (1869–1958) is the first film score by a significant Finnish composer during the silent era. It was also the first time in Sweden that music was especially composed for a film. Järnefelt belonged to a family of prominent cultural figures. One of his brothers was a writer, another a painter, and his sister, Aino was married to Jean Sibelius. Armas Järnefelt, a talented composer, had moved to Stockholm in 1907 to become a conductor at the Royal Swedish Opera. He dedicated three months to the composition of the film score. Mostly it was compiled from folk songs, but he composed original music. 'Shooting the Rapids' and 'The Fight' are still played as autonomous orchestral pieces.[17]

Finland, enjoying its 'golden age' of music, had a vast resource of magnificent contemporary compositions to draw from for accompanying films, and the music selections for the most prestigious films were indeed ambitious.[18] The documentary *Finlandia* (1922), commissioned from Suomi-Filmi by the State Department, boasted a particularly impressive score, culminating inevitably in Sibelius. Glancing at the glorious music programmes for Suomi-Filmi productions from *Koskenlaskijan morsian* (1923) to *Meidän poikamme* (Our Sons, 1929), one cannot help get the impression that music may have provided half of the enjoyment of the screenings.

Towards the end of the silent era, the best Finnish music theatre was also turned into films. It was a risk to tackle *Tukkijoella* in 1928 when Finnish films did not yet have soundtracks. The highly successful comedy written by Teuvo Pakkala has several memorable tunes by Oskar Merikanto. The cinema musicians knew how to play them, and probably half the audience knew the songs by heart anyway. Then came *Jääkärin morsian* (The Soldier's Bride, 1931), based on the romantic musical drama written and composed by Sam Sihvo: now there was a stirring music track although the film had no dialogue. Transitional films like *Jääkärin morsian* and *Laveta tietä* (The Broadway, 1931) with music tracks only and no dialogue are also important documents of film music before the talkies.

In the selection of music to accompany film, Sibelius was frequently used, although extracts were not limited to *Finlandia* and *Valse triste*. Even better suited for cinema was music by Oskar Merikanto such as *Romance*. From Armas Järnefelt, *Berceuse* was the best-loved

melody. Other Finnish composers active during the silent era who were favoured for accompanying film included Erkki Melartin, Heikki Klemetti, Leevi Madetoja and Toivo Kuula. Sibelius never composed for films, but consented to be filmed at his home Ainola, near Lake Tuusula, where Juhani Aho, too, had built his mansion. The short film *Jean Sibelius kodissaan* (Jean Sibelius At Home) was made in 1927, in the year when the silence of Sibelius started and when the silent era of cinema ended.

Finnish filmmakers of the silent era produced no landmarks that changed the course of film art. The directors of the silent era were still close to the theatre; directing actors in front of the cameras, they were often no more sophisticated than a traffic cop. The best actors, left to their own devices, managed to be effective, but the interplay between characters was often less successful. Although the cinematographers were experienced in composition, camera movement was often primitive. The filmmakers had yet to learn the finer points of continuity cutting, to speak nothing of the art of montage. However, Finnish cinema found its identity in the inspiration of the natural landscapes, in the fresh open air of the sea and of the forest. Almost invariably when the Finns tried drawing-room stories the result was contrived. But even in such a misguided effort as *Suvinen satu* (A Summer Saga, 1925),[19] there is a beautiful final scene on a moonlit pond, rippled by a sudden breath of wind (Fig. 9). And in the pedestrian military comedy *Meidän poikamme* (Our Sons, 1929, Fig. 10), the framing story is filled with images that are meant to represent all that is worth fighting for: the river, the fields, and the road through the woods are filmed with such devotion that they exist on a level different to the rest of the film. In such moments, Finnish silent cinema touched greatness.

Acknowledgements

I gratefully acknowledge the inspiration of Tytti Soila for this essay, and thank Sakari Toiviainen and Kimmo Laine for their comments.

Notes

1. The Finnish film magazines of the silent era were: *Bio* (1910), *Biograafi* (1915), *Bio* (1916), *Filmiaitta* (1921–32), *Filmrevyn* (1921–27), and *Elokuva* (1927–1931). See also Eila Anttila, Sakari Toiviainen, and Kari Uusitalo (eds.), *Taidetta valkealla kankaalla: Suomalaisia elokuvatekstejä 1896–1950* [Art On the Silver Screen: Finnish Writings on the Cinema 1896–1950] (Helsinki: Painatuskeskus and Suomen elokuva-arkisto, 1995).

2. *Laulu tulipunaisesta kukasta* (The Song of the Scarlet Flower) was published in 1905 and became the first Finnish international best-selling novel. It has been filmed five times (three times in Sweden and twice in Finland), see Tytti Soila, 'Five Songs of the Scarlet Flower', *Screen* 35, 3 (Autumn 1994): 265–274. Five key people behind *Sången* were born in Finland: besides the author of the novel, Johannes Linnankoski, the director Mauritz Siller, the screenwriter Gustaf Molander, the leading lady Edith Erastoff, and the composer Armas Järnefelt. Molander directed the 1956 remake of the film as his final feature film. *Juha* (*Johan*), published in 1911, has been filmed four times, once in Sweden and three times in Finland, the latest interpretation being Aki Kaurismäki's 1999 black and white silent version.

3. Roland af Hällström, *Filmi – aikamme kuva* [Film – The Image of Our Time] (Jyväskylä: K.J. Gummerus, 1936), 146–153. The passages on Stiller repeat almost verbatim the obituary published by the author in *Elokuva* 18 (1928): 14. I quote from the later source to show that this judgment was not a passing fancy of the writer, a respected authority in Finnish film culture.

4. Ibid., 146–147.

5. Ibid., 152.

6. See *Suomen kansallisfilmografia*, I, *vuosien 1907–1935 suomalaiset kokoillan elokuvat* [The Finnish National Filmography, I, Feature Films 1907–1935] (Helsinki: Edita and Suomen elokuva-arkisto, 1996) for information on the feature films, and Kari Uusitalo's *Eläviksi syntyneet kuvat; Suomalaisen elokuvan mykät vuodet 1896–1930* [Images Born Alive. The Silent Years 1896–1930 in Finnish Cinema] (Helsinki: Otava, 1972) for all the films. The latter volume contains the Filmografia Fennica 1904–1930, complete with the short films, compiled by Kari Uusitalo.

7. Roland af Hällström, *Filmi – aikamme kuva*, 221.

8. 'Eino Leino elokuvamiehenä' [Eino Leino as a Man of the Cinema], *Seura* 29–30 (1948): 3, 18. Written by Jaakko Saarikoski and based on an interview with Kaarle Halme's daughter Tyyne Jauri.

9. *Salaviinanpolttajat* was produced by Finland's best photographer's company, Atelier Apollo. The company's owner and manager, K.J. Ståhlberg, interested two directors in the film: Count Louis Sparre, who was a well-known artist and designer, and Teuvo Puro, an actor at the Finnish National Theatre, who became an important pioneer and whose career in film lasted until the late 1940s. The art director, Carl Fager, was launched on an equally long film career; the director of photography, Frans Engström, was the country's leading cinematographer during the earliest years, and his assistant, Oscar Lindelöf, was just starting a long and distinguished career in cinematography.

10. Kari Uusitalo, *Kuvaus - kamera - käy! Lähikuvassa suomifilmit ja Suomi-Filmi Oy* [Ready To Roll! Suomi-Filmi Oy In Close-Up] (Pieksämäki: Suomen Elokuvatutkimuksen Seura and Kirjastopalvelu, 1994), a history of the Suomi-Filmi company, established in 1919, the oldest Finnish film company still operating today. Kari Uusitalo, *Meidän poikamme. Erkki Karu ja hänen aikakautensa* [Our Sons. Erkki Karu and His Era] (Helsinki: Valtion painatuskeskus and Suomen elokuva-arkisto, 1988), a biography of the founding father of the Finnish film industry (1887–1935).

11. Finland was the first country in the world where women were given full political rights: in 1906, Finland's women were granted suffrage and the right to be elected to parliament. Minna Canth (1844–97) was a fearless champion of both women's rights and of social justice in general.

12. Although the epoch of the *häjys* ended in the nineteenth century, the stereotype still exists more than a century later, and may be seen, for instance, in *Häjyt* (The Badmen) which was released in 1999.

13. The people of Pohjanmaa have always been fond of dramatisation, and appear eagerly as extras even when big fight scenes are filmed. For the *häjy* scenes, descendants of actual *häjys* turned up. In the effective opening scene, the fighting was not totally simulated. Jalmari Lahdensuo, the director reported: 'As we were filming this scene, many got so carried away that despite all warnings they risked serious danger. Men were trampled under the hooves, others fell from the bridge, and a

couple of *häjys* rode against each other so violently that the horses fell to the ground. An ancient *häjy* survivor turned up with an axe believing that this was for real.' (*Filmiaitta* (summer issue 1925): 177).

14. The Biograph shorts and international cinema in general were well showcased in Finland during the silent era. The Lumière films came to Helsinki exactly six months after the world premiere in the Grand Café, Nick Carter got love letters from Finland in 1908, the Pathé and Gaumont productions were block-booked in the cinemas of Finland within months of their Paris release, and Charles Chaplin's films came to Finland well in advance of Sweden. Helsinki was one of the cities where Yevgeni Bauer's films were first shown. The Helsinki Police Department's censorship files of films are a complete register of films passed for exhibition in the city from 1911 to 1919. After the Declaration of Independence, municipal censorship was abolished. The film industry established a national self-regulatory censorship office in 1919. The historical files of the various censorship bodies are kept at the Finnish Board of Film Classification.

15. Mr. Jeremias, 'Filmi vuodelta 1918 – ja sen seuraajat' [A Film From The Year 1918 – And Its Successors], *Aamulehti* (daily newspaper), reprinted in *Filmiaitta* 23–24 (1927): 18–19. 'Stiller's film awakened the true film enthusiasm of our audience – it can be said to be the pathbreaker of film art', acknowledges Mr. Jeremias. After criticising the theatricality and the chilly nature worship of *Sången om den eldröda blomman*, Mr. Jeremias concludes by questioning the supposed progress of the cinema: 'the foundation, the contents, and the values are now the same as then … That contemporary film is not closer to the ideal of film art than Stiller was in his day is the fact to be regretted the most – that Stiller already in 1918 made a good film is of course only to be congratulated.'

16. Gösta Werner, *Mauritz Stiller. Ett livsöde* (Stockholm: Bokförlaget, Prisma 1991), 118–121. Werner estimates that neither Stiller nor his contemporaries fully understood the significance of the discoveries he made in *Sången om den eldröda blomman*.

17. *The Orchestral Music of Armas Järnefelt*. Compact disc (Sterling CDS-1021–2, recorded at Orkester-salen, Gävle, 1996). The sleeve notes by Heikki Saari include a long quote from a contemporary undated interview with Armas Järnefelt in *Svenska Dagbladet*: 'I had to do it foot by foot, piece by piece; as fixed points of reference I was given all of the more important episodes in the film in addition to information as to how many feet of film were to be shown per minute – information which in fact proved to be wholly inaccurate, because the film was shown at a much faster speed, so much so that I was quite horrified when I saw how ridiculously poorly the music and the pictures fitted together, and I had to cut out some of the score. Never before in my life have I composed according to such a method, where I needed to adjust myself to the pace of events – I who am accustomed to setting the tempo myself! But, in any case, it all worked out.'

18. *Suomen kansallisfilmografia*, I, 215, 227, 389, 480, 500, etc. Many music programmes of the silent era are reprinted in the volume. The restoration of the original scores from the 1920s would be a fascinating challenge.

19. Dubbed, in its day, 'savinen suti' ('a brush of clay').

Silents for a Silent People

Peter von Bagh

Stora Robertsgatan 44B 27, 00120 Helsinki, Finland

In theory, everything should have been fine. The Finns do have a reputation for being a strong silent people. Brecht had a phrase for it: 'Ein Volk, das in zwei Sprachen schweigt' (A people who remain silent in two languages). Surely, then, silent films should have been such a people's most natural mode of expression? Far from it. Finnish silent film cannot claim even a modest comparison with the achievements of the 'golden age' of the Swedish or Danish cinemas, unless the almost completely vanished pre-1920 Finnish output (the Finnish National Filmography lists only twenty-six titles) happened to include a number of gems. Search as we may there is little to indicate it. Moreover, there are but few strands leading from Finnish silent film to what came later. The first five years of the talkies constitute something of a black hole in Finland. So any interest shown in this period involves a kind of dramaturgy of absence.

Finland became a sovereign state at the end of 1917. Independence was followed by civil war in the early months of 1918. The distinguishing feature of the latter was the exceptional cruelty of the tit-for-tat acts of revenge on both sides. At this stage, cinema maintained an agonised silence over the crucial issues of the day; the trauma lay simply too deep. In the event, it is impossible to read into any film – or any one scene – produced in Finland at that time that in 1918 the country had gone through one of the century's bloodiest civil wars. That is, except for the fact that

many sagas of orphans and tales of human woe were being shown on the screen. The contributor to the first Finnish film magazine, *Filmiaitta*, reported:

> There is something infinitely human and touching in all these life stories passing before our eyes; there is an aura of still acceptance hovering over it all, something resembling the memories crowding into the countess' mind as she stands there at the graveside recalling the faces of her departed loved ones. Here pain is subdued, each tale of broken hearts and lost happiness is communicated in quiet and dignified tones.

It is significant that such a verbal report goes to the heart of the matter more than any film. At the same time, literature – from which the winning side understandably demanded silence – made several dagger-sharp sallies on civil war themes. It is ironic that the only 'civil war film', the infantile *Sotapolulla* (On the War Path, 1920) was directed by Teuvo Pakkala, a notable author and a master of the short story. This film takes on the trappings of some absent-minded concoction from a five-year old child, out of which you get the impression that all workers are to be considered drunkards and direct representatives of Original Sin.

It is clear that there was a great need to define, over-emphasise, and proclaim the concept of a Fatherland. Such a necessity looms up at its most simplistic in the Finnish national flag

fluttering at the end of several of Erkki Karu's films. Karu was also one of the two directors of the most important documentary that came out of the 1920s. It appears that *Finlandia* (Eero Leväluoma, 1922) was also well received outside Finland – it gave foreigners a chance to witness an enigmatic account of this far-flung land, to see her stark wilderness and changing seasons, as well as noting the people's livelihood, their industry, their way of life – and to observe that utterly Finnish landscape. Today's Finns similarly find the film a veritable treasure-trove: a most detailed and all-embracing look deep into an era long gone, an anthology of a way of life and of a lost time.

The basic tendencies in early Finnish cinema were towards a conservatism and an absolute conformism which, as far as the aesthetic sense goes, was tantamount to regressing to the level of literature for adolescents. One typical fossil of a film is Erkki Karu's *Meidän poikamme* (Our Boys, 1928) which aimed at merging the newly-formed army into some mythical national heritage. The focus of imagery was obtusely on the Fatherland, in other words on everything that was worth defending – Finland's natural bounty and the private property of her people (even the naive protagonist Matti owns a small plot of land), including all the lakes, woods, fields and meadows. Even if the film after a pastoral beginning moves to soldiers' barracks and sentry posts, these images of the countryside accompany Matti off into the army. Fiction pre-empted reality: the Winter War of 1939 was both invoked and lived through by creating myths on the silver screen well before the actual event ever occurred.

Even though cinema did not really take off, there was a cinema culture of a kind. We can read in newspapers of the day that Yevgeni Bauer's films, which remained unknown in most parts of the world, were quite popular and appreciated in Finland, which at the time was still part of the Russian Empire. And the chefs-d'oeuvre from neighbouring Sweden kept coming into Finland in a steady flow. In these expansive years of Charles Magnusson's regime at Swedish Biograph (Svenska Biografteatern), when the focus was on two directors (namely Stiller, who lived in Helsinki until

he was twenty-two, and Sjöström), we may recall that there was a third prominent film-maker, Konrad Tallroth, a Finn who directed eight films for Swedish Biograph in 1916. His films are seldom commented upon today. In the early 1920s, *Filmiaitta* magazine published an interesting list of the most popular films of the previous years based on the number of weeks they were screened. The two directors who took the lead were Lubitsch (*Carmen*, 1918, *Die Austern-prinzessin*, 1919) and Stiller (*Sången om den eldröda blomman*, Song of the Scarlet Flower, 1919) and *Johan* (1921). This prompted an optimistic remark from the compiler of the list; he regarded the list as a proof of 'the evolved taste' of the general public.

Everything had to be constructed in a country which had so recently gained her independence: national identity, the fiction of a national history, and national self-esteem. Later on, Finnish cinema was to take part in this enterprise in an energetic manner, but during the silent film era, its efforts simply lacked bite. It is noteworthy that in other fields there was always one name that rose above the herd: in sport it was Paavo Nurmi, in music Jean Sibelius, in literature (for starters) Juhani Aho (the author of *Juha/Johan*), in painting Akseli Gallen-Kallela, and in cinema just about – if not very prominently – Erkki Karu. Cinema was sending out only rather fudged signals. The following should at least, be noted as standard features.

Local tradition

Even though the best in foreign cinema was being actively followed, the composition of a local home-grown cinema turned out to be quite home-spun. A heavy dependence on literature and the theatre was a characteristic of early Finnish film, and this was to last for decades in so far as Finnish cinema, rather than reflect other art forms in their contemporary expression, derived its inspiration from earlier periods. *Anna-Liisa* (Teuvo Puro, J. Snellmann, 1922) is a typical example. It is based on a drama by Minna Canth, one of the female dramatists of the Finnish theatre whose contributions have always been crucial. The theme is a disconsolate nightmare from the past: Anna-Liisa gives birth to a child

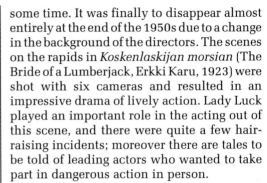

from her relationship with the farm-hand Mikko and kills the new-born infant. Canth's thesis would be as follows: in order to live in an archaic and intolerant society, a woman must conform with the prevailing double-standards and cover up all the traces of the error of her ways, even if that includes infanticide. In the true spirit of Finnish all-or-nothing, Anna-Liisa finishes up with absolutely nothing. Her telling last words are: 'She wanders along the road of eternal life. Happy she'. Even if such an end lacks a certain finality, Anna-Liisa's utterance does not consist of mere words; the film's indoor and outdoor imagery convey reflections of a particular world and its moral values.

The film is certainly one of the few films from Finland that can be mentioned in the same breath as the films of the Swedish masters; it is a minor work, but it is certainly on the same wavelength. The essential factor in this film is the meeting of two influences, the theatrical and the naturalistic. There are also scenes of delirium: a little girl wakes up, walks to Anna-Liisa (who is merely lying down), and lays flowers upon her. Perhaps the most memorable scene is when Mikko recalls how he seduced Anna-Liisa. It is a scene full of propriety and distinction, delicate and undiluted. First of all, a summer party and dance, then the lovers glide by boat along the length of a lake, they disembark, they embrace, and then the silent images of nature accompanying the woman's yielding. Anna-Liisa's numerous 'monologues' are like silent prayers, a true communion with nature. When she collapses, exhausted, at the edge of the rapids, or again in a wind-swept forest where trees seem to weigh down heavily upon her, nature takes part in her agony and seems to bewail the severity of life's punishments.

Rural anthology

As can be seen from the above, a kind of rural anthology dominated cinema and made it possible, in some way, to bypass action. The screen was drenched with images of the countryside for the potent reason that 83 per cent of the country's population still lived in rural areas. These images of nature were spontaneous and atavistic, and such treatment remained an emblem of Finnish cinema for

some time. It was finally to disappear almost entirely at the end of the 1950s due to a change in the background of the directors. The scenes on the rapids in *Koskenlaskijan morsian* (The Bride of a Lumberjack, Erkki Karu, 1923) were shot with six cameras and resulted in an impressive drama of lively action. Lady Luck played an important role in the acting out of this scene, and there were quite a few hair-raising incidents; moreover there are tales to be told of leading actors who wanted to take part in dangerous action in person.

Konrad Tallroth's *Suursalan häät* (The Country Wedding, 1924) is a beautiful example of the capacity of the still rather modest Finnish cinema to project the imagery of a receding world. When screened now, a good seven decades on, the film still catches the vitality of those half-recalled memories, and manages to reach the level of primitive documentary: the country dance, an untroubled baby in a cradle, the passionate actuality of a knife-fight, or men's heavy drinking out-the-back at country celebrations. Silent cinema lacked utterly the capacity for story narration, but there were compensations. The basic theme of *Pohjalaisia* (The Northerners, Jalmari Lahdensuo, 1924), which is a kind of Finnish interpretation of the American western, is a powerful drama from the flat western regions of Central Finland, and offers an anthology of essential locations and scenarios: appropriate landscape, a bridge, a fight, a card-game, dust rising from the field, the ploughing ritual. It does not really matter if you do not understand a thing about the plot, you are in the middle of events anyhow.

Metropolitan dreams

The urban world was, for the Finns of those days, like a metropolitan dream because the majority of cinema audiences, in different parts of the country, had never been to Helsinki. The capital depicted in the films of the 1920s was a kind of provincial replica of Paris or Berlin. Perhaps the most interesting example of these films would be *Korkein voitto* (The Highest Victory, Carl von Haartman, 1929) using a story to which Josef von Sternberg was to give brilliant treatment some years later in *Dishonored*. The film is far from being negligible because it is alive with self-mockery and a host of sprightly details, particularly since it was directed by a swindler, or at any rate, a hollow man. He was Carl von Haartman, an army officer, who left for America in 1924, and after a variety of exploits, finished up in Hollywood. There he held a somewhat questionable – at any rate, low-grade – job as a 'military adviser' on *Wings*. (This 'poor man's' von Stroheim claimed that he had made a brief appearance in a crowd scene in *The Wedding March*.)

Archaism

Many films reached back to the nineteenth century and are, in some respects, 'authentic films of the 1860s' in the sense Henri Langlois meant when analysing Danish cinema. There is a touch of the archaic about them which hearkens back to an entirely different period. In the most significant Finnish silent film of all, *Nummisuutarit* (The Village Shoemakers, 1923), Erkki Karu summoned up an highly impressive milieu, a melding of an imaginary world and social reality. The techniques of working, ways of earning a livelihood, and the represented life-style are all scenic elements (smoke rising from slash-and-burn cultivation, a symbol for the prospective audience of a dream landscape of times past) as well as the folk traditions of wedding rites and similar festivities. There is a comparable fine-focus tuning in Dreyer's film fragment *Der var engang* (Once Upon a Time, 1922). The countryside seems to breathe its very own life force which has moulded, tried and tested habits and customs over the centuries. In the film, woods and meadows, lakes and rivers, dwellings, lanes, and 'the loveliness of leaves rustling in the trees' (which fascinated audiences of the very first Lumière films) bestowed their own potent and authentic contribution. The film was based on a drama by Aleksis Kivi, the first Finnish professional author, and is one of the few truly creative screen versions of a literary work. This is the play reborn in images, in associations, in the warp and weft of language and drama, conquering a new dimension, and interwoven with symbols and flashbacks, fantasies of high hopes and icy fears. There is quite a mix of ingredients: 'realism', dreamlike passages, cross-cutting, fantasies, the best-known being Esko's drink-

ing scene which it dramatises Finnish 'mythic inebriation' to an overwhelming degree. The variations in perspective, above all the use of low-angle camerawork, create a dizzying effect of the protagonist at one with nature. Such shots render a sky-embracing sense of unity where man's conscious perceptions and nature's implacable presence form an inseparable whole.

Hardly a film is to be found where all the details I have described fall into place, but one single image may be worth all the trouble of shooting, one excellent gag may encapsulate the film. I mention this because the principal sources for Finnish film have been high-class fiction and drama, but the cinema circled around them like an uninvited guest, always the respectful and mournful outsider. That is why a bright little comedy such as *Kun isällä on hammassärsky* (When Father has Toothache, Karu, 1923) is so unusual. This is a nightmare fantasy about toothache. The father (in which rôle, Aku Korhonen employs a whole gamut of grotesque expressions) is the family's absolute authority, and has reached a state of frenzy. The whole family is seen fussing around; from this absurd point of view, a real-life drama develops. As the situation worsens, the father gulps down 'medicine' out of a twenty-litre bottle, collides with the walls, bangs his head on the ceiling, and so on and on – all this depicted as the typical and representative view of bourgeois family life of the time. Moreover, some single shots may be treasured for the self-same fragmented reason such as the particularly eerie sequence from the film *Elämän maantiellä* (On the Highway of Life, 1927) where the image of lovers frolicking in the forest may stay in your memory longer than dozens of feature films. Why is this? It may well be chance, rather than directorial vision, that brought to the screen a few phantom glimpses of what Finnish silent cinema could have brought to our attention had it been equal to the cinematic challenges of the time.

Laveata tietä (The Wide Road, 1931) was, nevertheless, a fine film directed by Valentin Vaala with actor Theodor Tugai (alias Teuvo Tulio) who later became a fine director of melodrama. The concerns of the film were almost symbolically both provincial and

European. Throughout the film scenes of Finland's snow-burdened trees and sparkling ski terrain alternate with cosmopolitan imagery: cars speeding through streets at night, art deco interiors, the stark modernism of the decor, European cosmopolitanism (the highlight here is the leading man hanging out in Paris). Even the public baths in central Helsinki bring to mind Roman baths. Multi-faceted details rest on the cinematic power of fragmentation and on a montage that sharpens the significance of a given moment like a whip lash.

This was the first occasion in Finland that we learnt what kind of modern cinema was being made out there in the wide world. It was thanks to such young directors as these that the tradition of silent film was held in respect for a long time, reaching its belated culmination in the major sound films of the 1930s and 1940s. It is ironic that now, seventy years on, it is the new wave of Finnish cinema that counts amongst the very few that have re-discovered the authentic language of the silent film. In Aki Kaurismäki's silent *Juha*, there are no traces of Finnish silent films, and how could there be? But there are so many lightning associations and snatches of dialogue pointing to the imagery of Tulio and Vaala, and, indeed, to Nyrki Tapiovaara who, in 1937 as his first directorial assignment, shot the first Finnish version of *Juha*.

3
Norway

Sisters of Cinema: Three Norwegian Actors and their German Film Company, 1917–1920

Gunnar Iversen

Department of Art and Media Studies, University of Trondheim, NTNU, 7491 Trondheim, Norway

Early Norwegian film history appears fragmented and sporadic compared with the strong national film industries emerging in neighbouring Denmark and Sweden in the first two decades of the twentieth century. A few attempts were made to establish a national film production, mainly by cinema owners, but with the municipalisation of the cinemas in the 1910s, this movement faltered.

During the 1910s, Aud, Gerd and Ada Egede-Nissen made a name for themselves in the Nordic and German film industries as actors, producers and directors. Like many female pioneers in the film industry, their work has been neglected. The rise of interest in feminist studies in the past decades has, however, led to renewed interest in the work of early women directors and producers. The contribution of the Egede-Nissen sisters to silent film in the 1910s is remarkable given the odds they had to overcome as female producers in a male dominated industry, and the lack of tradition and experience in filmmaking in their home country, Norway. This essay presents an outline of their career which took them from Norway to an international career in motion pictures, emphasising their role as female pioneers, and assesses their overall contribution to Norwegian, Nordic and German film. This essay also provides an outline of Norwegian film production in the 1910s.

A small sensation

In 1916 the Norwegian film magazine *Norsk Kinematograf-Tidende* reported what seemed like a small sensation: the three sisters Aud, Gerd and Ada Egede-Nissen, all actors, planned to establish a film production company. The eldest of the three sisters, Aud Egede-Nissen, was reported as being the one behind the plans, and the magazine noted that she would assume artistic control over film production. Her German husband, the actor Georg Alexander, was to be managing director, and all the sisters were to act in their films.[1]

Originally the sisters wanted to establish their company in Copenhagen, but in interviews

in Norwegian film magazines they always stressed that the company was *Norwegian*. The sisters also stressed their interest in filming Norwegian themes in Norway, even though they wanted to establish a base in Copenhagen. There they could use the studio owned by the Dania Biofilm where Aud Egede-Nissen had worked as actor in 1913.[2] Their company – Egede Nissen Filmsbyraa A/S – was registered in the Norwegian city of Stavanger on 20 September 1917 as a production and distribution concern. The Norwegian company probably ended up as a branch office and distributor of the films the sisters made, because earlier in the year, Aud Egede-Nissen and Georg Alexander (originally named Lüddekens) established a separate production company in Berlin. This production company – Egede-Nissen-Film Comp. GmbH, sometimes called Lüddeckens-Egede-Nissen & Co in censorship papers – produced thirty feature films in Germany in the period 1917–20.[3]

Aud Egede-Nissen (1893–1974) was the daughter of the radical politician Adam Egede-Nissen. In 1917 he was mayor and postmaster in Stavanger, and he also held the position as chairman of his daughters' Norwegian film company. Through her younger sisters, Gerd Egede-Nissen (1895–1988) and Ada Egede-Nissen (1899–1981), Aud became interested in the theatre, and made her stage debut in Trondheim in 1911. Her sister Gerd had her first engagement as film actor for Nordisk in Denmark in 1912, and a year later, Aud joined her in Copenhagen, working for the Dania Biofilm company. There she met the famous theatre director Bjørn Bjørnson, son of the Nobel-prize winning author Bjørnstjerne Bjørnson, who worked as a film director. When he went to Berlin to work as a film director in 1914, she joined him there, working at Kleinen Theater auf der Bühne for a short period, and appearing in her first German film as an actor in the Literaria production, *Teddy im Schlafsopha* (Bjørn Bjørnson, 1914). That same year she acted in at least three other German films, and by 1915 had made herself a name in the German film industry as actor. In 1915 she appeared in at least fourteen German feature films, and was about to become famous as a movie star.

In 1916 she met Georg Alexander who worked as actor and director. Alexander directed her in *Wer wirft den ersten Stein auf Sie?* in 1916, and in the same year, Aud Egede-Nissen and Georg Alexander married. Together with her husband and sisters, Aud Egede-Nissen began making plans, hoping to exploit the opportunities in Germany and, at the same time, establish a Norwegian film company. As noted earlier, these plans were regarded as a small sensation in Norway. Since early 1913, no feature films had been produced in Norway, and both film production, film distribution, and cinema ownership underwent radical changes. At the same time, film production experienced a massive creative drain. From 1912 on, Norwegian authors, directors and actors tried their luck in the film industries of, first, Denmark, and later, Sweden.[4] The combination of uncertainty about the role of films in Norway and the massive drain of creative talent, explains to some degree why no features were produced in Norway between 1913 and 1917. It also partly explains why Aud Egede-Nissen ended up making movies in Berlin in the late 1910s.

The pioneer era in Norway

The first exhibition of 'moving images' in Scandinavia took place in Norway's capital Kristiania – later renamed Oslo – on 6 April 1896, just a few months after the Lumière brothers' first public projections in Paris. Director Jacobsen at Circus Variété, a music-hall and circus, had seen the German pioneers Max and Emil Skladanowsky present their Bioscop films at the Wintergarten in Berlin in November 1895, and booked the brothers and their films for his music-hall. Between 6 April and 5 May 1896, the Skladanowsky brothers showed their programme of nine films as part of the entertainment at Circus Variété in Kristiania. After visiting Norway, the German brothers travelled to Denmark and Sweden.

For the next few years, itinerant cinema exhibitors roamed Norway, showing mostly French and English films. Film viewing was, in early years predominantly an activity for the bourgeoisie since ticket prices were high in the period of travelling showmen. This changed when cinema became a permanent entertainment attraction in its own right in the larger cities. On 1 November 1904, the first permanent-site cinema, Kinematograf-Theatret, opened in Kristiania. Before the end of the year, four more cinemas were opened, and ten years later, in 1915, Kristiania had twenty-one cinemas. A 'nickelodeon-boom' swept across Norway, and cinema-going became a popular urban form of entertainment that attracted all classes.

The most popular genre in these early years was comedy. French and Italian comedies were particularly popular in Norway, and film comedians like André Deed (his comic persona, Cretinetti (Foolshead), was called Lehmann in Norway and the rest of Scandinavia), and Max Linder were the most popular 'stars'. During the 1910s, Norwegian audiences slowly but steadily became more and more fascinated by American films. Vitagraph westerns were popular, and Chaplin became the new comic favourite. Danish films also enjoyed great popularity, with Danish erotic melodramas becoming infamous in Norway in the early 1910s. Besides comedies, erotic melodramas and, later, American westerns, actualities were popular. The British Boer War films in particular played an important role in the early programmes of short films. Domestic actualities enjoyed a special popularity, the first being produced in 1897. Around 1900, the production of actualities increased in Norway, and most of these first actualities showed winter sports or the Norwegian landscape and nature.

The first Norwegian feature film was the short *Fiskerlivets Farer – Et Drama paa Havet* (Dangers of a Fisherman's Life – An Ocean Drama) made by the cinema-owner Hugo Hermansen sometime between 1906 and 1908. This one-reeler tells the story about a fisherman whose son falls overboard in high seas. The son is pulled on board, but too late for him to be saved. On the shore, his mother sees the accident and tears her hair out. A dramatic intertitle ends the film: 'DEATH'. This first Norwegian fiction film has, unfortunately, been lost, and the written sources regarding the film often contradict themselves so, in many respects, details of the film are far from clear. One thing is certain, though: the photographer was the Swede, Julius Jaenzon, later to become the master photographer for Victor

Sjöström and Mauritz Stiller's famous films in the late 1910s and early 1920s.[5]

By 1910 film-going had become a major form of popular entertainment in Norway, but domestic film production was small, mainly actualities. Between 1906 and 1919, seventeen feature films were made, and reached a limited audience in Norway. These films seem to have taken their strongest inspiration from the Danish erotic or 'social' melodramas, showing either flirtation among the rich, or the temptations and dangers of lower-class city life. One early feature, *Demonen* (The Demon, Jens Christian Gundersen, 1911) was even made in a Danish studio. The earliest Norwegian films were made by different directors and production companies. They were not particularly well received, and were not widely distributed in Norway. Even if these early films differ sharply from the later 'national' films of the 1920s, when a 'national breakthrough' took place and an unbroken tradition of professional film production commenced, the 1910s may be divided into two different periods.

After Hugo Hermansen's tragic ocean drama, no feature films were made until another cinema owner, Halfdan Nobel Roede, made five features between 1911 and 1912. One of these films has been saved, and this film, *Under Forvandlingens Lov* (Under the Law of Change, 1911), is a clear example of what Tom Gunning has termed 'a cinema of attractions'.[6] The narrative is a loose string of attractions – mostly erotic titillations: kisses, embraces, female dances – inspired by Boccaccio's *Decameron*. The story concerns two married couples and how one of the husbands discovers his wife's marital infidelity. Together with the wife of the adulterer, he decides to punish the couple, and after drugging the two, imprisons the adulterous couple in two large cages until they become bored with each other. In the end, peace and harmony is restored, and the couples march happily on. This sketchy narrative is only to a limited degree integrated since the film mostly comprises a string of episodes, loosely joined together. The period 1911–13 thus differs from the later 1910s when Norwegian film production became a more narratively integrated cinema.

After 1913, when only one feature was made in Norway, no features were produced until 1917 when Peter Lykke-Seest established a production company. He was a prolific author of popular novels, and began a career as script writer in Denmark and Sweden in 1912. At Svenska Bio in Sweden he scripted many of the early films of Sjöström and Stiller. Lykke-Seest returned to Norway, and established the first film studio in Norway in 1916. He directed six features between 1917 and 1919. His most popular film was *Historien om en Gut* (The Story of a Boy, 1919). In this film, young Esben is falsely accused of stealing his teacher's watch. Disappointed because nobody believes him, he runs away from home. In several episodes, Esben is seen roaming the country until he finds out that the real thief has been found, and can safely return home. *Historien om en Gut* was Lykke-Seest's greatest success, both artistically and economically. It was exported to several countries, was well received in Sweden, and some years ago, a copy of the film was discovered in Czechoslovakia. Comparing Lykke-Seest's film with *Under Forvandlingens Lov*, made eight years earlier, one can easily see how a cinema of attractions has been replaced by a more strongly integrated narrative cinema which, offering more than just a string of attractive episodes, develops a more detailed story and offers a sketchy psychological portrait of a young boy. This more strongly integrated narrative cinema is also evident in *Revolutionens Datter* (The Daughter of the Revolution, Ottar Gladtvet, 1918), the only feature in the years between 1917 and 1919 made by a director other than Lykke-Seest. This feature is also made up of a dramatic journey in which a young worker saves the life of a factory-owner's daughter. They leave behind them a country ravished by revolution.

Film production in Norway in the 1910s is thus divided into two short, eruptive periods. Lykke-Seest's production company represented a most promising start to extensive and serious feature film production in Norway, but it was discontinued when the efforts to market films in the USA met with failure. Another obstacle to Lykke-Seest's ambitious plans was government legislation. The passing of the Film Theatres Act in 1913 would gradually change the situation in Norway regarding exhibition practices as well as film production. With the absence of film studios and with the halt of film production altogether after 1913, the Act is probably one of the reasons why Aud Egede-Nissen chose to develop the German production company, leaving the branch office in Norway mainly to distribute her German films.

Before the 1913 Act, local communities were responsible for films shown in their cinemas. Local police authorities controlled the cinemas, from a rudimentary form of censorship to building and safety regulations. Control measures varied greatly between communities, and many voices were raised against the new, popular, and powerful medium. Local protests from teachers and school authorities were followed by attacks on a nation-wide scale by the Society for the Promotion of Morality. In 1910 the Kristiania division of the Society passed a resolution calling for municipal by-laws to limit the number of cinemas, and recommending that a municipally appointed committee should oversee programming. Many citizens were concerned about the supposed effects of films on children.

The Film Theatres Act stipulated that municipal councils were to license all public exhibition of film within the area of their jurisdiction, thus controlling the rapidly growing interest in cinema, and established a Central Board of Film Censors in Kristiania which was to process all films prior to public screening. Shortly after the Act was passed, local municipalities started to take over cinemas by buying out their private owners. Municipalisation could have been restricted to granting licences to private owners, but many local authorities were moved by reasons other than moral anxiety. They saw the financial opportunities in running the cinemas themselves, thereby both controlling the new and powerful medium while, at the same time, earning a profit that could be used for other cultural purposes.

The first municipal cinema was established in Harstad, in the north of Norway, in 1913, and after a two-year lull, a spate of local authorities moved to municipalise cinemas during the years from 1915 to 1917. Private cinema owners tried to resist municipalisation, without success. The private rental companies boycotted municipal cinemas for a short period, but the establishment of a municipally-owned rental company in 1919 broke the boycott. The definitive breakthrough for municipalisation came around 1920, and the establishment of municipal ownership of all cinemas in the capital (now renamed Oslo) in 1925, saw the end of private ownership of cinemas in the big cities, or on a large scale in Norway. Some private cinemas continued their business, and still do today, but most cinemas in Norway are municipally owned. Film rental and film production were mostly left to private initiatives.

The municipal cinema system in Norway displays some undeniably attractive features. Owned by the municipalities, cinemas are supposed to operate for the common good of the local community. The system has effectively counteracted the establishment of any centralised cinema circuits, and being a local institution, municipal cinemas are thus seen less as commercial enterprises and more as a cultural service, a part of local cultural life.

The municipal system, nevertheless, has one serious flaw: it does not generate production capital. The municipal system broke the circular economy inherent in film industries or film production elsewhere, but municipalisation during the 1910s no doubt seriously hampered the development of a national film industry. Vertically integrated corporations, with profits from cinema attendance being used to produce new movies, have been virtually impossible since the early 1910s. The municipalisation of the cinemas made it harder to produce films in Norway, as pioneers like Peter Lykke-Seest or Ottar Gladtvet soon found out. The importance of domestic film production was gradually perceived in the early 1920s, but in the 1910s, investors were not interested in film production at a time when great insecurity attended municipalisation.[7]

This outline of the major events during the 1910s in Norway partly explains why news of the Egede-Nissen sisters' production company was regarded as a small sensation. The turbulence during municipalisation also partly explains why, first, Copenhagen and, later, Berlin were preferred to any Norwegian city. The development of the film industry in Germany, and the sisters' familiarity with film production in Germany also, perhaps, explains why Aud Egede-Nissen in the end chose Berlin.

Egede-Nissen-Film Company

Prior to the First World War, Germany, though the foremost power in Europe, relied overwhelmingly on imported motion pictures to supply its cinemas. Before 1914, German filmmaking remained relatively modest in scale. In 1912–13 the domestic share of the market reached only 13 per cent. At the same time, the German film industry went through a fundamental transformation. The new distribution system, the marketing concept of 'Monopolfilm' which was based on granting an exhibitor territorial exclusivity for exploiting a film, and the development of the feature-length evening programme supplanted short film programmes, and boosted domestic film production.[8]

When war broke out French, Danish and Italian production suffered a decline, and the closing of Germany's border eliminated French competition. The war would make imports from overseas increasingly difficult, so ensuring that the German film industry had its domestic market all to itself. Large companies like Ufa, and a host of smaller firms sprang up to exploit the new situation. Import regulations and the seemingly endless demand for motion picture entertainment, made the years during and immediately after the war an exceptionally successful period for the development of the German film industry.

One of these new firms was the Egede-Nissen sisters' film production company in Berlin. Egede-Nissen-Film Comp. GmbH produced ten features in 1917, the first being the comedy, *Ich heirate meine Puppe* (Georg Alexander, 1917) starring Aud Egede-Nissen in a comic role. Most of the thirty feature films the company produced were divided into three series, each with one of the three sisters as leading actor and star. The Egede Nissen series, centring around Aud Egede-Nissen, came in two waves, the first in 1917/18 and

the second in 1918/19, with a total of eleven features. Some of these were dramatic tragedies, like *Die Geburt der Venus* (Georg Alexander, 1917), others were detective films.

Detective films were one of the most important German genres at this time, and not only male detectives like Stuart Webbs, Dick Carter [sic], Harry Higgs, Tom Shark and Joe Jenkins solved exciting cases. In 1913, Karl Werner in Berlin produced the famous Miss Nobody series, dominated by thrilling chase sequences.[9] A year later, in 1914, another female detective was introduced: Miss Clever. Egede-Nissen-Film Comp. introduced the youngest sister, Ada Egede-Nissen, under the name Ada van Ehlers, in 1917, in a detective series comprising four films: *Ein Detektiv-Duell, Das Geheimnis der Briefmarke, Der Kampf mit dem Sturmvogel* and *Der Halsschmuck*. The first three films were directed by Georg Alexander, while the director is unknown in the case of the last feature; all the films were produced by Aud Egede-Nissen. The Ada van Ehlers series resumed in 1918 with four more features, and ended with two features in 1919. Not all of these movies were detective films; in the last film, *Erblich belastet* (Georg Alexander, 1919), Ada's rôle was smaller and more traditional. Although Gerd Egede-Nissen had been busy at Max Reinhardt's theatre, in 1918, Egede-Nissen-Film Comp. released three films in their third series, Gerd Nissen Meister-Syklus. These three films – *Die Rachegöttin* (1918), *Das Brandmal* (1918) and *Die Jugendsünde* (1919) – were all directed by Georg Alexander and produced by Aud Egede-Nissen.

The thirty features produced by Egede-Nissen-Film Comp. are thus mostly divided into three series, each starring one of the three sisters. Besides Georg Alexander, Valy Arnheim directed some films while Alexander was in the army, most notably *Der Roman der Herzogin von Corvy* (1918) and *Sturmschwalbe* (1918), both in the Egede Nissen series. Aud Egede-Nissen was the producer for all thirty features, and in interviews she is presented as the ruling force behind the film company. When a Norwegian journalist visited her company in 1918, he gave a vivid portrait of a large film production company, bursting with energy, making new films and copies of older films in their own laboratory, all ruled by one *will*, one person; 'die schöne Egede Nissen'.[10]

Very little information exists about the films today. Descriptions in trade papers and censorship cards give some indications of themes that ranged from fantasy-comedy to detective films. Of the thirty features, only ten were distributed in Norway (six in 1917 and four in 1919), and only three Egede-Nissen films reached Swedish audiences. Reviewers in Norway praised the cinematography and studio decor, but complained about script quality. The lack of originality was a typical complaint.[11] Unfortunately, it is hard for film historians today to assess the film production of the company. All but one of the films is lost, the only existing copy of a film by the Egede-Nissen-Film Comp. being rediscovered in the Desmet collection of the Nederlands Filmmuseum in Amsterdam. The film is *Erblich belastet*, a feature, which some sources date as 1917, but other sources, 1919.[12] The copy is not complete; only 802 metres of the orginal 1251 metres have been preserved. *Erblich belastet* (Georg Alexander, 1919) was probably the last film produced by Aud Egede-Nissen, although *Das Testament des Grafen Hammerstein* (?, 1920) was censored and released later. *Erblich belastet* was part of the Ada van Ehlers series, starring the youngest of the Egede-Nissen sisters as well as Georg Alexander in the leading role. This feature gives us at least one indication of the film production of the three Norwegian sisters in Berlin.

Erblich belastet

The film begins with an intertitle, presenting 'The famous American millionaire Harrington and his daughter Ellen'. The two are sitting at a café, and after paying the waiter, they leave. These two first shots establish the style as slow and measured, and early on, the film establishes an interest in composition in depth and a predilection for high contrast, shadows, and discrete masking. The next shots present the journalist Ferry Hudson, an orphan raised by the millionaire who treats him as if he were his own son. Ferry also works as Harrington's secretary.[13] Ferry and Ellen have fallen in love, and in a scene the couple

sneaks away from a party, the yellowish tinting turning to beautiful red as they kiss each other.

The expectations of the young couple are abruptly shattered when the millionaire tells Ferry that he is the son of a murderer, and that he will not give his daughter's hand to a killer's son. Ellen is heart-broken. Some days later a man breaks into the millionaire's office and steals some papers. On his way out, he encounters Ferry, and when he finds out that the millionaire's men are after him, he puts the stolen papers in Ferry's pocket and runs off. When Harrington and his men arrive they discover the papers in Ferry's pocket, and he gets the blame. Harrington scorns him, and tells Ferry that he has an inherited character trait. Ferry leaves Harrington's house, after saying goodbye to Ellen, and as a journalist for a big newspaper, leaves for the Wild West. There Ferry encounters the man that stole Harrington's papers and framed him by placing the documents in his pocket, and in a long action-packed sequence, a condensed mini-western, complete with several dramatic chases, cowboys and gun-slinging, the thief is mortally wounded. Before his death he confesses, and with a written confession, Ferry returns to Harrington and his beloved Ellen. In the meantime, Harrington's brother has returned to America after twenty-five years' absence, and Harrington changes his mind about Ferry when he sees how much Ellen loves him. In the end, Ferry returns, still in his cowboy outfit, and the millionaire's brother confesses that he was the murderer twenty-five years earlier, not Ferry's father, and kills himself. The last shot shows Ferry and Ellen as they embrace and kiss; their bodies, black silhouettes against a shining background of windows and glass doors.

Erblich belastet recounts a narrative that is set in America. The story is full of clichés, and changes tone abruptly in the middle when a slow melodrama changes into an action-filled western. In the end, though, the film returns to the slow melodramatic mode. Thus, the film is a curious mixture, presenting a mini-western bracketed by a tragic melodrama about old sins, love, suicide and triumphant love. This mix of genres and modes give the film an 'international' tone, as if it tries to combine all the most attractive elements of both the European slow tragic melodrama (even though the ending is happy) with the speed, rhythm and violence of the American cinema. If the story borders on the formulaic and the acting on exaggerated gesture, *Erblich belastet*, like many contemporary German films, explores stylistic expressivity in order to present a 'banal' story in an exciting manner. Egede-Nissen and Alexander use staging in depth and slow rhythm as well as framing and camera angles to promote expressivity. Often the staging alternates interest between the extreme foreground and rear field of action, or creates less than interesting areas within the shot. One example occurs in a chase scene in the Wild West when Ferry and the thief fight on a steel ladder on a construction that looks like a water tower or part of an industrial building. The two cowboys fight at the extreme right of the shot, while most of the image is dominated by the tower which tends to 'flatten' the composition. *Erblich belastet*, being both melodrama and western, mixes techniques from various stylistic and generic paradigms of the 1910s. Yet the film does not have an eclectic feel about it because the western sequences, to some extent, are modified by the film's overall stylistic strategy – staging in depth and framing – which create an expressivity that sometimes approaches the tradition of the art film after the war.

Conclusion

The Egede-Nissen sisters were active at a time when the German film industry had a transnational and international character, a fact that makes it problematic to label the Egede-Nissen sisters as 'Norwegian' filmmakers, but which also raises the question of a special category of 'European' or 'international' filmmaker. As *Erblich belastet* clearly shows, the films obviously had a vaguely 'international' tone. As with so many films in the 1910s, the film could have been made almost anywhere. Yet it still retains a fascinating mixture of genres and styles, and clearly shows that features from the Egede-Nissen-Film Company had definite qualities. *Erblich belastet* is an example of a film that, experimenting with genres and modes, demonstrates a sound, professional base.

In 1920 the company ceased production. Gerd Egede-Nissen left both stage and screen, and returned to Norway. Ada married a Norwegian musician, and returned to Norway to start a career on the stage under her new name, Ada Kramm. Only Aud remained in Berlin. She divorced Georg Alexander, and married the actor Paul Richter. Today, Aud Egede-Nissen is internationally known for her acting in German films of the 1920s. She is remembered for her rôles as Haidee in *Sumurun* (Ernst Lubitsch, 1920), as Jane Seymour in *Anna Boleyn* (Ernst Lubitsch, 1920) or as Cara Carozza in *Dr. Mabuse, der Spieler* (Fritz Lang, 1922). She also had major roles in Murnau's *Phantom* (1922) and *Die Austreibung* (1923), and in Karl Grune's *Die Strasse* (1923). From 1920 to 1929 she acted in at least thirty-seven German features, as well as a couple of Norwegian features. When sound film production started in Germany, she starred in *Zwischen Nacht und Morgen* (Gerhard Lamprecht,

1931), but returned to Norway in the late 1920s. As with her younger sisters, she returned to the stage in Norway. She worked mainly as an actor and director in the theatre for the rest of her life, but occasionally is mentioned as working on film projects. As late as 1962, a Norwegian film magazine noted that she had started work on a short drama-documentary about the Second World War.[14]

The three Egede-Nissen sisters were female pioneers in a male dominated industry, establishing a considerable track record in film production in the late 1910s. They left their mark on German cinema not only as female pioneers, but also in their own right as artists and producers. Aud Egede-Nissen was the most important person in their production company, making, as *Erblich belastet* illustrates, interesting and fascinating movies, combining genres, and at the same time experimenting with style and form.

Notes

1. *Norsk Kinematograf-Tidende* 4 (1916): 85.

2. *Norsk Kinematograf-Tidende* 5 (1916): 117, *Film og Kino* 1 (1918): 2–4.

3. Herbert Birett (ed.), *Verzeichnis in Deutschland gelaufener Film – Entscheidungen der Filmzensur 1911–1920* (Berlin, Hamburg, Munich, Stuttgart: K.G. Saur, 1980).

4. More information about this creative drain can be found in Sigurd Evensmo, *Det Store Tivoli* (Oslo: Gyldendal, 1967), and, from an actor's perspective, in Lise Lyche, *Norsk Teaters Mare – Agnes Mowinckel og norsk kunstnerliv* (Oslo: Grøndahl, 1990), 62–65.

5. For a discussion of the sources regarding this film, see my article 'Snarveier til fortiden – Kildeproblemer og formidlingsaspekter omkring Norges første spillefilm', *Norsk Medietidsskrift* 2 (1995): 49–55.

6. Tom Gunning, 'The Cinema of Attraction: Early Film, Its Spectator and the Avant-Garde', *Wide Angle* 8, 3/4 (1986): 63–70.

7. For a more extensive discussion of the early 1910s in Norway, and indeed Norwegian film history, see my chapter on Norway in Tytti Soila, Astrid Söderbergh Widding, Gunnar Iversen, *Nordic National Cinemas* (London: Routledge, 1998), 102–141.

8. On early German cinema, see Paolo Cherchi Usai and Lorenzo Codelli (eds.), *Before Caligari: German Cinema, 1895–1920/Prima di Caligari: Cinema tedesco, 1895–1920* (Pordenone: Le Giornate del Cinema Muto/Edizioni Biblioteca dell'Immagine 1990), and Thomas Elsaesser (ed.), *A Second Life: German Cinema's First Decades* (Amsterdam: Amsterdam University Press, 1996).

9. Elsaesser, op. cit., 97, 135, 145, 148.

10. Jonas Lie jr., 'Aud Egede Nissen – Norsk Kunstnerliv i Berlin II', *Ukens Revy* (1918).

11. *Film & Kino* 1 (1918): 2–4.

12. Cherchi Usai, op. cit., 486 follows Gerhard Lamprecht, *Deutsche Stummfilme 1917–1918* (Berlin: Deutsche Kinemathek, 1969), 163. Hans-Michael Bock (ed.), *Cinegraph. Lexicon zum deutschsprachigen Film*, (Munich, 1984) follows Birett op. cit., 455. After comparing the sources, and after seeing the film, where one of the intertitles, dealing with events in the past, mentions the date 16 April 18, I believe that the film was made and released in 1919.

13. The copy has two different types of intertitles, one green and the other blue. The green intertitles, relatively few in number, give the name of the millionaire as Harrison.
14. *Norsk Filmblad* 6–7 (1962):190.

Filmography

Ich heirate meine Puppe (1917)
Die Geburt der Venus (1917)
Peter mit der Posaune (1917)
Die Libe, sie war nur ein Traum (1917)
Drei auf der Platte (1917)
Ein Detektiv-Duell (1917)
Der geigende Tod (1917)
Das Geheimnis der Briefmarke (1917)
Das Verhängnis der schönen Susi (1917)
Der Kampf mit dem Sturmvogel (1917)
Der Halsschmuck (1918)
Der Roman der Herzogin von Corvy (1918)
Sturmschwalbe (1918)
Der Todestraum (1918)
Bobby und die süssen kleinen Mädchen (1918)
Bobby als Familienvater (1918)
Heddys Meisterstreich (1918)
Der weinende Dieb (1918)
Hoteldiebe (1918)
Der Rosenkranz (1918)
Die Rachegöttin (1918)
Leuchtende Punkte (1918)
Verkauftes Glück (1918)
Das Brandmal (1918)
Luxuspflänzchen (1919)
Die lachende Seele (1919)
Die Jugensünde (1919)
100 000 Dollars (1919)
Erblich belastet (1919)
Das Testament des Grafen Hammerstein (1920).

Travel Films in Norway: The Persistence of the 'View' Aesthetic

Bjørn Sørenssen

Department of Art and Media Studies, University of Trondheim, NTNU, 7491 Trondheim, Norway

On 4 February 1930, a Norwegian film was presented at one of the major cinemas in Stockholm to favourable press reviews. The film in question had the Swedish title *Det vackra Norge* (Beautiful Norway). It was photographed by Paul Berge and directed by Lyder Selvig, who was later to become manager of the municipal cinema organisation in Trondheim, Norway. According to the reviewers, the silent feature-length film was accompanied by an orchestra playing Norwegian music. The review in the major evening newspaper *Aftonbladet* was enthusiastic:

> The ... audience at the 7 o'clock performance was taken with the beauty shown on the screen and thunderous applause accompanied the final exceedingly beautiful winter images. The spectator sat captivated from beginning to end ... The photographer Paul Berge has learnt how to make a captivating presentation. The film is worth a visit above many other films being offered this week.[1]

Selvig's film had a similarly favourable reception at its first screening in Oslo in November 1929, where the film played three performances per night for five weeks with an expanded orchestra and eminent vocal soloists. What strikes us as remarkable today is the fact that in a period we may characterise as the transition to sound, none of the reviews found it worth mentioning that a travelogue such as this must have presented a strong contrast with other film premieres, seeming to treat it as just another attraction in the cinema repertoire. This response seems to indicate that the travel film may have represented a special aesthetic that in many ways remained unchanged for the entire period of silent film.

The silent travel film genre was one of the earliest popular and developed forms of film practice dating back to the period before the nickelodeon, and it represented, together with the 'actuality film', the major form of pre-documentary non-fiction film. As a result of the rise of the dramatic narrative film and, subsequently, the feature film, non-fiction subjects were relegated to the margins of the exhibition repertoire. Thus, actuality film survived in the form of the newsreel, while the travel film or 'travelogue' survived in sporadic appearances in the cinema repertoire or in alternative exhibition venues throughout the silent period. One interesting

aspect of the travel film is the amazing consistency of the subject, from the earliest days in the 1890s through and, in several cases, beyond the era of silent film.[2] This consistency becomes all the more remarkable when compared with the dramatic evolution of fiction film during the silent period. It may be argued that the travel film found its form in the first decade of the century after which it changed very little.

Tom Gunning has sought to characterise early non-fiction (pre-Griersonian) film as dominated by what he calls 'the aesthetics of the "view"', a mode which, he argues, possesses clear mimetic qualities:

> To my mind the most characteristic quality of a 'view' lies in the way it mimes the act of looking and observing. In other words, we don't just experience a 'view' film as a presentation of a place, an event or a process, but also as the mimesis of the act of observing.[3]

The 'view' is closely connected to what Gunning has termed the 'cinema of attractions', a general descriptive term for early cinema as opposed to the narrative form developed in fiction film between 1908 and 1912, with an emphasis on showing instead of telling.[4] Gunning contrasts the independence of the shot in the 'view' tradition with the later documentary mode with its argumentative use of shots, either as evidence or as a part of a logically constructed narrative. Gunning goes on to differentiate between what he calls 'place films' and 'process films', the latter being films that describe the processes of production or present certain events. The 'place film' is a series of shots presenting a certain landscape or locale, representing various views, often using the camera to create a panoramic view. The 'phantom ride' is a special version of such a 'place' film, in this case the attraction is closely connected to movement, the film being shot from a moving vehicle such as a train, an automobile or a boat moving through the landscape, combining the experience of the view with the sensation of movement.

The 'phantom ride' was very often used as an attraction in itself, being offered at amusement parks and fairgrounds as an exciting substitute for travel. The most famous of these early phantom ride attractions was the Hale's Tours concept of 'Pleasure Railways', offered by George C. Hale in Kansas City 'Electric Park' in 1905 and later expanded nationwide in the US. The Hale's Tours concept consisted in showing 'phantom ride' films in a mock railway carriage with several sound and motion effects emulating the experience of a train ride. Although the Hale's Tours venues did not last beyond 1912, the concept of the 'phantom ride' survived in travel films, and is seen re-emerging in today's IMAX cinemas.[5]

Tourism and travelogues in Norway

In March 1907 the photographer H.M. Lomas visited Norway in order to secure footage for Hale's Tours. True to the chosen subject, his visit resulted in shots from railways in southern and central Norway, and according to a newspaper interview at the time, Norwegian State Railways allowed him free travel and a permit to mount a camera in front of the locomotive.[6] These scenes no doubt were later incorporated into the regular programme at the various Hale's Tours exhibitions in the United States. Whether these railway 'phantom rides' were shown in Norway is unclear, though not very probable, given the institutional context of Hale's Tours. The concept of travel films or 'phantom rides' were, however, not new to the growing Norwegian audience for cinema.

The lack of film production companies and facilities in Norway during the first decade of the century, and the sporadic (and mainly unsuccessful) attempts to establish permanent film production in the 1910s, did not mean that there were no films made in Norway during this period.[7] In the early days of cinema, Norwegian exhibitors followed their colleagues in other countries by utilising the attraction of the local environment by supplementing their programme with the presentation of local actualities. Thus, a cinema owner in Trondheim was able to present moving images of the royal procession during the crowning of King Haakon VII on 27 June 1906 the very same evening in his cinema. Similar success had been achieved by a Kristiania (by which name Oslo was formerly known) exhibitor when Haakon VII (the former Prince Carl of Denmark) arrived in his

new country half a year earlier. The exhibitor had secured a place for his photographer aboard the ship bringing the young Danish prince to Norway to accept the throne of the newly-independent state.

These kinds of early 'media events' were augmented by other, less sensational local images, and very soon we find the travel film genre appearing also in Norway in the form of films shot in more exotic locations as well as films from various parts of Norway. In 1901 the spectacle of moving images was brought to the northernmost parts of Norway by an enterprising travelling exhibitor who had brought a camera as well as his projector. As a result, he was able to offer scenes from the land of the midnight sun, scenes that might appear just as exotic to an audience in southern Norway as images from Paris, the sky-scrapers of New York, or coolies in China.[8]

With the rapid development of tourism in Norway after the First World War, the production of travel films presenting a touristic view of Norway became more common. Several of the films dealing with Norwegian landscapes and attractions were admittedly made with a foreign audience in mind, particularly the American audience. Nevertheless, this subject fitted well with the overall effort of establishing Norwegian national identity. Being a Norwegian meant knowing and being proud of the natural wonders that set Norway apart from other nations. We find, not surprisingly, that the Norwegian travel films, the early short films as well as the feature-length so-called *Norway-films* (*Norgesfilmer*) of the 1920s, tend to reproduce the same images that belonged to the standard touristic repertoire of the day.

The early Norwegian tourist trade was primarily centred around the fjords and salmon rivers of western Norway. The salmon rivers had attracted members of the British upper classes since the last part of the nineteenth century, and this had in turn resulted in a spate of British travel books and memoirs about the area. The British *lakselord* (salmon lord) was an established character in these areas, and often spent a considerable part of spring and summer there becoming a key figure in establishing the early tourist trade.

Large and comfortable fjord and mountain hotels were built around the turn of the century in Swiss and Norwegian national romantic style to accommodate these early, affluent tourists. We find, not surprisingly, a number of travel films concerned with salmon fishing, notably in the Lærdal and Rauma rivers, favourites of the 'salmon lords'. These films can be categorised as 'process films', since the beauty of the landscape has to yield to the excitement of reeling in a 40-pound salmon.[9]

About the same time, pleasure cruise ships started to make summer excursions to the deep fjords stretching as much as a hundred miles inland, and this activity soon established a flourishing summer trade bringing cruise tourists from the fjords up to the mountains and glaciers, an activity which, in turn, necessitated the building of adequate roads for this purpose. The first decade of the twentieth century saw a strong development in cruise traffic, and the annual and well-publicised visits of the German Kaiser brought a large number of German visitors as well as British. No wonder, then, that the West Coast Grand Tour figures prominently in extant travel films from the period: the Folgefonna glacier above the calm waters of Hardangerfjord, the majesty of the hundred-mile long Sognefjord, and perhaps most famous of all fjord vistas, Geiranger fjord with numerous waterfalls cascading from the top of the steep mountain walls straight down into the fjord. Fjord vistas such as these would later find their way into the *Norway-films* of the 1920s.

From the 1920s on, the northern part of Norway was introduced as a tourist area, offering dramatic coastal panoramas during the summer all the way up to North Cape, adding the exotic touch of the indigenous *Sami* (Lapp) population and their reindeer herds. In 1925 and 1926 film teams boarded the flagship of the Norwegian-American Line, the *Stavangerfjord*, resulting in two films with the same title, the one made by Gustav Lund's Bio-Film company in 1925 having been preserved.[10] The film, with the title *Med 'Stavangerfjord' til Nordkap* (With the 'Stavangerfjord' to North Cape), is organised as a reportage of the cruise, starting with the usual west Norway fjord vistas, Geiranger and the Jostedal Glacier,

before proceeding north. The emphasis is clearly on the northernmost part, a part of Norway that generally was as little known to audiences in southern Norway as to foreign tourists. The cruise tourists are visited by King Neptune himself as the ship crosses the Arctic Circle and have to undergo his 'baptism'. The drama and beauty of the Lofoten isles is fully explored, as is the theme of the midnight sun and the lure of the North Cape, representing the northern end of the European continent. In the 1930s, the *Stavangerfjord* cruises would go even further north to the Svalbard Islands and Spitsbergen, as one of Thor Iversen's films documents, thus linking polar exploration with tourism.

Railway films

If the fjord film could be said to constitute one sub-genre of the Norwegian silent travel film, another sub-genre was constituted by the railway film. The railway film, was, of course, already established as one of the *Ur*-forms of the international travel film, and the proliferation of 'phantom rides', with camera mounted on a train, has been noted as one of the prime examples of the 'view' aesthetic.[11]

Railway building in Norway was challenged by the hard facts of Norwegian topography. Vast distances between few cities in a sparsely populated countryside offered major obstacles like the Hardanger and Dovre mountain plateaux separating Oslo and the east country from Bergen in the west, and Trondheim in the north. North of Trondheim, there was an additional 1200 kilometres up to the Finnish border on the edge of the Barents Sea containing still more mountain plateaux and intercrossed with deep fjords making the distance from the sea to the Swedish border, at one point, as narrow as four kilometres.

Nevertheless, during the first three decades of the twentieth century, Norwegian railway engineers managed to overcome the obstacles in southern Norway to construct railways that were the pride of the young nation and facilitated Norway's leap into the industrial age. The first breakthrough was the construction of the Ofoten railway in northern Norway, linking the ice-free port of Narvik with the Swedish Kiruna railway in 1904 as a means to ship out iron ore from the vast mines of Swedish Lapland all year round. The railway made a dramatic descent from the high mountains near the border through tunnels and trestles to the fjord below, and a film from this scenic railway was made a short time after its opening and shown in Norwegian cinemas. It is highly possible that this is the 'educational' film referred to in a satiric rendering of the cinematic repertoire in the New York *Herald* in 1908 when New York City authorities demanded the presence of a 'lecturer' at Sunday screenings to justify a screening of a film from a northern European country as 'educational':

> 'A railroad track', said the lecturer, the motion picture having been taken evidently from the front of a train.

> 'Some men', continued the educationalist presently, when a group of men on skis were shown. The next scene revealed them speeding downhill.

> 'Men skiing', announced the man.

> The picture again switched to the railroad tracks.

> 'Another railroad track.'

> The track led across a low trestle.

> 'The Brooklyn Bridge', bellowed the announcer.

> Pictures showing reindeers tramping about in the snow were explained as 'Animals eating snowballs'.[12]

The Ofoten railway was, however impressive, although only thirty-two kilometres long. By the time this mountain railway opened, work had been under way for several years on the project regarded as the great triumph of railway engineering in Norway: the Oslo-Bergen railway. The only stable means of communication between the two major Norwegian cities had so far been by boat along the coast, a trip that took three to five days by steamer. Land transport was impossible in winter due to the forbidding Hardanger Plateau raising up to 1301 metres above sea level, and the construction of a railway line here was considered extraordinarily complex because of the problem of snow in winter. Construction

proved to be extremely difficult, with many setbacks, but in 1909 the last stretch across the plateau was finished, and the railway could be officially opened on 27 November. An actuality film was made of the occasion and this film, *The Opening of the Bergen Railway*, is among the early Norwegian actualities that have been preserved. The concerns of this 1909 film confirm the thesis about the consistency of the 'view' aesthetic: apart from the clues given by fashion, there is very little to distinguish it from later films of the 1920s with the same subject. The camera is present when the king and his entourage enter the train from a red carpet in Kristiania. On the way to the mountains through the scenic Hallingdal Valley, a camera has been mounted at the end of the train sharing the speed, excitement and the vistas with the spectator. Near the highest point of the railway, Finse station at 1222 metres above sea level, there is a ceremony, speeches and a lunch before the train continues across the Hardanger Plateau and down to Voss. At this point the camera leaves the railway, and the rest of the film is used to extol the surroundings and the hotel at Vatnahalsen where the steep Flåm valley descends from the railway line to the fjord. In these sequences the panoramic quality of the film is enhanced by the use of a 'binocular mask', a device no doubt copied from contemporary foreign travel films.

The Bergen railway was the subject of several actualities and travel films during the 1920s, reflecting pride in the ambitious railway project. There might have been railways reaching higher altitudes in the Alps and in the Rocky Mountains, but no other railway ran for more than a hundred kilometres above the tree line, a fact that made winter maintenance a difficult – and spectacular – task. The main visual attraction was the 'rotation plough', a giant snow blower powered by a locomotive charging through the snow and sending cascades of snow up into the air and away from the track. The formerly desolate Finse now became a fashionable winter resort offering great possiblities for cross-country skiing and, as another attraction, an indoor skating rink.

Among several shorter films documenting the wonders of the Bergen railway, Ottar Gladtvet's *The Bergen Railway* (1925) is a typical example of the railway travel film. This film makes extensive use of the 'phantom ride' concept, with the camera mounted in front of the locomotive, presenting the viewer with an exciting ride through the snow-clad Hardanger plateau. We have a photo of Ottar Gladtvet posing proudly with camera and tripod on the wooden platform constructed in front of the locomotive. Intercutting between the moving camera and the interior of the engine driver's cab hints at an embryonic 'documentary' usage. Apart from this, there is no doubt about the *view* having prominence, with the added attraction of panning while moving. One of the main attractions of this film is the spectacle of the rotating plough, representing the triumph of modern technology over the forces of nature. There is also extensive coverage of the new tourist hotel at Finse, presenting the well-to-do at play, with skiing, skating, and curling, the lavish lunch table, and dinner and dancing in stylish evening attire. Thus this film shares the ambition of the cruise films by presenting Norway as a place where timeless natural beauty can be enjoyed with all modern comfort.

The Norwegian State Railways company no doubt supported these railway films, and as a result a considerable number of films present vistas and cover major events in the development of the railway system in the 1920s and 1930s. The next major accomplishment of Norwegian railway construction (the years of the First World War had seen a moratorium on all railway building) was the Dovre railway, creating a standard European-gauge link between Oslo and Trondheim at its completion in 1921. There had been a narrow gauge connection between the two cities since 1877 – the Røros Railway – but there was a need for a more modern and fast connection. An additional argument in the years following Norway's seccession from the union with Sweden, was to move the main railway link between southern and northern Norway further away from the Swedish border in case of war![13] Although it did not present the same construction challenges as the Bergen Railway, the Dovre Railway was in many ways as spectacular, crossing the Dovre Mountain Plateau at an altitude of 1025

metres above sea level and making a dramatic descent down the Drivdalen valley towards Trondheim.

A film celebrating the opening of the Dovre Railway in 1921, not unlike the 1909 film of the opening of the Bergen Railway, focuses on the royal entourage on the opening train, gives examples of vistas from the train at various points, and records the festivities in Trondheim for the occasion.[14] The opening of the railway, however, had a tragic post-script, also recorded on film, as one of the trains carrying dignitaries to the opening collided with a freight train, resulting in the loss of six lives.

There are a great number of railway films preserved in the Norwegian film archives in Oslo and Rana, although it is uncertain how many of these films were financed or how they were exhibited.[15] A considerable number were shot by Ottar Gladtvet, the dominant figure in Norwegian non-fiction film production in the years preceding the Second World War. Gladtvet was responsible for covering the opening of another of the Norwegian mountain railways in the 1920s and 1930s, the Rauma Railway, connecting the Dovre railway at Dombås with the western Norwegian fjord port of Åndalsnes in 1924. His *Raumabanen – Norges nyeste turistbane* (Raumabanen – Norway's newest tourist railway), probably made in 1925, is primarily concerned with presenting this railway as a new tourist attraction, combining the fjord cruise with scenic railway travel. The film opens with a shot of cruise ships off Åndalsnes harbour, before presenting the ride through the dramatic mountain landscape of Romsdalen valley, with shots of mountaineers climbing the Romsdalshorn peak, and a shot of the famous 1,100 metre high Trollveggen ('Troll Wall') rock face in Romsdalen. Although not as difficult to construct as the Bergen or Dovre railways, the Rauma railway nevertheless presented some amazing feats of railway engineering in taking the railway from the valley bottom almost at sea level up to an altitude of 670 metres in a short distance. This was achieved by constructing a so-called turning tunnel at Verma, where the railway also had to cross a dramatic gorge over the Rauma river on an elegantly designed bridge. All of this was duly presented in Gladtvet's film, using all the devices known to the classic travel 'view' film. At the high altitude point of the railway, Bjorli station, the restaurant, hotel and tourist facilities are presented and, as if to underline the possibilities of people from all over the world coming to admire the beauty and engineering ingenuity of Norway, an Indian couple is singled out for special presentation.

Tiedemann's travel films

The Norwegian travel films of the two first decades were produced either as actualities or for feature presentation. The 1920s saw another presentation form, the travel and/or culture film as advertising vehicle. The number of advertising films in Norway increased dramatically in 1927, from between five and seven a year to one hundred, and averaged around sixty the following years. The majority of these films were produced to promote tobacco products, above all, the products of the Tiedemann Tobacco Company of Oslo. One of the reasons for this rise has been linked to the fact that the Norwegian-owned tobacco company during these years was challenged by international competition which led Tiedemann to increase its advertising budget and to expand into the field of film advertising. [16] A considerable number of these advertising films were classified as 'culture films' or 'nature films', where the advertiser mainly functioned as a sponsor of a short educational non-fiction film, and within these categories we find many films that would fall into the established travel film genre. Among the advertising films censored in the 1920s and early 1930s, we find titles like *Travelling by reindeer sled in the Røros Area, Geiranger* (naturally!), *In the Romsdal Valley, Musk oxen in the Dovre Mountains*, and *Setesdalen*.[17] In *Flying to Jotunheimen*, the viewer is presented with exciting aerial photography of the highest mountains in Norway. The form and structure of these films adhere closely to the conventions of the travel film 'view', with one major exception: at regular intervals during the films, and guaranteed at the end, we find shots of people enjoying their *Teddy, Medina, Cromwell* or whatever

other cigarette brand advertised against a background of beautiful nature.

We find an excellent – and exotic – example of this kind of film in *Over Besseggen på motorcyklel* (Across Besseggen on a motor cycle, 1930). Besseggen is a dramatic ridge between two mountains in the Jotunheimen mountains in southern Norway. The sides of the narrow, mile-long ridge plunge into two lakes, several hundred metres below, and is well-known to Norwegians through Henrik Ibsen's *Peer Gynt*, where the main character boasts of having ridden the ridge on the back of a wild reindeer. 'Peer Gynt's ride' is an obvious reference in the film, where we meet a present-day Peer Gynt with motor bike, goggles, and a cigarette in his mouth, poised on his vehicle before setting off on the daring quest. A series of panoramic shots helps establish the dramatic beauty of the area and underlines the inherent danger. He pauses to light a cigarette (we are informed by an intertitle which make of cigarette gives relaxation and concentration in a moment like this), and sets off down the mountain and over the ridge. The final shot is a composite shot of a man and a woman lighting and smoking cigarettes, with Besseggen Ridge in the background.[18]

The increase in production of advertising films was an important factor in keeping Norwegian film production alive in the late 1920s and 1930s, and made it possible for at least two production companies to maintain the production of non-fiction film. Sponsorship by Tiedemann and other companies also made it possible to produce a number of nature, travel and other educational films for theatrical as well as school exhibition.[19] A special case in point is Ottar Gladtvet's Tiedemann film, *Grønlandsekspedisjonen* (The Greenland Expedition) which continued the tradition of the Norwegian 'polar expedition film'.

The polar expedition films of the 1920s and 1930s

The polar exhibition film, a sub-genre of the travel film, emerged as something of a Norwegian speciality. There are obvious reasons for this specialisation, closely associated with the increase in activity in Norwegian Arctic

and Antarctic exploration around the turn of the century and later, as well as with the rise of nationalism in the newly-independent country. Explorers like Nansen, Sverdrup and Amundsen evolved into important national icons for the young country through their expeditions, culminating in Amundsen's conquest of the South Pole in December 1911. An early Norwegian actuality fragment covers some of the expedition.[20] The 35mm fragment seems to belong to an early actuality presentation, and is introduced with the title 'Roald Amundsen has planted the Norwegian flag on the South Pole', and is followed by shots of Amundsen's ship, Nansen's legendary *Fram*, arriving in Norwegian waters. Amundsen had brought a film camera with him on this expedition (although it did not accompany the group making the final push for the Pole), and the ensuing *Roald Amundsens sydpolsekspedisjon* (The South Pole Expedition of Roald Amundsen, 1912) firmly established this new genre of travel film.

In ensuing years, this activity was stepped up, providing the country with an area of national excellence and identity, and even becoming an example of colonialism with the treaty of Svalbard in 1923 and the attempt to annex East Greenland in 1931 as culmination. Against this background, it is not surprising that actuality and travel films dealing with polar expedition evolved into a dominant trend in the modest output of Norwegian non-fiction film, and were, evidently, enthusiastically received by audiences.

A prominent role in this and other non-fiction film ventures was played by film pioneer and theatre owner Gustav Lund who, in 1911, established the Bio-Film Compagni in Kristiania. This company became central to the production of shorter and longer non-fiction films for theatrical distribution. In 1919 another Norwegian film pioneer, Ottar Gladtvet, joined Bio-Film as its actuality photographer. Before setting out as a member of a Swedish expedition to South America, Gladtvet instructed Bio-Film's title photographer, Reidar Lund, and then sent him off on another expedition to Novaya Zemlya in the Russian Arctic in 1921. Lund returned with material which was presented for theatrical distribution as *Under polarkredsens himmel* (Under the Sky

of the Arctic Circle) in December 1922. Reidar Lund and Bio-film was then involved in another arctic adventure, this time with Roald Amundsen himself. In 1918 Amundsen had set out with his new ship, the *Maud*, along the coast of Siberia in an attempt to drift towards the North Pole. The entire *Maud* expedition lasted until 1925 but, although it provided arctic exploration with a wealth of scientific data, it did not bring Amundsen any closer to his ultimate aim – the North Pole. Reidar Lund was among the participants as Amundsen, in 1921, set out from Seattle, where he had been forced to take *Maud* for repairs and new provisions. Lund then filmed aboard *Maud* during its voyage back north to the polar ice where it was to drift in the ice during winter, while Amundsen made his winter quarters in Wainwright, Alaska before making another attempt (which once again failed) at reaching the North Pole, this time by airplane. Back in Kristiania, Lund edited and released *Med Roald Amundsens nordpol-sekspedition til første vinterkvarter* (With Roald Amundsen's North Pole Expedition to the First Winter Camp) for Bio-Film in February 1923. Another photographer, Odd Dahl, stayed with *Maud* for the remainder of her journey through the ice back to Norway in 1925. This resulted in another non-fiction feature film for Bio-Film, *Med 'Maud' over Polhavet* (With *Maud* Across the Polar Sea), having its premiere on Norwegian National Day (17 May) in 1926.

Amundsen's polar exploits provided Norwegian filmmakers with more opportunities for popular and, presumably, profitable film presentations. Amundsen had by now turned to aviation, and the two next Amundsen expeditions were filmed by a pilot, Oskar Omdal, joining him on those expeditions. This resulted in two films for the company Spektro-film released in 1925 and 1926: *Roald Amundsen-Ellsworth's flying expedition 1925* and *Luftskibet 'Norge's' flugt over Polhavet* (The Flight of the Dirigible *Norge* Across the Arctic Ocean), the latter film capturing Amundsen's long-awaited passage across the North Pole in an Italian dirigible with Umberto Nobile. The reason for the popularity of these films can be explained by Amundsen's position as a Norwegian national hero. His

conquest of the South Pole in competition with the hapless Scott in 1911 had secured international fame for the young and insecure nation, and combined with the feats of Fridtjof Nansen, contributed to forging a strong link between polar exploration and Norwegian identity. Among the actuality material preserved from the 1920s, we find several films covering Amundsen's triumphant return from the 1926 expedition, showing how thousands of people would turn out to hail their hero. Amundsen's tragic death in an airplane crash while attempting to rescue his rival, Nobile, in 1928 undoubtedly enhanced his heroic image and secured his position in latterday Norwegian mythology.

The series of popular polar expedition films shown in Norwegian cinemas ended in 1930 with a film about the third *Norvegia* expedition to the Antarctic. Between 1927 and 1931 the ship, *Norvegia*, made four expeditions to the Antarctic financed by a Norwegian shipowner. The idea behind the expedition was to examine the possibilities for commercial whaling, and thus the expedition was instrumental in initiating large-scale whaling in the region. The expedition also formally annexed two small, uninhabited (and uninhabitable) islands for the Kingdom of Norway and circumnavigated the Antarctic continent. The leader of the third expedition was Hjalmar Riiser-Larsen, a pilot who had accompanied Amundsen on his arctic expeditions in 1925/26 and flown with him across the North Pole in *Norge*. Riiser-Larsen had brought filming equipment and the film was premiered in November 1930 as *Mot ukjent land* (Towards Unknown Land).

If this was the last of the polar expedition films in a commercial setting, the genre was supplemented in other distribution outlets. As mentioned previously, during the 1920s, Norwegian companies, especially the Tiedemann Tobacco Company, became interested in film as an advertising medium, and saw an opportunity to advertise by sponsoring short films with the clear understanding that the film would contain advertising sequences. In 1931 Norwegian seal hunters proclaimed East Greenland as a Norwegian administrative province in what more or less amounted to an 'occupation'. The Norwegian cabinet

seized this opportunity to divert public opinion from the rather precarious economic situation at home, and the young lawyer and arctic explorer, Helge Ingstad, was put in charge of Norwegian affairs in the area and despatched to East Greenland. Ingstad's expedition was covered by cameraman Ottar Gladtvet, and resulted in a film that was sent in four parts to the Norwegian bureau of film censorship to be given separate censorship numbers, indicating a form that would lend itself easily to exhibition at feature film presentations. The films showed various landscapes and activities in this harsh climate to which the Norwegian public had, by now, become accustomed through earlier expedition films. What was new about the *Tiedemann's Nature Films: The Greenland Expedition* (as this series was called), was the compulsory shot of Helge Ingstad and his colleagues puffing away at Tiedemann's excellent cigarettes.

In 1935 an educational film presented a coda to the Norwegian polar expedition genre. Made by a goverment fisheries official, Thor Iversen, a series of separate silent films from arctic fishery research expeditions between 1930 and 1932 was given one censorship number in 1935 as *Høit mot nord* (Towards the Far North). This film (or rather films) presents an interesting mirror image and summation of the genre as a whole. Iversen's expeditions took him to the northernmost shores of the Svalbard Islands and to the Norwegian islands in the polar North Atlantic: Bear Island, Jan Mayen and Hopen. One of the films records in graphic detail the hunt for polar bears in a way that would certainly shock today's ecologically correct audiences, but undoubtedly held an unmitigated thrill for a pre-war audience.

The *Norway-films:* modern communication and pre-modern national romanticism

During the 1920s the Norwegian tradition in touristic travel films culminated in a number of feature-length compilations for theatrical as well as non-theatrical distribution known as *Norgesfilmer* (*Norway-films*). The explicit aim of producing these films, one in 1923,

two in 1927, and two in 1929, seems to have been the promotion of Norway as a tourist destination for foreign audiences. The fact that most of the films were submitted to the Norwegian office of film censorship seems to indicate a wish to reach the Norwegian market as well, something which the long run of Lyder Selvig's film in Oslo indicates. The first of these films was produced by the film distribution of the Norwegian municipalities,[21] Kommunenes Filmcentral (KF) in 1923 as *Norge – En skildring i 6 akter* (Norway – A Description in 6 parts), 2074 metres.[22] Each of the six reels of the film was dedicated to one geographical area, ending with images from the Finnmark region in northern Norway. The film was first shown to a specially invited audience on 20 November 1923, and in a short notice in the Oslo newspaper, *Dagbladet*, the following day it was praised for being 'a film that will contribute to making the name of Norway and its natural beauty known and attractive in foreign countries'. This indicates that the film was primarily meant for distribution to a foreign non-theatrical market under the auspices of the Norwegian tourist industry.

Tancred Ibsen, grandchild of the two giants of Norwegian literature, Henrik Ibsen and Bjørnstjerne Bjørnson, spent two years in the United States in 1923–25, where, becoming interested in film as a medium, he spent a year working for MGM in Hollywood. Upon returning to Norway, he looked for opportunities to produce film in Norway, and his first project was a series of short films promoting Norwegian tourist sights in southern Norway. In this he cooperated with the Danish filmmaker George Schnéevoigt who played an important part in Norwegian fiction film projects in the 1920s. The first screening of the resulting film, which has since been lost, was shown to the press in October 1927 as *The Norway Film* and was reported in three of the Oslo newspapers. *Dagbladet* did not fail to make the connection with Ibsen's family background, while at the same time, underlining the importance of promoting Norway: 'Let it be said that lieutenant Ibsen in the most successful way has continued his grandfathers' work to make the name and nature of Norway known throughout the world'.[23] In

this review, Ibsen's film was favourably compared with a *Norway-film* by Lyder Selvig which had been shown earlier the same year. This is the only record we have of this film, which might have been withdrawn and included in Selvig's 1929 film. Since Ibsen's film was never submitted to the Norwegian Bureau of film censorship, it is reasonable to surmise that the film was mainly shown abroad after the first Oslo screening. In 1929, Gustav Lund's Bio-Film company produced a feature length film for the domestic and foreign market, *Se Norge* with the English distribution title *Norway Today*. The film was mainly a compilation made of various shorter travel films shot during the 1920s covering a wide range of areas and subjects. Unlike Selvig's *Norgesfilm* later that year, this film does not seem to have achieved widespread Norwegian distribution.

The common denominator for all the *Norway-films* seems to be the wish to present Norway and Norwegian culture abroad, and in the case of Selvig's film, also to a Norwegian audience. The choice of visual material is very much the same, and seems to have aimed at portraying Norway both as a beautiful country steeped in tradition and as a modern European nation. This dual focus reflects the desire to relate Norway's growing industrialisation to the same natural wonders that the films extolled. The first half of this century saw Norway's abundant waterfalls, which had hitherto been seen as either an outright menace or as majestic nature, being domesticated and brought under control as the source of hydro-electric power, making it possible to establish heavy industry in and around the Norwegian fjords. We find this reflected in the fact that usually after presenting the natural wonders of Norway, the films contain a sequence that presents major heavy industries such as the Rjukan and Herøya fertiliser factories, or the Borregaard paper and cellulose mills as representative of the new, modern Norway. Norwegian self-esteem is also reflected in the emphasis on winter sports, reflecting both the perceived Norwegian character and the wish to capitalise on this aspect in connection with the winter sports tourist industry.

In a broader context, it is also reasonable to make a connection to the establishment of Norwegian fiction film production in the 1920s. Rasmus Breistein's *Fante-Anne* (Anne the Tramp, 1920) opened up a string of popular Norwegian films that were well received, both critically and at the box office. These films represented a form of national romanticism which, in many ways, echoed the literary movement of the mid-nineteenth century, and it has been argued that perhaps this was necessary in order to create a national tradition for Norwegian film production. In this regard, the early twentieth-century cultural expression in Norway is very closely related to the fact that Norway, as a young nation, was trying to define a national identity.[24] This double bind of old and new may be found in all *Norway-films* of the 1920s, not as contradictory, but as complementary terms. The beauty of the waterfalls and the efficiency of industry is presented side by side, without a hint of the dramatic consequences that industrialisation had on the landscape. In the films, the modern and pre-modern co-exist in harmony, the modern even being presented primarily as a way that enhances the possibilities of enjoying the pre-modern through the wonders of modern communication. This attitude is reflected in the third (of six) sequence of Selvig's *Beautiful Norway*, where 'Tourist Norway' is presented. What sets Selvig apart from other *Norway-films* is the prominent place of the automobile. The sequence is introduced by presenting a trip from Oslo to Bergen by automobile across the Haukeli mountains, a trip only possible in summer. Selvig's photographer Paul Berge takes great care to show the automobile in the landscape as often as possible, and very often resorts to dramatic panoramic shots showing the automobile cortege driving up or down some of the roads criss-crossing the mountain passes. Here the 'view' concern has been adapted to a 'view with automobile' concern. After arriving in Bergen and presenting Bergen as a modern, busy city, the strict chronology of the sequence is broken to give the audience further examples of how the Norwegian mountains have been made accessible to the automobile, showing Selvig's automobiles traversing dramatic passes, gorges and waterfalls in the mountains of central and west Norway. The fascination

with the modern machine in the pre-modern landscape leads to repetitions and variations of the same visual theme with the wonder of the automobile in the foreground.

According to Gunning, the 'view' aesthetic as a mode of non-fiction film represented a remarkable coherence for 'nearly two decades of film history'.[25] The reception of Selvig's film in Sweden and Norway in 1930, as well as other examples, suggests that the 'view' aesthetic may well have survived as an acceptable and expected form of non-fiction film throughout the period of silent film. A part of this aesthetic is even carried over into the sound film documentary in the form of travelogues for theatrical distribution, like the MGM Fitzpatrick Traveltalks in the 1930s and 1940s. The story that Lyder Selvig and other enthusiasts of the Norwegian landscape and Norwegian culture wanted to tell was better suited to a different form of mediation than the classic narrative. Instead of 'listen to my story', *Norway-films* seem to say 'come and see what I saw!', giving evidence to the persistence of the 'view' aesthetic in the travel film genre well into the era of sound film.

Notes

1. *Aftonbladet*, 4 February 1930: 'Den fulltaliga publiken vid 7-föreställningen var hänförd över allt det vackra som visades på den vita duken och rungande applåder ljödo när som slutkläm rullades en rad utomordentlig vackra vinterbilder … Fotografen Paul Berge har föstått at göra skildringen oerhört fängslande. Filmen är värd att ses före mycket annat av vad som enna vecka bjuds i filmväg.'
2. There is an interesting comment on this consistency by Tom Gunning in Daan Hertogs and Nico de Klerk (eds.), *Nonfiction from the teens* (Amsterdam: Nederlands Filmmuseum, 1994), 35. See also Jennifer Peterson, ''Truth is stranger than fiction': travelogues from the 1910s in the Nederlands Filmmuseum', in Daan Hertogs and Nico de Klerk (eds.), *Uncharted Territory: Essays on early nonfiction film* (Amsterdam: Nederlands Filmmuseum, 1997), 75–90.
3. Tom Gunning 'Before documentary: early nonfiction films and the 'view' aesthetic' in Hertogs and de Klerk (eds.), *Uncharted Territory*, 15.
4. Tom Gunning: 'The Cinema of Attractions: Early Film, its Spectator and the Avant-Garde', in Thomas Elsaesser (ed.), *Early cinema: space, frame, narrative* (London: British Film Institute, 1990), 56–63.
5. See Charles Musser, *The Emergence of Cinema: The American Screen to 1907* (New York: Scribner, 1990) 429–431, and Tom Gunning 'The world as object lesson: Cinema audiences, visual culture and the St. Louis world's fair, 1904', *Film History* 6, 4 (Winter 1994): 422–444, 439–441.
6. Gunnar Iversen, 'Norge i levende billeder – Hale's Tours i 1907', *M* no. 2 (1997): 21.
7. For a short introduction to early Norwegian cinema, see Gunnar Iversen, 'Norway', in Tytti Soila, Astrid Söderbergh Widding, Gunnar Iversen, *Nordic National Cinemas* (London: Routledge, 1998), 103–107.
8. Hans Fredrik Dahl, Jostein Gripsrud, Gunnar Iversen, Kathrine Skretting, and Bjørn Sørenssen, *Kinoens mørke – fjernsynets lys. Levende bilder i Norge gjennom hundre år* (Oslo: Gyldendal, 1996), 22.
9. Such as *Laksefiske i Lærdal* (Salmon fishing in Lærdal), Spektrofilm, 1920, Norwegian National Library, Rana FP 2002 0203.
10. Lars Thomas Braaten, Jan Erik Holst and Jan H. Kortner (eds.), *Filmen i Norge* (Oslo: Ad Notam Gyldendal, 1995), 90.
11. Tom Gunning, 'Before documentary': 15–16.
12. Quoted in Tom Gunning, *D. W. Griffith and the Origins of American Narrative Film: The Early Years at Biograph* (Urbana, Chicago: University of Illinois Press, 1991), 154.
13. Børrehaug Hansen, Gundersen, Sando *Jernbanen i Norge* (Oslo: Pax, 1980), 98.
14. Nitrate copy in the Norwegian National Library, Rana FT 4331 0098, 198 metres.
15. Such as The Røros Railway (1930), The Kristiania-Kornsjø Railway (1924–25), The Norwegian National Library, Rana Negative Red 1112.
16. Cf. Kathrine Skretting, *Reklamefilm. Norsk reklame i levende bilder 1920–1990* (Oslo: Universitetsforlaget, 1995).
17. Ibid.
18. Copy in the Norwegian National Library, Rana R 214 1/22.

19. In fact, several of the early educational films produced in Norway were conceived and produced as advertising films. Examples include Hans Berge´s *Geografitimen* (The Geography Lesson, 1926), a combined place/process film following a shipment of coconuts from the Southern Sea to their processing as PARI Margarine in Oslo, and Ottar Gladtvet´s *Fra Gullkysten til Freia* (From the Gold Coast to Freia, 1926), describing the cocoa bean from picking the crop in Africa to a delicious chocolate bar at Freia in Oslo. Cf. Jan Anders Diesen, *Eit hugtakande læremiddel? Undervisningsfilmen i norsk skole*, Doctoral Dissertation, University of Trondheim, 1995.

20. Nitrate copy in the Norwegian National Library, Rana FP 2014 0083. The fragment seems to indicate a form of newsreel – *Verdensspeilet* (World Mirror) – presented by the distribution company, Kinocentralen.

21. For discussion of the unique Norwegian institution of municipally owned cinemas, see Nils Klevjer Aas, 'Municipal Cinemas 1910–1925: Building a Unique Exhibition System', in Jostein Gripsrud and Kathrine Skretting (eds.), *History of Moving Images Reports from a Norwegian Project* (Oslo: The Research Council of Norway [*Levende bilder* no. 1, 1994; *KULTs skriftserie* no. 20], 1994), 51–73.

22. Braaten, Holst, and Kortner (eds.), *Filmen i Norge*, 88.

23. *Dagbladet*, 24 October 1927: 'La det være sagt at det er på den mest vellykkede måte at løitnant Ibsen har tatt op sine store bedsteforeldres arbeid for å gjøre Norges navn og vår natur kjent i utlandet.'

24. See Anne Marit Myrstad, 'National romanticism and Norwegian silent cinema', in Richard Dyer and Ginette Vincendeau (eds.), *Popular European Cinema* (London, New York: Routledge, 1992), 182–193.

25. Tom Gunning, 'Before documentary', 16.

Caricatures, Cartoons and Advertisements: The Pioneers of Nordic Animated Film

Gunnar Strøm

Volda College, P. O. Box 500, 6101 Volda, Norway

The first attempts to produce animated films in the Nordic countries go back to the mid-1910s. Inspired by pioneers like James Stewart Blackton, Winsor McCay, and the German screen cartoonist, Robert L. Leonard, young cartoonists in the Nordic countries undertook their first animated experiments with a great deal of enthusiasm and with simple home-made equipment. The earliest Nordic animated films involved time-lapse photography where the cartoonist drew a caricature commenting on a news story or newsworthy event in the style of a newspaper cartoon or a drawing from a humorous magazine. Both the Norwegians, Sverre Halvorsen (1892–1936) and Thoralf Klouman (1890–1940), and the Finn, Eric Vasström (1887–1958), produced films in this way in 1913 and 1914.

Like most of the Nordic pioneers, Halvorsen, Klouman and Vasström were cartoonists for newspapers, humorous magazines, advertisements, posters and postcards. The growing advertising market offered money to cartoonists, and animated film was a fascinating new medium. In Norway, the cartoonists formed Tegnerforbundet (Cartoonist Society) in 1916, and through their magazine, annual exhibitions and meetings, Tegnerforbundet became a meeting place where colleagues could meet, discuss, and develop their work.[1]

Between 1915 and 1922, nearly forty animated shorts were made in Denmark, Norway and Sweden. Because of the War in Finland, Eric Vasström's early attempts were not taken up until the mid-1920s. But in the three other Nordic countries, the period between the late 1910s and the mid-1920s was the hey-day of the animated short film. Most of these filmmakers are today unknown to an international audience. Their films had only limited national distribution. Some of the films, such as Vasström's *Päivänkuvia* (Sketches for Today), were so local in their concerns that they were not even shown outside the Finnish capital.[2] The only Norwegian silent animated short which we know was screened outside Norway is *Fanden i nøtten* (The Devil in the Nut, 1917) made by Ola Cornelius. The film was well received in Stockholm and Copenhagen.[3] In Denmark, Robert Storm-Petersen was the best known cartoonist with an inter-

national reputation by the late 1910s, at least in the other Nordic countries, but his animated cartoons were not, as far as we know, shown outside Denmark.

One Nordic animator achieved international success: the Swede, Victor Bergdahl. Bergdahl's animation debut *Trolldrycken* (The Magic Drink, 1915) was sold to eight countries outside Scandinavia, including Brazil, and eight copies were sold to Russia. The first *Kapten Grogg* film (Bergdahl's most famous cartoon character) was *Kapten Groggs underbara resa* (Captain Grogg's Wonderful Journey, 1916) of which thirty-five copies were sold outside Scandinavia, including Latin America. Besides Russia, the German-speaking countries in Europe seem to have been the most loyal *Kapten Grogg* audience outside Scandinavia.[4] A few copies were sent to England and the US, but they were probably never distributed. This lack of success in the English-speaking world may be one reason for Bergdahl's lack of recognition in the international history of animation, even though his films were among the best made in the 1910s. In Norway, Bergdahl's *Kapten Grogg* films were the most popular, only rivalled by W.R. Bray's *Colonel Heeza Liar* films in the late 1910s. Bergdahl was a major inspiration for other Scandinavian animators of the time.

Some of the early animators in Denmark, Finland and Norway were quite well known but not necessarily because of their work in animation. Sven Brasch (1886–1970) is best known for his film posters, both for Danish films and foreign films. Ola Fogelberg (1894–1952), a Finn, is best known for his comic strip, *Pekka Puupää*, while Thoralf Klouman was, for years, the leading theatrical cartoonist in Norway, and Ottar Gladtvet is best known for his work as a live action filmmaker. Victor Bergdahl also worked as a cartoonist in newspapers and magazines, but he is the only Nordic animator who is more famous for his animated films than for his other work during the silent era.

Viking Eggeling, of course, is widely recognised as one of the great animation pioneers, and his *Diagonal Symphonie* (1925) is rightly recognised as one of the classics of experimental animated cinema.[5] The film was made in Berlin and, inasmuch as the film may more

properly be regarded as part of the avant-garde movement in Germany, it is not considered in this essay.[6]

Film caricatures and cartoonists

In all the Nordic countries, animated drawings were a regular feature of cinema programmes by the mid-1910s. The films used time-lapse photography, and the cartoonists often appeared in the film as he quickly completed a drawing commenting on news events or issues of common interest to the cinema-going public. These short films lasted approximately one minute.

The earliest Nordic film in this genre that I have viewed was made by the Norwegian, Sverre Halvorsen, in 1913. In an interview in *Helt og Skurk*, Halvorsen related:

> One evening we were sitting in Circus Tivoli with the director Randall watching some live drawings by Leonard.[7] Then director Randall says to me, 'Why can't you make something similar, Mr Halvorsen?' 'Oh, yes', I responded, 'I guess that should be possible for a man like me', 'Well', Randall said – with a 'w' he had learned 'over there in the States', 'give it a try'. 'Just give me a blackboard and some chalk, and a test will be quickly done.'[8]

Helt og Skurk included some stills from the film in which we can see Halvorsen drawing on the blackboard. Halvorsen refers to five

Fig. 1. Roald Amundsen paa Sydpolen, *Sverre Halvorsen, 1913. [Courtesy of the National Archive, Mo i Rana.]*

Fig. 2. Cartoon (self-portrait), Thoralf Klouman.

films in the article, including *Oscar Mathisen paa skøiter ved Nordiska Spelen* (The Skater Oscar Mathisen at the Nordic Games, 1913) and *Roald Amundsen paa Sydpolen* (Roald Amundsen at the South Pole, 1913), which latter film, recently found in the national archives in Mo i Rana, deals with the popular hero, Amundsen (Fig. 1). After these early films for Randall and Circus Tivoli, Halvorsen formed the company A/S Filmfotografen og jeg with the cinematographer Hans Berge, but the company went bankrupt before it completed any films.

The newspaper and theatre cartoonist, Thoralf Klouman (Fig. 2) was the next person to venture into animation in Norway. While at the Art Academy in Kristiania in spring 1914, Klouman made three caricature films (*karikaturbilder*): *Veirprofeten Strømberg* (The Weather Prophet Strømberg), *Tango*, and the most successful of the three, *Hedin rider kjephesten* (Hedin Rides the Wooden Horse) about the Swedish explorer, Sven Hedin. With Sverre Halvorsen's film about Roald Amundsen, this film is an early example of a major theme in early Nordic animation: explorers and expeditions. In an article in the Norwegian trade journal, *Film og Kino*, Klouman's caricatures were 'presented to the public so that they could see how the drawing was made, then it was shown on the screen for a minute, and then it was gone'.[9] In 1914, Eric Vasström also made his first *päivänkuvia* in Helsinki. These short films made for Finlandia Films were quite striking for their time, and were popular with Helsinki cinema-goers.

Because of the strong position of Victor Bergdahl and other Swedish animators in the late 1910s, Swedish film cartoonists have been overlooked. But a list of 'quick-drawers' in Torsten Jungstedt's study of Bergdahl shows that the film caricature was a well established genre in Sweden in 1916. The most popular of these artists was Paul Myrén (1884–1951) who later drew the animated sequences in the live-action feature, *Robinson i skärgården* (Robinson in the Archipelago, Rune Carlsten, 1920). Myrén regularly featured as a 'quick-drawer' in Swedish newsreels in the 1910s. Other artists working in this field included the painter, graphic artist, and set designer (John) Jon-And (1889–1941), the newspaper cartoonist Nils Melander (1895–1980), and Gustav Bergström (1899–1983). Even though their films employed time-lapse live action drawings, Myrén, Melander and Bergström also used short drawn animation sequences.

Other Swedish film caricaturists from the late 1910s include Nils Ringström (1880–1952) and Eigil Schwab (1882–1952). The tradition of film caricaturists commenting on the news continued as late as 1927. In the archive of the Swedish Film Institute, for instance, a drawing titled *Veckans skämtteckning* (The Caricature of the Week) by Ivar Starkenberg (1886–1947), who worked for the newspaper *Social-Demokraten* and *Konsumentbladet* for the Co-operative, has survived. This would seem to indicate that *Veckans skämtteckning* was regularly screened in Swedish cinemas as late as 1927. Jon-And also performed live action drawing in addition to his other artistic accomplishments, as did the Danish cartoonist Storm P. At the opening of the new Circus building in Copenhagen in 1913, Storm P. drew his comic strip characters *De tre smaa mænd* (The Three Small Men) being chased by a lion. Although this performance was live, the tradition of live action drawing was documented in *Storm P. tegner Tre Smaa Mænd* (Storm P. Draws The Three Small Men, 1920), a short 30-second film that shows Storm P. finishing a drawing of the Three Small Men on an easel. He leans back and watches the animated characters greet each other and walk out of the picture. Storm P. turns towards the camera with a satisfied smile.

Sweden

Sweden was the leading animation country in the Nordic countries in the late 1910s. Not only was Victor Bergdahl active in animation, two other Swedes produced animated shorts: Emil Åberg made three five-minute shorts in 1916, the same year that *Negren och hunden* (The Negro and the Dog) was completed at Svenska Biografteatern (Swedish Biograph). It is unclear who made *Negren och Hunden*, but the film is usually credited to M.R. Liljeqvist.

In additional to work by Åberg and Liljeqvist, Bergdahl completed three animated films concerning a circus, Circus Fjollinski, and the first two *Kapten Grogg* films in 1916, and made *Trolldryken* in 1915. As a 1916 issue of *Filmbladet* observed:

> Mr. Bergdahl got the inspiration for his living humorous sketches a couple of years ago when in a cinema he happened to see a cleverly done drawing, *Slumberland*, by Winston Mc Kee [sic]. Mr. Bergdahl realised that this was something to try out for a cartoonist with ideas and humour, and he went home directly from the screening and started work.[10]

In his study of Swedish animation, Torsten Jungstedt argues that several scenes in the *Kapten Grogg* films (as well as in films by Emil Åberg and by M.R. Liljeqvist) were inspired by newspaper comic strips by Winsor McCay in the early 1900s. It is easy to understand the excitement that young and enthusiastic Scandinavian cartoonists must have felt when they saw animated cartoon films for the first time, as animation was still quite rare in the Nordic countries in 1915. Probably a few Emile Cohl films were screened, but of this, we cannot be certain.[11] Wladislas Starewicz's puppet films were screened in Scandinavia,[12] but this did not inspire a Nordic puppet film. In Norway, animation films appeared as a regular attraction from 1916 with *Colonel Heeza Liar* films. This was soon followed by *Kapten Grogg*. In 1917 as many as twenty *Mutt and Jeff* films were imported to Norway. It seems likely that the 'boom' in Swedish animation paralleled the growing number of American animated films seen on Scandinavian screens.

Working for Pathé in Stockholm, Emil Åberg's animated film, *Lilla Kalles dröm om sin snögubbe* (Kalle's Dream about His Snowman, 1916), received better reviews than Bergdahl's *Circus Fjollinski* (Fjollinski's Circus).[13] After studies at Konstakademien in Stockholm, Åberg worked mainly as an illustrator, and his three films for Pathé from 1916 are well animated, and rank among the best animation films made in Scandinavia in the 1910s. *Lilla Kalles dröm om sin snögubbe* tells the story of a young boy who dreams about a snowman coming to life. In his dream, Kalle finishes his snowman by placing the head on the snowman and making its face. The snowman comes alive and puts on a hat, tries to smoke cigars, visits Kalle in his bedroom while he is asleep, melts in front of the oven, and plays hide-and-seek with Kalle. When Kalle wakes up the next morning, the snowman is still there as he left him – still without the head. *Mäster Tricks äventyr* (Master Trick's Adventure, 1916) is based on some visual gags which the main character, Master Trick, a magician, performs. It is not always clear what he is doing, but the film has some interesting visual manipulation where Master Trick plays with the illusionistic surface of the animated image. The film is an experiment in the possibilities of the medium. *Herr Klot, herr Spindelben och lilla fröken Synål* (Mr. Klot, Mr. Spider and Little Miss Needle) tells a love triangle story about a thin and loving couple, Spindelben (Mr. Spider) and Synål (Miss Needle), and the fat rival, Herr Klot. Herr Klot offends the little lady and Herr Spindelben challenges him to a duel. Spindelben wins by stabbing Herr Klott with his sword. The blood runs out of Herr Klot who becomes thin. To save him, Spindelben fills Herr Klott with liquid, and the film ends with all three characters becoming friends.

The film, *Negren och hunden*, by M.R. Liljeqvist is a mystery. Swedish films from this period are quite will documented, but the author and animator of this film is still unknown. No Swedish copy of the film exists, and it is even uncertain if the film was ever screened in a Swedish cinema, although the film was examined by the Norwegian censor on 1 February 1916. We know that at least thirty-two copies of the film were made,

twenty-four for destinations outside Scandinavia.[14]

After 1916, Victor Bergdahl was almost the sole animator in Sweden for a period of about ten years. The one exception is the live-action feature film, *Robinson i skärgården*, where Paul Myrén filmed a two minute animated scene and a few shorter animated sections. The leading character, Agathon, reading the famous novel about Robinson Crusoe, falls asleep, and the Robinson Crusoe of his dream comes alive as an animated character. The dream is quite scary, and Agathon wakes from his dream with a scream. The design of this animated sequence is quite detailed and advanced. The drawings of the natives dancing around a cauldron in which a character, quite similar to the live-action hero, is being boiled alive, is particularly lively.

The 1926 feature film, *Giftas* (Getting Married), directed by Olof Molander includes some animated sequences. In this wedding comedy based on a short story by August Strindberg, the animation is filmed by Arvid Olson who is most famous for his animated film advertisements, which I discuss later. He also filmed some animation for political propaganda films in the late 1920s and early 1930s.

The highly successful Swedish comic strip character, Adamsson, appeared in a short silent animated cartoon in 1930. *Adamsson fångar säl* (Adamsson Catching Seals, 1930) is based on original drawings by the comic-strip artist Oscar Jacobsson who also worked on the film, while the animation and direction was carried out by Berndt Erkéus and Åke Johansson. Adamsson was the first Scandinavian comic strip to be published in the United States as *Silent Sam* in 1922, and the strip was widely distributed internationally from the late 1920s.

Victor Bergdahl

There can be little doubt that Victor Bergdahl is one of the most important pioneers in the international history of animation. In a letter to Bergdahl in 1917, Asta Nielsen wrote:

> One day half a year ago I was in a movie theatre in Berlin suffering through a 'tragic' film and almost committed suicide

because of boredom. Then suddenly the Captain appears; I cannot describe how beautiful an effect he had on the audience and myself; there was laughter as never before in a theatre, I was almost sick with laughing. Naturally I have followed my beloved Captain on all his changes, and I long for his next voyage.[15]

Asta Nielsen had attended the premiere of the first *Kapten Grogg* film in Berlin, and he was an immediate success. From a traditional cartoon animation technique on paper, Bergdahl developed a time-saving technique where he printed several cards with the same background drawing on each card on which he drew the animations. This technique allowed him to use advanced backgrounds, not common in international animation in the late 1910s. Bergdahl's most advanced film is *När Kapten Grogg skulle porträtteras* (When Caption Grogg Was to Have His Portrait Painted, 1917). With a combination of live action and cartoon animation, Victor Bergdahl and Kapten Grogg are shown in the same shot in which Grogg is drawn by his creator. Bergdahl made this film on two different matted negatives which were processed together in the lab. The accuracy of registration is impressive, and shows Bergdahl's technical skills and inventiveness in his early productions.

Alcohol is a favourite concern in many of the *Kapten Grogg* films. Grogg's habitual drinking is a prominent aspect of his character. But while alcohol is drunk for pleasure in *Kapten Grogg* films, drinking is connected with alcoholism and delirium for the main character in Bergdahl's first film, *Trolldrycken*, which premiered in 1915. The three-minute film was made using simple drawings on paper, and tells the story of a fat man drinking and smoking a large cigar. The bottle changes into a baby which grows and becomes a grotesque monster that eats the man. The monster baby drinks what is left in the glass, but the mixture of the man and the alcohol is too much. The monster baby's stomach explodes, and transforms into something like a fireworks display. From the falling stars, a drawing of the man as he was at the opening of the film emerges, once again with a full bottle, a glass, and the fat cigar, but now the man is smiling. According to reviews in 1915, this grotesque story

was read as a funny film rather than a serious comment on alcohol addiction.

Bergdahl started work on *Trolldrycken* in 1912. At the same time he developed the first drawings for a film set in a circus. It took time before Bergdahl got access to a camera to shoot these films. *Trolldrycken* was shot over four days in 1915. *Circus Fjollinski* was shot, late 1915 or early 1916. There now followed a very active period for the animator. Two more Fjollinski films were drawn and shot during spring 1916: *Den fatala konserten i Circus Fjollinski* (The Fatal Concert at the Fjollinski Circus) and *Komisk Entré av Pelle Jöns i Circus Fjollinski* (A Comic Turn by Pelle Jöns at the Fjollinski Circus). We encounter the same clown, Pelle Jöns, in all the Fjollinski films which are all characterised by the inventive use of transformations and metamorphoses. In the first film, which was originally called *Dansösen och clownen* (The Dancer and the Clown), Pelle smokes cigars and a pipe, an activity which is not allowed at the Circus. He then draws a female character who comes to life, and the last half of the film shows the dancer and her performance on a horse. In *Den fatala konserten*, Pelle is playing the guitar when the chair on which he is sitting suddenly becomes alive and plays with Pelle. In *Komisk Entré*, which probably is the best of the three, Pelle's body is manipulated as it goes through several transformations. Pelle turns into a snake and starts to eat objects: first a cigar, then a sword. With considerable difficulty, he tries to swallow a canon, but the barrel becomes wedged in Pelle's mouth. The gun is loaded and fired, and after the explosion, parts of Pelle's body fall into shot and are pieced together again. The film ends where it began.

Between the last two Fjollinski films, Bergdahl animated and shot *Kapten Groggs underbara resa*. This, the first of the thirteen *Kapten Grogg* films Bergdahl made between 1916 and 1922, is a typical example of the series. Torsten Jungstedt relates the Captain Grogg character to Bergdahl's experience as a sailor on a tough voyage which Bergdahl undertook to Australia in 1899. After a year, Bergdahl returned to Sweden where he started work as a cartoonist, a tale that is recounted in *Till Antipoden som Beckbyxa*.[16] Even though the book relates a sad and unpleasant story, one can also read the fascination Bergdahl had for the sea and life as a sailor, and the excitement he felt for travelling. These aspects are, of course, central to the *Kapten Grogg* films.

Many of the *Kapten Grogg* films are set in exotic locations. In *Kapten Grogg i ballong* (Captain Grogg in a Balloon, 1916), Grogg and his companion, Kalle, travel over Vesuvius as far as Eygpt and the Nile. *Kapten Grogg och Kalle på negerbal* (Captain Grogg and Kalle at the Darkies' Ball, 1917), *Kapten Grogg bland vilda djur* (Captain Grogg Among Wild Animals, 1919) and *Kapten Grogg badar* (Captain Grogg Takes a Bathe, 1919) were set in Darkest Africa. In other films, Grogg and Kalle also visit the North Pole, a Pacific Island and Australia. And these journeys provide the basis around which the narratives are constructed. In short funny episodes, often including animals, Bergdahl shows his ability both as a humourist and as an animator. In several of the films, one of the animals finds Grogg's bottle and gets drunk.

A striking element in the *Kapten Grogg* films is the harshness of Bergdahl's caricatures. Many of the films would be thought today to be politically un-correct. His negro characters are drawn in a way which we today would categorise as racist. In *Kapten Groggs underbara resa*, for example, Grogg and Kalle end up on a tropical island where they are chased by a lion. They are saved by a black hunter and, by offering the natives some Swedish akvavit, make friends with the king and the natives. Kalle even gets the princess, and the last scene shows Kalle with the native beauty who embraces him under a shining moon as they look out towards the ocean. I doubt whether Bergdahl or his audience considered his films racist. Apart from the visual style in which the natives are drawn – with stereotypical faces and big lips – the end of *Kapten Groggs underbara resa* has a naïve beauty to it. His drawings were clearly inspired by the way in which African negroes were presented in popular books, comic strips and the popular press, but as Torsten Jungstedt writes: 'one should not forget that there is some kind of warm feeling in most of the scenes with negroes. Captain Grogg and Kalle enjoy being in

the negro village, and most of those in the village like their white guests. No one party ever exploits the other.'[17] In *Kapten Grogg har blivit fet* (Captian Grogg Becomes Fat, 1922), however, the last film in the series, a stereotypical caricature of a Jewish shopkeeper is portrayed. This characterisation is certainly not necessary for the story.

Unlike the black women and mermaids who appear in several of the films, Captain Grogg's wife Sylfidia, is a negative character in the series, especially in the film *Kapten Grogg och fru* (Captain Grogg and Wife, 1918) where she is presented as the angry wife who only wants to control her husband. Everything that Captain Grogg enjoys in life is, according to Sylfidia, forbidden. The love story that started as a charming romance in *Kapten Grogg gifter sig* (Captain Grogg Gets Married, 1918), ends with Grogg walking out of his marriage in the last scene of *Kapten Grogg och fru* with his wife shouting his first name, 'Fileas!' ('Phileas!'), after him. This story of Grogg and his wife has an unpleasant parallel in the marriage of Bergdahl himself. In 1910, he married a famous, beautiful and successful actress, Maja Johansson, from the Stockholm varieté stage. Shortly after the marriage, Maja turned extremely religious. She could not even see her husband's films since going to the cinema was part of the 'sinful life' she had rejected. Bergdahl took up sailing, and increasingly left Stockholm to spend weeks at a time on board his sailing boat. In a documentary by Gunilla Edin and Torsten Jungstedt, Victor Bergdahl's son, Bo, recounts his joyful memories of these sailing trips with his father. He also admits that the marriage in the *Kapten Grogg* films was influenced by Victor Bergdahl's own marriage.[18]

Bergdahl made his last *Kapten Grogg* film in 1922. After that, he made film advertisements for a few years, and ended his animation career with the educational film, *Från cell till människa* (From Cell to Man) in 1936. He died in 1939.

Denmark

Denmark was a leading force in early Nordic silent film, but never managed to produce an animated series as significant as *Kapten*

Grogg. The leading Danish cartoonist, Storm P. (Storm-Petersen), was inspired by Bergdahl, and probably could have been as important if his enthusiasm for animation had been maintained. But Storm P. became quite quickly bored with the time-consuming and hardly profitable work, and returned to his newspaper and magazine cartoons after a few years of animation experiments around 1920. These films, however, are filled with Storm P.'s special humour, and represent a fresh chapter in the history of early animation. Even if his output is small, Storm P. is the real Danish animation pioneer, and the father of quality animated cartoons in Denmark.

Storm P. was not the first Danish animator. In 1917, the illustrator and cartoonist, Sven Brasch (1886–1970), made an animated film, *Meningen er god nok* (A Rather Good Intention) with the subtitle *Som det er – som det føles* (As It Is – As It's Felt). Brasch was a well-known cartoonist, but he is best known for the many film posters he designed for Danish and foreign films. Many of his early posters show slightly decadent but charming female characters, and he was associated with Film-Centralen which represented Palladium and MGM in Denmark for many years. As a poster designer, he worked in a simplified Art Deco style, and is known for the use of silhouettes in many of the films starring the Danish comic duo, Fyrtaarnet and Bivognen (Long and Short).[19] In 1917 he set up a film company with the photographer Aas, but as far as I know, made only one film. According to the registration card at The Danish Film Museum, the film was not premiered until January 1919. The most remarkable aspect of the film is its elegant design as the filmmaker is an exceptional illustrator. The pace of the animation is slow, and appears more like an animated drawing where we follow the creation of the drawing without seeing the artist. The film does not have a linear narrative, but is built around six episodes from everyday life where the artist first presents the situation, then gives his version of how the situation can also be experienced.

Storm P.

For a few years, Danish animation was dominated by Robert Storm-Petersen (1882–1949)

and his collaborator Karl Wieghorst. Storm P. already had a position as cartoonist, and as an actor and humourist in the theatre and in film. After a few minor appearances in the early 1900s, he played leading roles in many of the first films Ole Olsen produced at Nordisk in the period 1906–08. He even claims to have been the person who suggested to Ole Olsen that he should start to make films, and relates how he bought the first colony garden at Mosedalsvej from which Olsen developed the Nordisk film studios.[20] He played principal characters in the six *Happy Bob* comedies that Nordisk produced in 1907, the first attempt in Denmark to make a film comedy series. Storm P. also painted the sets and contributed to the scripts. While he was working for Ole Olsen, he made what was probably his first animation with Axel Graatkjær Sørensen as camera operator. In the tradition of Blackton, he drew a short blackboard animation of a flower opening up and blossoming. But this was never intended to be shown as it was an experiment as Storm P. relates in his diaries.[21]

Storm P. also performed on stage as a cartoonist. At the opening of the new Circus building in Copenhagen, Christmas 1913, he performed with his new comic strip characters, De tre smaa mænd (The Three Small Men), who later became his principal animation characters (Fig. 3). It is not known which is his earliest animated film, but because of the relatively simple technique and overall roughness of the film, *Øen* (The Island, 1919) is generally regarded as the earliest.[22] The film tells the story of The Three Small Men on an island where a submarine digs the island loose so it can float freely on the sea.

Back from the US, and inspired by the cartoons and animated films that he had seen, Storm P. advertised for a cameraman, and found Karl Wieghorst who had made animated propaganda films for the Germans during the First World War. Storm P. managed to obtain 10,000 Danish kroner from the businessman, Dethlef Jürgensen, and Storm P. and Karl Wieghorst started to work in their studio in Bredgade in the centre of Copenhagen (Fig. 4). In the contract, they agreed to make four films. *Gaasetyven* (The Goose Thief, 1920) and *Foryngelseskuren* (Rejuvenation, 1921)

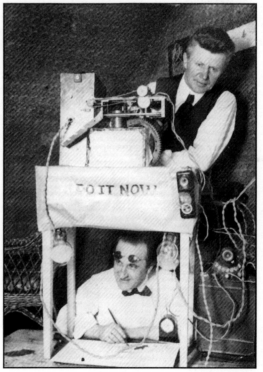

Fig. 3. Gaasetyven *(The Goose Thief) or* De tre smaa mænd – Et Andeeventyr *(The Three Small Men: A Duck Adventure), the earliest animated film starring* De tre smaa mænd *drawn by Storm P. [Courtesy of the Storm P. Museum, Copenhagen.]*

Fig. 4. Storm P. *(below) and Karl Wieghorst (above) in their studio at Bredgade 25, Copenhagen, circa 1921. [Courtesy of the Storm P. Museum, Copenhagen.]*

were made with a great deal of enthusiasm, but after the third film, *Jernmiksturen* (The Iron Tonic, 1921), Storm P. tried to get out of the deal with Jürgensen. In his diary, Storm P. wrote: '*No* and *No* – never again no more animated cartoons'.[23] Fragments from a couple of other Storm P. animated shorts are preserved in the Danish archive. There can be little doubt, however, that Storm P. was proud of his first animated film when, in an interview in the Danish daily newspaper, *Politiken*, he observed: 'This new work has absolutely consumed me. I have given up

painting and will never again perform on stage. I'm tired of performing in person, now I will let my three small men dance throughout the world.'[24] In the interview, Storm P. proudly declared that two more films starring The Three Small Men were in production.

The first film that Storm P. and Karl Wieghorst made has no specific title. In the press it was announced as *Storm P.s 1. Tegnefilm De tre smaa Mænd* (Storm P.'s 1. Animated Film, The Three Small Men); in the archive of The Danish Film Museum, the film is known both as *Gaasetyven* and *De tre smaa mænd – Et Andeeventyr* (The Three Small Men – A Duck Adventure), which latter title is the one by which the film is commonly known. The film is a cross between the cartoon in which the cartoonist himself appears as the main character, and the animated film (or cartoon series) in which the drawn characters play the leading roles. There is no main title at the beginning of the film. The film starts by giving credit to Storm P. as the cartoonist and Wieghorst as the photographer before showing a live action shot of Storm P. smoking his pipe. Then the story about a duck being stolen by a thief starts to develop. The duck makes it possible for the thief to fly. After several visual gags where The Three Small Men chase the thief, Storm P. appears as a drawn character in a studio in front of a large canvas. He starts to draw a bottle and a glass, pours liquor into the glass, and drinks it. An intertitle appears: 'Will Denmark be knocked down by prohibition? – NO!'. Storm P. then draws a woman in the kitchen in front of a stove. He disappears and the thief enters with the duck. The thief notices the bottle, empties it, and gets drunk. A ship in a painting on the wall starts to roll, mice creep out of the canvas, and a policeman appears in the drunken imagination of the thief. The woman takes the duck, transforms it into a piece of wood that is put in the oven, and the duck is cooked. Storm returns and draws a sofa on the canvas. The drunken thief lies down on the sofa, and Storm puts him behind bars. In the end, Storm is joined by The Three Small Men and they eat the duck. A pun on the Danish for 'end'/'duck' on the end card declares: *Naar Aanden er god, er alting godt* (When the end/duck is good, everything is good). This first film demonstrates a

confident technique in the use of rapid transition and metamorphoses. As Storm P. stressed in an interview in *Politiken*: 'the cartoonist should always remember that he should not compete with the normal film camera. An animated cartoon should only give situations which are impossible to create in any other way.'[25]

Although the studio scene at the opening of *Gaasetyven* may have been made using cels, in interviews Storm P. had great fun in keeping the secret about how he actually made his films to himself. In *Politiken*, Storm P. was asked directly how he made his films, to which he replied:

> That's our little secret which we won't even tell you in our sleep. For an animated cartoon that plays for 15 minutes, 16,000 pictures are required. You will understand that someone who makes such a film cannot be lazy. The cartoonist must together with the cameraman do all the work. It's no use letting others do it because new input and improvisation are made constantly. Wieghorst and I sit the whole day with dark glasses over white paper in strong artificial light, we are quite relaxed, mumbling constantly numbers and figures to each other, moving around in the higher spheres of Mathematics. When you make such a film, what's important is to calculate! Any unnecessary image is spoiled labour and money. One should always find the shortest way to reach a goal and, at the same time, use the possibilities that are offered to the utmost. First I write a draft for the film, but during filming, I improvise all the time, and it's the improvisations that give humour and attractiveness to the whole. Artistic skill, arithmetic, and dedication is what's needed.[26]

Storm's inventive and improvisational humour is present in all his animated shorts, as may be seen in the next two films by Storm P. and Wieghorst, *Foryngelseskuren* and *Jernmiksturen*. The first is also known as *Professor Steinacks Metode* (Professor Steinack's Method) and concerns a professor who discovers a formula for rejuvenation. The Three Small Men give this wonder medicine to an old man who becomes younger and younger,

and who ends up as a baby chasing a fly. Visual gags involve giving the cure to an old horse, a cow and an old beggar. In the end, the old man reflects on the episode of the baby and the fly, and concludes that it was only a dream, but a most pleasant dream. The film starts with the same live action shot of Storm P. as *De tre smaa mænd – Et Andeeventyr*.

The opening of *Jernmiksturen* is missing, so we do not know if the familiar opening live-action shot of Storm also opened this film, but The Three Small Men are involved in a story in which a hen drinks an iron tonic and lays a giant iron egg. The hen eats the hat of one of the Small Men. After a series of gags in which the farmer tries to break the iron egg, the egg, having been used as a cannon ball, finally breaks open in front of The Three Small Men. The lost hat emerges from the egg.

These three films are about 170 metres in length, a standard length for animated cartoons in the early 1920s. But the archive of The Danish Film Museum has also preserved several shorter cartoons credited to Storm P. One is *Storm P. tegner Tre Smaa Mænd* (Storm P. Draws Three Small Men, 1920) in which we see Storm P. draw. He leans back and The Three Small Men come alive and walk out of the frame. Storm turns to the camera and smiles.

In addition to *Øen* (75 metres), the Danish archive also has an incomplete version of *Gendarmen* (The Gendarme, 1921). With typical Storm P. humour, a policeman chases a driver who has broken the traffic regulations. The policeman fails repeatedly to catch our hero. *En dejlig drøm* (A Wonderful Dream, 1921, 15 metres) shows a fat man who is looking through a key hole at a woman eating a wonderful meal. The man only has a carafe of water, but he dreams of whisky and delicious food. This film clearly comments on the pleasures of good food and drink that Storm P. so often extols in his drawings; some of his best-known advertising cartoons were made for Tuborg.

Several other fragments and unidentified short animated cartoons that may have been made by Storm P. are held by The Danish Film Museum. Some of the short films may be exercises or tests that Storm and Wieghorst carried out in 1920–21. After Storm P. lost interest in animated film, Karl Wieghorst continued to make animation films under the name of Storm P. He mostly shot animated advertising shorts, but he may well be responsible for some of the shorter Storm P. films in the archive.

After Storm P.

In 1928 Wieghorst made three films based on stories by H.C. Andersen. The visual style is very different from the earlier films he made with Storm. They lack humour, and the narrative is kept very close to the original stories. The films comprise drawings which accompany extensive intertitles that provide an abridged version of the familiar fairy tales. The drawings are not poor and when they are animated, they move fluidly, but neither the drawings nor the animation adds much to the intertitles. *Den lille pige med svovelstikkerne* (The Little Match Girl, 1928) is hardly animated at all, but the animation sequence gives a nice touch to the scene where the little girl lights matches to warm herself. *Den standhaftige tinsoldat* (The Steadfast Tin Soldier, 1928) is more effective in its animation, especially when the toys become alive, but the images mainly reiterate the intertitles. *Den grimme ælling* (The Ugly Duckling, 1928) with the subtitle *En billedbog med levende billeder* (A picture book with living pictures) principally comprises live-action footage.

Two other Danish animated films from the mid-1920s are also preserved in the archive of The Danish Film Museum. According to the registration cards, *Le Theatre de Hula Hula* (50 metres) is a Danish animated film. The film includes an amusing scene in which a group of musicians accompanies a female hula-hula dancer on stage. *Flyvning uden motor* (Flying without Motor, 110 metres) is, according to the registration card, credited to the work of Richard Johansen. The film tells the story of Ole Bims who is putting the finishing touches to his new invention. As Marguerite Engberg has written on the registration card: 'A man has made a pair of wings and flies to the sun which gives him a three star cognac. Drunk, he falls back to earth. Complete, and a cute little film.' I have no information regarding the director Richard

Fig. 5. Aito
sunnuntaimetsästäjä
*(The Real Sunday
Hunter), Yrjö
Nyberg [Yrjö
Norta],
Lahyn-Filmi, 1924.
[Courtesy of the
Finnish Film
Archive.]*

Johansen, but this short film stands out as a forgotten treasure of early Danish animation.

Finland

Yrjö Nyberg (1904–88) worked as a producer for the film company Lahyn-Filmi in Turku from 1919. In 1935 he changed his name to Yrjö Norta, under which name he is known today in the few publications that exist on early Finnish animation. After a few film advertisements in the early 1920s, Norta and his colleagues at Lahyn made the first Finnish animated short in 1924. *Aito sunnuntaimetsästäjä* (The Real Sunday Hunter, 1924, Fig. 5) is a cut-out animation shot on glass plates and concerns a hunter who dreams of a rich and successful hunt. Inspired by comic strips, the dialogue was written in speech bubbles, not in intertitles. The film was inspired by American animation and, particularly, by the *Kapten Grogg* films which were very popular at the time. The film is lost. Yrjö Norta later related:

> We thought about making the first [Finnish animated film], so we made it. We were fascinated by the new technique. When we had finished it, the fascination was gone. We never even thought of making another animated film.[27]

In a later interview, Norta observed:

> It didn't suit my style to undertake such mechanical work. One picture after an-

other, one frame, two frames, and so on. We thought, well, we can do this – and that's that. Then we got more extensive work, real film work, and this [animation] got left behind. We saw we could do it, so we stopped with that.[28]

Although Lahyn-Filmi continued as a film production company until 1934, no further animation was undertaken.[29]

The most popular Finnish strip cartoon character was Pekka Puupää (Willy Woodenhead) who first appeared in 1925. Pekka was drawn by Ola Fogelberg (1894–1952) and, later, by his daughter Toto (Ruth) Kaila. Pekka was the hero of at least thirteen live-action features, and occupies a unique position in Finnish popular culture. He appears, however, in only one animated film, a five-minute short made in the late 1920s.[30] Ola Fogelberg, who went to the United States in 1927, tried to establish an animation studio on his return to Finland. The project was supported by the Elanto Cooperative Association who used Pekka Puupää (an eager supporter of the cooperative movement!) in their advertising. After making test drawings, several artists were hired, and production was set up in the Elanto buildings. His daughter Toto Kaila later recalled:

> We were small, my brother and I, four and six years old, when one day my father came home with a kind of ghastly black arrangement, a film projector of the time – and our small fever-beds were moved from the children's room into the adults' room where we hung a sheet on the wall. Then my father showed the Pekka Puupää film … Pekka was rather big. He wasn't always seen as a whole figure, but he was large. Then there was, if my memory serves me correctly, some kind of open car – one with a folding hood and spoked wheels, things like that. This much I do remember: in those figures, the Pekka figures, movements were jumpy because they were made with joints.[31]

Unfortunately the film is lost. It probably was not a big success, and Fogelberg gave up animated films to go back to comic strips which he continued to draw until his death in 1952.

The silent animated film continued will into

the 1930s in Finland, where Hjalmar Löfving (1894–1952) started to make animated film advertisements including an impressive short, *Muutama metri tuulta ja sadetta* (A Few Metres of Wind and Rain, 1933, Fig. 6). This two-minute paper animation is an animation masterpiece, and concerns a cloud burst that takes everyone by surprise, and develops into true chaos. In the end, the sun shines again. Löfving had a background as a comic strip artist, and experimented with animation from the early 1920s. He was probably the most ambitious of the Finnish animation pioneers. His dream was to make animated films based on popular comic strip heroes, and to create an animated series. In the mid-1930s, he started to use cels in his animated advertisements, but *Muutama metri tuulta ja sadetta* was the only animated short he made. Lauri Tükkülainen, in the closing voice-over of his documentary, praises Löfving's work:

> *Muutama metri tuulta ja sadetta*, a bold and telling example of one man's skill, gives a hint of how high Löfving could have soared had he continued. War cut short the development, and the tradition was broken. The work of the Finnish cartoon sank into oblivion for decades.[32]

Norway

In an article in *Film og Kino*, the caricaturist Thoralf Klouman is mentioned as 'the first to have made living drawings in Norway'.[33] For *Admiral Palads* (Admiral Palace, 1917), Klouman made fifty drawings, some of which he used several times, to tell a story about the American president, Woodrow Wilson. These fifty drawings, however, could not have made the film a fully animated short, so the film, more likely, was something between the caricature drawings for which he was known after 1914 and an animated cartoon. The article went on to note:

> The technical quality of these living drawings could have been more perfect, but as they were, they showed that the artist has both humour, talent, and fantasy for caricatures on the screen. Without doubt he is heading in the right direction.[34]

The Norwegian film censor passed *Fanden i nøtten* by Ola Cornelius, a fellow member of

Tegnerforbundet, on 9 October 1917. This 160-metre animated cartoon was made for the advertising company E & O Co., but even though parts of the film were used in an advertisement for Melange margarine a few years later, the film is not so much an advertising film but an ambitious project to make an animated version of the Norwegian folk tale 'Gutten og fanden' (The Lad and the Devil) as collected by Peter Christen Asbjørnsen and Jørgen Ingebrektsen Moe. These collections of folktales (*Norske Folkeventyr*) have been a continuous inspiration for Norwegian illustrators, and *Fanden i nøtten* marks the beginning of a long tradition of animated films based on these stories, the best-known examples being those by the puppet animator, Ivo Caprino, in the 1950s and 1960s.

The drawings in *Fanden i nøtten* are quite detailed. As a newspaper and magazine cartoonist, Cornelius was a more realistic illustrator that his colleagues, and the film stands out as the most ambitious project in early animated shorts in Norway. Luckily about half of the film is saved in the extant advertisement, and parts of the animation, especially when the smith tries to break a nut with numerous sledgehammers of ever increasing size, is impressive. Unfortunately, this film is, as far as I know, his only venture into animation. In an interview, he was asked if he would continue making animated films. The interviewer noted:

Fig. 6. Muutama metri: tuulta ja sadetta *(A Few Metres of Wind and Rain), Hjalmar Löfving, 1933. [Courtesy of the Finnish Film Archive.]*

'That depends on available time and how well the work will be paid' ...[and] with a face as if he had drunk vinegar, he showed better than words can tell how the art of cartooning is paid in the world of film.[35]

The cinematographer Hans Berge, who had worked with Sverre Halvorsen and Thoralf Klouman on their pioneering films, collaborated with Cornelius on *Fanden i nøtten*. Berge was one of the leading cinematographers in Norway in the 1910s and 1920s, and he is best known for his many live-action shorts documenting everyday life in Norway. He returned to Norway in 1906 after a career as a still photographer in the United States. He then formed Fram Film which, apart from live-action films, is credited as the production company of *Heimebrennerens mareritt. Drikkens følger* (The Moonshiner's Nightmare. The Result of Drinking, 1924). This animated film is lost, and the censorship card, unfortunately, reveals nothing about the content of the film, but since it was made during the prohibition period in Norway, it almost certainly satirised the misuse of alcohol, in common with many early Scandinavian animated films.

Ottar Gladtvet

The producer, director, and cinematographer Ottar Gladtvet (1890–1962) was a creative force in Bio-Film in the early 1920s, and became a leading producer of film advertisements in the 1920s, including several animated film advertisements. The prohibition theme, noted in Ola Cornelius' work, is also common in the animated films of Bio-Film. The prohibition of alcohol is explicitly the subject of *Det nye aar?* (The New Year?, 1921) produced by Bio-Film, and credited as a caricature drawn by Sverre Halvorsen. This short 90-second film begins with a pixillation sequence which features an old man with a long beard dressed like Santa Claus. A slogan on his back proclaims: '1921 – Prohibition, Language, Taxes, Visitation, Inquisition, and Pressure'.[36] Then the year '1922' appears, and a monkey in uniform stands beside a large champagne bottle shaped like a cannon. At midnight, a live action hand lights a matchstick. The bottle opens like a firework

hopefully bringing greater pleasure in the year to come.

At the same time as *Det nye aar?* received its premiere, another Bio-Film animated film in the same vein was submitted to the censor. *Jul i Norge* (Christmas in Norway, 1921, 58 metres) was viewed by the censor on 21 December 1921. This two-and-a-half minute film shows 'how one believes Christmas is celebrated in Norway and how it is actually celebrated'.[37] Given that the animation in *Det nye aar?* is credited to Halvorsen, it seems reasonable to assume that Sverre Halvorsen also animated *Jul i Norge*. He may also have animated *Kuffertsyken* (The Suitcase Sickness, 1922, 60 metres) which Bio-Film submitted to the censor one month later. Unfortunately, both films are lost, and the only information the censorship card gives relating to *Kuffertsyken* is that it is an animated film.

Two more Norwegian animated films were premiered in 1921. Both *Serenaden* (The Serenade) and *Båtsmann Dick's eventyr* (Boatsman Dick's Adventure) were made by Kinografen, originally a Danish film company that had recently opened a Norwegian production unit. Both films are lost, and there is little information available on *Båtsmann Dick's eventyr*. With regard to *Serenaden*, the censorship card notes:

> Animated cartoon. A man chases two black cats who are performing a concert on the fence. He holds them by their tails, and arrives at the top of the church tower, falls down, and is arrested by a guardsman.[38]

This description sounds almost like an American cartoon, but since Kinografen is credited as *rekvirent* (distributor) and *filmfabrik* (production company) on the censorship card, I doubt that the film is a foreign production. Since Kinografen, however, was a Danish company, the film could be Danish.

One more animated cartoon, according to Norwegian censorship cards, is probably of Norwegian origin: *Robinson Crusoe paa gamle tomter* (Robinson Crusoe in Old Familiar Places, 1927), an eight-minute animation film in which 'Robinson returns to the island to see the place again, but is very surprised to see how modern the island has become'.[39]

The film is credited to the production company, Grafisk.

Norwegian animated film advertisements

In all the Nordic countries, film advertising had an important place in cinema programmes in the 1920s. While animation played a minor role in film exhibition, it had a more prominent role in film advertisements. In Sweden, film advertisements were introduced in the animated films of IRE-film and in the work of Arvid Olson, and in Denmark, Storm P. and Karl Wieghorst were among the pioneers of film advertising. When the leading Norwegian company, Tiedemann Tobaksfabrik began to use film to advertise its products in the mid-1920s, half of their advertisements used animation. In Finland, advertising also represented a new possibility for animators.

It is difficult to date the beginning of film advertising. Film had probably been used in advertising from the earliest years. In the context of German cinema, Günter Agde refers to a note in *Der Komet*, and claims that the first German cinema commercial was made in 1897. In a catalogue of films for hire from Oskar Messter, the following year, Agde mentions an advertisement for Wellenband-Schaukel.[40] In Denmark, the first film advertisements were shown in the first years of this century, and the Danish pioneer, Peter Elfelt, produced several advertising films in the years 1903–06. He might even have made his first film advertisements earlier as part of a programme which he first presented in 1898–99.[41] Ottar Gladtvet claims to have made his first film advertisements as early as 1913/14, though advertising films are usually regarded as having commenced in Norway in the 1920s.[42]

The films of Julius Pinschewer, so central to the development of advertising in German cinema in the 1910s, were also screened abroad in versions for foreign exhibition.[43] In Norway, Pinschewer collaborated with Ottar Gladtvet on the Norwegian versions of three silent *Persil* advertisements in 1929.[44] Pinschewer made films using a wide range of techniques. In addition to live action, he used

the whole spectrum of animation techniques from animated cartoons through puppet, cut-out, and object animation. Very often he combined these animation techniques with live action.

Many of the advertisements Ottar Gladtvet made in Norway have similarities with Pinschewer's work. Although Gladtvet mainly produced live-action films, at least sixteen of his preserved silent advertisements are animated. He also used object animation in many of his live action advertisements, especially in the presentation of the product at the end of the advertisement. Together with his animated shorts, these animated advertisements make Gladtvet the most significant producer of animation in Norway in the silent era.[45] Gladtvet probably shot stop-motion animation himself since, as a cinematographer, he had particular interest in trick photography. Among his most interesting object animations are *Det mystiske kjøkken (Noget at glæde seg til)* (The Mystical Kitchen [Something to Look Forward to], 1927) and *Sportsproviant, eller Bord dekk deg!* (Sports Provisions, or Table Cover Yourself!, 1929). For his cartoon animations, Gladtvet collaborated with other animators. Some of these films were made with Ths. W. Schwartz who had a cartoon film studio and who also distributed film advertisements.

J.L. Tiedemann Tobaksfabrik

Several of the early Gladtvet-Schwartz cartoon advertisements were made for J.L.

Tiedemann Tobaksfabrik (J.L. Tiedemann Tobacco Company). Of the sixty silent Norwegian animated advertisements I have identified, twenty-two were made for Tiedemann. Given that Tiedemann made many more live-action advertisements, this makes Tiedemann the most important advertiser in Norwegian cinema in the silent era, an importance the company maintained until the Second World War.[46]

The popular Tiedemann tobacco, *Teddy*, was named after the American president Theodore Roosevelt, and used the logo of a teddy bear as its mascot. This character was an obvious choice for animation, and several of the early Tiedemann cartoons used the animated teddy bear as the leading character. *Teddy paa biltur* (Teddy Drives His Car, 1927, Fig. 7) was made by the director and producer, Walter Fyrst (1901–93), who was the other major producer of film advertisements besides Gladtvet in Norway during the 1920s. Fyrst proudly tells how he constructed an animation table and a camera set-up modelled on drawings in *Filmen, dens midler og maal* by Urban Gad.[47] This short two-and-a-half minute film is a good example of the inventive humour of the *Teddy* films. Teddy is driving his car, and stops in front of a restaurant to eat. While he is eating, the bad guy attacks his car, and flattens its tyres with a knife. When Teddy gets back, he wonders what to do – he lights a cigarette, and blows four smoke-rings round the wheels of the car so that he can happily continue his drive. 'Tiedemann's Teddy – Everybody's Friend!' To make *Teddy paa biltur*, Fyrst brought in his old school-mate, Niels Sinding-Hansen, for the drawings. And while Fyrst gave up animation after this first exercise, Sinding-Hansen continued production, and made at least five more animated films for Tiedemann in 1927–28, three of them starring Teddy.

Fyrst claims to be the first to have made animated cartoon advertisements in Norway, but in the January 1926 issue of *Filmen og Vi*, an article on film animation states:

> Now it seems that cartoons have in some way became a regular part of the typical cinema programme. But they are used even more extensively in advertising. And cartoons for soap and tooth-paste,

washing- and baking-powder, are almost part of daily life.[48]

The article indicates that quite a few animated advertisements must have been shown in Norwegian cinemas no later than 1925. But an extensive search through the censorship cards for this year has not yielded many results. A few films that might have been made before 1926 are preserved in the national archive. Four short cartoons made for Mustad margarine on Kodak stock from 1924 may be included amongst the oldest animated advertisements in Norway. But these films exist as Swedish version, and it is hard to tell whether the films were produced in Sweden or in Norway. Two other short Mustad cartoons – *Mustad F. Margarine* and *Mustad Mono* – were made by Storm P. and Karl Wieghorst in Copenhagen in the early 1920s. The soap commercial, *Maaneprinsessens gave* (The Present of the Moon Princess, 1923), made by Norwegian Film Co., has an animated opening scene. In 1924–25, Norvegia-film made an advertising film for the *Rex* electric iron. In this film, O. Trygve Dalsegg combined cartoon animation on paper and cut-out animation with live action, and even though there are some registration problems with the drawings, the animations are quite good, although I do not know if Dalsegg animated the film himself. It is possible that Dalsegg was behind other films that have survived such as the Viking adventure story, *Erobreren* (The Conqueror, film stock from 1924) for Freia Chocolate Rollo, the Mustad folk tale, *Prinsessen paa glassberget* (The Princess on the Glass Mountain), and the politically un-correct, *En verdenreise, eller da Knold og Tot vaskede negrene hvite med 13 sæpen* (A World Voyage, or When the Katzenjammer Kids Washed the Negroes White with 13 Soap, film stock from 1925). A mis-spelling in one of the titles in *En verdenreise* may indicate that the film was made in Sweden. Maybe all these films were Swedish productions?

Cinema advertisements were not registered on a regular basis on censorship cards in Norway before 1927. That is probably one reason why 1927 is thought to be the breakthrough year for cinema advertising in Norway. About one hundred different advertising films were registered in 1927; Gladtvet

alone made fifty. Of these, at least twenty-two were animated films, thirteen of which were made for Tiedemann. The preponderance of Tiedemann films and the increase in cinema advertising by Tiedemann in 1927–28 add to the impression that 1927 was a break-through year for cinema advertising.

Walter Fyrst with his *Teddy* film, however, was not the first to make an animated cartoon for Tiedemann. Fyrst related that his strategy was to browse through advertisements in magazines and newspapers, make a rough script, and then suggest it as a film advertisement to the company behind the product.[49] The *Teddy* advertisements may very well have developed in this manner, but both Gladtvet and Ths. W. Schwartz presented Tiedemann animated cartoon advertisements to the censor months before *Teddy paa biltur*.

Ths. W. Schwartz

Gladtvet presented *4 Generationer* (4 Generations) and *To om en pipelill* (Two for a Little Pipe) to the censor in early Febraury 1927. Schwartz presented *Den store sultan i Oslo* (The Great Sultan in Oslo) and *Tyverier fra Bagdad* (Stolen from Baghdad) at the same time. All of these cartoons were made for different Tiedemann products. From the censorship cards it would seem that Gladtvet and Schwartz competed for the Tiedemann account. On the title credit of *Tyverier fra Bagdad*, however, Gladtvet and the advertising company Atelier E-O are given as the filmmakers. In 1927 the two companies also collaborated on several live action advertisements. Since Gladtvet did not draw his own cartoons, it is highly probable that many Gladtvet films produced in 1927 were made with the help of Ths. W. Schwartz. We know that Schwartz had his own cartoon studio in Roald Amundsens gate in Oslo, where Martin Christoffersen was in charge of cartoon work. The 16-year-old Tore Dejnbol started his career in this studio as well, and there may also have been other employees.[50]

Schwartz started producing and distributing film advertisements in 1924, but as Sverdrup Dahl soon obtained a virtual monopoly for the distribution of film advertisements in Norway, Schwartz concentrated on production.

His first cartoons were made in late 1926 or early 1927, and if most of the Gladtvet film advertisements were made in Roald Amundsens gate, the studio had an impressive output of at least fifteen animated cartoon advertisements in a short two-year period. Both *Tyverier fra Bagdad* and the Tiedemann cartoon, *Chefen's cigaretter* (The Boss' Cigarettes, circa 1927), are credited to Gladtvet and Atelier E-O. Again I believe that the film may well have been made at the Schwartz studio. In addition to Schwartz, we know that Niels Sinding-Hansen continued to produce animated cartoons in 1927–28 after he had left Walter Fyrst.

The advertising pioneer, Knut Spange, who had studied animation in the Storm P./Wieghorst studio in 1925, also made animated cartoons in Oslo in 1927. The only Spange film for which I have found any concrete information is *Søndagsfiskern 'Flag'* (The Sunday Fisherman 'Flag', 1927) made for the BATCO cigarette brand *Flag*. But from advertisements in *Aftenposten* which, in one instance, shows that Spange was looking for an assistant, it seems likely that his studio must have been quite active. From this information we can be certain that there were no fewer than three operating cartoon studios in Oslo in 1927.

Another Tiedemann cartoon, *Ship O-Hoi*, opens up the possibility of a fourth studio. Both the film and the censorship card credits this 64 metre cartoon to Alb. Jærn. *Ship O-Hoi* was censored in June 1927. It is a simple cut-out film based on rhyming titles, and it looks different to the other Tiedemann cartoons. On these grounds, I do not believe that the film is a Schwartz production. It could have been made by Knut Spange using the Storm P.–Karl Wieghorst camera in Copenhagen as a model. But Knut Spange could not remember working with any assistant or collaborator when I interviewed him in October 1988. Albert Martinius Jensen Jærn (1893–1949) was a Norwegian cartoonist and graphic artist, who as far as I know, made only this type of animation. He is best known for his extensive and elegant production of ex-libris inscriptions. He worked briefly in advertising, but I doubt whether he had the

Fig. 8. Fiinbeck har römt, *1927, Ottar Gladtvet/Victor Bergdahl? [Courtesy of the National Library of Norway.]*

technical skill for film production himself. Who his collaborator was, is still unknown.

Fiinbeck

The film *Fiinbeck har römt* (Jigg Has Run Away, 1927, Fig. 8) makes the far from clear state of Norwegian production in 1927 even more complicated. This film was censored on 20 January 1927. Gladtvet is credited as *filmfabrik* (producer), and the distributor was the advertising agency, Merkantil. The censorship date makes this the oldest of the registered Tiedemann cartoons. The problem is that it is also the best, both in terms of narration and animation. Adopting George McManus' characters from the comic strip, *Bringing Up Father*, the plot centres on Fiinbeck's (Jiggs') need for a drink at the pub and his wife's fight to keep him home. She buys him a packet of *Tiedemanns Gul Mixture* for his pipe, and this ensures family happiness. With Tiedemann's mixture in his pipe, Fiinbeck prefers to stay at home. The film uses a cut-out technique, and resembles the style of animation that Bergdahl used in film advertisements in the mid-1920s.

Swedish animated film advertisements

After the last *Kapten Grogg* film in 1922, Bergdahl made *Lilla Kalle på Göteborgsut-*

ställningen (Little Kalle at the Gothenburg Exhibition, 1923) where much of the cartoon is set in the Liseberg amusement park in Gothenburg. The film is lost. We next hear of Bergdahl in the context of animation for Industri- och Reklamfilm (IRE-film) an industrial advertising company in Kungsgatan, Stockholm, where he was employed as *chefstecknare* (main cartoonist).[51]

Two of the animated Bergdahl films made at IRE-film are known. *Missionären i Afrika* (The Missionary in Africa, 1926) was a film promoting Stomotal toothpaste, and is preserved at the Swedish Film Institute. *Finbruken* (1926?), made for a Swedish writing-paper firm, has been reconstructed after the artwork for the film was found by Bo Bergdahl among papers left by his father. This material shows that Victor Bergdahl had changed from using paper cards to an advanced form of cut-out animation. *Fiinbeck har römt* is very similar to the reconstructed *Finbruken*, so it seems likely that Bergdahl and his colleagues at IRE-film may have made the first of the Tiedemann animated cartoons.[52] *Finbruken* is an engaging story involving a young couple who go out on a date to a restaurant. The following day, flowers and a letter are delivered to the young woman, and the young man asks to see her parents. Her father reads the letter and obviously dislikes it. The closing titles reveal why: 'Obviously a thoughtless young man. Writing on bad foreign paper when we have the best from Finbruken.'

The Stomatol advertisement has a lot more in common with the *Kapten Grogg* films. A missionary, probably a Swedish protestant, arrives in Africa where he stops to pray. On the beach, he sees two natives performing something mysterious: they are bending down towards the water as if in prayer. The missionary goes over to them and when they turn around, they proudly show what they are doing: brushing their teeth with Stomatol toothpaste. The missionary apologises and retires. The natives are drawn in the same caricatured style as the natives in the *Kapten Grogg* films.

According to the censorship cards at Statens Biografbyrå (the Swedish State Cinema Bureau), the advertising cartoon, *Ströms herrekipering* (Ström's Gentlemen's Clothing,

1927), was also made by IRE-film. The film was viewed by the censor on 5 October 1927, and is a late production from the short-lived company, but I have not yet established whether this film is the same as a film in the archive of the Swedish Film Institute that is titled *Ströms – den søvniga rockvaktmestaren* (Ströms – the Sleepy Cloakroom Attendant).

Arvid Olson

One of the leading names in early Swedish film advertising is the cartoonist Arvid Olson (1886–1978). Four of Olson's films for Stomatol are known to exist: *Negern* (The Negro), *Tyngdlyftaren* (The Weight-lifter), and *Baksmälla* (The Hangover), all made in early 1926, and other footage exists of a film which was presented in a television programme on Olson in 1976.[53] *Negern* is stereotypical in its use of black Africans as a contract to the whiteness of the Stomatol toothpaste in the tradition of Bergdahl. In *Tyngdlyftaren*, the athlete manages to lift even the heaviest weight with his teeth after brushing them with Stomatol ('the only way to get fresh and strong teeth'), and in *Baksmälla*, Stomatol mouthwash cures a terrible hangover when devils, banging inside the head of our unlucky hero after a heavy night on the town, are driven out by Stomatol. These films are all nicely animated on paper, some scenes even indicate the use of cels, though they are very different from the Bergdahl cut-out advertisements of the same period. In a way they are more like Bergdahl's earlier work.

The leading production company for film advertisements in Sweden from the late 1920s was Kinocentralen. Olson was one of their filmmakers, and he was also probably responsible for the Philips advertisement, *Locktoner* (Calling Tunes, 1929). This film, starring Felix the Cat, tells how everybody is entranced by the house from which beautiful music is heard, the source of which is revealed to be the new Philips radio and speaker. The animation is of a high standard, and it may well be a Swedish version of an international advertisement that has survived because during the 1930s, many Philips advertisements were made in several different language versions for the international market. On the other hand, a number of famous cartoon characters were also used in Nordic film advertisements in the mid-1920s. Since Kinocentralen is credited as *tilverknings-firma* (manufacturing company) on the censorship card, and as Olson worked for them regularly, I believe that this is probably another fine advertising film made by Arvid Olson.

A couple of other animated advertisements from the late 1920s are registered in the collection of the Swedish Film Institute. *Pix tabeletter* is a 32 metre cartoon concerning a man who has a cold so strong that he sneezes himself to the moon. By eating *Pix* tablets, the man is cured of his cold. The end-title proclaims: 'In the difficult and dark times of life, Pix is a gift, a help, a wonder'. Two films, *Tomtens Skurpulver* (Tomten's Scrubbing-powder) and *Tomtens Trolltvål* (Tomten's Troll Soap), combine live action with animated drawings. Both *Pix* and *Tomten* were part of the Andersén chain of cinema advertising.[54] The *Pix* film is the most satisfying of these, and may well have been made by Arvid Olson.

Danish animated film advertisements

Even though Storm P. renounced animation in 1921, he soon returned to work in animated film advertising with Karl Wieghorst for Danish and Norwegian film in the mid-1920s. Although it would appear that Storm P. was more interested in other cartoon work and left the animation to Wieghorst, his name was very probably used for its commercial value. Several of the films also included well-known Storm P. characters, and I believe that Storm was involved in the design work and in developing story lines, while Wieghorst did most of the time-consuming work under the camera. The animated shorts Storm P. made around 1920 were quite advanced in their technique and required a lot of artwork. The complexity of some scenes makes it look as though they were done on cel. In the advertisements, cut-out is the major technique. One reason for this change in technique may have been the need to reduce the amount of time spent on drawings in favour of manipulating characters directly under the camera. In this way, more of the work could be carried out by Wieghorst.

Storm, however, was still an important force in developing story lines and design. In a three minute advertisement made in 1926 for the weekly magazine, *Hjemmet*, Storm even appears live in the film reading the magazine. But most of the film is devoted to comic strip characters from *Bringing Up Father* to *The Katzenjammer Kids*, although *De tre smaa mænd* also appear in the film. As in Norwegian and Swedish advertising films of the period, American popular comic strip characters were used to sell Nordic products to a Nordic audience. In the case of *Hjemmet*, this function was closely connected with the magazine, since comic strips were an important part of its content, and both *Bringing Up Father* and *The Katzenjammer Kids* were run weekly in *Hjemmet* in the mid-1920s.

C.L.O.C.

Drinking was a central activity in the Storm P. universe. His famous advertisements for Tuborg lager are perhaps the best known, so it is no surprise that Storm also worked on animated advertisements for De Danske Spritfabrikker (The Danish Liquor Factories). According to E. Kjeldgaard, De Danske Spritfabrikker was the leading sponsor of film advertising in the 1920s, and at the time when his book was published in 1959, negatives for twenty of the films produced in the years 1923–28 were still extant.[55] Most of these films were animated cartoons made by Storm P. Kjeldgaard terms the films *forvandlingsfilm* (transformation films) because the films relied heavily on Storm P.'s skills in transforming images. As an example, Kjeldgaard mentions the Storm P. film *Huset der løber rundt* (The House that Runs Around) starring the well-known Storm characters, Peter and Ping. A house starts to rotate faster and faster, changing into a bottle of C.L.O.C., while the streetlight shrinks and changes into a glass. Other examples are a man sitting with a glass which suddenly changes height and width to become a bottle of C.L.O.C., and a clown and his dog juggling a ball which changes into a C.L.O.C. bottle.

Kjeldgaard's next category is the 'surprise film'. In these films, the C.L.O.C. bottle, usually giant-size, appears at the least-expected moment. In *Peter og Ping på Fisketur* (Peter

and Ping Go Fishing), the two friends are fishing from a bridge. Peter catches the C.L.O.C. bottle and Ping reels in the much-needed glass. *Grog er nysgjerrig* (Curious Grog) stars Grog the dog who snoops around a suitcase which suddenly opens to reveal a giant C.L.O.C. bottle. In another film, Pierrot and Harlekin magically transform a miniature house into a C.L.O.C. bottle. Children shout their usual, 'Say something Pierrot!' and Pierrot answers: 'C.L.O.C.' Magic is a popular theme in several of the Storm P. films. A bottle of C.L.O.C. issues as a result of magic in *Peter og Ping som Tryllekunstnere* (Peter and Ping as Magicians), and in *Aben* (The Monkey), the letters the juggling ape throws into the air change to form the letters 'C.L.O.C.' In *Tre smaa mænd*, the three friends juggle their hats, bottles and glasses until the text, 'Aalborg akvavit' closes the film. This is the only film which was still extant in 1959 and which did not advertise C.L.O.C. liquor.

A few of these films are preserved in The Danish Film Museum, including *Peter og Ping på fisketur* and *Aben*. *Peter og Ping drikker kaffe* (Peter and Ping Drink Coffee) is another C.L.O.C. commercial not mentioned by Kjeldgaard. In addition, there is a short live-action film advertisement in which Storm P. drinks C.L.O.C. On the registration cards at the Museum, the production year for the Peter and Ping films is given as circa 1930; Kjeldgaard's assignment to the period 1923–28 seems more likely. This period also accords with a visit which Knut Spange, the Norwegian cartoonist, made to Storm and Wieghorst's studio in 1926.[56] I also believe that the two advertisements Storm P. and Wieghorst made for the Norwegian margarine company, Mustad, were made in this period, probably around 1925. In both films, Storm P. characters appear with the Mustad-Man mascot. In the last scene of *Mustads Mono*, a signature occupies the right-hand corner of the picture: a 'W' is erased and replaced with the well-known Storm P. signature. It is hard to interpret this as anything other than a comment on the working relationship between Storm P. and Karl Wieghorst. Hopefully, it is a friendly and humorous gag from Wieghorst, and not an assertion of authority on the part of Storm P.

In the Storm P. Museum in Copenhagen, two puppet figures of Peter and Ping are exhibited. According to Jens Bing, the director of the Museum, these puppets have moveable parts as if they were made to be animated. We do not know if they were used in animation films as no extant film includes these puppets, but their existence indicates that such films may have been planned. Maybe such a film exists in an archive somewhere?

Storm P. and Karl Wieghorst were not the only Danes to make animated advertisements in the 1920s. The young Danish cartoonist, Jørgen Müller (1910– ?), made advertising films in England in the late 1920s, and returned to Denmark in 1931 where he established a studio in Copenhagen before going back to London in the mid-1930s. In a documentary film interview, Müller recounts how another young Dane, Niels Skjoldborg, was also active in the production of animated film advertisements in the late 1920s.[57]

According to E. Kjeldgaard, 'it seems as though animated cartoons were the favoured form for advertising' in the 1920s,[58] and while Storm P. made most of them, others were also involved. Kjeldgaard mentions the film, *Vikingerne* (The Vikings, 1924), which Skibstrup made for the American Tobacco Co. This film shows a bunch of Vikings fighting and even killing each other to get a packet of *Viking* cigarettes. In the Danish trade journal, *Biograf-Bladet*, there is a discussion about the coming of sound and the new 'talking advertisements' in the spring 1929 issue. Company director, Francois Monterossi, was asked to give his opinion of this development, and from the article, it would appear that Monterossi was an important though little-known figure in the Danish advertising and animation scene in the 1920s.[59]

A most interesting cartoon, the two-minute *Danske arbejde* (Danish Labour, circa 1925), is held in the Danish archive. The film is a strong appeal for Danes to buy Danish goods instead of foreign goods, and shows two factories on each side of a border. A man is dressed in foreign clothes and the Danish factory is the loser. Then a Viking comes up and gives new spirit to the production of Danish clothes, shoes, and other goods. Rhyming titles then declare that the viewer should not cross the river to fetch water but support him or herself by buying Danish goods. The film balances national sentiment by stressing that the Danes are not negative to what foreign people make and stand for, but the Number 1 choice in Denmark should be Danish goods. The film was made by Sct Peder filmen, but to date I have not found out who was behind this company. Could it be Skjoldborg, Skibstrup or, perhaps, Richard Johansen?

As in Norway, Sweden and Finland, where almost all animation pioneers were involved in the production of film advertising, animated advertisements were central to the experience of cinema in the 1920s. Recently, quite a lot of attention has been directed to the proud history of Danish animated cartoons. But as in most countries, the focus has been on theatrical shorts and features. The rich and fascinating history of animated film advertisements in the 1920s, not to mention the use of animation in documentary film, newsreels, industrial films and educational films, is almost forgotten.

Acknowledgements

Details of films in this essay come mainly from viewing films at the various national film archives in Copenhagen, Helsinki, Oslo/Mo i Rana, and Stockholm. I am very grateful to the staff of these institutes and archives for their generous help. I would also like to thank Jens Bing at the Storm P. Museum in Copenhagen, Niels Plaschke, Jan Anders Diesen, Heikki Joikenen and Jeanpaul Goergen.

Notes

1. For insight into the development of Tegnerforbundet, see the four annual publications of the society, Kristiania (present day Oslo), 1917–20.

2. Juho Gartz, *Elävöitettyjä kuvia – raportti soumalaisesta animaatioelokuvasta* (Helsinki: Soumen Elokuvasäätiö, 1975), 9.

3. 'Flisa', 'Norsk Tegnefilm. Ola Kornelius', *Helt og Skurk* no. 7 (1918), n.p.

4. Torsten Jungstedt, *Kapten Grogg och hans vänner* (Stockholm: Sveriges Radio förlag/Svenska Filminstitutet, 1973), 88–89.

5. See Louise O'Konor, *Viking Eggeling, 1880–1925: Artist and Filmmaker, Life and Work*, trans. Catherine G. Sundström and Anne Bibby (Stockholm: Almqvist and Wiksell, 1971), and Gösta Werner and Bengt Edlund, *Viking Eggeling Diagonalsymfonin: Spjutspets i återvändsgränd* (Lund: Novapress, 1997).

6. For discussion of this film, see Gösta Werner's essay, 'Spearhead in a Blind Alley: Viking Eggeling's *Diagonal Symphony*', in this anthology.

7. The German cartoonist, Robert L. Leonard, was a well established graphic artist in Germany in the 1910s, and was well known to readers of *Helt og Skurk*. In the Danish Film Archive I have viewed two films by Leonard presented as *Ugens karikatur* (The Caricature of the Week): *Fredens Engel* (The Angel of Peace, 1919), and *Farvel til Vinteren* (Farewell to the Winter, 1919). The first film comments on the recent war in Europe, the second, on such everyday matters as the weather and the changing seasons. Both films use time-lapse photography to show Leonard drawing. Each film runs for approximately one minute. A longer cut-out propaganda animation film, *Das Säugetier* (The Mammal, 1917) is preserved in the Bundesarchiv, Berlin. Leonard's caricature films are rarely discussed.

8. 'Flisa', 'Norsk tegnefilm. En samtale med tegneren Sverre Halvorsen', *Helt og Skurk* no. 6 (1918).

9. 'Raymond', 'Norges første filmtegner. Skuespiller Thoralf Klouman', *Film og Kino* no. 3 (1917).

10. 'Linsen', 'Den levande skämtbilden: Våra svensk 'cartoon'-tecknare', *Filmbadet* no. 24 (1916): 347–349, 347. Torsten Jungstedt also refers to a screening of *Little Nemo in Slumberland* in a newspaper interview conducted with Bergdahl by Märtha Lindqvist ('Quelqu' une'), *Svenska Dagbladet*, 2 January 1921, see Torsten Jungstedt, *Kapten Grogg*, 43.

11. *Luki vil ha en hund* (Luki Wants a Dog) was censored in Norway in June 1914. This is probably a Norwegian copy of the Emile Cohl film *When He Wants a Dog, He Wants a Dog* (1913) based on George McManus' comic strip *The Newlyweds*.

12. *The Grasshopper and the Ant* (1911) was censored in Norway in 1915.

13. *Stockholms-Tidningen*, 29 February 1916, quoted in Torsten Jungstedt, *Kapten Grogg*, 47.

14. For further discussion of this film and its attribution to M.R. Liljeqvist, see Torsten Jungstedt, *Kapten Grogg*, 100–103.

15. Letter form Asta Nielsen to Victor Bergdahl, Copenhagen, 4 March 1917, quoted in Torsten Jungstedt, *Kapten Grogg*, 61.

16. Victor Bergdahl, *Till Antipoden som Beckbyxa* (Stockholm: Bonniers, 1906).

17. Torsten Jungstedt, *Kapten Grogg*, 83.

18. Gunilla Edin and Torsten Jungstedt, *Mannen bakom Kapten Grogg*, Sveriges Television, Stockholm, 1971. The television programme was published on video by Metafilm, Stockholm in 1989 as were all the *Kapten Grogg* films.

19. See Ulla Hjort Nielsen, *Danske Filmplakater* (Copenhagen: Filmhuset, 1996), 10.

20. Storm-Petersen, 'Storm-Petersen om de første danske film', programme for Paladsteatret, Copenhagen, 18 February 1921.

21. See Jens Bing, 'Storm P.'s tegnefilm', in Ellen Tange Mortensen (ed.), *Tegnefilm – fra Storm P. til Valhalla*, exhibition catalogue, Kunstmuseet Køge Skitsesamling, 17 October – 9 November 1986, n.p.

22. See, for example, Giannalberto Bendazzi, *Cartoons: One Hundred Years of Cinema Animation* (London, Paris, Rome: John Libbey, 1994), 45.

23. Karen Hammer, 'Dansk Tegnefilms barndom – Fra Brasch til Barfod', *Kosmorama* no. 215 (Spring 1996): 42.

24. 'Jean', 'Storm-Petersen fortæller om sin Tegne-Film', *Politiken*, 22 December 1920.

25. Ibid.

26. Ibid.

27. Juho Gartz, *Elävöitettyjä kuvia*, 1975, 13.

28. Juho Gartz and Lauri Tükkülainen, *Muutama Metri Piirrettyä elokuvaa – kuvia suomalaisen animaatioelokuvan varhaisvuosilta 1914–39*, video (Helsinki: Suomen Elokuvasäätiön tuotantotuki, 1981).

29. In a list of Finnish animation before 1945, Lauri Tükkülainen credits Lahyn and Norta with making a 20 metre 'magic pen' test film on a Möller Tricktisch. This footage was probably shot to test the performance capabilities of the new camera.

30. Gartz and Tükkülainen (1981) specify that the film had a running time of 10 minutes.

31. Gartz and Tükkülainen (1981).

32. Gartz and Tükkülainen (1981).

33. 'Raymond', 'Norges første filmtegner. Skuespiller Thoralf Klouman', *Film og Kino* no. 3 (1917): 93.

34. Ibid.

35. 'Flisa', 'Norsk Tegnefilm. Ola Kornelius', *Helt og Skurk* no. 7 (1918).

36. In Norwegian, *maal* (language) more precisely refers to the struggle between the two Norwegian languages. The fight for the new Norwegian language (ny-norsk) is considered a negative influence in this film.

37. Censorship card 11029, Statens Filmkontroll, Kristiania (i.e. present day Oslo).

38. Censorship card 10059, Statens Filmkontroll, Kristiania (i.e. present day Oslo).

39. Censorship card 10103, Statens Filmkontroll, Kristiania (i.e. present day Oslo).

40. Günter Agde, *Flimmernde Versprechen. Geschichte des deutschen Werbefilms im Kino seit 1897* (Berlin: Verlag Das Neue Berlin, 1998), 9f.

41. E. Kjeldgaard, *Biografreklamen i Danmark* (Copenhagen: Einar Harcks Forlag, 1959), 10f.

42. Ottar Gladtvet, 'Filmkameraen Går!', in Jan Anders Diesen (ed.), *Filmeventyret begynner. Av og om filmpioneren Ottar Gladtvet* (Olso: Norsk Filminstitutt, 1999), 64.

43. For a discussion of Pinschewer, see André Amsler, *'Wer dem Werbefilm verfällt, ist verloren für die Welt'. Das Werk von Julius Pinschewer 1883–1961* (Zurich: Chronos, 1997).

44. *Kan sol undværes* is a Norwegian version of *Sonnenersatz* (1924); *An en skjortes liv* is a Norwegian version of *Aus dem leben eines Hemdes* (1925), and *Det var en gang. Blækhusfantasier for store og smaa* (Once upon a Time: Ink-well Fantasies for Big and Small, 1929), is a Norwegian version of a German film, title unknown.

45. On his first feature film as cinematographer, *Unge hjerter* (Young Hearts, 1917) which Gladtvet photographed for Peter Lykke-Seest, Gladtvet worked with Storm P.'s future collaborator, Karl Wieghorst. For studio shooting, Gladtvet acted as Wieghorst's assistant, but according to Gladtvet's autobiography, Wieghorst was not willing to teach the young Gladtvet his professional secrets (see Ottar Gladtvet, 'Filmkameraen Går!', 51). I do not know if Wieghorst's experience in animated cartoon production in Germany occurred before or after *Unge hjerter*, but collaboration with Wieghorst may well have inspired Gladtvet to work in animated film.

46. For discussion of Tiedemann's pre-war sound advertisements, see Gunnar Strøm, 'Fumes from the Fjords', *Animation World Magazine* 2, 2 (1997), and Gunnar Strøm, 'Desider Gross and Gasparcolor. European Producers: Norwegian products and Animated Commercials from the1930s', *Animation Journal* 6, 2 (1998).

47. In a letter to the author, 26 February 1985.

48. 'Tegnefilm', *Filmen og Vi* (January 1926): 17.

49. In letters to the author 26 February 1985 and 6 June 1988.

50. This information is based on telephone calls with Ths. W. Schwartz Jr, the son of the studio owner, see Gunnar Strøm, *Frå 'Fanden i Nøtten' til 'Fargesymfoni i blått'*, *Animasjonsfilm i Norge 1913–1939* (Volda: Møreforsking/Møre og Romsdal Distrikshøgshule, 1993), 54ff.

51. Torsten Jungstedt, *Kapten Grogg*, 77. Colleagues at IRE-film included Einar Norelius, Uno Stallarholm, Kjell Viborg, and Hallkvist.

52. Statsarkivet in Oslo holds the international correspondence of Tiedemann Tobaksfabrik. In connection with ordering *smalfilm* (16mm?) copies of films in 1927, among them *Fiinbeck er rømt*, IRE-film refers to some unspecified earlier contact between the two companies.

53. In this footage, Arvid Olson is seen sitting by his drawing board with his daughter on his lap as he draws a scene with a King and a Princess. The drawing comes alive, and a Prince arrives to ask for the hand of the Princess. The King refuses, and the Prince climbs down the live-action chair under which he hides. Olson's daughter asks why the King refused the Prince's request, and Olson replies: 'Didn't you see his ugly teeth?' Olson's daughter then takes a bottle of Stomatol mouthwash and some toothpaste, and gives them to the Prince. The Prince's proposal is now accepted, and the loving

couple embrace in front of the smiling King. In its combination of live action, still photography and cel animation, this is a charming short film.

54.   Bertil Andersén, head of advertising at Stomatol, established himself as a leading force in film advertising distribution in Sweden in the second half of the 1920s.

55.   E. Kjeldgaard, *Biografreklamen i Danmark*, 35. These negatives seem no longer to exist. At least four films are preserved in The Danish Film Museum. My description of lost films is based on Kjeldgaard.

56.   A brief announcement appeared in *Berlingske Tidende*, 14 August 1926, which reported: 'The young cartoonist, Knut Spange, from Oslo is in town at present studying at the Storm Petersen & K. Wieghorst Atelier for Tegnefilm [studio for animated cartoons].' In an interview with Knut Spange, 10 October 1988, Spange told me that he did not have much contact with Storm P., but learned his craft from Wieghorst.

57   *Det begynte med Storm P. Fra den tegnede reklamefilms historie kommenteret af Jørgen Müller*, documentary produced for Gutenberghus, Copenhagen, by Kai Thegler, Bellevue studio, Copenhagen, 1983.

58.   Kjeldgaard, *Biografreklamen i Danmark*, 36.

59.   Francois Monterossi, 'Tavse og talende Reklamefilm', *Biograf-Bladet* no. 17 (15 April 1929): 4f.

4
Sweden

Exchange and Exhibition Practices: Notes on the Swedish Market in the Transitional Era

Jan Olsson

Department of Cinema Studies, Stockholm University, 105 21 Stockholm, Sweden

The provisional sketch below is inspired by two Pordenone events: first, the 1986 Scandinavian series memorable for salvaging Georg af Klercker from oblivion and confirming the stellar qualities of Danish cinema from the early 1910s; secondly, the reappraisal of films from 1913 that pitched a cornucopia of landmark titles in a characteristic mix of revivals and revelations. For more than a decade, Le Giornate del Cinema Muto has positioned itself as an unrivaled cutting-edge forum gradually redefining the coordinates for silent cinema. The Festival has contested current historiographies and in the process shaped new frames of reference through inventive programming. Swedish scholars, and the silent community at large, have benefited immensely from the annual disclosures at Cinema Verdi.

Featuring the film year 1913 as the fulcrum for the 1993 Pordenone Festival was by no means an innocent choice. From a Swedish perspective, 1913 is the year of *Ingeborg Holm* and the gradual dissemination of Swedish Biograph features via Phoenix, a brand promoted by Pathé for the international marketing of Swedish titles. The memorable aspects of 1913 ran parallel to a market meltdown affecting a host of domestic producers. In each case, the collapse was triggered for a variety of fine-grained reasons. One way or another, history caught up with vulnerable enterprises that particular year. In the main, 1913 marked a global restructuring of market relations and exhibition patterns in the film business, kindling portentous changes in production and distribution structures. The production capacity in several European countries peaked that year boosted by the triumph of the feature format. The surging demand for features during 1911 and 1912, ignited by European exhibitors, rapidly turned into overproduction and market crashes. In the wake of the crisis, a drastic reorganisation of the European industry took effect, and new alliances were formed when undercapitalised producers were evicted from the arena.

In the US, the Motion Picture Patent Company, as a joint venture, gradually faded from the scene; neither the courts nor the market sustained their aspirations for control in the

long run. Pathé, once an unrivalled screen-time provider for American nickelodeons, had lost its dominance years earlier, and suffered marginalisation as the unattractive foreign other even as a patent partner and licensee. At this critical juncture, the American industry, licensees as well as independents, commenced the move to scenic California with its pleasant climate and ample opportunities for outdoor shooting irrespective of season. The relocation westward had its symbolic overtures in the persecution, by trade press and reformers, of French *grand guignol* melodramas and alleged decadence. The targeting of the Red Rooster coincided with a search for a national cinematic identity removed from European genre preoccupations. Men struggling with rugged nature and other not always friendly elements in scenic settings provided an alternative and highly appealing backdrop for one aspect of the Americanisation of American cinema in the early 1910s, as Richard Abel has convincingly argued.[1] On the feature front, a slow transition to longer domestic titles is detectable from circa 1910. The success enjoyed by prestigious multi-reel films screened on road shows attested to the viability of a format that the well-oiled one-reel machinery otherwise had blocked as a resistance-to-changes spinal reflex. Exchanges and nickelodeons were tuned and interlocked to the one-reel format, and saw little need for changing a flourishing programme model. Their resistance spilled over to the production end of the industry. From such a perspective, Eileen Bowser provides an in-depth account of the market for the expansion of features.[2] High-class exhibition venues, by way of European, primarily Italian features, successfully marketed longer films as a full evening's entertainment, thereby substituting nickels and dimes for more sizeable ticket prices in catering to affluent patrons. Nickelodeons operated on a programme slot from 30–60 minutes with a daily change of programme. The notion of brisk business spelled multiple audience changes rather than multiple reels, this to make the nickels count.

Pathé was an equally important supplier of material for the Swedish screens as for the American nickelodeons from 1905 and on-wards, especially given the absence of the domestic production of fiction material prior to 1909, excepting dance films and attempts at sound synchronisation produced in 1907–09. During this period, Swedish Biograph (hereafter SB [Aktiebolaget Svenska Biografteatern]) built an impressive exhibition empire from its headquarters in small-town Krisitanstad, a city the company outgrew in 1911. The business strategy after the move to Stockholm is an intriguing exercise in balancing alliances between different partners. In 1912, the feature format was *the* given production vehicle, although interspersed with a few one-reel comedies and short non-fiction subjects as fillers. By all standards, SB was a small emerging studio. Notwithstanding such a predicament, it managed to take advantage of two major corporation resources – on the one hand Pathé, with a Swedish affiliate Red-Rooster branch opened in 1910 and, on the other hand, Nordisk Films Kompagni (Great Northern) in Copenhagen. Great Northern operated in a weak domestic market due to government regulations of exhibition, but commanded sizeable laboratory resources as well as gateways to all major markets. Polar-bear offices were opened in Berlin, London and New York in 1907 and 1908, and Olsen, the CEO, later provided production differentiation by way of, for instance, offering alternative endings to his films to satisfy the Russian market's taste for tragic closures. For SB, the Polar bear's muscles and the Red Rooster's mighty crow respectively could clear the way for a company in need of international sale and visibility. SB had gained domestic strength thanks to exhibition revenues from its numerous cinemas, while Great Northern predominantly had to reap its profit as producer chiefly in the international arena. In Denmark, after Great Northern's and Fotorama's successful feature gamble and later merge of distribution after major clashes in 1910, new studios mushroomed. However, few of the producers that entered the market in 1912 survived 1913. Copenhagen Film Company, founded by veteran exhibitor O.E. Nathanson, suffered the most spectacular demise after only a few months in operation. Great Northern's unprecedented revenues and dividends in the early 1910s created a frantic demand for film stocks on the Copenhagen Stock Exchange. Copenhagen Film Company capitalised on Great Northern's goodwill, but the lofty prospects failed to convert into rapid turnovers. Rather the reverse: after only a few months of capital bleeding, the figures were alarmingly in the red. Court battles ensued and, eventually, bankruptcy and scandal-blazing newspaper headlines for weeks. This painful experience for a legion of small-fry investors forced the market to sober up.

The Danish situation was far from unique; other countries followed a similar, bleak trajectory. For the time being, however, Pathé was still a stabilising factor in most European markets, but more vulnerable than during the heyday of unrivaled worldwide screen preponderance.

Swedish Biograph was founded in Kristianstad in 1907, incorporating Handelsbolaget Kristianstads Biografteater (from 1905) in order to expand its scope of operations. Soon enough, SB was managing a chain of cinemas in smaller, provincial cities. To guarantee access to a sufficient number of titles for weekly or bi-weekly programme changes, SB secured copies from most of the major producers. Shortly, in the fall of 1907, the company decided to venture into production, initially focusing on topicals and scenics. In 1909, SB was ready for the next production step: thus, sound synchronisation and a few fiction titles hit the scoreboard. The interest in 'sound films' was an offshoot from Messter's Biophone that SB marketed in Sweden during 1908. When SB hired Robert Olsson as photographer, his first assignments were to shoot promotional films from the cities where SB owned cinemas. Local affairs and the prospect of being, perhaps, part of the spectacle still riveted audiences to the neighbourhood screens. Outside the 'shooting area', such films were useful to programme as scenic material, still an integral part of the regular offering. Pathé was even in this respect a dependable provider to help fill that slot. The company had, in fact, opened a cinema in Paris dedicated to non-fiction in 1908 to underscore the diversity of its operations, and was soon to inaugurate its weekly newsreel. Swedish reform groups, on the warpath in 1907–10, championed the educational value

of scenics and topicals, and hoped they would if not curb, at least hold the fiction material in tighter reins. In the process, Danish features, many of them screened in Pordenone in 1986, were singled out as scapegoats by vigilant reformers in lengthy diatribes in the Stockholm newspapers.[3]

The non-access to cinemas in the major cities, particularly Stockholm, soon became a concern for SB. After the move of operations to Stockholm in 1911–12 and various temporary arrangements for exhibition, SB reached an agreement with a competing rental exchange and exhibitor, Svenska Film Companiet (SFC), resulting in a combination of their respective chains of cinemas into Svenska Förenade Biografer. SFC was at that time representing Great Northern in Sweden. Eventually, and after several temporary solutions, Swedish Biograph built an elegant, up-to-date movie palace in Stockholm, Röda Kvarn, and refurbished another one in Malmö, Metropol. The background for the agreement with SFC was a conflict concerning Great Northern's access to the Swedish market when both SB and Great Northern opted for attractive cinemas in key cities, primarily Stockholm. The combination secured Great Northern titles for SB exhibition via Fotorama, with whom Great Northern had entered into a distribution deal earlier. A side effect was a sales guarantee for all SB titles via Great Northern. This gradually undermined the SB alliance with Pathé and the currency of the Phoenix brand.

From the outset in 1906, Ole Olsen and Great Northern's production efforts reaped handsome revenues from Swedish exchanges and exhibitors acquiring their films. An early title like *Fiskerliv i Norden* (1906), for instance, sold six copies to Sweden: to SB, to Gunnar Goes and Christian Svensson, both in Stockholm, to A. Myrin, Norrköping, Anders Skog, Gothenburg, and Axel Ahlström, who managed the Scala in Malmö and a small exchange on the side. In 1907, a Swedish company, Jönköpings Biografteater, later SFC, volunteered to represent Great Northern in Sweden; the offer was declined.[4] By then, Olsen and his partner, Niels Le Tort, had divided the assets between them: Ole Olsen focused on production while Le Tort managed the movie

theatre, A/S Biograf-Theatret. In a letter to Pathé Frères informing them of the change, Le Tort mentioned that he was an erstwhile Pathé customer in 1902–05 when he was heading Malmö Biograf-Teater and Blanch's Teater, the latter in Stockholm. After a short interlude when Numa Peterson represented Great Northern in Sweden, the agency was handed over to SFC in 1911.

In addition to expanding production efforts, after having given up the theatrical part of the business to Le Tort, Olsen managed the exchange leg of the business, and also supplied film stock to Scandinavian companies. When SB contemplated shooting titles of its own, Olsen was the natural provided for film stock. In a letter dated 13 April 1908, Olsen complained that SB no longer seemed to care about his production. Before being represented by Swedish companies, that is up until mid-1909, Great Northern regularly sent inspection copies directly to a handful of key Swedish exhibitors/exchanges, but SB, it would appear, no longer purchased any films. SB's ledgers confirm that the company depended heavily on local exchanges in 1906 – Axel Ahlström, K.O. Krantz, Frans Lundberg and Malmö Biograf-Teater – but foremost on Great Northern.[5] The Pathé material was acquired via Numa Peterson. In 1907, SB purchased material directly from international producers, mostly via Berlin, instead of from domestic exchanges. SB followed the market by subscribing to German, French and British trade papers. Company correspondence has been destroyed, but its financial records from 1906–07 detail all transactions, including the fading interest in Great Northern's production. In 1906, SB bought material from Great Northern for little more than 14,000 Swedish kronor (corresponding to 560,000 Swedisk kronor in 1999). Numa Peterson sold material to SB for almost 12,500 Swedish kronor in 1906. In 1907, when SB secured cinemas in a host of new cities, Pathé material from Numa Peterson became increasingly important. The Peterson sale to SB tripled to 36,000 Swedish kronor, while the Great Northern sales plummeted to 6,000 Swedish kronor. One still finds minor acquisitions from local exchanges, primarily from Ahlström and Krantz, but, more importantly,

heavy international trading. SB bought material from the Berlin branches of Edison, Cines, Urban and Gaumont, from Deutsche Bioscope, Messter, Eclipse, Théophile Pathé, Raleigh & Robert, Georges Mendel, Carlo Rossi, Cricks & Sharp, Walturdaw and Vitagraph. Towards the end of 1907, the London-based Swedish exchange manager, Oscar Rosenberg, became a major supplier, primarily of American material. Unfortunately, there are no financial records after January 1908. The films SB accumulated were first screened within the company's own exhibition chain, but several independent cinemas used SB as full-scale programme providers, while others rented on a more irregular basis. In the process, several SB suppliers from 1906 had to retreat from the exchange business in the wake of new business protocols.

Sweden, like most markets, made the transition to permanent-site exhibition primarily thanks to the scope and regularity of new Pathé releases. The quality as well as genre diversity of the films seems to have appealed to local audiences almost worldwide. SB's rapid exhibition sprawl is a case in point: Pathé material goaded the process. For a producer without exhibition support within the company, exchange activities offered the only other possible source of revenue. For Great Northern, therefore, it became paramount to be able to offer the Pathé brand to local customers. In 1906, Numa Peterson enjoyed the sole rights for Pathé in Sweden and Norway, and he apparently received new titles before they reached Denmark. The shrewd Ole Olsen hoped to outsmart his Danish competitors by channeling Pathé titles to Denmark via Stockholm. In late December 1906, Olsen enlisted a straw man in Stockholm, one Gustaf Möller, and promising financial rewards if Möller could get his hands on new Pathé titles without giving the scheme away to Peterson. Olsen particularly looked for longer films, pre-features. The list of titles delivered by Möller, however, proved to be material already available to Olsen. Later on, Pathé was represented in Denmark by Edward Partsch, a former Olsen employee, who had set up Great Northern's branches in Berlin and London before he was fired by the non-sentimental CEO.

From the outset, Ole Olsen backed Pathé's attempt to form a European production trust in order to regulate production, and in the process downplay the importance of the exchanges. In a letter to Charles Pathé (17 November 1908) Olsen wrote:

> I think your intention is to form a new syndicate, gathering the good firms and leaving out the unsound, which are only spoiling the trade.
>
> If this is your idea, I can give you my full approval and I shall do everything in my power to assist you in this. Of course you have the best chances of doing this through Eastman.
>
> I shall once more point out to you the advisability in doing all that must be done as soon as possible.

Olsen had a vested interest in supporting Pathé, hoping to continue to make money on the popular brand if local competitors were out-trusted and emerging producers put on a minimal quota. Replying to a lost letter from Pathé, Olsen, in colourful English, revealed more of the cards up his sleeve:

> I duly received your esteemed letter, and beg to say, that I am quite sure, that you are in this case working too slow, because you are not aware what is being done behind your back.
>
> I have to a certain party pledged my word of honor not to say any thing, but I have written to you plain enough to show you that a conspiration (*sic*) is being made against you and several big names are between them.
>
> This is all I could do and will now leave the rest to you.
>
> I have also been informed, that you are going to start branch offices as well in Scandinavia as in other places. It is my opinion, that this will be a great loss to you, if you are not combined with other manufacturers.
>
> I beg to inform you, that Gaumont is also starting branch business in Scandinavia. (23 November 1908)

In spite of Olsen's offer to join forces, Pathé established an unofficial Copenhagen office in the name of Edward Partsch, and in 1909 there was fierce competition between Pathé and Great Northern spilling over to the Swedish market. In a letter to Frans Lundberg, Malmö, dated 7 December 1909, Great Northern offered to match all metre prices Pathé might be offering.

Olsen approached Charles Pathé again early 1910 hoping to rekindle the combination process, this time in colourful and less than correct French:

> Comme un an a maintenant passé depuis la combination à Paris, òu 'la Convention' était formée, et comme aucune base réelle pour coopération entre les éditeurs de film a été produit, veuillez bien me dire, si vous croyez pas, que le propre moment est maintenant venu pour votre maison à faire une proposition, qui doit être profitable aux maisons assez *viables quant à fonds et à productions*.
>
> Je penserai que vous nommerai ces maisons, dans la condition que celles-ci se combinent s'obligent à éditer seulement une nombre de négatives à raison de la présente grandeur des affaires. C'est la seule mode, dans laquelle les affaires peuvent marcher par une trace saine.
>
> Nous avons recu [sic] aujourd'hui les nouvelles d'un de nos succursales, qu'une grande maison anglaise et deux maisons francaises [sic] soient pour le moment très mal ètablies [sic], et d'ailleurs c'est chose connue, que plusieurs maisons sont mal établies, et pour se sauver elles nuirent au marché de tous les manières. (5 January 1910)

Nothing came of Olsen's proposal; instead Pathé decided to set up a Stockholm branch. From the outset, Siegmund Popert, the veteran who managed the Stockholm office, sought arrangements via London exchanges to secure American titles to facilitate contact with Swedish exhibitors who wanted material from more than one producer. Films from the American Biograph Company were of particular interest for Popert, who praised the superior quality of the films from American Biograph in his correspondence with the London exchanges. The local censor in Malmö,

Fig. 1 (top). Georg af Klercker supervising sets at the Lidingö studio in 1912. [Courtesy of Professor Jan Olsson.]

Fig. 2 (right). Mauritz Stiller frolicking between takes. The snapshot was caught by the omnipresent Julius Jaenzon. [Courtesy of Professor Gösta Werner.]

the most noteworthy in a 'report card' for the 1910-season published in two installments in a local newspaper.[6]

SB's ledgers and financial records from 1906–07 underpin Numa Peterson's role as the dominating Swedish exchange prior to 1910 when Pathé established its Stockholm outlet. A few years later, the Peterson empire went down for a variety of reasons; the film division represented only one aspect of their diverse business interests.

After years of clashes and drawbacks on the American market, and plagued by less than successful attempts at monopolising film sales in Europe, Pathé decided to target new markets. A minor component in that strategy was to open the Stockholm office in the summer of 1910. The filial, as it was called, later established sub-branches in Malmö, in 1912, and in Gothenburg in 1914.

Swedish Biograph's production of features from 1909 onwards came to the fore during the unruly days of early features with French, Italian and Danish titles furnishing the models. The SB titles produced in 1909 and 1910 (prior to the move to Stockholm) had limited impact outside Sweden. Nonetheless, an avid reader can find traces of some of the titles in the German trade press from advertisements by Ludwig Gottschalk in Düsseldorf, an exchange with a longstanding interest in Scandinavian films. Despite Charles Magnusson's misgivings concerning the quality of the first years of limited feature output, he persisted in exploring the format. Magnusson took over the SB helm in 1909 after a career as producer of topicals and scenics for a small company in Gothenburg. Several timely topicals shot by Magnusson were sold in a host of copies; SB was among his regular customers. In conjunction with SB's move to Stockholm, Magnusson hired Georg af Klercker as head of production (Fig. 1), and Victor Sjöström and Mauritz Stiller (Fig. 2) as directors and actors. All three were well-known stage personalities on the travelling circuit, but with no experience of screen-related work. During the period of studio construction in 1911, the zealous Magnusson took a small group of actors and the cameraman Julius Jaenzon on an extended globetrotting trip shooting films in the US and, in passing,

Frans Hallgren, seconded this contention when singling out Biograph's production as

covered scenic spots and metropolitan vistas in Europe.

Notwithstanding SB's new studio, a contending Swedish producer, Frans Lundberg, enjoyed a higher level of international visibility in 1912 and 1913. Lundberg produced his first two features in 1910: *Värmlänningarna* (The People of Värmland) and *Massösens offer* (The Victim of the Masseuse). The latter film was shot in Denmark, and featured a Danish cast in addition to the capable Alfred Lind behind the camera. The laboratory work was turned over to Great Northern. Lundberg's strategy, when entering the production market after several years of exhibition and exchange business, was to produce two distinct types of films. *Värmlänningarna* was a domestically inspired production, a 'classic' Swedish folk play, performed outdoors in a summer theatre by a local amateur cast that Lundberg later persuaded to act for his film camera. In fact, SB had shot a version of the same play in 1909 also taking advantage of local amateurs; Magnusson generally favoured this type of material during the first two years of production. Lundberg's cameraman, Ernst Dittmer, was hired from SB in 1910; Lundberg thus capitalised on SB experience in several respects. Simultaneously, the resourceful Lundberg produced a sensational melodrama in the Danish vein, and in Denmark, no less, with a cast of well-known actors. The film was shot as an interlude while on the road with a theatrical tour spearheaded by the famous impresario Otto Jacobsen. The success of *Massösens offer* and its sensational melodrama formula was underpinned by featuring popular veteran Oda Nielsen as the mother of a young man gone astray. In her rôle, Mrs. Nielsen masquerades as a prostitute in order to retrieve her son, the title's designated victim, from the clutches of masseuses and usurers. After soliciting his desires, she discloses her identity at a critical juncture in the proceedings. Thwarting everyday-logic, this titillating quasi-incestuous strategy proved to be narratively effective. After a showdown, the young man is reunited with his family at their country manor leaving the temptations of the big city behind. *Massösens offer* enjoyed considerable success in Denmark and Germany and, more importantly, its following inspired new seasons of Lundberg production in 1911 and 1912. In preparation for the 1911 season, Lundberg advertised his upcoming films in the German trade press. This paved the way for a liaison with the Berlin exchange, Robert Glombeck, and a high-profile marketing of the films and their star, Ida Nielsen, in the trade press, lavishly so in the case of the German trade press. The exhibitor's predilection for features catapulted Lundberg and his production into international recognition during a period when the German market was a gold mine for sensational films marketed as *Kunstfilms*, soon to be superseded by *Autorenfilm*.

1912 proved to be a resilient year in the history of Swedish cinema. SB moved into the new studio in Stockholm; Lundberg was busy shooting features in Malmö; N.P. and Axel Nilsson, Stockholm's foremost exhibitor, hired a modest production unit headed by Anna Hofmann-Uddgren, and Viking Film, based in Linköping, added a few features to their production of scenics and topicals. Viking struggled with a financially precarious situation after an unsuccessful investment in Kinemacolor; the features did not remedy the company's financial concerns. In addition to these domestic initiatives, Pathé decided to produce films in Sweden, initially in close alliance with SB. Pathé made a substantial investment in SB's new studio complex on Lidingö in preparation for a more active involvement in the Swedish market. Sjöström and Magnusson visited the Pathé plant in Paris, and Paul Garbagni came to Sweden where he co-directed one film in 1912. At this time, both companies were under reconstruction: Pathé incorporated the Swedish branch as Pathé Film, and Swedish Biograph registered their studio operation under the company name Nordiska Filmfabriken. The Phoenix trademark was launched as a production label for titles produced in Stockholm and marketed internationally by Pathé. Magnusson thereby secured worldwide high-profile distribution for his production.

A letter dated 15 December 1915, from the sales department at the Compagnie Générale des établissements Pathé Frères to the Stockholm branch of the company, marks the definite dismantling of the cooperation be-

tween Pathé and Swedish Biograph.[7] The letter lists negatives returned to Stockholm, negatives primarily relating to Phoenix titles produced by SB in 1912 and 1913 and marketed internationally by Pathé. This letter also lists seven Swedish films distributed via Pathé. A few more titles were part of the deal, for instance, *Med vapen hand* and *I livets vår/Första älskarinnan* (distribution title, 'Le printemps de la vie'). Although Sjöström is credited as the director of the latter film on the poster for the film, *I livets vår/Första älskarinnan* (In the Spring of Life) was supervised and co-directed by Paul Garbagni, who came to the Lidingö studio in 1912 to superintend and share expertise after Victor Sjöström's visit to the Pathé studio in Paris earlier that year. The quantities specified in the return shipment of negatives would appear to indicate separate scenes. One can assume that the films consisted of as many shots as the list specified. Extant screenplays support this conclusion, particularly in respect of *Löjen och tårar* (distribution title, 'Les bijoux'). Unfortunately, none of the films survive in a complete version; 'Sous la coupole du cirque', directed by Klercker, is the only one preserved in fragmentary form.

The returned negatives include the following films:

> Sous la coupole du cirque (*Dödsritten under cirkuskupolen* (The Death Ride under the Circus Tent), 43 shots specified);
>
> Mariage secret (*Ett hemligt giftermål* (A Secret marriage), 49 shots specified, 49 scenes according to the screenplay);
>
> Les bijoux (*Löjen och tårar* (Smiles and Tears), 44 shots specified, 45 scenes according to the screenplay);
>
> Fausse alerte (*Falskt alarm* (False Alarm), 25 shots specified);
>
> L'enfant (*Barnet* (The Child), 52 shots specified);
>
> Mariage de Mr. Muller (*Äktenskapsbyrån* (The Marriage Bureau), 25 shots specified);
>
> Roman d'un pauvre enfant (*En skärgårdsflickas roman* (A Story of a Girl from the Archipelago), 27 shots specified).[8]

The sales revenues for the seven titles (listed above) in the letter of 15 December 1915 were included in monthly reports from Pathé's Stockholm office to SB, and include sales from both the Berlin and New York branches in addition to sales via Paris.

In 1913, Pathé temporarily discontinued its production of features in Sweden after censorship altercations surrounding their first feature, *Tvenne bröder* (Two Brothers), directed by Georg af Klercker and, instead, agreed to acquire SB titles for international distribution via Phoenix. A national censorship body, Statens Biografbyrå, came into operation in December 1911 after several years of campaigning by reform groups. Moreover, the reform movement's spokespersons became the first generation of uncompromising national censors. Pathé was not the only victim. The Board banned Victor Sjöström's first film, and was particularly relentless on Frans Lundberg, banning most of his titles and cutting others so that they could not be exhibited. Lundberg decided to dismantle his business in 1913, due to the many unpredictable market glitches. The veteran exhibitor N.P. Nilsson died in 1912, which curtailed his firm's production initiative. The films released by N. P. and Axel Nilsson were by and large not very successful. Their efforts included the first screen adaptations of works by August Strindberg. *Fröken Julie* (Miss Julie) faced a dismissive reception in the press; *Fadren* (The Father) fared slightly better, but only slightly. Adapting Strindberg plays was, of course, a challenging cultural gambit, in spite of the author's magnanimous carte blanche for shooting. Nilssons' strategy was prone to elicit dissent: a new medium, branded as the cultural other, should not tamper with high art. The extant copy of *Fadren* has few endearing qualities; for a film produced in 1912, an outdated mode of cinematically unimaginative tableaux.

Both Viking Film features produced in 1912 are lost. They attracted little attention from Swedish exhibitors, and it does not seem as if the advertisements in a British trade paper paid off internationally. Consequently, Viking Film gave up the struggle early in 1913, and a reorganisation of the business as Discus Film proved unsuccessful. All of a sudden,

SB found itself as the only remaining Swedish film producer.

The business aspect of Swedish film history starts with Numa Peterson's Trading Company. Peterson won the concession for the 1897 Stockholm Exhibition, and operated a cinema in the exhibition grounds together with the Lumières of Lyon during the summer. Subsequent catalogues from the Peterson firm, a business predominantly dealing in pharmaceutical goods, photochemical matters, phonographs and cylinders, offered film cameras and projectors in addition to film titles from Lumière and other producers. From 1901, the company listed phonograph cylinders to be synchronised with French film titles. Alexandre Promio represented the Lumière brothers during the Stockholm exhibition event. He brought in titles from earlier film expeditions, but in line with Lumière practice shot new material in Stockholm, titles that later found their way into the Lyon firm's catalogue. On the side, Promio educated apprentices from the Peterson firm, for instance Ernest Florman, and thereby helped to implement local film activities. A few domestic titles, produced by Numa Peterson, were screened during the exhibition: *Byrakstugan* (The Village Barbershop), and *Akrobat har otur* (Unlucky Acrobat). *Slagsmål i Gamla Stockholm* (Fistfight in Old Stockholm) – parts of medieval Stockholm were rebuilt at the exhibition site – is credited to the Lyon firm. As a spin-off from the exhibition, Numa Peterson operated a permanent-site cinema in 1897–98. After an almost year-long stint at exhibition, cut short mainly due to lack of films, the Peterson firm took part only in special events during the next few years, selling and renting films, first to travelling exhibitors and then, later, to permanent-site cinemas. Their only production venture, besides the films shot in 1897 was a series of domestic films synchronised with phonograph cylinders which the firm produced in 1903. The opening for these films took place in conjunction with an exposition in Helsingborg. The production was marketed as The Swedish Immortal Theatre (Svenska Odödliga Teatern), taking the initiative for this title from the French Phono-Cinéma-Theatre whose products Peterson marketed in Sweden.[9]

In his licentiate dissertation, Rune Waldekranz maps the first ten years of film exhibition in Sweden.[10] He charts the travelling showmen's routes and venues across the country via police records, newspaper advertisements and posters, and, in addition, provides an account of the material screened. Waldekranz's heroic archival efforts have given us a far more detailed account for the period 1896–1906 than what is available for the first years of permanent-site exhibition, 1906–09. By all standards, Rune Waldekranz is a revisionist film historian *avant la lettre*, an inventive scholarly pioneer, although internationally unrecognised since his work has not been translated.

For the period immediately following the time frame of Waldekranz's investigation, evidence of an emerging market for film sales and regular exhibition can be gleaned from the 1906–07 financial records and film inventory for SB at Kristianstad. The records go back to January 1906, listing box-office earnings on a daily basis from the various cinemas. The cinema in Kristianstad, for example, had receipts of little more than 82 kronor per day in January. Business was particularly brisk on Sundays, providing as much as 173 kronor. Later that month, a cinema opened in Karlskrona, earning 99.25 the first day, 29 January. February saw cinemas in Kalmar and Karlshamn, and the one in Sölvesborg opened in March. Throughout the year, new venues were added to the chain. Below a sample of box-office receipts:

April 1906:
Kristianstad: 91 kronor per day; Karlskrona: 110; Kalmar: 132; Karlshamn: 43.

September 1906:
Kristianstad: 129 kronor per day; Karlskrona: 97; Kalmar: 73; Karlshamn: 61.

December 1906:
Kristianstad: 102 kronor per day; Karlskrona: 88; Kalmar: 82; Karlshamn: 60.

During December cinemas in Sala and

Visby opened, in addition to the recent ones in Nyköping, Visby, Uddevala, Söderhamn, Västerås, Örebro, Boden, and Köping.

February 1907:
Kristianstad: 93 kronor per day; Karlskrona: 89; Kalmar: 88; Karlshamn: 63; Visby: 102.

September 1907:
Kristianstad: 115 kronor per day; Karlskrona: 61; Kalmar: 111; Karlshamn: 148; Nyköping: 68; Västerås: 91; Örebro: 76; Visby: 88.

Finally, January 1908:
Kristianstad: 116 kronor per day; Karlskrona: 66; Karlshamn: 64; Kalmar: 73; Visby: 75.

By 1908, SB operated cinemas in the following cities: Boden, Köping, Åmål, Uddevalla, Filipstad, Vänersborg, Kristianstad, Kalmar, Malmö, Karlskrona, Karlshamn, Sölvesborg, Söderhamn, Västerås, Örebro, Nyköping, Köping, Visby, Gävle, and Härnösand. SB's inventory from 1 July 1906 lists sixty-three brown chairs and forty-three yellow, thus, it seems as if the cinema could accommodate around one hundred patrons. Kristianstad had a population of 11,000 in 1908. Admission prices varied between cinemas: 25–50 öre for adults; 10–25 öre for children. If we assume that the average ticket price was 35 öre in 1908 and relate that to the box-office receipt of 116 kronor per day for the Kristianstad cinema, the number of admissions was just over 330, i.e. 3% of the local population. And Kristianstad had at least one more cinema.

1907, the year of incorporation, was highly volatile. In the process of acquiring enough material to keep the cinemas going, SB turned into an exchange, renting to several independent exhibitors. The small domestic exchanges were, no doubt, affected by SB's new strength, this in addition to losing the sales to SB. The next logical step for SB was to develop a production division in addition to exhibition and the exchange. In the long run, a small town like Kristianstad could not support a regular production unit. The actors had their bases in the legitimate theatre in

Stockholm, and the company had out-grown the studio space. Thus the move to a more culturally diverse scene for the company's operation became increasingly necessary.

The interplay between permanent-site cinemas and distributors/exchanges provides a given focus for the formative years of local exhibition. As we have seen, several Swedish exchanges were established in and after 1905, often as offshoots of permanent-site cinemas. A few notes regarding the mercurial flux for one venue illustrate the short half-life for exhibition businesses during the transitional era. Aktiebolaget Bioblanche, registered in July 1905, incorporated a Stockholm business managed by Carl Edberg and Albin Bjurman. Ole Olsen's partner, Niels Le Tort, was involved at Blanch's prior to Edberg and Bjurman. Bioblanche was dismantled in July 1906; one can find traces of their activities in the SB account books for early 1906. Blanch's (without the prefix bio-) was a vaudeville-like entertainment establishment that housed a film venue on the side. The film theatre reappeared almost immediately after Bioblanche's bankruptcy. Files from the latter Blanch's (at Föreningen Stockholms Företagsminnen) include a list of film titles for sale. The Kristianstad firm bought some of these titles from Jarl Östman, who ran Blanch's in 1907 and 1908 together with Christian Svensson. The latter year, Östman shot dance films and two synchronised sound titles.

The dates for the oldest film sale and distribution catalogues preserved at the Royal Library, Stockholm, and at the University Library, Lund – not counting the vintage ones from Numa Peterson – coincide with the period in which permanent-site cinemas were established in Sweden. One finds, however, no surviving material from the veteran exchanges ran by Axel Ahlström and K.O. Krantz respectively. A 1906 List of Films from the Sewing Machine Company Nornan in Sundsvall offers 'Short loop films', that is 3- to 16-feet film loops. The items are numbered from #31 – #94 and include the following titles: #36 *American Infantry*; #49 *The Man With Two Heads*; #52 *The Monkey at the Table*; #71 *La Belle Otéro*, #86 *Peasant and Clown* (Transformation). Some of these titles were also offered in 'original' format. The latter

category, 'Films in Original Length (large films)', list titles 25–100 feet long. The list covers items from #210 to #278, for instance: #250 *Through The Key Hole*; #258 *The Flea Hunt*; #262 *The Kiss in the Tunnel*, #278 In the Boudoir. The longer titles are described in one or two sentences. For example, #278: 'Exhausted, the young lady returns home from the theatre. She undresses and goes to bed. Piquant'. Finally, there is a separate category devoted to films from the Russo-Japanese War, listing five, more recent titles. Besides the war titles, the films – predominantly French, American and British – seem to be hold over material perhaps for arcade viewing in slot machines. The film list is Nornan's only sign of film-related activities.

A 1907 list of films, issued by C.A. Friberg, based in Karlskrona where he operated one of his many cinemas, offers around three hundred titles. Friberg's catalogue includes local and international scenics, in addition to fiction material from Denmark, France and the US. Besides giving the Swedish distribution title, only the film's length in metres and a one-word genre descriptor are given, for instance: Tale, Toned, Drama or Comedy. The titles are all fairly recent: #16, *Tour du monde d'un policier* (Pathé, 1906); #149 *Den hvita slafvinnan* (Great Northern, 1906); #195 *Kathleen Mavourneen* (Edison, 1906). The Pathé titles were probably acquired via Numa Peterson. The catalogue runs from #3 to #387 with some gaps for discarded titles.

Hugo Silow, Linköping, issued one undated catalogue, probably in 1907, consisting of 103 titles. The last title on the list is one of several actualities shot during a military drill in September 1907. Rental price: 10 öre per metre per week, except for the military title which was offered at 20 öre. Silow was a former travelling exhibitor.

From 1908 there is a film catalogue from Montogomery & Wahlberg, a Stockholm-based exchange related to a cinema in Stockholm (at Sankt Paulsgatan 13) managed by Wahlberg, and a second cinema in Norrköping under the management of Erik Montgomery. Erik was the son of Gothenburg film pioneer Otto Montgomery who in 1907 and 1908 relied predominantly on SB as supplier of films for his cinema. The list comprises 152 titles offered for sale as well as for rental. The quoted price per metre probably relates to sale. The price range varies from 30 öre to 1 krona; topicals – with their shorter market appeal – are at the expensive end. All types of non-fiction material are categorised as *Naturbild*. Some films are toned. For one of the titles (*The Great Train Robbery*), the genre is substituted for an indication of manufacturer: Edison.

An undated catalogue from Svensk Films Compani, based in Jönköping (Catalogue No. III), probably dates from 1908. One of the last titles on the list, #157 out of a total of 159, is a Gaumont title from May 1908, *Mr. Farman's Airship*. This catalogue lists many Great Northern and Pathé titles. For some of the films, Comedy or Drama is indicated, a few titles are toned, some partly or entirely colourised, probably tinted. No prices are given, but there is information regarding length for each title.

The Stockholm-based Svensk-Franska Handelsaktiebolaget issued a film catalogue in 1909. Several hundred titles are listed. Apart from Swedish distribution titles only information regarding length is available. The first item is #336, the last as #877. The catalogue has some omissions. Overall, it displays the same mix of news items, short comical, and dramatic subjects from international producers as the other catalogues. The business was incorporated and registered in October 1906.

Svensk-Amerikanska Filmkompaniet opened in 1908 as Globe Films. The business expanded in 1910 and at that time the company published three bulletin issues, including extensive film lists offering titles from the leading American, French and Italian producers. True to their American affiliation, the company also marketed, for a limited time, illustrated songs. These were introduced during the Stockholm Exhibition in 1909, with a limited following. More important, the company started a trade paper in 1909, *Nordisk Filmtidning*, the first one in Swedish. In addition to the Stockholm office, there were local branches in Copenhagen and Kristiania (Oslo). According to the bulletins, new programmes were offered twice a week. Prior to the bulletin issues, the company printed an extensive film catalogue in 1909, listing titles

by genre from a score of producers. *Heard Over the 'Phone* was one of twelve dramas from Edison alone, and one could choose between thirty Gaumont comedies.

Orientaliska teatern, the jewel in the crown of N.P. Nilsson's chain of Stockholm cinemas, issued a catalogue in 1909. The list is extensive, and divided into topicals/scenics, comedies, and dramas, representing all major producers.

No catalogues have survived from Frans Lundberg's exchange, but the scope of his business can be assessed via the number of films he submitted to the censorship board for inspection in 1911 and 1912. He then owned a multitude of titles from the leading French, American, Italian, Danish and British producers. From the outset in the fall of 1910, Lundberg relied heavily on the local Pathé outlet for a substantial part of his programming. Pathé's rental records list all the transactions. Lundberg had only one cinema, apart from one in Copenhagen, but he ran a longstanding exchange prior to production in the period 1910–12.

Pathé did not issue a catalogue until March 1914, but supplied weekly programmes to many exhibitors, in addition to selling cameras, projectors, film stock, and film-related equipment. Their exchange records from 1910 and 1911 are preserved. The Stockholm office bought between one to five copies of titles from Paris and other production legs of the empire, for instance American Kinema. Some copies were 'sold' to other Swedish exchanges; that is, the exchanges received a distribution option for a limited time (often close to a year) and then had to return the copy. One or two copies were used for renting to minor exhibitors. An example: four copies of *Max tager ett bad* ('Max prend un bain') were bought from Paris for 235.20 kronor each in mid-November 1910. Three were immediately sold: to SB, Numa Peterson and Frans Lundberg respectively. Peterson, as a former agent, paid 157.50 kronor, while the other copies amounted to 178.50 kronor. Peterson's copy was returned on 15 September 1911; Lundberg's in early October. There is no return date for the SB copy, but it was re-rented to SB in April 1912. Pathé's own copy was normally first rented to N.P. Nilsson and circulated for a few weeks at his Stockholm cinemas; in this particular case, for three weeks, before it was sent to the next customer. Nilsson paid 68.25 kronor for the film. The revenues from his screenings were always more substantial than those from other exhibitors. In July 1913, copy A was sold for 20.50 kronor to an exhibitor in Öresund. Sales of old material were not uncommon, but in most cases, copies were returned to Paris after a few years.

The fact that no film catalogue survives from SB underscores the general scarcity of paper material. However, the unearthing of sources, particularly from the censorship board from the period after 1911, still has a lot to offer, especially in terms of text lists for lost films. The programme and poster collections at the Royal Library and the university libraries are not taken into consideration here at all, and local newspapers can provide important insights into exhibition and reception practices. As Gregory A. Waller has shown, research based on in-depth local material can provide profound insights.[11] The work continues . . .

Notes

1. Richard Abel, *The Red Rooster Scare: Making Cinema American, 1900–1910* (Berkeley, Los Angeles, London: University of California Press, 1999), particularly Chapter 6.

2. Eileen Bowser, *Transformation of Cinema* (Berkeley, Los Angeles, London: University of California Press, 1994; [1990]), 191–215.

3. Much of the material is quoted in my essay 'Svart på vitt: film, makt och censur', *Aura. Filmvetenskaplig tidskrift* 1,1 (1995): 14–46.

4. The information on Great Northern comes from uncatalogued sales ledgers and copies of outgoing letters from the studio held by the Danish Film Institute.

5. Swedish Biograph's financial records from 1906–07 are part of the SB-collection at the Swedish Film Institute.

6. See Jan Olsson, *Sensationer från en bakgård. Frans Lundberg som biografägare och filmproducent i Malmö och Köpenhamn* (Lund, Stockholm: Symposion Bokförlag, 1988), 48–49.

7. In records pertaining to the Swedish branch of Pathé at the Swedish Film Institute.

8. *Svensk filmografi*, I, lists five titles under Phoenix: *Med vapen i hand*; *Vampyren*; *När kärleken dödar*; *En skärgårdsflickas roman*; *Lady Marions sommarflirt*. Revenues for *Vampyren*; *När kärleken dödar*, and *Lady Marions sommarflirt* have not found been in the records of the Stockholm Pathé office.

9. The 1897 Stockholm Exhibition gave the new medium a more diverse resonance than the scattered screenings in Sweden during 1896 had provoked. The very first event, opening in Malmö 28 June 1896, was an undisputed success. Subsequent screenings in Stockholm, unrelated to the season in Malmö, did not create a stir. During the summer of 1896, Stockholm had three film exhibition venues: Charles Marcel showed living pictures at Victoria-Teatern commencing 21 July; the brothers Skladanowsky visited Kristallsalongen in August, and around the same time Anette Teufel screened her film show at Berns. *Dagens Nyheter*'s unimpressed reviewer concluded:

    > The Cinematograph has no luck in Stockholm. The first item, exhibited at the Victoria Theatre, was bad, the version of the invention demonstrated at Kristallsalongen (The Crystal Palace) under the heading the Brothers' Skladanowsky's Bioscope, was even worse, and even Anette Teufel's kinematograph, displayed at Bern's was pretty unsuccessful. (20 August 1896)

    In passing, the critic mentioned that the machine displayed in Malmö was said to be far superior in quality. It is worth emphasising that the brothers Skladanowsky during the short stay shot the very first film in Sweden, a spoof called *Komische Begegnung zum Tiergarten im Stockholm*, a film that has survived. For further information, see Jan Olsson, *Från filmljud till ljudfilm. Svenska experiment med Odödlig teater, Sjungande bilder och Edisons Kinetophon 1903–1914* (Stockholm: Proprius förlag, 1985) and Jan Olsson (ed.), *I offentlighetens ljus* (Stockholm/Stehag: Symposion Bokförlag, 1990).

10. Rune Waldekranz, *Levande fotografier: Film och biograf i Sverige 1896–1906*, Licentiate Dissertation, Institutionen för Teater- och filmvetenskap, Stockholm University, Autumn 1969.

11. Gregory A. Waller, *Main Street Amusements: Movies and Entertainment in a Southern City, 1896–1930*, (Washington, D.C.: Smithsonian Institution Press, 1995).

Educational Cinema and Censorship in Sweden, 1911–1921

Åsa Jernudd

Department of Humanities, Örebro University, 701 82 Örebro, Sweden

According to Ellen Strain's reading of Martin Heidegger, 'science, technology, culture, the loss of the gods, and the artwork as *Erlebnis*'[1] are the essential phenomena through which the modern age can be discerned. As Heidegger observes, '[t]he fundamental event of the modern age is the conquest of the world as picture'.[2] For Western, urban, turn-of-the-century populations, familiarity with the world became an educational goal, part of a process of locating and establishing the self within a rapidly changing, secular world. This involved an educational practice that was interrelated with the pedagogical discourses of science and its view of a structured universe. The technological base for the conception of a structured image of the universe, which provided the vehicle for the conquest of the world by man, was found in a new and expanding visual culture represented by graphic illustration, the reproduction of photographs in books, newspapers, posters, postcards, and by exhibitions, museums and cinema.

In the past two decades a revisionist tradition within cinema studies has been devoted to the emergence of cinema and its early period within the conceptual framework of moder-

nity.[3] From this work I would like to recall Tom Gunning's description of the pedagogical dimensions of an emerging visual culture when discussing turn-of-the-century World Exhibitions. In his article 'The World as Object Lesson: Cinema Audiences, Visual Culture and the St. Louis World's Fair, 1904', Gunning outlines the key aspects of the new visual culture in an analysis of the World Expositions which, he writes, embodied and proselytised this new culture, and shaped the emergence of cinema by offering a training ground for a new kind of spectating. The key aspects were: 'a new faith in the power of visual knowledge; a conception of the world itself as a consumable picture, imaged through the collapse of space and time; and an aggressive visual address aimed at dazzling the viewer with a new control over the gaze'.[4]

Through a reading of the discourse surrounding the World Expositions, Gunning shows how the experience of the event was described as a mediated one, organised as knowledge, and experienced as a picture; in short, the World Exposition as an educational text:

> But this was a peculiarly modern text, one embodied less in verbal signifiers than in visual ones, exemplifying a new conception of education which made use of

things themselves rather than conventional signs. By the turn of the century the World Exposition served as a demonstration of the latest theory in education, the 'object lesson', an approach pioneered in schools and museums which depended less on language to convey knowledge than on pictures and, when possible, scrutinised actual objects for the lessons they contained.[5]

In Sweden as elsewhere in the Western world, a modern visual culture emerged in the late nineteenth century with close ties to scientific and technological culture, exemplified by pedagogical institutions such as Naturhistoriska Riksmuseet (the National Museum of Natural History),[6] biological museums,[7] Skansen (an open air museum exhibiting national culture),[8] and the technical exhibitions in Stockholm in 1897 and 1909, in Malmö in 1914, and in Gothenburg in 1923.[9] The late nineteenth century also saw the emergence of cinema, an event that is conventionally told in the light of its indebtedness to the legacy of science since many of the techniques and instruments that contributed to the emergence of cinema were developed and used within scientific culture. Then the historical narrative quickly shifts, as Lisa Cartwright has pointed out, from science to popular culture.[10] However, the rise of a popular film culture neither implied that scientific film culture suddenly ceased to exist nor that the two cultures evolved as two entirely separate and independent entities. On the contrary, as scholars such as Lisa Cartwright,[11] Alison Griffiths,[12] Ellen Strain,[13] Fatimah Tobing Rony,[14] and Tom Gunning[15] have demonstrated, the two cultures were at times uneasily but nonetheless intertwined.

The discourse surrounding early Swedish cinema offers an example of the interaction between scientific and popular culture based on the dichotomy of fiction and non-fiction film. The cultural elite which organised public opinion in a negative reaction to the establishment of narrative cinema, regarded film and cinema as a wonderful and valuable scientific and educational tool. Influenced by the German film reform movement, this group of intellectuals agitated in the weekly press, in cinematic trade journals, as well as in political pamphlets, against the spread of sensationalistic film melodramas and for an understanding of cinema as a popular educator. They also enthusiatically promoted the educational use of film/cinema for schools, emphasising the pedagogical value of film in the method of teaching known as object lesson. In this essay, I shall consider the discourse associated with educational cinema, initially a loud and strong voice within the field of modern visual culture in Sweden at the beginning of the twentieth century. A discussion of the film reformer's discourse of educational cinema not only adds to our understanding of an emerging modern visual culture in Sweden, but because the reformers made a clear distinction between non-fiction and fiction film, it also reveals something about the reception and status of non-fiction film and its relation to early narrative cinema.

Educational (non-fiction) film and the institutionalisation of narrative cinema in Sweden

Shortly after the turn of the century, non-fiction film lost its worldwide dominance with the rise of narrative film. Yet, as Charles Musser has pointed out, non-fiction programmes continued to be shown in a wide range of venues in the industrialised nations.[16] In Sweden, the rise of narrative film relegated non-fiction film from its central position in the cinemas, yet non-fiction film continued to be imported, produced and exhibited in the early 1910s. Leif Furhammar writes in his standard history of Swedish cinema that non-fiction shorts and newsreels were incorporated within mainstream cinema programmes. He also attests to an increase in the production of documentary film in the late 1910s and early 1920s, which included feature-length expedition films, and attempts by various cultural institutions to include non-fiction film in their practices.[17]

In a study inspired by Michel Foucault's understanding of social relations and power, Jan Olsson has explored early Swedish narrative cinema as an institutional practice constituted through censorship as a process. Censorship is defined as both productive and

repressive, and is reconstructed as a complex net of discourses relating to cinema. The advent of Swedish narrative cinema is characterised by Olsson as having been a harmonious process in which the government, commercial industry and the press shared ideas and ideals concerning cinema.[18] However, in narrative cinema's nascent period in Sweden, there existed a fourth party who expressed a different version of cinema's value and function than those who were, in the long run, the most powerful. This fourth party consisted mainly of teachers associated with Svenska Pedagogiska Sällskapet (the Swedish Pedagogical Society), who struggled to enforce an understanding of cinema as a pedagogical institution and, as such, suited for non-fictive representations. Non-fiction film was favoured by the teachers and thus their reform efforts supported the continued importation, production and distribution of non-fiction film after the establishment of the narrative feature as the dominant screen interest.

To be fair, a large part of Olsson's article is devoted to these spokesmen and women of educational film, but because their ideas did not prevail in the dominant discourse of cinema, their perspective is largely neglected in Swedish film historiography, much as non-fiction film is generally marginalised. Guided by Olsson's approach to censorship and cinema, I shall explore the discourses surrounding non-fiction film and the idea of cinema as pedagogical institution around the time when the narrative feature was in the process of becoming the predominant screen practice. I propose, to paraphrase Annette Kuhn,[19] that during this transitional period an uncertainty existed regarding the means by which cinema in Sweden was to be understood, valued and regulated, thus allowing for the contesting of ideas concerning cinema to circulate in the public domain. I shall be concerned with the period between the establishment of Statens biografbyrå (the National Board of Film Censors) in 1911 and the institution in 1921 of a unique department, Skolfilmsavdelningen (the School Film Department), by the leading commercial film company AB Svensk Filmindustri, which had as its sole purpose the promotion of film for

educational purposes. Both these events mark key moments in the history of non-fiction film and thus of the institutionalisation of Swedish cinema in general.

In tracing the discourse on educational film and cinema as a pedagogical institution, I shall refer to publications of the teachers who led the film reform movement in Sweden, and who became film censors when Statens biografbyrå was established. I shall follow the rhetoric of Statens biografbyrå, in particular, Gustaf Berg who was appointed the new head of the bureau in 1914, and who later crossed over into the commercial industry and founded Skolfilmsavdelningen, thus providing an infrastructure for educational (non-fiction) film in co-existence with that of narrative cinema. I propose that the two institutions not only co-existed; they were interlocked. To give an indication of the nature and degree of their interdependence, I shall discuss the discourse surrounding the public opening of a feature length non-fiction programme with the title *Bland vildar och vilda djur* (*Among Wild Men and Beasts*, 1921),[20] which was commissioned by Skolfilmsavdelningen and which was its first promotional project.

The film reform movement, Statens Biografbyrå, and the idea of educational cinema

The first public reaction to, and in this case, against the constitution of cinema in Sweden is dated by Elisabeth Liljedahl to 1905.[21] Cinemas were opening in cities throughout the country, establishing a new form of entertainment open to a mass audience. A large part of that audience were children, which was the alleged reason for the initial protests against 'the wretched cinema', as it was called by protesting teachers and parents. A meeting held by Pedagogiska Sällskapet in Stockholm in 1908 initiated the reform campaign that led to the founding of a central censorship authority in 1911. As in earlier protests, it was children's presence in the cinemas that was invoked as the primary motivation for the campaign.[22]

For the leading figures of the cinema reform

movement, Marie-Louise Gagner, Walter Fevrell and Dagmar Waldner, the goal of reform was not merely to regulate the conditions of cinema exhibition and the demoralising content projected on the screens.[23] Their dedicated reform work was also aimed at advancing an understanding of cinema as an educational institution. The kind of films these intellectuals considered to be the most suitable for cinema were *naturbilder*. A direct translation of the term would be 'nature pictures', i.e. pictures of natural locations and phenomena. In contemporary discourse, *naturbilder* were contrasted with fictional films termed *inspelade bilder*, 'recorded pictures'. In the reformers' use of the term the emphasis is on the idea of recording as a construction; fictional pictures were construed, they were artificial, non-natural.

Marie-Louise Gagner offered a descriptive analysis of the repertoire of contemporary cinema at the pedagogical society's meeting in 1908 mentioned above. Olsson describes how the dichotomy between natural pictures and artificial ones, between non-fiction and fiction film, was clearly articulated by Gagner. She described geographical films, and films depicting industrial work, sports and actualities in positive terms. Gagner admitted that some attractions were indeed pleasant ('beautiful' is the adjective she used), though she added that this kind of film could also be disagreeable and ugly. Comical numbers and drama were spoken of in negative terms.[24] Olsson also gives an account of Walter Fevrell's typology of film from 1913 which offers a similar dichotomy between non-fiction and fiction film. Non-fiction film included the categories geography, educational films, sports and actualities. Fiction film included drama and comical numbers as well as adventure and trick films. According to Olsson, Fevrell concluded his analysis with the following evaluation: 'narrative film may have its eligibility, and its popularity, its psychological explanation, nevertheless, film's foremost and finest function ought to be to represent nature's and culture's diversified realities'.[25] In this regard, the film reformers regarded non-fiction film as the true practice of cinema. It can be assumed that when they spoke of cinema as educational practice, they referred exclusively to the screening of non-fiction film to this end. Thus, in promoting educational cinema, they were in fact supporting the continued circulation of non-fiction film at a time when narrative film was overtaking the cinemas.

Both Marie-Louise Gagner and Walter Fevrell (later also the earlier-mentioned Dagmar Waldner) became censorship officials when Statens biografbyrå was established in 1911. Walter Fevrell was appointed head of the authority. The third and last pioneering censor was the medical doctor Jakob Billström. All three had been active in the preceding campaign: Fevrell as chairman of the cinema committee formed by Pedagogiska Sällskapet in 1908, Gagner as leading agitator in the campaign, and Billström as a medical doctor who had given the campaign psycho-medical legitimacy.

The primary purpose of Statens Biografbyrå was to examine all films viable for public screening in order to categorise them for different age groups and to prohibit the screening of pictures 'the showing of which is contrary to law or morality or is otherwise liable to have a brutalising or agitating effect or to cast doubt on the concept of legality'.[26] The English-language title for the authority, the National Board of Film Censors, is misleading because the terms 'censors' and 'censorship' were consciously avoided by its founders as they did not wish to emphasise the prohibitional aspects of the authority's activities. Certainly, prohibition dominated and still dominates its practices, yet the early censors wanted their work to involve productive values and practices, such as the promotion of educational film. In an article in a trade journal from 1913, Fevrell wrote:

> Ever since the work to reform the cinema in our country started, I have claimed that this work should not be reduced to only negative practices, such as censorship, but should also involve strictly positive practices, such as emphasising good pictures and giving prominence to the educational use of cinematography in schools and for the public. That is why our bureau was named the State Cinema Bureau and not the Censorship Bureau, and I have, therefore, as an examiner, worked for the

purpose: that this excellent illustrative and instructive medium be used in education.[27]

The film reformers all shared a similar optimistic and enthusiastic attitude towards film's and cinema's instructive and illustrative capacity. They were influenced by Comenius' pedagogical ideas of teaching by object lesson, and regarded film as an excellent means for realising them. Fevrell and his colleagues objected to the word-based intellectualism of traditional education and, in tune with modern ideas circulating at the time, they believed in an education that moulds a person's physical and emotional character as well as her aesthetic sensibility. In line with these ideas, Fevrell and those of his colleagues who were active in the reform movement championed an educational approach in schools and in a broader, popular context, that was characterised by a confrontation with objects in the world, and with life itself. As an instrument to represent life, cinematography was considered ideal.[28]

Dagmar Waldner published a pamphlet in 1915 in which she gives an introduction to the film reform movement, a survey of various cinematographic techniques as well as numerous examples and suggestions of its possible use in various scientific, cultural, social, educational and judicial practices. In her concluding argument for reform, Waldner sums up the ideal of cinematography as educational practice. In a discussion of the ideal conditions for teaching and learning, she writes:

> Where no emotional elements are present, where life, secret, intriguing life, is missing, interest and delight will abate. Through observation, examination, study, the spirit is trained and the mind is sharpened. Education mediated by the best possible lucidity, perspicuity, graphically presented is, since the days of Comenius, what must be demanded within all forms of education if it is to prove effective. ... Can anyone deny that in film one finds both the example, as well as the accurate, objective, true observation personified which we only have to take into our possession, so that it can, when properly used, become something

self-experienced or at least something which comes close to self-experience. Alas, only that which is newly experienced by the self, that which has assumed form in our consciousness, that which comes closest to reality or in itself is reality can make a lasting psychical impression.[29]

Learning is here described as a process involving psychical impression and spiritual growth. Rather than using logical or rational methods, learning is founded on simulating or recreating an accurate experience of reality. Waldner not only conceived of cinematography as a joyous, educational experience through mediated observation, she also wrote that it was a better apparatus for teaching by object lesson than any other available visual technology, such as photography, illustration, and natural objects, explaining that film can provide a contextualised understanding of an object and, more importantly, convey a sense of movement, life. Cinematography was, moreover, described by Waldner as superior as an educational device to an actual experience of the field because film structures and disciplines perception.[30] Waldner's text can be interpreted as a celebration of cinematography as a modern technological wonder involving its potential to offer the viewer a mediated, emotional and perspicacious experience of 'life, secret intriguing life'.

Educational cinema was not only regarded as relevant for educational institutions such as schools, but also as a more general, public service. The influential social reformer Ellen Key, for instance, wrote in a widely circulated publication in 1914 that cinema could be an ideal place for recreation for the working class, provided that the repertoire became more genteel. Recreation was entertainment which contributed to a person's spiritual or physical resurgence, and could thus be called productive and educational. In this category, Key included the kind of non-fiction film that gives 'genuine and atmospheric pictures of our time; living landscapes and city views with an authentic local touch; pictures of natural scientific objects and processes, as microscopes and experiments show them to us; intimate insights into the animal and vegetal kingdoms'.[31]

Gustaf Berg and Statens Biografbyrå's new rhetoric

As the narrative feature film grew in importance, the rhetoric from the censorship authority changed. In 1914, Walter Fevrell was replaced by Gustaf Berg as head of the authority. Berg did not enter the institution of cinema by way of Pedagogiska Sällskapet, and viewed the industry with different eyes to the members of the film reform movement. Reflecting on his time at the bureau, Berg wrote: 'One can say that from the very beginning, the censorship bureau was ruled by pedagogical objectives, and that it would not have fared well, in the long run, if these had persisted unchallenged.'[32] Jan Olsson's article on early Swedish censorship demonstrates that Berg regarded the future of cinema as interlocked with the narrative feature. Consequently, his ambition as head of Statens Biografbyå was to encourage the film industry to cooperate with the censorship authority in the collective goal of improving and refining the audience's cultural taste as consumers of narrative cinema.[33] Rather than maintaining the discursive dichotomy of non-fiction and fiction film characteristic of the film reformers, a dichotomy which favoured non-fiction film, Berg accepted the idea of cinema as a commercial institution suited for the exhibition of narrative feature films.

The new discursive agenda that this twist involved is exemplified by the theatre critic Bo Bergman. He was the first journalist from a leading newspaper in Sweden to treat a feature film as equivalent to a theatrical drama. Bergman wrote in his review of *Terje Vigen* on 30 January 1917: 'The scientific and pedagogical significance of film is clear. It is its artistic significance which has been and is disputed'.[34] In an attempt to create film art, *Terje Vigen* was produced by one of the leading companies with a considerably higher production value than was common at the time. The success of *Terje Vigen* led to a series of art films produced by the Swedish industry in the years to come.[35]

Despite the industry's attempt to associate cinema with highbrow culture, its status was dubious at the end of the 1910s.[36] In a bill presented in the Swedish parliament in 1919 suggesting a new tax on entertainment, cinema was discussed in the same category as the circus, cabaret and dance hall entertainment. Members of the cinema industry responded with indignant protests and managed to elevate cinema to a slightly more respectable category.[37] Cultural prestige was obviously important to the industry, and because non-fiction film was associated with recreation and education rather than with cheap entertainment (and was therefore highly valued by the social and cultural elite), there was good reason to maintain the production and distribution of non-fiction film. Newsreels and non-fictive shorts were routinely incorporated into the mainstream programme which commonly featured a narrative film.

Skolfilmsavdelningen and public cinema

Gustaf Berg left the State Cinema Bureau in 1918 to join a film company as literary adviser. That same year he founded a society which aspired to create a new forum for non-fiction film. Svenska Kinematografiska Sällskapet (the Swedish Cinematography Society) expressed an interest in film as culture rather than as entertainment. With the term *värdefilm* (valuable film), which the society coined, they referred to 'cinematography in the service of science, education, trade, and other propagandistic or informational functions'.[38] Among the initial members of its board were Walter Fevrell (who had inspired Skolmuseet (the School Museum) to acquire and distribute film and apparatus for screenings in schools, and headed its Skolfilmsavdelning (School Film Department) between 1917 and 1920),[39] Charles Magnusson who was head of AB Svensk Filmindustri, the leading film company in Sweden at the time, and Per Fischier, principal from a secondary school in Stockholm that had integrated film screenings as a regular part of its educational practice.[40]

It is likely that in bringing together advocates of educational film with the head of Svensk Filmindustri, the Swedish Cinematography Society paved the way for Gustaf Berg to establish, in 1921, a special department in

Svensk Filmindustri devoted to the promotion of educational film in schools. The School Film Department was a department which distributed educational film, provided advice and support to schools, arranged screenings, and also engaged in the production of film. Svensk Filmindustri states that the purpose of this department was not economic profit, but to create goodwill for the company, and to lend the institution of cinema cultural legitimacy through associating it with valuable edifying qualities and practices.[41] Only a few months after the School Film Department was established, approximately seventy cinemas in Sweden were engaged in regular screenings for school children.[42]

In promoting the new department, Gustaf Berg wrote frequently and extensively in pedagogical and cinema journals, echoing the film reformers in his arguments for the educational value of film. However, Berg confined his rhetoric on the benefits of educational (non-fiction) film to schools, side-stepping the idea of a popular cinema of education. It appears as if the School Film Department helped to establish a position for school film separate from the popular practice of mainstream cinema. A publication in 1922 signed by Gustaf Berg supports this idea: 'The only link which remains between the cinema and educational film is that educational cinema … should be able to continue to render possible the production of films suitable for pedagogical use, and also that the cinema, outside of its ordinary programmes and activities, and during a transitional period, can offer its machines, premises, and technical knowledge as a service to schools.'[43]

The ties between the public, commercial industry, and educational film were stronger than Berg anticipated or chose to acknowledge. The industry continued to provide films for circulation through the department. Part of the department's film archive was made up of imported non-fiction films, from the United States, Ufa, Gaumont and British Instructional Films. Svensk Filmindustri also included its own non-fiction films in the school film archive, and produced new ones which were incorporated into the archive. Most of these films were intended for both commercial and educational distribution. Before being listed in the school film archive, a film received commercial exhibition and, after a print had been commercially exploited, was re-edited by Svensk Filmindustri to suit an audience of school children.[44] Thus, Skolfilmsavdelningen did not cut short the screening of non-fiction film in public cinemas; it offered a new arena for their circulation. In commercial terms, the organisation offered an extended market for non-fiction film.

Another connection between educational film and public cinema involved the use of cinemas for screening films to parties of school children. In the extract quoted above, Gustaf Berg expressed a hope that schools would invest in technical equipment which would make it possible to screen films in schools.[45] Due to the expense involved and the fire hazard that came with nitrate film, film screenings in schools remained rare for decades to come. Instead, groups of school children continued to attend public cinemas for screenings of primarily non-fiction, educational film programmes.

A case study of the reception in the daily press of a feature length non-fiction film gives an indication of the status of non-fiction film in the public domain at a time when narrative film was predominant on cinema screens. For this purpose I have selected the press response that attended the opening of *Bland vildar och vilda djur* on Monday, 28 November 1921 at Brunkebergsteatern, a cinema situated in the central part of Stockholm. The feature was shot and edited by the cameraman Oscar Olsson, and was the outcome of his film expedition to British East Africa in 1919–20 commissioned by Svensk Filmindustri. It is an example of a non-fiction film that became very popular within the Swedish film industry when the First World War came to an end and extensive travelling became possible again. Film expeditions were sent to different corners of the world by all the major Swedish film companies; in most cases a cameraman accompanied and documented an expedition led by a scientist.[46] *Bland vildar och vilda djur* is especially significant among this wave of expedition films because it was Skolfilmavdelningen's first promotional project. Thus the press reception of the film can be assumed to have established a precedent.

The public screening of *Bland vildar och vilda djur* was marketed by Svensk Filmindustri as a family event, the film having passed the censorship requirements for screening to children. The opening screening at 7 p.m. was sold out with an audience primarily composed of children. On the opening night, Oscar Olsson introduced the film in person, sharing with the audience the technical difficulties involved in shooting the film, and offering a personal reflection on the East African landscape. He added extrafilmic qualities to the evening programme by describing the colours of the landscape and the scorching heat.[47]

Several critics described the film as a series of views compiled into a feature length film programme. For example: 'It is a series of selected pictures from the scientific expedition';[48] '[t]he film company has realised the excellent idea of arranging a family programme composed of a series of pictures from Svensk Filmindustri's African expedition'.[49] Featuring a non-fiction programme was a novelty, and this novelty in Swedish cinema is described not as a feature film, but as a series of films or a selection of pictures arranged into an evening programme. In an anthology describing Svensk Filmindustri's corporate history, its feature length non-fiction films are presented as 'SF Nature Films Which Were Screened as Evening Programmes'[50] confirming that this kind of event was regarded as a screening of a film. Furthermore, it associates the event with the illustrated lecture rather than with entertainment.

The critics in the Stockholm newspapers, a few with national distribution, were unanimously enthusiastic about *Bland vildar och vilda djur*:

> The photographer, Mr. Oscar Olsson, has in an absolutely exceptional way captured on film the wildlife of the plains and the great forests such as baboons, hippopotamus, buffalo, crocodiles, lions, etc. However well books depict animal life, they don't come close to the life-like quality of representation in these films.

There is so much more to learn from watching a splendid film such as this.[51]

> The pictures were exceedingly varied and interesting. A better object lesson concerning exotic animal species in their natural habitat is hard to find, and the scenes showing the life of the Negro tribes were both entertaining and instructive. The film is an excellent complement to natural history museums and geography textbooks.[52]

> The film, which was composed of six acts, was extremely well-shot and exceedingly entertaining. Its instructional value can hardly be overrated. ... This is a film one wishes success, which it will also surely win.[53]

As an evening programme, *Bland vildar och vilda djur* is characterised by the journalists in the context of modern cultural and educational practices, including the museum and the textbook. The reference to the discourse of the textbook perhaps indicates that school children were assumed by the critics to be the film's target audience. In their reviews the critics praise the film for its pedagogical qualities. They describe *Bland vildar och vilda djur* as instructive and life-like, as an excellent object lesson. The journalists also admire the film as entertainment. They observe that it is amusing *and* interesting, entertaining *and* instructive, thus echoing Dagmar Waldner's idea of learning as a joyous, mediated experience of natural objects, indeed, of life. With the reviews of *Bland vildar och vilda djur* the journalists partook of the film reformer's celebration of educational cinema, testifying that Walter Fevrell's, Dagmar Waldner's, and their film reformer colleagues' ideas of educational cinema had made their way into the public discourse of cinema by the early 1920s.

We may conclude that The School Film Department put an end to the film reformer's agitation for film as education since the commercial film industry, in establishing the educational film department, incorporated the reformers' ideas and practices, and provided a home for non-fiction (educational) film which harmonised with the Swedish institution of cinema.

Notes

1. Ellen Strain translates *Erlebnis* as 'subjective experience with the connotation of adventure and event', see Ellen Strain, 'Exotic Bodies, Distant Landscapes: Touristic Viewing and Popularized Anthropology in the Nineteenth Century', *Wide Angle* 18, 2 (April 1996): 70–100, 76.

2. Martin Heidegger, 'The Age of the World Picture', in *The Question Concerning Technology and Other Essays*, trans. William Lovitt (New York: Harper Colophon Books, 1977), 130; quoted in Ellen Strain, 'Exotic Bodies, Distant Landscapes': 77.

3. See, for example, Thomas Elsaesser (ed.), *Early Cinema: Space, Frame, Narrative* (London: BFI Publishing, 1990); Leo Charney and Vanessa R. Schwartz (eds.), *Cinema and the Invention of Modern Life* (Berkeley, Los Angeles, London: University of California Press, 1995); Richard Abel (ed.) *Silent Film* (London: The Athlone Press, 1996); John Fullerton (ed.) *Celebrating 1895: The Centenary of Cinema* (Sydney, London, Montrouge, Rome: John Libbey, 1998) and *Aura. Filmvetenskaplig tidskrift* 4, 2–3 (1998).

4. Tom Gunning, 'The World as Object Lesson: Cinema Audiences, Visual Culture and the St. Louis World's Fair, 1904', *Film History* 6 (1994): 441.

5. Ibid., 425.

6. For a *smörgåsbord* of the scientific research that has been conducted at Naturhistoriska riksmuseet, see Kjell Engström (ed.), *Naturen berättar. Utveckling och forskning vid Naturhistoriska riksmuseet* (Stockholm: Naturhistoriska riksmuseet, 1989).

7. Biological museums exhibiting mounted animals, flora, and fauna, were common throughout the cities of Sweden by the turn of the century. In 1893 a national biological museum was inaugurated in Stockholm which became one of Stockholm's greatest attractions by the end of the nineteenth century, perhaps due to its spectacular display of Nordic scenery and biological specimens in a circular panorama exhibit, see Karen Wonders, 'Kolthoffs museiprogram och dioramatraditionen', in *Natur och illusion. Biologiska museet* (Stockholm: Informationsförlaget, 1993), 34–45, 39. In her dissertation on the habitat diorama (a kind of exhibition which typically contains mounted zoological specimens arranged in a naturalistic foreground that merges into a painted landscape background), Wonders discusses the national traditions which contributed to the emergence and popularity in Sweden of habitat diorama exhibits. These involved the Linnean heritage of emphasising the role of visual observation and communication in science, a hunter-naturalist tradition, and an acute awareness of landscape inspired by the national romantic movement, see Karen Wonders, *Habitat Diorama: Illusions of Wilderness in Museums of Natural History* (Uppsala: Acta Universitatis Upsaliensis, 1993).

8. For a discussion of Skansen's life group displays and the modern gaze, see Mark B. Sandberg, 'Effigy and Narrative: Looking into the Nineteenth-Century Folk Museum', in Leo Charney and Vanessa R. Schwartz, *Cinema and the Invention of Modern Life* (Berkeley, Los Angeles, London: University of California Press, 1995), 320–361.

9. For a description and ideological discussion of the Swedish exhibitions with special reference to the first exhibition in Stockholm in 1897, see Anders Ekström, *Den utställda världen. Stockholmsutställningen 1897 och 1800-talets världsutställningar* (Stockholm: Nordiska museets förlag, 1994).

10. Lisa Cartwright, *Screening the Body: Tracing Medicine's Visual Culture* (Minneapolis, London: University of Minnesota Press, 1995), 3.

11. In *Screening the Body*, Lisa Cartwright traces imaging systems in medical science and reveals how cinema has colluded with other techniques of a scientific visual culture to produce and manage a specifically modern view of the human body.

12. See Alison Griffiths, '"Animated Geography": Early Cinema at the American Museum of Natural History', in John Fullerton (ed.), *Celebrating 1895*, 190–202, and Alison Griffiths, '"Journeys for Those Who Can Not Travel": Promenade Cinema and the Museum Life Group', *Wide Angle* 18, 3 (July 1996): 53–84.

13. See Ellen Strain, op. cit.

14. See Fatimah Tobing Rony, *The Third Eye: Race, Cinema, and Ethnographic Spectacle* (Durham, London: Duke University Press, 1996).

15. See Tom Gunning, 'The World as Object Lesson'; Tom Gunning, 'In Your Face: Physiognomy, Photography, and the Gnostic Mission of Early Film', *Modernism/modernity* 4, 1 (1997): 1–29.

16. Charles Musser, 'Documentary', in Geoffrey Noel-Smith (ed.), *The Oxford History of World Cinema* (Oxford: Oxford University Press, 1996), 86–95.

17. Leif Furhammar, *Långfilmen i Sverige. En historia i tio kapitel* (Stockholm: Förlags AB Wiken, 1991), 54–56, 70–73.

18. Jan Olsson, 'Svart på vitt: film, makt och censur', *Aura. Filmvetenskaplig tidskrift* 1, 1 (1995): 14–46.

19. Annette Kuhn, *Cinema, Censorship and Sexuality, 1905–1925* (London, New York: Routledge, 1988), 1.

20. The English-language title is adopted in accordance with the text list of the film in the Library at Svenska Filminstitutet (the Swedish Film Institute).

21. Elisabeth Liljedahl, *Stumfilmen i Sverige – Kritik och debatt. Hur samtiden värderade den nya konstarten* (Stockholm: Propius förlag, 1975), 110.

22. Jan Olsson, 'Svart på vitt: film, makt och censur': 20–21.

23. The cinema reform movement was part of a larger movement, with equally moral overtones, against popular entertainment such as wax cabinets, pornographic postcards, and literary pulp fiction. Pedagogiska Sällskapet took an active part in this larger, reform movement along with Svenska riksförbundet för sedlig kultur (the National Organisation for Moral Culture), ibid., 28.

24. Marie-Louise Gagner, *Barn och biografföreställningar. Ett föredrag av Marie-Louise Gagner. Jämte ett uttalande av professor B.E. Gadelius* (L. H., 1908); rpt. in Jan Olsson, 'Svart på vitt: film, makt och censur': 31–32.

25. '[D]en episkt berättande filmen kan ha sitt bestämda berättigande, och dess popularitet sin folkpsykologiska förklaring, men icke desto mindre torde väl filmens förnämsta och vackraste uppgift vara att återge naturens och kulturens mångskiftande verklighetsbilder.' Quoted in Jan Olsson, 'Svart på vitt: film, makt och censur': 32.

26. *Film Censorship in Sweden. The National Board of Film Censors.* Pamphlet produced and distributed by Statens biografbyrå.

27. 'Allt sedan arbetet på biografväsendets reformering började i vårt land, har jag yrkat på att detta arbete ej skulle inskränka sig till en del mer negativa åtgärder, till censur, m. m., utan att det skulle omfatta rent positiva anordningar, framhävandet och befodrandet av allt det myckna goda på området samt brukandet av kinematografien i undervisningen och det bildande, fostrande folknöjets tjänst. Det var därför vår byrå fick namnet: Statens Biografbyrå och icke Censurbyrå, och jag har därför såsom granskningsman hela tiden strävat för det målet: tillgodogörandet för undervisningen av detta vår tids ypperliga åskådningsmedel, kinematografien.' Walter Fevrell, 'Ordet fritt. I en aktuell fråga', *Biografen* no. 3 (March 1913): 12.

28. See Elisabeth Liljedahl, *Stumfilmen i Sverige*, 138–145.

29. 'Där inga emotionella faktorer spela in eller tillåtas medverka, där livet, det hemlighetsfulla, intressanta livet saknas, slappas intresse och lust. Genom iakttagelser, granskning, studier skolas anden och skärpes förståndet. Uppfostran härtill förmedlad genom möjligast klar åskådning är också allt sedan Comenius tider den huvudfordran, som måste uppställas för vinnande av effektivitet inom all undervisning. ... Kan någon förneka, att man i filmen finner såväl exempel, som även den noggranna, objektiva, sanna iakttagelsen personifierade, att vi således endast ha att taga den i vår tjänst, för att den, rätt använd, skall bliva till något självupplevat eller åtminstone något som kommer självupplevelsen närmast. Ty endast det självupplevda, aktuella, det som tagit gestalt i vårt medvetande, det som kommer verkligheten närmast eller själv är verklighet förmår göra ett bestående psykiskt intryck.' Dagmar Waldner, *Filmen som kulturfaktor. En inblick i kinematografiens värld* (Stockholm: Ivar Haeggströms bokförlag A. B., 1915), 58.

30. Ibid., 56.

31. '... trogna stämnings- och tidsbilder; levande landskaps- och stadstavlor med äkta lokalfärg; naturvetenskapliga föremål och förlopp, sådana microskop och experiment uppenbara dem; förtroliga inblickar i djur- och växtvärlden.' Ellen Key, *Nöjeskultur* (Stockholm: Laboremus skriftserie, 1914), 9–10; quoted in Elisabeth Liljedahl *Stumfilmen i Sverige*, 129.

32. 'Från allra första början kan man nog säga, att censuren inrättades efter pedagogiska linjer, och det skulle troligen icke ha gått väl i längden, om dessa fått förbli alldeles orubbade.' Gustaf Berg, *Svensk lagstiftning och biografutveckling* (1919); quoted in Jan Olsson, 'Svart på vitt: film, makt och censur': 38.

33. See Jan Olsson, 'Svart på vitt: film, makt och censur': 35–36, 38–40.

34. 'Filmens vetenskapliga och pedagogiska betydelse är klar; det är den konstnärliga betydelsen varom striderna stått och stå.' Bo Bergman, *Dagens Nyheter* (30 January 1917): 6.

35. The period 1917–24 is commonly referred to as the 'golden age' of Swedish cinema due to the many Swedish art films which gained national and international acclaim, see Bo Florin, *Den Nationella Stilen. Studier i den svenska filmens guldålder* (Stockholm: Aura förlag, 1997), 10–12.

36. John Fullerton argues in a study of cinema as milieu in Stockholm, that the attempts to establish cinema as a prestiguous cultural institution in the 1910s was not so much to secure or expand the patronage of the middle-class cinema-goer, but to redefine the experience of cinema-going in order to align the experience with those of the cultural establishment, see John Fullerton, 'Intimate Theatres and Imaginary Scenes: Film Exhibition in Sweden Before 1920', *Film History* 5 (1993): 457–471.

37. Leif Furhammar, *Filmen i Sverige. En historia i tio kapitel* (Stockholm: Förlags AB Wiken, 1991), 69.

38. See unsigned editorial, 'Riktlinjer', *Kinematografisk tidskrift* 1, 1 (1921): 1.

39. The School Museum, though active from 1917 and into the 1920s, never acquired the funds and contacts necessary for widespread and lasting school film activities, see Elisabeth Liljedahl, *Stumfilmen i Sverige*, 142.

40. Ibid., 143.

41. Christian A. Tenow, 'Filmen i skol- och bildningsarbetet', *Svensk Filmindustri tjugofem år* (Stockholm: AB Svensk Filmindustri, 1944), 163.

42. Gustaf Berg, 'Skolan och filmen. Det modernaste åskådningsmedlets tillgodogörande.' *Folkskollärarnas tidning* 2, 47 (1921): 659.

43. 'Det enda samband som består mellan biografen och skolfilmen är det att biografen . . . torde komma att bidraga till att möjliggöra framställandet av filmer, lämpade för undervisningsbruk, samt att biografen vid sidan om sin ordinarie verksamhet kan under en övergångsperiod erbjuda sina 'resurser av installerade maskiner, lokaler och teknisk sakkunskap' till skolornas tjänst.' Gustaf Berg, *Från hembygds- till världsbild* (Stockholm: Zetterlund & Thelanders Boktryckeri A.B., 1922), 16.

44. Christian A. Tenow, 'Filmen i skol- och bildningsarbetet', *Svensk Filmindustri tjugofem år* (Stockholm: AB Svensk Filmindustri, 1944), 164; see also Gustaf Berg, 'Skolan och filmen. Det modernaste åskådningsmedlets tillgodogörande.', *Folkskollärarnas tidning* 2, 47 (1921): 658–659.

45. The reformers also expressed a similar idea; see, for example, Dagmar Waldner, *Filmen som kulturfaktor. En inblick i kinematografiens värld* (Stockholm: Ivar Haeggströms bokförlag A.B., 1915), 57; Walter Fevrell's speech as summarised in 'Biograferna och folkbildningen. Varmt erkännande åt filmmännen.', *Biografbladet* 2, 10 (15 May 1921): 317.

46. Leif Furhammar, *Filmen i Sverige. En historia i tio kapitel* (Stockholm: Förlags AB Wiken, 1991), 70–73.

47. See *Svenska Dagbladet* (29 November 1921); see also *Stockholms-Tidningen* (29 November 1921).

48. *Folkets Dagblad Politiken* (29 November 1921).

49. *Arbetaren* (29 November 1921); see also *Stockholms Dagblad* (29 November 1921) and *Social-Demokraten* (29 November 1921).

50. 'SF-naturfilmer som körts som helaftonsprogram.' This list, covering the period 1921–40, included a total of eight programmes. Six of the programmes were produced in the first half of the 1920s. *Svensk Filmindistri tjugofem år* (Stockholm: AB Svensk Filmindustri, 1944), 274.

51. *Folkets Dagblad Politiken* (29 November 1921).

52. *Stockholms Dagblad* (29 November 1921).

53. *Svenska Dagbladet* (29 November 29 1921).

Seeing the World with Different Eyes, or Seeing Differently: Cinematographic Vision and Turn-of-the-Century Popular Entertainment

John Fullerton

Department of Cinema Studies, Stockholm University, 105 21 Stockholm, Sweden

I open with a series of observations concerning *Visite à Stockholm*, a film in the category of *scènes de plein air* that Pathé Frères shot in Stockholm, and released in 1908.[1] In the third shot of the film, the viewer, thanks to the prosthetic device of the camera, 'ascends' a lift to a belvedere affording panoramic views of the city. The camera, representing the movement announced in an intertitle,[2] tilts upwards to follow a lift-car as it ascends the Katarina Lift (Katarinahissen). Later, the viewer 'walks' through the city[3] as a 'phantom ride', filmed from a tram, transports the viewer along one of the city's busy thoroughfares. A series of matte shots affords us views of various scenes and panoramas of the city, supposedly seen from the Katarina Lift, and we witness the excited response of a woman who, standing on a simulated observation platform, views the city through a pair of binoculars. We also sense the thrill she experiences as she displays to camera a stereoscopic viewer (Fig. 1) with which she, in turn, 'takes a picture' of the city (Fig. 2). Attentive to the ways in which the intertitles equate camera movement with the movement of the viewer through space, while vicariously experiencing the excitement that accompanies the act of viewing the city from an elevated position, we are catapulted into that heady and heterogeneous mix of actuality footage, simulated views and scenes, figurative intertitles, and a concern for reflexivity which we recognise as the hallmarks of a relatively new and popular medium displaying the prosthetic fascination that the cinematographic apparatus represented for the historical spectator. We shall return to a consideration of this type of footage in due course.

I offer here some initial thoughts relating to

Figs. 1 & 2. Frame enlargement, Visite à Stockholm, *1908.*

 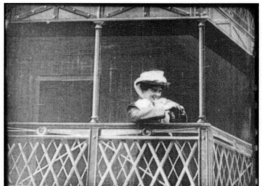

Swedish film in the early years of the twentieth century, and the ways it transformed existing forms of popular entertainment. In particular, I will consider in what ways the *cinématographe* redefined the representational systems associated with the theatrical scene, the panorama, the stereoscope, and the photographic scene. I will argue that this development – at times, so exhilarating – could, on occasion, induce a response in the spectator that might border on momentary sensory overload. Arising from this discussion, and adapting László Moholy-Nagy's notion of *foto-auge*,[4] I will characterise what may be termed the emergence of 'cinematographic vision', a distinct way of representing and giving coherence to the world, a multimedial mode which not only drew upon existing modes of representation, but exploited heterogeneous forms of visual pleasure to promote fascination in the medium.

Cinematographic vision and the theatrical scene

In an article concerned with the development of deep staging in Swedish film,[5] I argued that composition in depth, the defining characteristic in the early 1910s, was predicated on a practice that inscribed the spectator in the visual field, a process which, in the context of institutional practices film shared with theatre, announced priorities different to those of the later classical style. Taking, as my example, the revenge scene staged before a mirror in Konrad Tallroth's *Allt hämnar sig* (Everything takes its revenge),[6] I argued that the mirror, placed perpendicular to the camera and articulating space 'behind' the spectator, obviated the need for reverse-field cutting since the spectator could see action both in front of the camera and, through the device of the mirror, behind camera (Fig. 3). I also observed that the mirror, in drawing attention to the ways in which the framing of pro-filmic space aped that of the camera, inscribed a self-referential discourse. I propose to examine this notion more closely, to consider the ways in which framing was not only central to the process of articulating narrative space, but highlights a number of metafilmic concerns which help characterise the ways in which film redefined the theatrical scene. Central to this process is the way in which film, capitalising upon the *cinématographe*'s single vantage-point perspective, redefined the spectator's relation to narrative space. Important in this context is that the cinematic spectator views a given scene from a single point in space unlike the theatre spectator who views the theatrical scene from the relative position of his or her seat in the auditorium.[7] This difference not only had ramifications for the ways in which the film actor was blocked, but also for the ways in which framing and the inscription of off-frame space became significant concerns as may be observed in the final confrontation scene in *Mysteriet natten till den 25:e* (The mystery of the night before the 25th), a *sensationsfilm* which Georg af Klercker directed for Hasselbladfilm in 1916.[8] In this instance, a large mirror occupies the right-hand third of the shot and reflects space off-frame left and partly behind camera. The scene, preceded by a narrative intertitle,[9] opens as Cony Hoops, a master detective, is alerted at home

Fig. 3 (top left). Frame enlargement, Allt hämnar sig, *1917.*

Figs. 4 (top right), 5 (middle left), 6 (middle right), 7 (bottom left) & 8 (bottom right). Frame enlargement, Mysteriet natten till den 25:e, *1917.*

by the approach of the master criminal, Craig (Fig. 4). The camera frames Hoops' study so that the apex of the set is at extreme rear frame left. A curtained window (and a window visible beyond) occupy the left-hand half of the rear wall framed perpendicular to the camera. A large door, framed by draped curtains, stands reflected in the mirror which occupies the right-hand side of the shot. The mirror is angled towards the camera so that the doorway reflected in it lies behind and to the left

of the camera. Hoops, who has been standing behind the curtain to the left of the window, quickly moves out from behind the curtain and, approaching camera, exits at mid-field frame left. Shortly, he is seen reflected in the mirror as he hides behind one of the curtains surrounding the double doorway leading into the study (Fig. 5). The door opens, and Craig, reflected in the mirror at frame right, enters Hoops' study (Fig. 6). Craig closes the door behind him and, still off-frame left but re-

*Figs. 9 & 10. Frame
enlargement,*
Mysteriet natten
till den 25:e, *1917.*

flected in the mirror at frame right, advances into the study. As Craig's reflection leaves the mirror, he enters the space in front of the camera at foreground left (Fig. 7). Craig goes over to the curtain by the window, and, as he begins to advance towards the table at centre foreground, Craig's reflection and that of Hoops, as he peers out from behind the curtain by the doorway, are reflected in the mirror. As Craig crosses to mid-field centre, Hoops, still reflected in the mirror, comes out from behind the curtain by the doorway with a gun in his hand. He calls to Craig to halt (Fig. 8). Hearing and seeing the detective reflected in the mirror, Craig turns to face off-frame left as Hoops (still off-frame) shakes the revolver a number of times. As Craig raises his arms, Hoops slowly enters the field in front of the camera at foreground left (first the revolver appears (Fig. 9), then Hoops (Fig. 10)). As Hoops comes more clearly into view at foreground left, he reaches out with his left hand to disarm Craig, then, gesturing with the revolver, invites Craig to sit down. As Hoops, still covering Craig with his revolver, sits down in the chair near his desk, Craig sits down in the chair by the mirror. Shortly, the film cuts to an intertitle.[10]

With action reflected in the mirror, the scene is framed so that space to the side of the camera is emphasised. Much of the action takes place either at the edges of the frame or, inasmuch as there are brief moments when both actors are not visible in the shot, at the narrative threshold which the frame and mirror variously constitute. Those interstices in the action which fixed framing and single vantage-point perspective define – when

Hoops, preparing to hide behind the curtain leaves the screen for a moment before his reflection is seen in the mirror, or when Craig, entering the room leaves the virtual space of the mirror before appearing in the field in front of the camera – provide momentary hiatus in the action. The decision to stage the action in one continuous shot rather than alternate shots of Hoops hiding while Craig enters the room promotes spectator anticipation. In other words, fixed camera placement, the long take, a complex, lateral extension of pro-filmic space through the device of the mirror, and the play upon presence and absence of characters in pro-filmic space create suspense. In so doing, the film not only marks a system for articulating narrative space that is different to the conventions of the theatrical scene or classical cinema but, by presenting an absolute and totalising view of the action facilitates a relation to narrative space that would have been almost impossible to achieve in the context of theatrical staging.

In this process, not only does the momentary thrilling of narrative intelligibility hinge upon the presence and absence of characters who, while off-frame, are nonetheless, through the device of the mirror, on-screen, but the potential confusion between the space in front of the camera and the space reflected in the mirror, a confusion which the scale of the mirror promotes, draws attention to the very limits of the frame. In so doing, those moments when a character appears at the threshold of the image – when Hoops's entry is announced by the appearance of the revolver (Fig. 9) – draw attention to the frame if not the picture plane itself. Awareness of the formal proper-

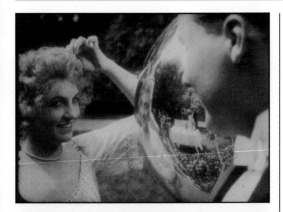

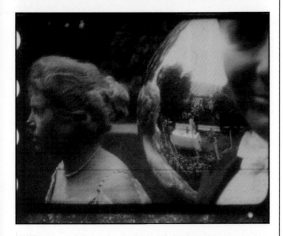

ties of the image is further heightened by those elements which define either strikingly symmetrical compositions (as when Hoops, standing at frame left, disarms Craig at centre foreground, which action is reflected (in reverse field) in the mirror at frame right) or destabilise the composition by emphasising non-centred elements (as when Hoops leaves the space in front of the camera to hide behind

the curtain). This play upon framing and the picture plane, understood not as a modernist response wherein the image 'bares the device' of its construction, but, as Sabine Hake has argued in the context of Wilhelmine cinema, as marking the site where the exigencies of presentation and narration are negotiated,[11] promotes an awareness that Swedish film in the mid-1910s not only constituted a practice which celebrated the act of display, but one which drew attention to the ways in which framing constituted an attraction in its own right. Moreover, inasmuch as the scene evidences the ways in which characters perceive one another through the device of a mirror, the scene also thematises character vision. This concern became common in Swedish film in the late 1910s as the following two brief examples demonstrate. The first, from *Mästerkatten i stövlar* (Puss in Boots), directed by John W. Brunius for Filmindustri AB Skandia in 1918,[12] represents a particularly intense articulation of off-frame, but not necessarily off-screen, space; the second, *Gyurkovicsarna* (The Gyurkovics Family), also directed by Brunius,[13] thematises the issue of vision through representing character fantasy.

The scene from *Mästerkatten i stövlar* occurs during a party where it is expected that the engagement of Jörgen to Rose will be announced. During the party, Kattrup attempts (unsuccessfully it transpires) to make Jörgen declare his love for Pips by kissing her as she serves drinks at a buffet in the garden, which action is observed by Rose reflected in a mirrored ball or garden-glass in a formal part of the garden. The film cuts from a shot of Kattrup kissing Pips to an Extreme Close Shot of the garden-glass at foreground right[14] which evidences considerable depth of field in its reflective surface (Fig. 11). Pips and Kattrup, by the buffet table off-frame left, are reflected in the ball to the right of the centre of the shot. Rose, standing at foreground left, is brushing her hair as she looks at her reflection in the garden-glass. A man in evening dress is talking with her at foreground right.[15] As the guest looks away, the film cuts to an explanatory intertitle before cutting back to the same shot of the garden-glass.[16] With a look of consternation on her face, Rose is looking at the surface of the garden-glass in

Figs. 11–13. Frame enlargement, Mästerkatten i stövlar, *1918.*

Figs. 14 & 15.
Frame
enlargement,
Gyurkovicsarna,
1920.

which she sees, reflected off-frame left, Kat-trup kissing Pips (Fig. 12). She turns away from her guest to look off-frame left (Fig. 13). The film cuts to an Extreme Long Shot of the buffet with Jörgen, responding to Kattrup's advances towards Pips, striding from the shrubbery at foreground left.

By using a convex surface to inscribe off-frame space, the garden-glass constructs an elaborate and distorted pictorial field in which space to the side of the camera is reflected in the surface of the mirrored ball. By articulating off-frame space and inaugurating a discrepancy between spectator knowledge and character knowledge, the surface of the garden-glass not only stages the dramaturgy of narrative perspective, but displays optical distortion as an attraction and raises the issue of vision as a concern in its own right.

This latter issue has been addressed by Bo Florin in his discussion of the use of the lap dissolve in Sjöström's *Körkarlen* (The Phantom Carriage).[17] While Florin argues that the lap dissolve marks ambivalence in the narration regarding the thematisation of space and time, he also notes that the lap dissolve was, on occasion, used as a metonymy for character vision.[18] I will examine this issue in a scene from *Gyurkovicsarna* where Géza encounters Jutka with her mother in one of the streets of the garrison town to which he has been posted.

The scene opens with an Extreme Long Shot as Géza, walking down a street, stops to look at himself in a mirror outside a second-hand shop. The film cuts to a Long Shot of the street with a large framed mirror occupying mid-field centre. Géza is standing in profile at

foreground left. As he turns his back towards camera, the film cuts to an exterior Medium Long Shot of the street taken (as it transpires) from the opposite side of the street. Jutka and her mother, standing at foreground centre, are looking towards off-frame left. They smile, look towards each other then advance towards frame left. After they leave the shot, the film cuts back to Géza,[19] and then cuts once more to a two-shot of Jutka and her mother before cutting back to Géza, this time with a closer framing so that the mirror now occupies almost the whole shot (Fig. 14). Jutka (on the right) and her mother (on the left) are visible at rear left reflected in the left-hand part of the mirror. As the two women laugh and joke, they look at Géza as he (off-frame, behind camera) continues to look in the mirror. The shot is held a moment before a lap dissolve (Fig. 15) figures a subjective shot of Géza as he fantasises standing in an officer's uniform in front of the mirror (Fig. 16). The shot is held a moment before the films cuts to an explanatory intertitle,[20] and then back to Géza looking at the fantasy image of himself. As he looks, a lap dissolve (Fig. 17) figures the return to the non-subjective image of Géza seen earlier in the scene (Fig. 18).

Not only does the shot series evidence an elaborate staging of reflected action in depth, but the lap dissolve, used to denote character fantasy, is staged so that Géza's point of view coincides with the spectator's view of the scene. In so doing, the shot and accompanying explanatory intertitle draw forcefully to attention the way in which the camera figures character fantasy, so constituting the lap dissolve as a metonymy for character vision. To what extent, then, did awareness of the

Fig. 16 (top left), 17 (bottom left) & 18 (right). Frame enlargement, Gyurkovicsarna, 1920.

specifically cinematographic mode of representation which, as we have already observed, could be figured through framing, optical distortion, and the lap dissolve, impinge upon a more general understanding of the metafilmic potential of film discourse? To what extent, in other words, does Swedish film evidence metafilmic concerns not at the diegetic 'level',[21] but in terms of their textual operation? We can begin to answer this question if we examine the ways in which cinematographic vision was inscribed in contemporaneous non-fiction film.

Cinematographic vision, the panorama, and the stereoscopic scene

I will consider three short films which conform either to the genre of the panorama or the 'phantom ride'.[22] The first, with an unknown original title, is catalogued as *Stockholms bilder 1909–10* (Pictures of Stockholm 1909–10) in the collection of Swedish Television;[23] the other two films, in the collection of the Swedish Film Institute, are *Med Jordens Nordligaste Järnväg: en färd Narvik –*

Riksgränsen (On the World's Most Northern Railway: a journey Narvik – Riksgränsen), a tinted print of a film produced by AB Sveafilms, Stockholm in 1911,[24] and *Sveriges Huvudstad* (Sweden's Capital City), a film Pathé produced in 1917.[25] Two of these films – *Stockholms bilder 1909–10* and *Sveriges Huvudstad* – include footage shot from the Katarina Lift.[26] The site of numerous photographic panoramas and postcard views at the turn of the century, Katarina Lift affords insight not only into the ways in which the historical spectator found metafilmic concerns pleasurable, but exemplifies one of the ways in which the *cinématographe* incorporated a variety of visual registers to make film-viewing a multimedial experience. Two points, however, should be made. By the late nineteenth century, the panorama, as a mass medium, had changed dramatically: no longer, as in the case of the photographic panorama[27] (or, indeed, the view that awaited the person who ascended Katarina Lift), did panoramas replicate that type of panoptic vision which, either by virtue of distance and

*Fig. 19. Biologiska
Museet, Stockholm
(detail of
panorama).*

height, or by virtue of sharp focus and per-spectival illusionism (as in painted panoramas) constitute the view as a unified pictorial field. Rather, in its late nineteenth-century manifestation, the panorama, through ever more elaborate 'false terrains', epitomised a more general ambition wherein three-dimensionality was structured, as with stereoscopic photographs and slides, by receding depth cues. Yet one has only to look at the various scenes represented in a panorama such as Biologiska Museet in Stockholm[28] to perceive that the series of receding cues defies optical unity (Fig. 19).[29] Notwithstanding its pedagogic ambition,[30] the 'reality effect' to which the late nineteenth century panorama aspired, emphasises artifice (as was apparent to visitors at the turn of the century)[31] through displaying the optical principles which the panorama and the stereoscope variously employed to animate vision. Aspects of this process may be observed in *Stockholms bilder, 1909–10.*

Just as forward motion through the streets of Stockholm constitutes the principal attraction in the early part of the film, panoramic views, and ascending and descending shots from the lift constitute the principal attraction

in a later part of the film. What is particularly striking is the almost hypnotic fascination that the passage of girders and struts past camera creates as the camera travels up and down the lift. Both the regularity of their appearance and the way in which they variously articulate foreground space, draw the viewer's attention to the extreme foreground of the shot, if not the picture plane itself. What the shot series, then, establishes is a strong dichotomy between, on the one hand, those shots which, in the tradition of the nineteenth-century painted panorama, exhibit extreme depth of field and inscribe the viewer in a discourse associated with a mastery of space (Fig. 20),[32] and those shots which, on the other hand, draw attention to the extreme foreground of the image. Constantly denying the plenitude and mastery of space that the panorama traditionally inscribed, the shots representing the ascent (Fig. 21) and descent of the lift (Fig. 22), structured by the regular passing of the lift gantry, draw attention not only to the lift but the mechanism through which they were recorded. While we should not overemphasise the ways in which the passage of the lift-frame past camera constitutes a metonymy for the cinematographic apparatus with its process of intermittent

registration, by drawing attention to the vehicles – lift *and* camera – through which the views are secured, the various ascents and descents emphasise the mechanical process by which the film was shot, and render that process hypnotic.

By drawing attention to process, *Stockholms bilder* also demonstrates (at least for a viewer familiar with the location) that some of the views, given their, at times, pronounced foreshortening, are not only simulated, but are defined by the optical system of the camera (Fig. 20). In this respect, the film may be understood to stand in a tradition of nineteenth-century illusionism in which the simulated nature of the viewing experience was not only apparent to the viewer, but arose from the optical system that the apparatus employed, be that the stereoscope as commonly used in middle-class domestic entertainment or those peep-hole shows which vied with the introduction of the mutoscope, kinetoscope and *cinématographe* into the public sphere. Just as matte shots, used to simulate key-hole views, telescope views, or microscope views in a number of early film genres, attest to a fascination for surveillance through optical devices, we should not underestimate the extent to which the optical nature of the apparatus would have impinged on the consciousness of the historical spectator, thus qualifying the medium's capacity for stimulating phantasmal reverie. In this context, *Stockholms bilder* not only draws the viewer's attention to the apparatus that was used to register the panoramas, but inscribes optical foreshortening as an attraction in its own right.

Cinematographic vision in the late nineteenth century, however, not only inscribed metafilmic concerns; it also incorporated a number of visual registers which it inherited from earlier technologies of the moving image. Pre-eminent amongst these was the stereoscopic panorama which, operated as a franchised outlet from the same German parent organisation that ran the famous Kaiser Panorama in Berlin, opened in Stockholm in January 1896. Housed in a building near the variety theatre, Svea-Salen in Hamngatan, the Panorama International and, later, the Passage Panorama (which opened in the

Figs. 20–22. Video print, Stockholms bilder, 1909–10.

fashionable arcade, Birger Jarls Passagen, in December 1899) not only presided over the transformation of the stereoscopic slide from domestic sphere to public sphere, but, through the policy of circulating stereoscopic slides between franchise-holders, established a form of distribution which the film industry would later emulate. However, similarities between early film exhibition and the stereoscopic panorama do not end there. Just as the 25-seat Passage Panorama in due course made

Figs. 23 (top left), 24 (bottom left) & 25 (right). Frame enlargement, Med Jordens Nordligaste Järnväg, *1911.*

way for the 75-seat Biograf Varieté when a cinema took over the site of the former panorama in September 1905, so too many of the genres that the stereoscopic panorama instituted were adopted by the early film industry: weekly programmes that might alternate, as in the case of the Panorama International, scenes from Java and Sumatra in one week with scenes from Norway the next,[33] or alternate scenes of topical events with scenes of a sensational nature. We should, therefore, not be surprised to find that film also sought to induce those quasi-stereoscopic pleasures which had attracted audiences to the panorama, so making film-viewing, potentially, a multimedial experience, as *Med Jordens Nordligaste Järnväg: en färd Narvik - Riksgränsen* demonstrates.

A number of strategies are apparent in this example of a 'phantom ride' shot from a moving train. Stereoscopic effects may momentarily be observed when the viewer's eye, accustomed to scanning deep space (i.e. focusing on or near the centre of the image

(Fig. 23)), has to adjust to the sudden appearance of a large detail that appears in the extreme foreground of the shot, as in shot 13 where a large rock outcrop appears from off-frame front left past camera (Fig. 24), before it recedes across the picture space as the train rounds a bend in the track. The effect is induced, in this example, by the fact that the eye has to switch attention rapidly from one area of concentration (on or near the centre of the image) to the extreme periphery of the image, an effect which disappears as soon as the eye adjusts to the new stimulus. A similar effect may also arise from a cut, as is evident at the end of the shot where a panoramic Extreme Long Shot gives ways to a shot in which rocks are seen in the foreground (Fig. 25). What is apparent in this example is the way in which the transition from one shot to the next is central to the production of the effect since it is not reproducible in the single frame, nor does it continue to be generated once the eye adjusts to the movement of the train in the following shot.[34] The effect, there-

fore, can only be understood as one generated by sudden contrast in form since the viewer, scanning a shot with extreme depth of field, has quickly to adjust to new subject matter entering the shot from the extreme foreground. Once the eye adjusts to this new stimulus, the effect is lost. Although studies in the psychology of perception would help us understand such effects better, the longevity of the 'phantom ride' would seem to indicate that not only did this genre continue to induce pleasurable effects well into the 1910s but, as with the stereoscope, one of its principal attractions arises as a consequence of bifocal vision.

While these effects are, in the main, induced involuntarily and may, in cases where the viewer is versed in the tradition of perspectival painting, be predicted with a degree of certainty, other effects are more self-consciously generated as the viewer, submitting to the protocols of the 'phantom ride', gives him- or herself over to the pleasures of viewing. In the first eight shots of the film, a number of quasi-stereoscopic effects may be noted: disjunction (at times extreme) between foreground subjects and mid-field or background space (trees in shots 1 and 4, Figs. 26, 27, telegraph poles in shot 7, Fig. 28); marked changes in perspective occasioned by movement in foreground and mid-field space relative to the background landscape (Figs. 29, 30) due to the movement of the train round a long bend during shot 2 or a gradual re-framing of view in shot 4; or the presence of a series of receding depth cues provided by a post or rail lying by the track, or rocks, mountain scrub, and trees etc. in shot 3 (Fig. 31).

On the one hand, then, film viewing may stage the dramaturgy of animated vision, of involuntary response, in which respect, *Med Jordens Nordligaste Järnväg* exhibits affinity to a panorama like that at Biologiska Museet. On the other hand, and contrary to what Lauren Rabinovitz has observed in her comparison of the 'phantom ride' with the present-day vogue for 'ride films' in the US,[35] in its relatively gentle ordering of stereoscopic effect, the film demonstrates a concern with orchestrating shifting depth cues in a manner not only similar to that of the stereoscope or the late nineteenth-century panorama, but similar to that tradition of staging in depth which Swedish film, in common with European production more generally, instituted in the early 1910s. While I have argued, elsewhere, that staging in depth responded to innovation in theatrical staging with regard to the introduction of the asymmetric set,[36] we may now propose that this development was a more complex process, one which was modelled as much on the stereoscope and panorama as on middle-class theatre. We may observe, therefore, that some films not only simulated those optical effects which the stereoscope and panorama induced, but mobilised a multimedial response in the historical spectator. In such an account, not only do the distinctions between so-called fiction and non-fiction film become less than tenable, but our understanding of the turn-of-the-century viewer as a person switching between a number of visual registers as he or she views a given film privileges a multimedial account of the medium wherein the development of film form responds, in part, to an elaboration of earlier technologies of the moving image.

Figs. 28 (top left), 29 (top right), 30 (bottom left) & 31 (bottom right). Frame enlargement, Med Jordens Nordligaste Järnväg, *1911.*

If what I have said so far may be summarised by the observation that film intensified innovation in theatrical staging while developing a multimedial visuality that drew upon earlier traditions of popular entertainment in the domestic and public spheres, there are two further ways in which we may characterise cinematographic vision. The first involves issues relating to framing and editing, involves issues, in other words, that concern its temporal organisation. The second raises issues relating to the way in which the camera is used, to the ways in which it could, on occasion, be an active prosthesis for the body in motion.

Cinematographic vision, the photographic scene, and temporal organisation

The ways in which cinematographic vision incorporated seemingly non-composed views will be considered by examining *Sveriges Huvudstad* (Sweden's Capital City). This film fragment is unusual in that it presents a series

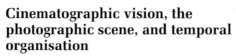

of bird's-eye views from the Katarina Lift that would not be out of place in the photographic work of László Moholy-Nagy or in the work of Dziga Vertov in the 1920s.[37] By invoking Moholy-Nagy, I am not alluding to a proto-modernist consciousness that may be said to have attended the viewing of cinematographic scenes. Rather, I refer to that type of excitement for formal experimentation which Moholy-Nagy and fellow photographers working in the Bauhaus during the 1920s felt for a representational practice that, in framing space, challenged traditional notions of the photographic view predicated on artistic practices which, as Moholy-Nagy argued, had hardly changed since the time of Daguerre. Observing that the photographic camera can '*make visible* existences which cannot be perceived or taken in by our optical instrument, the eye',[38] Moholy-Nagy argued that what became known as 'photo vision' (*foto-auge*) may be observed in scientific photography and in views that seemed 'faulty' or 'accidental' in their framing of space. In this context, Moholy-Nagy cites 'the view from

Figs. 32 & 33.
Frame
enlargement,
Sveriges
Huvudstad, *1917.*

above, from below, the oblique view';[39] views, in other words, that disconcert not only because they compel us to see the world in a way which is seemingly accidental (and which Moholy-Nagy characterised as 'optically true'),[40] but in ways which draw the viewer's attention to the unique capacity of the photographic camera (and, by extension, the cinematographic camera) to envision the world optically. In advocating such practice, Moholy not only referred to a type of practice that would redefine what we understood to be 'photographic', but, in drawing attention to the optical nature of photographic representation, would make the viewer *'see the world with entirely different eyes'*.[41] Openly indebted, then, to the non-traditional or seemingly 'accidental' framing of space, *foto-auge* celebrated that type of framing which was thought to characterise a mechanical and optical mode of representation. While there was nothing specifically new in photographs that framed the world in unusual or seemingly arbitrary ways, what Moholy emphasised was the prosthetic nature of photographic representation. In this respect, photography not only offered an opportunity to see the world liberated from the traditions of the nineteenth-century fine art academy or those of *salon* painting, it drew attention to the prosthetic nature of the medium. Just how different this process could be when applied to the *cinématographe* will be demonstrated by my last extract. For the moment, however, an example that demonstrates the medium's capacity for seeing the world in a different way, for framing arresting images of the world.

Sveriges Huvudstad opens with a fade up from

black on the title card, and then cuts to a second title card: *Stockholm from above. View from the Katarina Lift.*[42] What strikes one immediately on viewing the film is the way in which pro-filmic space is framed, particularly in the opening shots. Not only are the first three shots composed as bird's-eye views, but, given the pronounced vertical tilt of the camera, they accentuate the abstract organisation of the picture plane. This is particularly evident in the first two shots where the camera frames a network of roads and pavements in shot 1 (Fig. 32) or a network of road, pavement and railway lines in shot 2 (Fig. 33). Not only does framing accentuate the graphic organisation of the picture plane, but the angle of view flattens perspective so marking a further formal correspondence between the first three shots. Shots 2 and 3 also evidence a formal homology in terms of the graphic organisation of the image: the road in shot 2 diagonally bisects the shot, so echoing the framing of shot 3 where the angle at which the railway lines are framed is counterbalanced by the motif of the road crossing the railway at right angles in the top right-hand corner of the image (Fig. 34). The film thus inscribes a series of views which are not only visually arresting but, in flattening perspective, draw attention to the way in which optical distortion could be employed as a significant strategy in both fiction and non-fiction film. In this respect, the film also shares a concern for the formal organisation of the picture space in a manner similar to that of the *foto-auge* movement in Germany in the 1920s.[43] The point I wish to make is not that a film such as *Stockholms Huvudstad* directly influenced avant-garde practice but, in organising seemingly non-

Figs. 34–36. Frame
enlargement,
Sveriges
Huvudstad, *1917*.

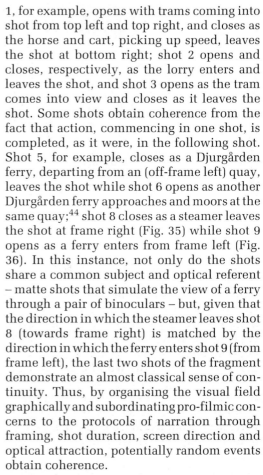

1, for example, opens with trams coming into shot from top left and top right, and closes as the horse and cart, picking up speed, leaves the shot at bottom right; shot 2 opens and closes, respectively, as the lorry enters and leaves the shot, and shot 3 opens as the tram comes into view and closes as it leaves the shot. Some shots obtain coherence from the fact that action, commencing in one shot, is completed, as it were, in the following shot. Shot 5, for example, closes as a Djurgården ferry, departing from an (off-frame left) quay, leaves the shot while shot 6 opens as another Djurgården ferry approaches and moors at the same quay;[44] shot 8 closes as a steamer leaves the shot at frame right (Fig. 35) while shot 9 opens as a ferry enters from frame left (Fig. 36). In this instance, not only do the shots share a common subject and optical referent – matte shots that simulate the view of a ferry through a pair of binoculars – but, given that the direction in which the steamer leaves shot 8 (towards frame right) is matched by the direction in which the ferry enters shot 9 (from frame left), the last two shots of the fragment demonstrate an almost classical sense of continuity. Thus, by organising the visual field graphically and subordinating pro-filmic concerns to the protocols of narration through framing, shot duration, screen direction and optical attraction, potentially random events obtain coherence.

In terms of film discourse, therefore, *Sveriges Huvudstad* demonstrates that framing is all-important in defining shot duration and pro-filmic event. In this context, not only is the camera a veritable prosthesis for the immobile viewer but, by ensuring that everything that comes within its field is subject to a determining logic, editing is constituted as *the* decisive organising principle. In this respect, the film demonstrates that cinematographic vision did not merely represent a new way of seeing the world; it provided a new means for organising spatial and temporal coherence, of structuring events *temporally*. Not only does this indicate a very different understanding of film as material form (that the film strip, rather than pro-filmic space, may be manipulated), but it highlights the ways in which the cognitive processes invested in film discourse become central to

composed views, the film evidences a common interest in redefining the subject matter that was deemed appropriate to photography.

Given that many of the shots also open as an action commences or close as an action concludes, the film also demonstrates that framing determines shot duration which, through editing, ensures that seemingly random action is structured as a series of brief narrative events. Thus, the film not only evidences a concern for formal abstraction, but is organised in terms of pro-filmic event. Shot

Figs. 37 & 38. Frame enlargement, Hantverksmässan i Falkenberg, 1907.

our investigation, which recognition signals concerns that lie outside the scope of this essay.

However, central to my argument in this essay is that film did not merely constitute formal innovation, it stimulated multimedial response. This was the key to its fascination for the historical spectator, its guarantee of success in the short term over rival forms of popular entertainment. While reformulating the ways in which the world could be envisioned, the *cinématographe* also *recast* established forms of visuality. In this respect, cinematographic vision did not merely involve seeing the world from unusual vantage points, it required viewers to *see differently* as the medium placed unprecedented demand upon their capacity to respond to a new mode of representation. Just how different may be judged from the last film I shall discuss; one which demonstrates that the *cinématographe* may not only be an active prosthesis for the body in motion, but one which probably took its viewers, as much as its practitioners, the best part of a generation to assimilate.

Bodies in motion

Hantverksmässan i Falkenberg (Handicraft Fair in Falkenberg) was shot in 1907 in the town of Falkenberg on the west coast of Sweden.[45] With a considerable number of in-camera 'edits' marked by jumps accompanied by flare in the first two shots of the film,[46] and with a number of camera movements which would nowadays be described as zip pans, surviving footage comprises material shot from ten different locations. From this

description, clearly, there is much that warrants discussion, but I shall examine three shots in particular, shots which register pronounced movement in and of pro-filmic space.

Shot 4, comprising 50 frames, with intermittent evidence (as do all the shots discussed here) of considerable chemical decomposition, opens with an upwardly-tilted Long Shot of a man standing on the platform of a delivery cart as, with horse's reins in his hands, he speeds towards frame right (Fig. 37). As the cart crosses the shot, the camera re-frames to the right, blurring both the foreground and background of the shot (Fig. 38). There is a brief jump in the print and, as the man draws rapidly away from camera and the camera re-frames to the right, the man goes momentarily out of shot (Fig. 39) before reappearing as the camera re-frames dramatically to the right. As the man continues down the street, the camera again re-frames to the right, so bringing the man on the cart and signs on the side of a shop (for Algot Nilsson's Velociped business) and on the side of a building (for Falkenbergs-Posten, the local newspaper, print workshop and office) into view (Fig. 40). Finally, the camera re-frames to the right to bring the edge of a building on the right-hand side of the shot into view. The shot is noteworthy for the camera's proximity to dynamic movement at the opening of the shot, the speed of movement within the frame and of the camera as it re-frames right during the course of the shot, and the way in which the driver and cart go momentarily out of shot before they are brought back into view as he rushes down the street.

Figs. 39 (top left),
40 (top right), 41
(bottom left) & 42
(bottom right).
Frame
enlargement,
Hantverksmässan i
Falkenberg, *1907.*

Shot 5, comprising 64 frames, has a similar subject and evidences a similar concern with movement within the frame. A man, seated on a cart with a blanket over his legs, rides towards camera from deep space as he rides down one of the streets bordering the town square (Fig. 41). As he approaches camera, the camera re-frames to the left and tilts up slightly (Fig. 42). As the driver gets closer, the camera begins to re-frame rapidly to the left (Fig. 43). As the cart draws parallel to the camera, the camera continues to re-frame left as it follows the movement of the cart past camera. As the cart begins to pass the camera, the driver and cart (backlit by sunlight), and the brick building at the rear of the shot become very blurred as the camera continues to re-frame left as it follows the movement of the cart to the left (Fig. 44). As the image (with flare) becomes blurred, the film cuts to shot 6 which opens with a similarly blurred view of a stucco building (Fig. 45, lower frame) which comes more clearly into focus as the rate at which the camera re-frames to the left slows down. Shot 5, like the preceding shot,

thus evidences considerable movement at close range to camera, and displays a concern for rapid camera movement to the extent that the shot becomes very blurred, an effect which is exploited in the ensuing shot by similarly blurred camera movement.

Camera movement is even more pronounced in the final shot of the film where, as with the other shots discussed here, in all likelihood attached to the operator's body, the camera records both pro-filmic action and traces its movement through space as it re-frames through approximately 135 degrees during the course of the shot. Comprising 98 frames, shot 10 is inaugurated by a brief and highly mobile re-frame to the right (Figs. 46, 47, 48, the last with momentary optical glare) and is followed by an upwards tilt and re-frame to the right as the principal object in the shot (two horses and a cart) enters, very blurred, at extreme frame right in the fourth frame of the shot (Fig. 49). As horses and cart advance into shot (Fig. 50), their movement is rendered highly dynamic as the camera begins to re-

Figs. 43 (top left), 44 (bottom left), 45 (right). Frame enlargement, Hantverksmässan i Falkenberg, 1907.

frame to the left (Fig. 51) and tilts up as the horses advance towards foreground centre (Fig. 52). As the cart draws parallel with the camera (still with a pronounced upwards tilt Fig. 53), the driver and assistant, high in the frame, cross the shot as the camera re-frames dynamically left and arcs once more through space as it follows the two men through the shot (Fig. 54). As the two men pass the camera, the assistant (the nearer of the two men to camera) looks towards camera as three other people, seated on the cart, enter the shot (Fig. 55). The cart rises and falls in the frame relative to the movement of the camera (Figs. 56, 57) as the latter arcs and re-frames left. The dynamic organisation of movement within and relative to the frame induces a pronounced sensation of bodily movement in the viewer. As the cart draws away (Fig. 58), the camera tilts down momentarily, then tilts up slightly and re-frames left more evenly as the cart, continuing down the street, approaches a shop (Fig. 59). The camera continues to re-frame left until, towards the

end of the shot, it tilts up again, which movement is maintained until the final frame of the shot (Fig. 60).

What is striking in this group of shots is that the camera is so mobile and that its direction of movement, particularly at the opening of the final shot, is dynamically set against movement within the frame. Even when foreground detail is not particularly sharp in focus, the proximity of action to camera, the arcing movement of the latter, the rapid and blurred movement of background detail relative to foreground subject, and the organisation of counter movements within the frame induce a pronounced sense of bodily movement in the viewer. Rarely does the camera pause sufficiently long for the viewer to feel a mastery of pro-filmic space since, in making it difficult to perceive figure-ground relations, many of the shots articulate a more haptic representation of space. Rendered thus highly unstable, the film bears ample testimony to the way in which the camera acts as a prosthesis for the viewer's body in motion.

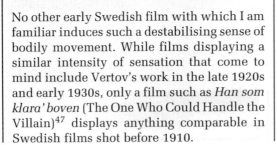

Figs. 46 (top left), 47 (top right), 48 (middle left), 49 (middle right), 50 (bottom left) & 51 (bottom right). Frame enlargement, Hantverksmässan i Falkenberg, 1907.

No other early Swedish film with which I am familiar induces such a destabilising sense of bodily movement. While films displaying a similar intensity of sensation that come to mind include Vertov's work in the late 1920s and early 1930s, only a film such as *Han som klara' boven* (The One Who Could Handle the Villain)[47] displays anything comparable in Swedish films shot before 1910.

In the course of this essay, I have examined some of the ways in which early Swedish film thematised vision and inaugurated metonymies for vision in film discourse. I have considered some of the ways in which Swedish film also elaborated a multimedial register that developed from the theatrical scene, the panorama and the stereoscope. Central to my argument is that these developments did not

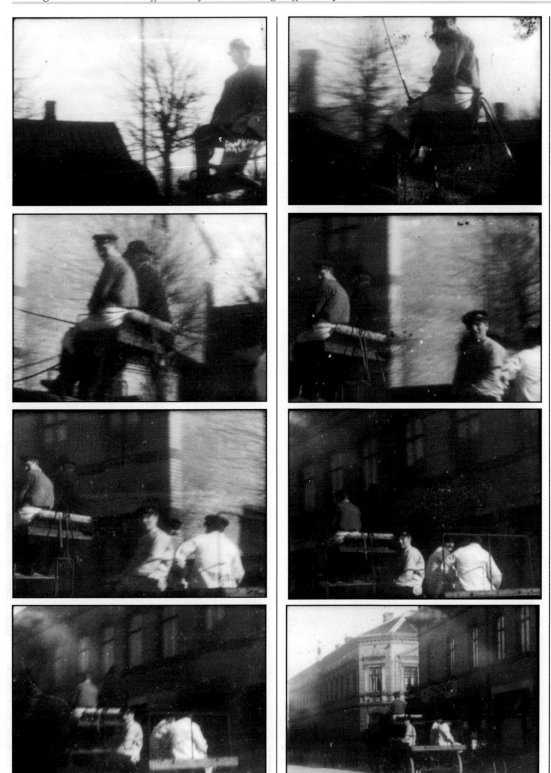

Figs. 52 (top left), 53 (top right), 54 (upper middle left), 55 (upper middle right), 56 (lower middle left,) 57 (lower middle right), 58 (bottom left) & 59 (bottom right). Frame enlargement, Hantverksmässan i Falkenberg, 1907.

merely redefine established modes of representation, they recast visuality so making the turn-of-the-century viewer *see differently*. In this respect, our understanding of the variety of visual registers which viewers were required to mobilise is not only a good deal more complex than we may previously have thought, but demonstrates that fascination in the *cinématographe* intersected with a fascination for the ways in which optical media recast representational strategies, so making viewers see the world with different eyes. In this respect, I have argued that some avant-garde practitioners not only developed this interest in the 1920s in the concept of *foto-auge* (and Vertov's concept of *kino-glaz* would also be relevant in this context), but shared a fascination with practitioners earlier in the century for the ways in which optical technologies provided new means for envisioning the world.

Notes

1. Two versions of this film have been preserved, one in the archives of Swedish Television, the other, at the National Film and Television Archive, London, loc. no. 602611A. I have viewed both versions. The 35mm viewing copy preserved by the NFTVA is the version that was exhibited in Sweden since the order in which the shots appear conforms to the contents of the film as announced in a poster that advertised the exhibition of the film at Stanley-Biografen, Kristinehamn, 28–31 January 1908, see poster printed by Grundels tryckeri, Kristinehamn, 1908, in the collection of the Department of Cinema Studies, Stockholm University. Unless otherwise indicated, 35mm viewing copies held by Svenska Filminstitutet were used to analyse films discussed in this essay.

2. In the German-language version preserved in both archives, the intertitle reads: *Aufstieg zum Aussichtsturm* (A*scent to the observation platform*).

3. The intertitle reads: *Spazierfahrt per Strassenbahn* (*Walk by tramway*).

4. Literally translated as 'photo-eye'.

5. See my essay, 'Contextualising the Innovation of Deep Staging in Swedish Film', in Karel Dibbets and Bert Hogenkamp (eds.), *Film and the First World War* (Amsterdam: Amsterdam University Press, 1995), 86–96.

6. Svenska Biografteatern, premiere 1 October 1917, Kungsholmsbio, Stockholm.

7. For consideration of this issue, see Ben Brewster and Lea Jacobs, *Theatre to Cinema: Stage Pictorialism and the Early Feature Film* (Oxford: Oxford University Press, 1997), 164–187 and their discussion of *Klovnen* (*The Clown*, Nordisk Films Kompagni, Ander Wilhelm Sandberg, 1917), 177–179 which is particularly relevant to my analysis. In the context of a discussion of mirrors in early Russian film, see Yuri Tsivian, 'Portraits, Mirrors, Death: On Some Decadent Clichés in Early Russian Films', *iris* nos. 14–15 (1992): 67–83. For a more general discussion of these issues in relation to staging in depth, see David Bordwell, *On the History of Film Style* (Cambridge, Mass., London: Harvard University Press, 1997), 178–198 in particular.

8. The film was banned from exhibition in Sweden on 14 February 1917, censorship number 17.147.

9. The intertitle reads: *En obehaglig överraskning* (*An unpleasant surprise*).

10. The intertitle reads: *'Ni ursäkter väl, att jag ringer efter polisen.'* (*'I suppose you won't object to my calling the police.'*)

11. See Sabine Hake, 'Self-referentiality in early German cinema', *Cinema Journal* 31, 3 (Spring 1992): 37–55.

12. The film received its premiere 11 November 1918, Sture, Stockholm. The viewing copy preserved at Svenska Filminstitutet currently has flash intertitles.

13. In production at Filmindustri AB Skandia 1919–1920, the film received its premiere 20 September 1920, Sture, Stockholm.

14. In point of fact, an intervening shot of Jörgen, looking at Kattrup and Pips, occurs before the shot of Rose and the mirrored ball, but since the shot of Jörgen functions only to inaugurate narrative misunderstanding on Jörgen's part, it is not important to the articulation of space considered here.

15. His position, framed in Extreme Close Shot, is unusually close to camera, and dominates the right-hand half of the shot so concealing the presence of the camera which would otherwise have been reflected in the surface of the garden-glass. Garden-glasses were popular in ornamental gardens in the early part of the twentieth century, and an example may be seen in the formal herb garden at Skansen, Stockholm.

16. The intertitles reads: *En spegel, som den fiffige Katten inte tagit med i räkningen.* (*A mirror which the cunning cat has not taken into account.*)

17. Bo Florin, *Den nationella stilen: studier i den svenska filmens guldålder* (Stockholm: Aura förlag, 1997), 175–178. *Körkarlen*, Svensk Filmindustri, Victor Sjöström, premiere 1 January 1921, Röda Kvarn, Stockholm. It should also be noted that in discussing shots incorporating a mirror, Florin argues that mirrors were used in *Erotikon* to problematise issues relating to sight and identity, see Florin, 155–158.

18. Ibid., 208–210 and footnote #62, 231 where Florin argues that fades, lap dissolves, matte shots, and double exposure were variously employed to thematise visual perception.

19. Using the same camera set-up as that employed in the previous shot of Géza.

20. The intertitle reads: *Så här tyckte Géza själv han såg ut.* (*This is what Géza thought he looked like.*)

21. As films such as *Vingarne* (Svenska Biografteatern, Mauritz Stiller, premiere 4 September 1916, Röda Kvarn, Stockholm) and *Thomas Graals bästa film* (Svenska Biografteatern, Mauritz Stiller, premiere 13 August 1917, Röda Kvarn, Stockholm) evidence with their film-within-a-film diegetic concerns.

22. For discussion of the panorama, the diorama, and the development of related technologies in the nineteenth century, see Stephan Oettermann, *The Panorama: History of a Mass Medium*, trans. Deborah Lucas Schneider (New York: Zone Books, 1997), but also see Angela Miller, 'The Panorama, the Cinema, and the Emergence of the Spectacular', *Wide Angle* 18, 2 (April 1996): 34–69, and Vanessa R. Schwartz, *Spectacular Realities: Early Mass Culture in Fin-de-Siècle Paris* (Berkeley, Los Angeles, London: University of California Press, 1998), in particular, 149–176.

23. The film is included in the collection of non-fiction films produced by Svensk Filmindustri (SF 2061 A), archive catalogue number 14.387. I have viewed a 16mm print of the film. The box containing the 16mm prints has a latter-day title: *Stockholms bilder 1909–10*. Although this is a generic title denoting the subject matter of the film, I have adopted this title so as to distinguish it from the other non-fiction films of Stockholm I discuss.

24. The viewing copy held by Svenska Filminstitutet has a length of 110 metres and 43 frames (running time at 18 fps of 5 mins 24 secs and 01 frames).

25. The surviving 35mm viewing copy runs for just over 2 minutes. The film, with an original length of 127 metres, was passed for universal exhibition by Statens Biografbyrå on 26 May 1917, censorship number 17.794. The censorship record card indicates that footage from much of the latter part of the film is missing since the viewing copy held at Svenska Filminstutet has a length of 41 metres and 04 frames (running time at 18 fps is 2 mins 00 secs and 02 frames) The film's incompleteness, however, would not appear to qualify my discussion of footage shot from Katarinahissen since the censorship record card indicates that subsequent footage was shot in other locations: *Värtahamnen – Utsikt, Hur åldringar kunna bo, Vad kommer?/Bondetågsgåvan/.*

26. Katarinahissen, a lift at Slussen, gave an unrivalled view over Slussen and Gamla Stan in the heart of Stockholm, and of the commercial centre to the north. With an overall height of 35 metres and with a walkway 151 metres long, Katarinahissen provided easy access from Slussen to Mosebacke Torg on Södermalm, an industrial and residential island to the south of the city. The lift was designed by a former military engineer, Knut Seve Lindmark, and was constructed at a cost of 177,000 kronor by Lecoq & Co., Belgium, Opened to the public on 19 March 1883, the lift carried in its first year of operation no fewer than 1,667,000 persons, i.e. more than six times the population of Stockholm in

the late nineteenth century. Katarinahissen was powered by a steam engine designed by Weeks & Halsey, Brooklyn, and twin lifts, holding a maximum of 12 persons each, rose at the rate of 0.8 metres per second, taking 45 seconds to complete the 34.1 metre ascent. The steam engine was replaced in 1915 by an electric system, and the lift was rebuilt in 1935. This latter construction is still in use, see Henrik Ahnlund (ed.), *Samfundet Sankt Eriks Årsbok, 1964* (Stockholm: P. A. Norstedt, 1964), 102–104; Birger Kock and Fredrik Schütz, 'Knut Lindmark, En pionjär inom kommunikationstekniken', *Dædalus* (Stockholm: Tekniska Museet Årsbok, 1973), 61–85, and Hans Eklund with Holger Blom, Rolf Gerlofson, Björn Hallerdt, Elizabeth Hatz, Tore Hellmark, Ove Köhler, Tord O:sson Nordberg, and Bo Wingren, *Se på Slussen: Från Söderbro till Karusellen – Historik, projekt, framtidsperspektiv* (Stockholm: Stadsmuseet, Kulturhuset, 1981), 15, 17.

27.   See, for example, Ernst Roesler's panorama taken from Mosebacke in 1897, reproduced in *Stockholms panoramor* (Stockholm: Stockholms Stadsmuseum, n.d.), plate 11.

28.   Biologiska Museet (The Biological Museum), founded by Gustaf Kolthoff, a naturalist, hunter, and taxidermist, and housed in a 'fornnordisk' (i.e. national romantic) building designed, in imitation of a medieval Norwegian stave church, by the architect, Agi Lindegren, opened on 11 November 1893. The panorama, more properly, a 'habitat diorama', painted by Bruno Liljefors with the assistance of Gustaf Fjaestad, employs a large canvas with three-dimensional foreground, a two-level viewing platform with interconnecting floors reached by a double spiralled staircase, and overhead natural illumination. The museum was visited by 30,078 people before the end of 1893, and attendance reached an all-time high of 106,490 visitors in 1897 when the museum was included in an international exhibition of art and industry, Allmänna Konst- och Industriutställningen. The popularity of the museum soon waned, however, and in June 1970, the museum was sold to the city of Stockholm who donated it to Skansen. The museum was renovated in 1993, and constitutes one of Europe's few surviving nineteenth-century panoramas, see Karen Wonders, *Habitat Dioramas: Illusions of Wilderness in Museums of Natural History* (Uppsala: Acta Universitatis Upsaliensis. Figura Nova Series 25, 1993), 56–57. Gustaf Kolthoff also established habitat panoramas in Uppsala (1889, no longer extant), Åbo (i.e. Turku, Finland, 1907, extant), Uppsala (1910, no longer extant), and Södertälje (1913, extant). I use the term, 'habitat diorama' to denote a more general form of (popular) scientific exhibition in which natural history specimens are displayed in environments designed to simulate the natural landscape. In this respect, Biologiska Museet confirms the more general tendency towards multiple-sense realism which Vanessa Schwartz has identified in her study of early mass culture in *fin-de-siècle* Paris, see Vanessa R. Schwartz, *Spectacular Realities*, 149–176. I am quite aware that displays such as Biologiska Museet, which allow the spectator a degree of ambulatory freedom, more properly belong to the tradition of nineteenth-century panoramas, but, to distinguish the panorama (a topographically accurate, 360-degree representation of a continuous view or locale) from the habitat diorama is a distinction worth keeping, particularly since the term, 'diorama' had currency at the end of the nineteenth century and was used to designate the panorama at Biologiska Museet.

29.   Of course, the sharply-focused photographic image reproduced here displays an optical unity quite contrary to the experience of standing before the panorama.

30.   A function which Gustaf Kolthoff noted: 'In such a museum, the animals could be shown in their natural Gestalt. The thoughtful viewer would understand why, for example, the crane had such a [sic] elongated body when he saw the birds among the high grass; why brooding birds, their eggs and young ones, had the same colour as the sandy beaches on which they nested, and so on. In other words, a short visit to such a museum would give the viewer a deeper insight into animal life than was possible from a long period of studying books', Gustaf Kolthoff, 'Biologiska muséet i Stockholm', June 1902, unpublished hand-written manuscript, 8–9, Skansen archive, Stockholm, quoted in Wonders, 55.

31.   See the report in *Dagens Nyheter* cited in Wonders, 58.

32.   For discussion of the panopticon and panoptic vision, see Oettermann, *The Panorama*, 39–45, Jonathan Crary, *Techniques of the Observer: On Vision and Modernity in the Nineteenth Century* (Cambridge, Mass., London: The MIT Press, 1990), 17–18, Anne Friedberg, *Window Shopping: Cinema and the Postmodern* (Berkeley, Los Angeles, London: University of California Press, 1993), 17–29, and Angela Miller, 'The Panorama, the Cinema, and the Emergence of the Spectacular': 48–50, 52–55.

33. See programme announcement for the Panorama International in the clippings archive (location 36,155) at Tekniska Museet, Stockholm.

34. Clearly, when observing a stereoscopic effect that is induced by a shot transition, it is important to establish whether the cut between a given shot and the following shot is original or merely the result of later damage to the film. Where analysis seeks to determine the likely response of the historical viewer, clearly this requirement is paramount. In the case of *Med Jordens Nordligaste Järnväg*, we can be certain that the cut in the surviving print is original since the splice, like most of the original splices that occur at the point of a shot transition, comprises a thin white splice visible towards the bottom frame-line and parallel to the bottom frame-line in the last frame of the shot in question. Of the 27 splices used to effect shot transition in the film, 23 examples are almost certainly original (constituted by a thin white splice (although, in a few cases, thin dark splices) visible towards the bottom of the frame-line and parallel to the bottom frame-line, usually occurring in the last frame of the shot preceding the cut); 3 examples are clearly not original (messy splices in all three cases, two of which occur in the first frame of the shot following the cut), and 1 example is impossible to determine.

35. See Lauren Rabinovitz, 'From *Hale's Tours* to *Star Tours*: Virtual Voyages and the Delirium of the Hyper-Real', *iris* no. 25 (Spring 1998): 133–152.

36. See my essay in Karel Dibbets and Bert Hogenkamp (eds.), *Film and the First World War*, 86–96.

37. I have in mind photographs such as Moholy-Nagy's famous *Photograph from above* (1925) or the less well-known gelatin-silver print, *View from Port Transbordeur, Marseilles (Aerial View of Cords Piled in a Circular Pattern)* (1929) reproduced in, respectively, László Moholy-Nagy, *Painting, Photography, Film*, trans. Janet Seligman (London: Lund Humphries, 1969), 93 (originally published as *Malerei, Fotografie, Film*, Volume 8 in the *Bauhausbücher* series, 1925) and Eleanor M. Hight, *Picturing Modernism: Moholy-Nagy and Photography in Weimar Germany* (Cambridge, Mass., London: The MIT Press, 1995), 126. In the interrelation of film with photographic practice, it is interesting to note that the Marseilles location also provided Moholy with inspiration to shoot *Impression vom alten Marseiller Hafen* in 1929, see Jan-Christopher Horak, *Making Images Move: Photographers and Avant-Garde Cinema* (Washington, London: Smithsonian Institution Press, 1997), 119–125. In the context of my discussion, it is also interesting to note that Moholy and Bauhaus photographers were attracted to the distorting properties of the garden-glass, see, in particular, photographs by Georg Muche reproduced in *Painting, Photography, Film*, 100, 103, and plates #228, #230, #229, 170, 147 in Jeannine Fiedler (ed.), *Photography at the Bauhaus* (London: Dirk Nishen Publishing, 1990), and also the title page of the prospectus for the *Film und Foto* exhibition (*Fifo*), Stuttgart, 1929 reproduced in Hight, 204 and Fiedler (ed.), 147. For general discussion of Moholy-Nagy's photographic practice and its relation to the *foto-auge* movement, see Victor Margolin, *The Struggle for Utopia: Rodchenko, Lissitzky, Moholy-Nagy 1917–1946* (Chicago, London: University of Chicago Press, 1997), 124, 135–150, 155–159. In the case of Vertov, I have in mind shots such as those reproduced as frame enlargements in Vlada Petric, *Constructivism in Film: 'The Man with the Movie Camera', a cinematic analysis* (Cambridge, New York, Melbourne: Cambridge University Press, 1987), frame enlargements #64(a), #94, 265, 273, or the (unnumbered) bottom-right frame enlargement reproduced on page 314.

38. Moholy-Nagy, 28, emphasis in the original.

39. Ibid., 28.

40. Ibid., 28.

41. Ibid., 29, emphasis in the original.

42. The Swedish-language intertitle reads: *Stockholm ofvanifrån. Utsikt från Katarinahissen.*

43. For framing of a street similar to that in shot 3, see the photograph by Hans Finsler (plate 54) in *foto-auge/œil et photo/photo-eye* edited by Franz Roh and Jan Tschichold (London: Thames and Hudson, 1974, originally published by Akademischer Verlag Dr. Fritz Wedekind & Co., Stuttgart, 1929).

44. A coherence which is all the more apparent, of course, if the viewer has local knowledge. However, even without this knowledge, the movement of a ferry towards frame right in shot 5 and the approach of a ferry towards frame left in shot 6 creates a certain symmetry.

45. No production details are available.

46. Shot 1, a relatively oblique framing of a procession down a road in the town, includes 6 jumps

accompanied by flare arising from the camera being stopped while filming the scene; shot 2, filmed from a high vantage point overlooking a square, includes 4 jumps accompanied by flare, and shot 3, taken outside a house, includes 1 jump but neither flare, nor original splice nor damage to the print from which the viewing copy was struck is visible. Including a number a short sections of black leader which have been cement-spliced into the viewing copy, the film has a length of 53 metres and 05 frames, and a running time at 18 fps of 2 mins 35 secs and 04 frames.

47. Biorama-Teatern Kristianstad, Frans G. Wiberg, 1908 includes a number of disorienting zip pans but not to the same degree as *Hantverksmässan i Falkenberg*.

Towards Classical Narration? Georg af Klercker in Context

Astrid Söderbergh Widding

Department of Cinema Studies, Stockholm University, 105 21 Stockholm, Sweden

The road to the classical style is sometimes characterised, a bit schematically, as if it were a matter of some evolutionary theory, where development is supposed to have advanced step by step towards a goal as inevitable as it is desirable: the integration of classical narration according to the American paradigm within the frame of different national film cultures. I am not sure, however, that this is a completely relevant model of description. This becomes clear in the analysis of a small Swedish production company such as Hasselblads Fotografiska AB in Gothenburg (hereafter Hasselblad), which produced thirty fiction films in the period from 1915–17, all but one directed by Georg af Klercker.[1] These films have often been characterised as static or as too theatrical when compared with the norm of editing-based narration.

If one considers 1917 as the year when the classical Hollywood style had been generally codified, and if moreover one turns this into a rule for European narration more generally, the fact that Hasselblad and thus also Georg af Klercker lag behind the norm is as indisputable as it is uninteresting. What is interesting, however, is to observe the character of the divergences, such as different stylistic versions and variants, to better describe a development that seems to afford a complex pattern with a network of paths and by-paths. Support for such a critical view may be found in *Theatre and Cinema* by Ben Brewster and Lea Jacobs, who sum up the relation between early cinema and the theatre in a number of ways, and take a sceptical attitude towards the idea of classical narration as the royal road in the history of cinema:

> First, it should be obvious that we reject the view that the history of the cinema is one of a steady emancipation from theatrical models. Early filmmakers had other models (still photography, lantern slides, cartoons, vaudeville acts, short stories, novels), and gave the theatrical ones short shrift if they proved inconvenient. ... On the other hand, when those models became appropriate, as they did with the development of longer films after 1910, theatrical models came back with a force that overwhelmed all of the others except perhaps the literary ones. ... we are reluctant to concede the priority many accounts give to the development of film editing as the 'spine' of film history. ... An editing-centered approach also tends to privilege the American cinema, as most

editing innovations started in the USA and were only slowly adopted in Europe, if at all, in the 1910s. However, the ways the cinema of this decade assimilated features of theatrical pictorialism have complex relations to film editing.[2]

The perspective of Brewster and Jacobs is of utmost interest especially as regards Swedish cinema, where an obvious theatrical inspiration in the composition of the image is generally manifest in many of the productions of the Hasselblad company – a style of composition which seems, moreover, to be closely connected to a more cautious attitude towards adopting classical American editing. In the following, I will focus on the problem of style in Hasselblad films, especially the relation between what is called by Brewster and Jacobs 'the pictorial style in European cinema' and editing.

Models of dissection

Of the characteristics of any particular film style, classical or non-classical, editing is one of the most important, and particularly the methods of cutting into a scene which Barry Salt has called scene dissection.[3] Yuri Tsivian as well as Jan Olsson have pointed out that the term is very appropriate in so far as it suggests a violence towards the long shot, the tableau.[4] Historically, however, it is likely that the quality associated with scene dissection diminished to the same extent that the audience became more familiar with narrative conventions, and that the term thus also to a certain degree loses its relevance. Still, it remains highly relevant in the context of modernity: Giuliana Bruno and Miriam Hansen, among others, have proposed that the cinematic montage principle might be interpreted as an embodiment of modernity's obsession with the fragment or the accidental joining of disparate units. Hansen also more specifically discusses the notion of film as symptom of a crisis in modernity.[5] Dissection (in the concrete sense of the word) and montage here appear as two sides of the same coin, both related to the modern fascination with the body in pieces ('le corps morcélé'), mechanically reconstructed. Both function according to the same principle of dissecting and rejoining, thus in this very connection

constructing a synthesis for the spectator. Dissection also frequently appeared in early trick films as an allegory of the medium.

It is clear that methods of scene dissection have varied between different countries and periods. Barry Salt offers a way of comparing these differences by means of his statistical style analysis. In his analysis of feature films he presents a series of diagrams of different shot scales in films from the period 1915–29. Two Swedish examples are mentioned in this context: *Havsgamar* (1916) by Victor Sjöström, and *Thomas Graals bästa film* (1917) by Mauritz Stiller. The former consists mostly of long shots and about half as many distance shots, whereas the latter appears as considerably more varied, with an alternation between distance shots, long shots, medium shots and medium close ups. Salt notes that *Thomas Graals bästa film* constitutes an exception, while *Havsgamar* represents the 'typical European scale of shot distributions of the time'.[6] In this context, he also refers to Klercker as one of these directors lagging behind. The question, then, is what do these statistics really show? How is shot space constructed in Klercker in relation to other elements?

Mirrors and scenic space

John Fullerton's analysis of the system of representation in early Swedish cinema clearly indicates that an independent spatial system developed during the 1910s in Sweden, which may not only be seen as an off-spring of the cinema of attractions:

> However, while there is much that is attractive in such an argument – one which emphasises the degree to which cinema in the so-called period of transition evidences a common lineage with the cinema of attractions – we can also propose that such a practice may mark a system for articulating space which is different to either the cinema of attractions or classical cinema. In developing this observation, we shall consider further the inscription of off-frame space, particularly as it relates to the way in which gazes towards off-frame space are articulated, for, if *Mysteriet natten till den*

25:e evidences a highly complex articulation of narrative space, other films contemporary with it evidence a use of space which places emphasis upon the diegetic gazes of characters. In being different to those practices which preceded it and different to those which were being developed contemporaneously in the United States, we can begin to define the contours of a system of spatial articulation which is largely autonomous.[7]

In two Hasselblad films, *Kärleken segrar* (1916) and *Mysteriet natten till den 25:e* (1917), Fullerton finds examples of a more developed spatial articulation than in Svenska Bio films from the early 1910s. Through the use of mirrors, pro-filmic space is broadened to include space either beside or behind the camera. *Kärleken segrar* contains a shot where Olga is in her room when she receives a message from the blackmailer Hans Brandt telling her to meet him. She leaves the room to go into the adjacent nursery, where she still remains visible through a mirror. Simultaneously, her husband enters her room without her noticing and finds the message on the floor where she had dropped it. Following Jan Olsson, Fullerton traces this mirror construction back to Frans Lundberg's productions, with *Svartsjuka* (1913) as a main example, and to Danish films from the beginning of the decade, and draws a parallel to a scene from *Ved Fængslets Port* (Nordisk, 1911) directed by August Blom.[8] According to Fullerton, this development occurs in response to the problem of the overloaded foreground plane in shots where actors were framed in *plan américain*, a problem he identified earlier in Sjöström. The two other strategies adopted to counter this problem were, according to Fullerton, the cut-in, which he identifies in *Ringvall på äventyr* (1913), and a more theatrical use of screen space where actors are filmed in long shot or extreme long shot with furniture and other scenic elements in the foreground.[9]

It is striking, though, that the two films chosen as examples are the only two Hasselblad productions containing mirror effects of the kind mentioned. In both cases – which Fullerton also discusses in relation to *Mysteriet natten till den 25:e* – the use of mirrors is also linked to the diegesis. Through the presence and function of mirrors it becomes possible to create suspense in a *mise-en-scène* which does not make use of the usual narrative conventions: different camera set-ups, the use of shot-reverse shot, or the anticipation of a given course of events by the spectator. The mirrors also make it possible to create a certain spatial disorientation: for a moment, the spectator becomes unaware of the difference between mirror space and 'real' screen space. In the scene from the end of *Mysteriet natten till den 25:e* analysed by Fullerton, Cony Hoops prepares himself for the visit of Craig, the villain, by hiding behind the curtain. First, he is seen leaving the room, but then his image returns reflected in the mirror where Craig also appears when he enters the room. Craig then moves off-screen for a moment, before returning to 'normal' screen space.

In addition to this mirror scene, there is also a scene earlier in the film with a secret door behind a mirror, which widens space considerably. After two intertitles that follow in succession ('The tragedy at the Valincourt castle', 'The secret door'), a cut introduces what seems to be an empty space with a corridor leading away from camera. A man appears in this corridor, seemingly walking towards camera. Soon, however, this turns out to be an illusion: the man walks into space to the right in front of the camera and meets his own mirror image. He turns around, examines the mirror, opens it, and then disappears through the secret door which closes again behind him. The shot ends as it began, with the illusory image of the corridor. The secret door figures again later in the same reel (after the intertitle, 'The helpers are let in') which is followed by the same set construction as earlier with the empty corridor. The secret door is opened, and the helpers enter, but this time in the opposite direction, towards camera. An interesting parallel earlier in film history is offered by the secret mirror door in Pathé's *Max Linder contre Nick Winter* (1912). Here, Max is chased by the detectives, and finds refuge in a wardrobe with a mirror door. The detectives enter the room and draw the conclusion that he is hiding in the wardrobe. Thus, leaving the room, they lock the door. Cut to the detectives

in the office where they show the confiscated key and leave again. The next cut leads back to a closer shot of the room with the wardrobe mirror filling the shot. Max is now seen in double exposure, stepping directly out of the mirror. The film cuts to a wider view of the room. As the detectives enter the room and unlock the wardrobe, they find the bird escaped, while at the same time, Max is visible in the mirror from a position off screen. When the disappointed detectives leave the room, he waves mockingly. The function of the mirror is the same in the Linder film as in Klercker. On the diegetic level it reveals a passage, while on the narrative level it also broadens screen space to include space in the foreground of the shot. But while *Max Linder contre Nick Winter* uses an attraction in the manner of a film by Méliès, *Mysteriet natten till den 25:e* uses the device of a mirror in a totally realistic way. This also emphasises its narrative function.

In addition to the mirror in *Kärleken segrar* described above, the film also contains an indirect mirror effect when Olga and her husband, travelling by train, are approaching their country estate where they are about to begin their new life together. At first, he sits opposite her concealing the window, but then moves to sit beside her. Now, her mirror image appears with sharp contours in the window. The husband points to something outside the carriage, which action is followed by a cut to an intertitle ('There lies your new home …') whereupon a pan, motivated by the movement of the train, reveals the stately home. A cut back to the train compartment reveals Olga's image in the window, still as sharp as before. It is easy to interpret these shots as implying the doubleness which characterises her attitude towards her new life, since she has hidden her past from her husband. This is confirmed in the next shot, where Olga is seen strolling in the garden with the stately home in the background of the shot. She picks a flower to put into her décolletage, and thereby takes out a locket which she carries around her neck. After a worried and guilty look about her, she opens the locket and looks at the image of her daughter.

Yuri Tsivian has analysed the use of mirrors in Russian films from 1911 which he charac-

terises as part of the redefinition of screen space from theatrical to cinematic conventions. This strategy functioned in similar ways in painting as a method of integrating off-frame space, in this case, 'behind' the camera. He points to 1912 as the year of the great 'mirror boom' in Russian cinema, and notes that towards the end of the 1910s, the use of mirrors had developed into a visual mannerism, especially in Danish or Russian cinema.[10] Compared with this early frequency, the use of mirrors in Hasselblad's productions seems rather late. However, the thematic device of the mirror – which according to Tsivian appears in Russian cinema about 1914 – is also integrated in Klercker's films, which the above-mentioned examples clearly demonstrate. Among the thematic concerns mentioned by Tsivian in particular – theatre in cinema, death in the mirror, and doublings/duplicity – Hasselblad obviously belongs to the last category. Concerning a Russian film from 1913, *Za Dveriami Gostinoi*, Tsivian writes:

> [M]ultiple exits and entrances from/into the field of the frame as well as from/into the field of the mirror foreground the issue (or, as Victor Shklovski would put it, 'make us sense the forms') of 'image-within-the-image' construction and its cultural connotations.[11]

If the heroine of *Kärleken segrar* leads a double life, which is suggested by the mirror effects in the film, the mirrors in *Mysteriet natten till den 25:e* also function according to the same pattern, in connection with duplicity and fraud. Still, the formal aspects of doubling are equally important, and doubling and duplicity thus join into a stylistic-symbolic unity.

Frames within the frame

With the same ambition to broaden pro-filmic space, split set and split screen effects were also frequently used in early cinema. In his analysis of these devices in the films from Nordisk in the period 1910–16, and of telephone scenes in particular, Jan Olsson notes that in Swedish cinema there are few triptych images of the kind that were so dear to the Danes. However, he offers a few examples of split sets from Sjöström's *Havsgamar* and

from Klercker's *Fången på Karlstens fästning* (both from 1916) related, like most of the triptych images from Nordisk, to telephony.[12]

In *Fången på Karlstens fästning*, the split screen shot is inserted into the context of the chase after Mary Plussman and her kidnapper in the first reel of the film. The split screen shot follows shortly after an intertitle: 'The departure had witnesses, who notify the police'. This is immediately followed by a shot of two women running towards a house and then a shot from the policemen's office, showing a policeman in the company of Doctor Johnson, Mary's fiancé, and some other people. The phone rings, the policeman picks up the receiver, and then turns to Dr Johnson – all filmed in one shot. Then follows the split screen effect which, quite conventional in execution, links a telephone scene split into two with a third image in the middle showing a roof with smoking chimneys and telephone wires crossing the image to link the other two parts of the shot together. To the left, two women (the witnesses), and to the right, the policeman whom they have called from a phone near the port. After this split screen shot, a dissolve leads to a flashback showing the kidnapping. The flashback reproduces exactly the moment of departure, which has already been shown from the perspective of the two women. The sequence then closes with a cut back to the policeman as he puts down the receiver.

As an example of a split screen construction, the shot from *Fången på Karlstens fästning* is rather late, however not excessively; Abel Gance's *Barberousse* from 1916 also contains a triptych image structured according to the same principle, even though the context in this case is much more fateful and eventful. The left part of the shot shows a woman calling, the right part a man answering, and in the middle, a man who has climbed a telephone pole, thus completely corresponding to the convention. The shot is followed by an intertitle decorated with telephone wires that details the content of the call. What is interesting in Klercker's case, however, is that the content of the call is not shown through intertitles, but only figures as visual description. The fact that the use of split screen effect only occurs once in the history

of Hasselblad is not particularly astonishing, given that they were generally rare in Swedish cinema. Jan Olsson has pointed out that in Nordisk films, many split screen effects were planned at the manuscript stage but never realised: 'the directors wanted to avoid a device that had become a cliché'.[13] Also, Klercker's hallmark seems to be to use an undivided screen space where dissections and doublings take place within the general frame rather than through the introduction of several frames. Beside the mirror constructions, Klercker also uses door-frames within the image, often in combination with deep focus cinematography.

Ben Brewster and Lea Jacobs briefly discuss a scene in *Kärleken segrar* from an automobile salesroom, where they claim that the background is sharp whereas the foreground is markedly blurred. The villain is in the background plane, and the unconventional composition could thus be motivated by his reintroduction in the narrative (he has been absent since the beginning of the film). Brewster and Jacobs claim, however, that this does not appear to be the real motive in the film: 'it seems more likely that it was a mistake on the part of the cameraman, but not one felt to be sufficiently serious to warrant reshooting'.[14] They refer to several other examples of partly unfocused compositions, a quite common device in the 1910s (*The Coming of Angelo*, Biograph, 1913; *The Inherited Taint*, Vitagraph, 1911). I disagree, however, with the definition of the foreground in the actual scene, an exterior from a courtyard, as blurred. First, Olga and her husband are standing in the foreground with a perspective opening towards an archway in the background through which the street is clearly visible. Here, Hans Brandt appears as they move slightly to the left, as if to leave room for his entrance. A cut-in on Brandt underlines the importance of his appearance, as he stares intensely at Olga. The next cut returns to the original set-up where Brandt hides behind a car as Olga leaves through the archway. Rather than an ill-concealed photographic mistake, the sequence thus might figure as a clear example of Hasselblad's deep focus composition combined with the use of an extended screen space backwards, a strat-

egy which Brewster and Jacobs analyse in another context.[15]

Roman d'un mousse (Perret, 1913) is mentioned by Barry Salt as a classic example of this kind of deep focus composition combined with the use of space behind; a practice which he claims spread from French cinema to other European film cultures close to France: Denmark, Sweden, Italy.[16] Among early examples, Andréani's *Le Siège de Calais* or August Blom's *Expeditricen*, both from 1911, might be mentioned. *Ingeborg Holm* is a Swedish example from the same year as Perret's film, where frequent use is made of deep focus narration in combination with space behind. Later, it also figured frequently in Hasselblad productions. One example is offered by *Förstadsprästen* (1917) in the scene at General von Tillisch's when the scandalous news of the prostitute Stella's nightly visit to the clergyman has reached the press. In the drawing-room the General, his god-daughter Elin, and his wife who is also the clergyman's mother are placed in different planes of the shot. To the rear of the drawing-room there is another salon, and between these two spaces, the General's son, Ove, wanders. The deep focus is remarkable, and the multi-layered construction of the shot gives the adequate impression of a complex course of events: the different positions in screen space are diegetic as well as purely spatial markers. The consistent use of deep focus narration as well as space behind in Gance's *Mater Dolorosa* (1918) among others also shows that *Förstadsprästen* cannot be considered as exceedingly late.

Two trial scenes

To clarify the differences between Klercker's films for Hasselblad and films from other companies or directors, it is worth comparing a few sequences in detail. I have chosen two sequences staged in a courtroom, one from Sjöström's *Tösen från Stormyrtorpet* and the other from Klercker's *Förstadsprästen*. Both films date from 1917, the year when, according to Bordwell, Staiger and Thompson, the classical style was established. The sequence from *Tösen från Stormyrtorpet* is taken from the second reel, whereas the sequence from *Förstadsprästen* is in the fourth reel. Both,

though, are central to the plot. In *Tösen från Stormyrtorpet* the course of events starts outside the courtroom and continues after the trial. In this context, however, I will only discuss the part that is directly comparable to *Förstadsprästen*: the scene in the courtroom from the beginning of the trial to its end.

Tösen från Stormyrtorpet

1. *Plan américain* framed frontally with the Judge in the middle behind the Judge's bar (which remains off screen), with Per Mårtensson to the left and the girl to the right.

2. Medium shot of the girl from a position close to the Judge.

Text: She knew how severe people were out in the country as soon as marriage was concerned. They knew of no sin worse than the one that she had committed.

3. Medium shot of people in the courtroom.

4. Like 1. The Judge speaks.

Text: 'Does Per Mårtensson maintain that he is not the father of the child?'

5. Medium close shot of the Judge obliquely from the right, from a position close to the girl.

6. Medium shot of Per Mårtensson obliquely from the right – he nods.

Text: 'Are you ready to take your oath?'

7. Like 2. She turns her head to the right with a frightened look.

8. Like 5.

Text: 'Place two fingers on the Holy Bible!'

9. Like 6. He nods again.

10. Like 2. She looks even more frightened.

11. Like 1. Per Mårtensson passes a note to the Judge who reads it.

12. Close up of the Bible which is pushed forward to the left by the Judge. The book is opened with the Judge's hand pointing.

13. Like 1. The Judge points to the open Bible.

Text: Helga knows, that there is no sin more horrible than perjury. It leaves no room for grace or forgiveness. The gates of hell open as the name of the perjurer is mentioned.

14. Like 1. Per Mårtensson is getting ready.

15. Like 2. Helga turns around and looks appealingly at the Judge.

16. *Plan américain* with Per Mårtensson in the middle and the head of the Judge obliquely framed from behind in the right corner of the shot. The Judge's head then leaves the shot.

17. Like 12.

18. Like 2.

19. Like 16.

20. Like 5. The Judge is speaking.

Text: 'I, Per Mårtensson, solemnly swear …'

21. Long shot from an oblique angle behind the Judge. Per Mårtensson to the right.

22. Like 2.

23. Like 16.

24. Medium shot. Per Mårtensson to the right, seen in profile, Helga to the left. She looks horrified.

25. Like 5.

26. Like 2. Helga takes the Bible.

Text: 'He must not take the oath!'

27. Like 21. There is turmoil in the courtroom.

28. Medium shot of people looking off-frame right.

29. Like 5.

30. Like 21. Helga is speaking.

Text: 'He must not commit perjury!'

31. Medium close shot of Helga with the Bible and people in the background. She looks left.

32. Like 5, the Judge now turned to the right.

33. Like 31.

34. *Plan américain*. The table framed obliquely from the left. The Judge to the left, Helga to the right. Three men are watching while she is talking.

Text: 'He is the father of the child, but I don't want him to commit perjury! I want to withdraw the trial!'

35. Like 31.

36. Medium shot of Gudmund Erlandsson smiling, looking left towards camera.

37. Like 5.

Text: The Judge no longer despairs of his people, having found so much charity and fear of God in one of the most insignificant.

38. *Plan américain*. Like 1, but more to the right.

Text: 'The trial is withdrawn!'

39. Medium shot. Per Mårtensson from the perspective of the Judge.

40. Like 5, the Judge now looking left.

41. Like 39.

42. Like 21. Per Mårtensson leaves the shot to the right. The Judge, now to the left, shakes hands with Helga.

Text: 'Thank you!'

43. Medium shot. The Judge, left, continues to shake hands with Helga.

44. Like 28.

45. Like 38. The Judge leaves the shot to the right while other people hug Helga.

46. Like 28, now with the people in the courtroom moving.

47. Long shot with the exit left of centre. People leave. Gudmund makes his way towards the courtroom door.

48. Like 38. Helga alone.

Förstadsprästen

Text: Before the Judge.

1. Long shot obliquely framed behind the Judge to the left and out towards the hall and the people in the courtroom. To the right of the centre of the shot, the accused woman, Stella. To the right of the head of the Judge, the clergyman, seated; between the clergyman and Stella, in the courtroom, Elin von Prangen and Ove von Tillisch can be seen standing. To the right of Stella, her pimp, Starke Rudolf. Stella is speaking.

2. *Plan américain*. Camera moves from the left past the people in the courtroom. The camera then stops for a moment by Elin and Ove. Then the tracking shot continues right until the pimp appears standing on the right of the shot.

3. Medium close shot of the pimp, who is looking right past the camera.

4. *Plan américain* of a man, probably the prosecutor, to the right of the shot, people in the courtroom at the rear. To the left, Elin and Ove.

5. Like 1. The prosecutor is still to the right of the shot. Stella is speaking, addressing the court.

Text: 'The lieutenant there can bear witness that I was with the clergyman that night.'

6. Like 1. Stella turns round and points.

7. Medium shot of Elin and Ove, who is looking distressed.

8. Like 1. The Judge points to Ove who stands up and comes forward. The clergyman also stands up and moves forward towards the centre of the shot. Elin is also standing. Stella has moved a bit to the right. The Judge points to the Bible and Ove reaches out his hand.

9. Close up of the Bible and fingers.

10. Like 1. Ove takes his hand away.

Text: Ove tells, that he has seen Stella coming out from Erik's place.

11. Like 1. Ove is speaking, and the clergyman comes forward and begins to speak. People in the courtroom stand up in agitation, and then the clergyman turns towards the courtroom. In the middle of the shot, Elin can be seen.

12. Medium shot of Elin leaning forward.

13. Like 1. Ove goes back, the Judge turns towards Stella.

Text: 'Can you take your oath upon your explanation?'

14. Like 1. The clergyman moves out left. Stella turns round towards the people in the courtroom.

15. Medium shot of the pimp.

16. Like 1. Stella is at the point of laying her fingers on the Bible. The clergyman stretches out his arm and begins to speak.

Text: 'Do not swear! … I take my accusation back.'

17. Like 1. The clergyman continues to speak. Elin comes between the clergyman and Stella, turns towards the Judge, takes the clergyman's hand, and then turns towards Stella.

Text: 'Swear now, if you dare! Face to face with his future wife.'

18. Like 1. The people in the courtroom stand up again. Stella is once more going to put her fingers on the Bible but stops herself, and turns to the Judge as she speaks.

Text: 'It is his fault. He conjured up the whole story.'

19. Like 1. She turns towards the courtroom and points to the pimp.

20. Like 15. He turns round, on his way out of the courtroom at the left of the shot.

21. Like 1. Stella breaks down. The clergyman and Elin move right and the pimp is brought forward. After a short question from the Judge, the pimp is led away. The

Judge stands up. The clergyman comes forward, thanks the Judge, then turns round and moves to the centre of the shot accompanied by Elin, on her way out of the courtroom, while people in the courtroom shout and clap their hands.

Spatial strategies

Many ingredients are to be found in common in both films: the two scenes afford a fundamental parallel in addition to the theme of trial because the threat of perjury is the focus of narrative interest and functions as a climax in both films. Connected with this concern, both sequences employ a close up of the Bible that is cut into the shot series. The trials conclude in a similar way with the shaking of hands after the prosecuting party, avoiding perjury, wins public acclaim.

At the same time, however, the narration is totally different in the two sequences.[17] The extract from *Tösen från Stormyrtorpet* comprises forty-eight shots with seventeen different framings; *Förstadsprästen* comprises twenty-one shots with eight different framings. The latter shot series is wholly built on what may be termed an establishing shot (here shot 1) which recurs on no fewer than thirteen occasions.[18] This composition is similar to shot 21 in *Tösen från Stormyrtorpet*, but is only used four times.

The static character of the film by Klercker in contrast to the dynamic narration of Sjöström is highlighted in an interesting way by a stylistic parameter established by Barry Salt. In an essay on the comparative stylistics of early German film, Salt details the average shot length (ASL) of a number of European and American productions from this period. As regards Swedish films, he provides the ASL for no less than eight films by Klercker, three by Sjöström, and two each by Stiller and Tallroth, all from the period 1912–17. In this context, comparison with *Förstadsprästen* and *Tösen från Stormyrtorpet* is instructive: *Förstadsprästen* has an ASL of 15.0, *Tösen* only 6.0. The latter value is also the lowest for a Swedish film during this period, with Stiller's *Thomas Graals bästa film* (in second place) having an ASL of 9.0.[19] While Salt's calculations confirm the impression made by

the two scenes, the ASL indicator is, in itself, too mechanical a computation for a complete characterisation of the narrational system of the two films.

In spite of these data, it would oversimplify analysis if one drew the conclusion that Klercker's film provides an example of 'primitive' narration in contrast to the classical one represented by Sjöström. That *Tösen från Stormyrtorpet* has been obviously inspired by American narration was observed by Oscar Hemberg.[20] Also Barry Salt notes that 'In Sweden, Victor Sjöström had all the devices of continuity cinema working properly in *Tösen fra Stormyrtorpet* [sic]', whereas he is of the opinion that Sjöström's other films of the period lag a bit behind from the point of view of style, a conclusion wholly in line with the ASL values he has calculated.[21] The trial scene in many respects also gives a splendid example of the dynamic style of continuity cutting typical of Hollywood. Still, it is completely obvious that Sjöström's narration in the sequence in question does not totally conform to classical norms – and this is not possible to demonstrate by means of the calculations made by Salt. By cutting across the 180-degree line between shot 42 and shot 43, a circular sense of narrative space is constructed (a cut across the line had also been employed shortly before the sequence opens). The editing technique is on the whole similar to that used in a sequence in *Berg-Ejvind och hans hustru* (1918) which Bo Florin has analysed where, in addition to cutting across the line, a multitude of different framings 'encircle' action.[22]

Neither can the narration of Klercker be called outrightly 'primitive' – and this in spite of the tableau-like theatrical framing of narrative space. On one side there is an advanced use of deep focus as elsewhere in Klercker's work. The spectator may on the base of a total view of what happens read the reactions both of Elin and Ove, and of the pimp, but also the simultaneous reactions of the courtroom which Sjöström chose to cut into the shot series as separate shots. On the other hand, this use of deep focus may be seen as founded on an understanding of pictorial space as a space for the spectator's gaze to traverse. An example is the tracking shot which guides the

spectator to an independent investigation of narrative space. Finally the four cut-ins that are used are all well-justified by the directions of the diegetic gazes, and thus accord with classical norms as when Stella turns to look at her pimp. Whereas Sjöström transforms a courtroom drama into an intimate event, an interaction of persons between whom a close connection is established by means of the camera, Klercker insists on the objectivity in the drama which is enacted in front of the Judge's bar.

The trial theme also occurs in a film by Léonce Perret from 1913, *Roman d'un mousse*. The comparison with Perret's film is instructive as this film is strikingly similar to the later Hasselblad productions in setting and in narration. It uses the same kind of somewhat elaborate bourgeois interiors with heavy furniture, curtains and plants, where the events may be acted out on different planes; sometimes the furniture dominates the foreground of the shot whereas the characters are located on a more distant plane in the shot. The narration in *Roman d'un mousse* is also rather static, mainly concentrating on long shots with few variations in framing. Contrary to the film as a whole, however, the trial is filmed from many different perspectives with shot scale varying from distance shot to medium shot. The use of different camera angles also implies that in the scene cuts are made between adjacent parts of the room as well as directly opposing parts, thus creating in the spectator a general sense of the space of the law court. In this way Perret's film differs from Klercker's or Sjöström's trial scenes: if Klerker represents space and the reactions of the court from almost one and the same angle, Sjöström renders the characters and their reactions in such detail that spatial orientation is weakened or totally lost.

In addition to *Roman d'un mousse*, however, another interesting comparison recommends itself, so complicating or possibly diversifying the problem; in all events it demonstrates that it is not possible to establish an unambiguous chronological development with regard to Hasselblad films. I refer to another trial scene in the production of Klercker, one from *Nattens barn* produced in the previous year. Here, shot composition is quite different. The cam-

era has been angled obliquely towards a corner to the left of the centre of the shot. The Judge and his assistants are framed to the left of the shot, by a table alongside the wall. The other characters are seated to the right, with the accusing party well forward in the shot. Violet, the accused, is seated on the diagonal, face towards camera, and by her side the late Count's widow is standing, giving evidence. After a short view of the scene as a whole which ends as the Countess returns to her seat, a medium shot of the Judge fades in frontally, i.e. the shot transition involves both a change in framing and a change in shot scale. This shot, however, is matched with action in the previous shot by means of gesture as the action of moving the Judge's left hand, which commenced in the establishing shot, is concluded in the cut-in. He is fingering the stolen jewels, occupied with formulating the accusation. After a fade out, the shot fades in on Violet in medium close shot, energetically shaking her head as she protests her innocence. The Judge's gaze, to the left, alternates between the necklace and the girl, whereas Violet's gaze seems to be turned inwards although she continues to look straight ahead. The space constructed through the two cut-ins thus implies that the position of the camera in pro-filmic space should be identical, although the camera reframes approximately 90 degrees to the right. This is a clear 'transgression' of the shot reverse-shot system, which is not completely covered by the direction of looks motivating the alternation of shots. Moreover, in the cut-in to Violet, the courtroom has been replaced by a neutral background which gives the shot an emblematic status.

Despite changes in framing, this series of shots functions in the same way as an establishing shot in the classical system followed by an alternation between two parties in conversation. After a fade out, the sequence continues within the initial camera set-up where the Count now gives his testimony at the centre of the shot as a lap dissolve announces a flashback to an earlier part of the film where Violet was looking at the necklace. After a further lap dissolve back to the courtroom the trial is adjourned, and everybody leaves the room except for the public, the Count, and

the widow of the late Count. The framing remains identical. After a flash title, there is a cut to a new angle, now with the camera more to the right and closer to the Judge's bar. Thus, the composition of the shot becomes more focused, the Judge and the widow of the late Count constituting two centres of attention, one on each side of the shot. Violet appeals to the accusing party, obviously in vain, and as the sentence is pronounced, faints and is taken away. The shot fades.

If the trial scene from *Förstadsprästen* takes place in a theatrical space where only the matching of diegetic gazes conforms to American conventions, this earlier example points in another direction. There are clear tendencies towards classical narration in the overall construction of space, through the cutting in to characters at the dramatic peak of the trial – where the accused denies her guilt – as well as in the insertion of a flashback, or the change in framing in the middle of the sequence. On the other hand, the staging seems to point backwards in time, calling to mind a film such as *Foul Play* produced by Vitagraph ten years earlier. After having discovered a mode a narration which corresponds well with classical norms in Stiller's *Alexander den Store* (1917), Jan Olsson proposes a comparison with *Nattens barn*, 'where directions of looks, cut-ins and continuity are not exclusively submitted to classical stylistic norms'.[23] That this is true is evident from the courtroom sequence. However, it is worth analysing another sequence from this film in detail. I have chosen a sequence from the fourth reel, comparable to the one analysed by Olsson, with several contiguous spaces and a number of people involved in the action. The heroes – Count Berkow, detective Tompson, the villain's butler, Dick Holmes, and Violet Holmes – are setting a trap using Violet's necklace as bait. At the beginning of the sequence in question, everybody arrives at the villain's house.

1. Exterior, extreme long shot. A car approaches slowly from the right and moves to the left in a slow tracking shot. Three men jump out, the car goes off-frame left. The three men enter through a gate (tracking left), then go up a flight of steps and enter the house through a porticoed doorway.

2. Interior, hall, long shot. The three men – Count Berkow, the detective, and the butler – enter left. A lamp is lit. The camera frames a corner of the hall at the centre of the shot. To the left, a transparent pearl curtain, to the right a door and a telephone table, and at far right a cloakroom. The three men look around and seem to hear sounds. Berkow and the butler enter the nearby room through the pearl curtain but immediately return. The butler points to the cloakroom.

3. Exterior, extreme long shot. The porticoed doorway seen frontally from the street. A new car approaches from the right. The international criminal Harry Bresky accompanied by his female partner Lucile d'Odette gets out of the car.

4. Like 3. Violet Holmes gets out of the car, which then goes off-frame left. They enter the gate, go up the flight of steps, and enter through the door.

5. Like 2. The butler leaves frame left. The other two remain mid-field centre.

6. Long shot framed perpendicular to the wall with door, telephone, and cloakroom. The detective and Berkow hide in the cloakroom. The butler and Bresky accompanied by the ladies enter from the right. They take off their coats. Bresky shows them in through the curtain to the left.

7. Long shot, dining-room with the camera angled towards a corner of the room. A table occupies the greater part of the room. To the left a double door through which the four people now enter. Three of them sit down and Bresky – in the middle – starts a conversation. The butler disappears right and returns three times, then he leaves through the door to the left. Match on action.

8. Like 6. The butler enters the hall through the curtain, goes up to the cloakroom, and lets out Berkow and the detective. All three then leave the room through the curtain to the left. Match on action.

9. Long shot, office – a room between the hall and the dining-room, with a double door to the dining-room to the left. The butler, Berkow and the detective enter from the right, go to the door and open it.

10. Like 7. The door is opened a little, and the three men look furtively at the three diners.

11.Like 9. They discuss, gesticulate, and close the door. Then the butler opens the door and enters (Berkow and the detective stay back, each on one side of the door).

12.Like 7. The butler enters, approaches Lucile d'Odette and gives her a message.

Flash title: 'Telephone, miss.'[24]

13. Like 7. Berkow is seen furtively looking through the door. D'Odette stands up.

14. Like 9. Berkow and the detective now stand hidden behind the curtains.

15. Like 2. D'Odette enters through the curtain, approaches the telephone. The two men follow, capture her, and lock her in the cloakroom. Berkow returns through the curtain.

16. Long shot almost like 7, but with the table to the right. Bresky stands up talking to Holmes and tries to examine her necklace. Berkow is seen furtively watching through the door, then he locks it.

Flash title: 'Violet pretends to be sick.'

17. Like 16. Bresky takes out a liquid and, believing that Holmes does not notice, pours it into a glass. Berkow can be seen again through the door-chink.

18. Medium shot. Berkow in front of the door which occupies the whole shot. Through the door-chink Bresky is seen pouring something into a glass. Berkow is looking around, frightened.

19. Long shot, almost like 16, but now with the table still more to the right. Bresky is feeling her pulse, and slowly she seems to go numb. She 'wakes up'. Berkow is looking on, she stands up, laughing, and points to the necklace in Bresky's hand.

Flash title: 'The jewels are false!'

20. Like 19, she is laughing. Berkow, the detective, and the butler come rushing in. Bresky pushes Holmes towards them and sneaks away to the door. Match on action.

21. Long shot, almost like 9, but the door further to the left; thus the window behind the white curtains is visible to the right. Bresky enters and locks the door to the dining-room.

22. Like 19, the four who have been locked in try to get out through the locked door.

23. Like 21. Bresky escapes through the window, the door opens, and the pursuers enter.

24. Exterior, extreme long shot. The house can be seen behind a fence with a gate. Bresky, leaving the window, exits through the gate and leaves the frame to the right, followed by the detective and the butler.

25. *Plan américain*, the hall from the front with a telephone in the middle, the door to the left. The cloakroom with d'Odette (locked up) is seen in a split set on the right of the shot. Holmes enters from the left. Berkow makes a phone call.

26. *Plan américain*, the police station. A policeman on the left is answering the telephone (another policeman is sitting to the right, reading a newspaper).

27. Like 25. The phone call is finished, he stands up, puts on his hat, gives Holmes a revolver, and leaves frame right.

28. Like 26. Two policemen enter through the door, are given instructions, and disappear again.

29. Like 3. Berkow comes out of the door, goes out through the gate, and then exits frame right.

This sequence is among the most dramatic in the film, with a comparatively high narrative tempo and frequent changes between heroes and the villains. The twenty-nine shots contain thirteen different framings which create a dynamic narration alternating between various spaces. Most of the shots, however, are long shots or *plan américain*; there is only

one cut-in (to medium shot) on Berkow outside the dining room door (shot 18). Still, this doesn't strike the spectator as a cut-in since there is a change of space: the previous shot presented the dining room. The cut-in is used to create suspense as it shows Berkow's reaction to the attempted poisoning. Compared with the classical sequence in *Alexander den Store* it is once again the distance that is maintained towards action that is striking in Klercker. The way of establishing screen space, the direction of characters' looks, and the use of match on action, however, mostly correspond to the norm. Among the exceptions is a recurring 180-degree cut, between shots 9–14 and shots 16–23. As reverse-field cutting this might be acceptable since the construction of the overall space remains perfectly clear; still, it violates classical rules by crossing the 180-degree line. In the narrative, it is used as a method, albeit unorthodox, to cut to both sides of the action. Another smaller exception to the norm is to be found in the transition between shot 6 and 7: whereas shot 6 shows Bresky and the ladies leaving the hall, in shot 7 the camera is already in the dining-room. The cut suggests that the spaces should be contiguous which, however, is not the case. As an attentive spectator may note, an office is visible in shot 2 through the transparent curtain in the hall, a space that has also been established in a previous episode in the film. In spite of this, shot transition creates a certain spatial ambiguity.

The room shown in cross-section, according to a frequent pattern in the cinema of attractions, is also worth examining. It is clear that the house is empty after Bresky's escape, except for Berkow, Holmes and Lucile d'Odette. The use of cross-section thus facilitates their presence within one single space. The shot is split into three which creates a kind of split set effect not unlike the example from *Fången på Karlstens fästning*, with the telephone in a bright part of the frame in the middle flanked by two darker areas on each side. This may not be very innovative, but it is still efficient from a narrative point of view since within one single frame, it allows the spectator to account for the fact that the villains are capable of anticipating the actions of their opponents. The set-up does not differ

much from its many cinematic predecessors; an example may be found in *Max Linder contre Nick Winter* where it is combined with an attractional mirror effect. The shot in split set in *Havsgamar* discussed by Jan Olsson – where young Anton listens to his father and brother in an adjacent room as they plan a smuggling operation – is structured according to the same pattern.[25]

Comical and classical

Considering the sequences that have so far been analysed, it might seem reasonable to draw the conclusion that Klercker's Hasselblad films constitute a clear alternative to classical narration. Even though there are some classical components, the basic pattern in the films seems to correspond to the cinematic stage as defined by Brewster and Jacobs. However, any such conclusion is defied – somewhat surprisingly – by a close reading of one of the comedies: *Löjtnant Galenpanna* (1917). The opinions of the critics on this film differed somewhat. Where the critics in Gothenburg generally were benevolent, the Stockholm press was more sceptical, in so far as the film was reviewed at all. There was a common denominator, though: many critics mentioned the speed of the action, either positively ('The action runs with the necessary speed')[26] or negatively ('the actors move with an irritating speed').[27] That this remarkably high tempo was not only a question of comedy convention concerning the speed of the action proper or the movement of the actors becomes clear when you study the construction of space in one of the scenes in the film.

The film opens in a restaurant with a long shot where Professor Loris is in the foreground to the left. He is picking up a newspaper. In the background, at the centre of the shot, Lieutenant Juncker can be seen with two accomplices at another table, gesticulating. There is a 180-degree cut to a shot with the Professor in the background to the right, now with his back to camera, and the accomplices centred in the foreground, in medium shot. Each of the two set-ups are cut-in on two further occasions though with varying shot scales: the first shot of the three accomplices shows them in medium shot, the next one in

long shot, while the last one returns to medium shot. The deep focus effect, however, also gives the medium shots a sense of depth. In addition to its spatial mobility, this introduction clearly establishes the two central characters of the film, at the same time suggesting a parallelism between them which is later materialised when Lieutenant Juncker, inspired by the mixed up overcoats later during the same restaurant visit, assumes the temporary identity of the Professor.

Another scene, spatially the most dynamic in the film, takes place in the same restaurant when Juncker goes to have lunch in Loris' place. His accomplices are already there, then Ina Floor, Loris' niece, arrives to whom Juncker has taken a fancy.

1. Medium shot, interior, frontally framed showing Lieutenant Juncker dressed up as Professor Loris, and another man, Clasik, side by side at a restaurant table.

Flash title: 'An interesting conversation.'

2. Like 1.

3. Long shot, at an angle of about 135 degrees from 1, the camera now behind their backs and towards the entrance to the restaurant through which Ina Floor and another lady enter.

4. Like 1.

5. Like 3.

6. Long shot, at an angle of about 180 degrees to the previous shot. The ladies sit down at a table. At the centre in the background the two gentlemen can be seen.

7. Like 1.

Flash title: 'Isn't uncle Josef sitting over there?'

8. *Plan américain* showing the ladies at the table from a new position somewhere between the ladies and the two gentlemen.

9. Like 1.

10. Long shot frontally framed towards the entrance, the ladies sitting at the table

in the centre. Professor Loris enters and walks up to the ladies.

11. Like 1.

Flash title: 'There is something wrong here.'

12. Like 10. Loris sits down with the ladies, his back towards camera.

Flash title: Reel III

13. Like 1. The conversation goes on.

Flash title: 'How can you say that flea from Mississippi is only a common louse?'

14. Like 1. Clasik takes out a little box and opens it.

Flash title: 'I really shudder at that kind of abominable tiny creature!'

15. Like 1. Juncker stands up. Match on action.

16. Long shot from the entrance of the restaurant with the ladies' table in the foreground where Juncker is seen passing the table. He pushes a waiter, Loris reacts by standing up, the two identically-looking men remain, looking at each other for a moment; then Juncker rushes out right, past camera.

17. *Plan américain* from the cloakroom where Juncker is entering; he then disappears through a door rear left.

18. Like 1. Clasik tries to catch the disappearing vermin with a glass.

Flash title: 'So he was saved for the time being.'

19. *Plan américain* in which the entrance door of the restaurant occupies the right part of the shot. Juncker in his normal dress is waving and then disappears past the camera to the left to join his companions.

20. Like 8. Floor is pointing.

Flash title: 'Mummy, look – there is the man who bought the flowers.'

21. Like 8.

22. *Plan américain* showing the Lieuten-

ant's accomplices side by side at a table (this table was shown earlier immediately before shot 1, and is thus located by the spectator to the right, slightly in front of Loris' customary table where Juncker was sitting earlier). Juncker enters from the right in front of the camera, and sits down facing them, to the right.

Flash title: 'Now we have almost succeeded!'

23. Like 1. Loris enters and sits down where Juncker was sitting earlier.

24. Like 11. They are talking. Juncker takes a watch out of his pocket.

Flash title: (The text is missing).

25. Like 22. Juncker glances to the left.

26. Medium close shot showing Floor looking obliquely to the left.

27. Medium shot of Juncker who is looking obliquely to the left.

28. Like 26. Floor is coquetting.

29. Like 22. All three are looking to the left.

30. Like 1. Loris and his companion are quarrelling. They then start to read their newspapers.

31. Like 22. Juncker takes out Loris' diary and shows something to the others.

Flash title: (A page in a note book which earlier has been shown in an intertitle. An index finger follows the fifth line. Insert.) 5. 4 o'clock. Visit Ina Floor, St Allégatan 7, try to get a definite answer.

32. Like 22. One of the accomplices is waving his hand negatively.

33. Like 8. The ladies stand up, Floor first looks embarrassed, slightly to the left, then to the right towards Loris.

34. Like 1.

Förstadsprästen is characterised by a certain flatness of the image despite deep focus, and a limited movement from left to right in the tracking shot. In the sequence analysed from *Nattens barn*, dynamism is created by move-

ment between different spaces, whereas the change of perspective within a single room is only of small relevance. *Löjtnant Galenpanna*, on the contrary, makes use of several spaces – the restaurant interior as well as the cloakroom – but at the same time, establishes several spaces within the set through careful placing of the tables in pro-filmic space and through the exchange of looks between characters. Narration in the sequence analysed here is classical almost without exception; in spite of an elaborate spatial construction, the spectator is easily oriented with regard to plot as well as space. The most recurrent framing is a medium shot of the two men, Clasik and the false Loris, later replaced by the real one: this framing occurs thirteen times, and both introduces and closes the sequence. Apart from this, there are framings from ten other camera set-ups, of which one (shot 22) occurs five times, one (shot 8) three times, and three (shots 3, 10, 26) twice. The most common framings recur throughout the extract. In general, shot transitions respect directions of movement and gaze, with an interesting exception: shots 25–28. Here, Juncker looks left, and Ina, who according to the shot/reverse-shot pattern that the shots obviously are meant to establish, should have looked right, is instead throwing a coquettish glance to the left. However, the general space, being so well established that the spectator is perfectly aware of the positions of the different tables, camouflages this lack of continuity, and thus renders it not confusing. The change between shots in this instance corresponds to the shot/reverse-shot pattern in function, if not in form. The change of shot scale also contributes to this impression, i.e. the medium close up of Ina in shot 26 followed by a medium shot of Juncker in shot 27 confirms that a relation has been established between the two of them. Thus, the sequence makes it clear that Hasselblad productions as a whole may neither be defined as entirely pre-classical, nor as an unambiguous alternative to classical narration.

Clearly, the central interest in Hasselblad's productions is to be found in the *mise-en-scène* rather than the editing. The deployment of comparatively static spatial construction with relatively few changes of camera angle

or shot scale appears as a parallel mode of narration rather than a late occurrence of an earlier mode. This particular mode privileges deep focus compositions and efficient scenographies, i.e. the possibility of using space within rather than between shots.

However, it is also clear that genre hierarchies or prejudices concerning the complexity of certain kinds of stories tend to block the understanding of narrational structures. One might not expect to find the clearest example of classical narration in Hasselblad's productions in *Löjtnant Galenpanna*, which as a story has little complexity; it might also be easy to overlook the fact that the detective story *Mysteriet natten till den 25:e* or the war film *För hem och härd* (1917), produced for military purposes, are among the simplest as regards the general structure of the story. By pointing to the principles of continuity cutting in *Löjtnant Galenpanna*, I hope to have contributed to nuancing the much too schematic dichotomy between montage and *mise-en-scène* in European cinema of the 1910s.

Acknowledgements

The author gratefully acknowledges permission from Aura förlag to publish this essay in *Nordic Explorations*. The essay first appeared (in Swedish) in a longer version in Astrid Söderbergh Widding, *Stumfilm i brytningstid. Stil och berättande i Georg af Klerckers filmer* (Stockholm: Aura förlag, 1998). Translation by the author.

Notes

1. Nineteen of these films are preserved in the Archive of the Swedish Film Institute.
2. Ben Brewster and Lea Jacobs, *Theatre to Cinema* (Oxford: Oxford University Press, 1997), 214.
3. Barry Salt, *Film Style and Technology: History and Analysis*, second edition, (London: Starword, 1992), 328.
4. Yuri Tsivian, *Early Cinema in Russia and Its Cultural Reception* (London, New York: Routledge, 1994) 197; Jan Olsson, 'Förstorade attraktioner, klassiska närbilder: anteckningar kring ett gränssnitt', *Aura. Filmvetenskaplig tidskrift* 2, 1–2 (1996): 37.
5. Giuliana Bruno, *Streetwalking On A Ruined Map: Cultural Theory and the City Films of Elvira Notari* (Princeton: Princeton University Press, 1993), 272 f; Miriam Bratu Hansen, 'America, Paris, The Alps: Kracauer (and Benjamin) on Cinema and Modernity', in Leo Charney and Vanessa R Schwartz (eds.), *Cinema and The Invention of Modern Life* (Berkeley, Los Angeles, London: University of California Press, 1995), 365 f.
6. Salt, 144–146.
7. John Andrew Fullerton, 'The Development of a System of Representation in Swedish Film, 1912–1920', Doctoral Dissertation, University of East Anglia, 1994, 226.
8. Ibid, 219–220; Jan Olsson, *Sensationer från en bakgård* (Stockholm, Lund: Symposion bokförlag, 1988), 276.
9. Fullerton, 223–225.
10. Yuri Tsivian, 'Portraits, Mirrors, Death: On Some Decadent Clichés in Early Russian Films', *iris* 14–15 (1992): 70–71.
11. Ibid., 74.
12. Olsson, 'Förstorade attraktioner, klassiska närbilder', 54–55.
13. Ibid., 54.
14. Brewster and Jacobs, 172.
15. See also David Bordwell, *On The History of Film Style* (Cambridge, Mass, London: Harvard University
16. Press, 1997), particularly the chapter 'Exceptionally Exact Perceptions: On Staging in Depth', 158–205. Bordwell here draws the conclusion that the duality between a tableau aesthetics prior to 1918 followed by a classical narration·based on editing must be revised, considering the richness of the *mise-en-scène* during the transitional period 1909–1920.
17. Salt, 102 ff. Salt also refers to Ben Brewster in this context, who also with Lea Jacobs discusses space behind in *Theatre to Cinema*.
18. The sequence from *Tösen från Stormyrtorpet* lasts about 3 minutes, whereas the duration of the *Förstadsprästen* sequence is 4 minutes.
19. In a review of *Förstadsprästen*, the critic noted that '[t]here is something disappointing about this

film like all Hasselblad films, namely that the interiors are too small and too theatrical', *Dagens Nyheter*, 4 September 1914. This probably refers to the long shot narration that makes the shot scale comparatively small.

20. Barry Salt, 'Early German Film: The Stylistics in Comparative Context', in Thomas Elsaesser (ed.), *A Second Life: German Cinema's First Decades* (Amsterdam: Amsterdam University Press, 1995), 225.

21. *Aftonbladet*, 30 December 1917. See also Jan Olsson, 'Förstorade attraktioner, klassiska närbilder', 59–60, 78.

22. Salt, *Film Style and Technology*, 146.

23. Bo Florin, *Den nationella stilen, Studier i den svenska filmens guldålder* (Stockholm: Aura förlag, 1997), 72–78.

24. Olsson, 'Förstorade attraktioner, klassiska närbilder', 79 n. 29.

    Nattens barn has not been restored. The texts are taken from *Nattens barn*, Script IV, SFI Archive.

25. Olsson, 'Förstorade attraktioner, klassiska närbilder', 54.

26. *Göteborgs Handels- och Sjöfartstidning*, 11 September 1917.

27. *Social-Demokraten*, 18 September 1917.

'A Dangerous Pledge': Victor Sjöström's Unknown Masterpiece, *Mästerman*

Tom Gunning

Department of Art History, University of Chicago, Chicago, Illinois 60637, USA

A rediscovery

Mästerman (Masterman, 1920) stands as one of the neglected masterworks of world cinema. While I may claim I do not believe in the 'masterpiece theory of film history' (because history chugs on whether films are great or not), I must confess I do believe, as a film viewer at least, in great films, and that film history helps us appreciate them (and that their importance has to do partly with their place in that history). This essay, therefore, will verge from an analysis as a film historian to a pure appreciation of a great film. Readers unsympathetic with one viewpoint or the other are welcome to take the part that works for them and leave the rest.

Recent historiography has made great strides in re-exploring the largely unknown first two decades of film history, the 1910s and pre-1910s, unearthing a series of previously uncelebrated directors and films: Franz Hofer and Max Mack in Germany, Yevgeni Bauer in Russia, and to some degree, Georg af Klercker in Sweden. Most of these remain names known only to a few scholars (especially af Klercker, and the recent work of Astrid Söderbergh Widding makes an important contribution to rectifying this) which need

wider appreciation. But works by well-known directors also need to be rediscovered, not only because acknowledged masterpieces must be dusted off and re-examined, but because certain films which were thrust into the shadows by previous historians may now attract more attention than the masterworks which previously overshadowed them. In my opinion nothing will ever dethrone *Berg-Ejvind och hans hustru* (The Outlaw and his Wife; French title: Les Proscrits, 1918) as Sjöström's masterpiece and one of the key works in the history of cinema. However, while my admiration for *Intolerance*, *The Birth of a Nation*, or *Broken Blossoms* remains undiminished, I in some sense find *True Heart Susie* to be Griffith's most remarkable film. *Mästerman* is, I believe, Sjöström's *True Heart Susie*, and, like that film, one of the most delicately conceived of masterworks, expanding film language in its portrayal of desire and renunciation.

Mästerman has been eclipsed, I would claim, twice. At the time of its release it was not received as a major film, probably because of its unpretentious length and plot. I would also imagine that as a collaboration with Hjalmar Bergman, based on an unpublished short story, the film fell into the shadow cast by the

spectacular Bergman/Sjöström film which followed it, *Vem Dömer* (Love's Crucible; French title: L'Epreuve du Feu, 1922). This extraordinary tale of passion and courage in Renaissance Florence was undoubtedly the film that brought Sjöström (and Bergman) a Hollywood contract with MGM.[1] Ironically, now it is also a neglected film, in spite of its great critical success at the time, with the more nationalistic adaptations from Selma Lagerlöf undoubtedly seeming more conducive to founding a tradition of Swedish cinema rooted in national themes and images. *Vem Dömer* (which I also consider a masterpiece of a very different sort from *Mästerman*) was intended very much as an international film with broad appeal (although I would claim it remains resolutely Swedish and Protestant in its narrative logic).

In contemporary historiography, *Mästerman* remains eclipsed by a film which preceded it slightly, Sjöström's *Körkarlen* (The Phantom Carriage; French title: La Charrette Fantôme, 1921). I don't intend to deny the beauty and quality of this famous film but, frankly, I think it is unfortunate that for many people, if they know one silent Swedish film, this is the one. Its representative role is unfortunate, I believe, and in this respect I find it inferior to such Sjöström films as *Berg-Ejvind*, *Ingmarssönerna* (The Sons of Ingmar; French title: La Voix des Ancêstres, 1919), or *Mästerman*. The other films portray more complex characters, and their engagement with film language, while less flamboyant than the superimpositions and flashbacks of *Körkarlen* are, to my mind, actually more elegant and innovative. *Körkarlen* wears its technique on its sleeve, overtly displays its unquestionable mastery of superimposition and complex narrative structure. *Mästerman* tucks its mastery of editing and composition up its sleeve, so to speak, and refuses to make explicit its character's psychology as does the rather too-pat allegory offered by *Körkarlen*. *Mästerman* remains a film ripe for rediscovery, and I hope in this essay to offer both an appreciation and a sketch of its place in film history. It is very much as an individual film – with a powerful narrative and unforgettable characterisations – that *Mästerman* claims its rank as a great film. Although I want very much to deal with

Mästerman as an individual work, with it own unity and aesthetic logic, first I want to place it within the evolution of Sjöström's style and the unique position that I believe Swedish cinema occupied at the end of the 1910s.

From single shot to scenic breakdown

Swedish silent cinema was discovered by the French in the 1910s who celebrated it as no other critics or historians have. Knocked out by *Berg-Ejvind* and Stiller's *Herr Arnes Pengar* (Sir Arne's Treasure; French title: Le Trésor d'Arne, 1919), Louis Delluc initiated a tradition which approached Swedish cinema through the lens of landscape romanticism, a tradition followed and made canonical by the general and comparative histories of silent film written by Georges Sadoul and Jean Mitry in the post-war era. Even the most recent important history of world cinema, Kristin Thompson and David Bordwell's *Film History: An Introduction* while adding Klercker to the discussion of Swedish cinema, still privileges the landscape tradition, and stresses the use of flashbacks and superimpositions found in Sjöström's *Körkarlen*.[2] There is a reason for this unbroken continuity. There can be no question that the use of landscape in silent Swedish cinema represents one of the glories of film history. The sense of sky and river, sea shore and meadow, snow banks and frozen lakes, mountain and forest introduced in the Swedish cinema of the 1910s inaugurates a dialogue between cinema and nature, man and the cosmos, that offered a legacy to filmmakers around the world. But as filmmakers of the 1910s, and as inheritors (and in some sense maintainers) also of the tradition of Danish cinema, Swedish cinema of the 1910s needs also to be examined in terms of the key stylistic issue of that era: the construction of scenographic space – both its construction through blocking and composition within single shots, and the development of the breakdown of scenic space through editing, an approach that Thompson and Bordwell initiate in their treatment of Sjöström's intricate work within the single shot in the farewell sequence of *Ingeborg Holm* (1913).[3]

During the 1910s one can recognise a broad opposition between two styles of filmmaking: one style more dependent on editing, another

Figs. 1 & 2. Frame enlargement, Ingeborg Holm, 1913. [Courtesy of John Fullerton.]

style working more within single long-lasting shots. We must avoid posing this opposition as a restatement of the opposition in the early silent era described by film historians such as Sadoul and Mitry between a cinematic film style based on flexibility of space, and a less cinematic style rooted in 'theatricality', the fixed viewpoint of 'le monsieur d'orchestra'.[4] Mitry and Sadoul's concept of theatricality has limited relevance to the 1910s as the research, especially of Yuri Tsivian, has demonstrated. Tsivian shows that cinematic composition within a single shot in the films of Bauer and Hofer worked in an extremely different and even oppositional manner to theatrical staging by emphasising the unique optics of the camera's single viewpoint.[5] In discussing these two styles I am neither saying (with Bazin) that one is more realistic than the other, nor (with Mitry) that one is more cinematic. On the contrary, these are both carefully arranged cinematic styles, but their opposition and, in fact, interaction forged a flexible and expressive film language in the 1910s and early 1920s.

This opposition balances a greater reliance on editing (shorter shots, more intercutting, and the increased breakdown of single scenes into shots of different angles and sizes) against the resources of the single shot (longer takes, more developed acting sequences, pictorial effects, deep staging, careful blocking of actors to conceal and reveal each other, deep sets carefully lit). Frequently this contrast is posed as an opposition between American and European styles.[6] Broadly conceived, the opposition works; Griffith, Sennett and Ince (united in the 1910s for a while at Triangle Pictures) clearly contrast with the style of

most Danish, Italian and French films of the early 1910s. But there are exceptions: Tourneur and DeMille in the US seem to blend the two styles, while certain French comedies and Italian thrillers use shorter and more numerous shots to convey action and gags. By the later 1910s, Swedish cinema seems to be a place where the convergence of the two styles was especially strong, providing a seed bed for styles of narration that emerged in the 1920s.

Danish cinema, especially that of August Blom and Benjamin Christensen, represents one of the high points of the single shot school. The sequence of the son's theft from his mother in *Ved Fængslets Port* (At the Prison Gates, 1911) stands as both a masterpiece of this style and an illustration of its distance from theatricality, as Yuri Tsivian has demonstrated.[7] The single shot style called for great ingenuity in the precision of framing, the use of mirrors, the sub-dividing of the scenic space by the borders of the film frame or by doorways within the set, and the layered blocking of characters. Sjöström had mastered this method to perfection, as *Ingeborg Holm* demonstrates. Most key scenes in that film take place within a single carefully staged shot. The scenes of Holm's loss and later regaining of her sanity employ finely calibrated performances within carefully staged deep spaces. The final scene of the film (when Ingeborg's son comes to the poor house, learns of his mother's madness, observes her distracted behaviour, and then finally makes contact with her and seems to restore her sanity) takes place in one shot.[8] Although its temporal compression may beggar our understanding of therapeutic processes, Sjöström's

Figs. 3 & 4. Frame enlargement, Ingeborg Holm, 1913. [Courtesy of John Fullerton.]

careful staging makes the scene work as drama articulated through entrances and exits, use of different layers of the shot, careful blocking, and clearly modulated performances. This final shot of the film takes about four minutes.

In the office of the poor house a large desk dominates the foreground right at which the warden of the institution sits. In the background left there is a doorway through which an attendant enters, speaks to the warden, announces the son, and exits. The son then enters and comes to the warden's desk, sitting in a chair to the left of it (Fig. 1). They talk, the warden informing the son of his mother's insanity. The son stands up in alarm, grabbing the warden to make him affirm his statement, then sits back down, looking at the floor in despair. He speaks to the warden, jumping up again for emphasis. The warden rises and goes to the door at the back (a slight jump occurs in the print at this point, possibly indicating a place a title was spliced in or a camera stoppage).[9] The warden re-enters. The son rises and they stand speaking together, moving to the right.

The second dramatic section of the shot begins with the entrance from the doorway of Ingeborg Holm and her nurse. Sjöström has carefully staged this dramatic moment by having the two men move to the right, balancing the entrance of the two women in background left, framed by the door (Fig. 2). Further, the two men turn their backs to the camera, both looking towards the doorway, drawing our attention to it. The son moves a bit, so that, as his mother enters, his figure has blocked out that of the warden. Holm comes forward, cradling the piece of wood that in her delirium she believes is her lost

child (Fig. 3). The warden crosses to speak to the nurse. Sjöström now has arranged the shot so that mother and son occupy the foreground, Ingeborg on left, son on right, these key figures framing the nurse and warden in the midground. Ingeborg moves towards her son blocking out the nurse and warden. The son crosses behind her to speak to the warden and nurse. They agree to leave and walk through the door in the background, leaving mother and son alone. The son closes the door. Ingeborg has moved to the foreground right.

Entrances and exits break the scene into a variety of different sorts of encounters with different moods. The blocking of actors prepared these transitions through carefully balanced choreography of dominant and less important characters. Attention shifts naturally throughout the scene. Now, with only two characters in the foreground, a choreography of gestures and smaller movement takes over, bringing us into a more intimate proximics. The son comes forwards from the door standing in the foreground left and takes out the photo he has preserved of his mother. He holds it out to her (Fig. 4). Ingeborg turns to him, not quite understanding. The son urges her to examine the photo, coming closer to her. Ingeborg's eyes widen as she looks at him, then looks at the photo he holds. She drops the piece of wood that embodied both her loss and her madness, her hands now hanging empty at the end of her arms. She looks at her son again, and raises her hands to stroke his face. She takes his hand holding the photo, looks at the image, and hangs her head sadly. Her son now kneels before her (Fig. 5, the opposite of his repeated hopping to his feet in his conversation with the war-

Fig. 5 (left). Frame enlargement, Ingeborg Holm, 1913. [Courtesy of John Fullerton.]

Fig. 6 (right). Frame enlargement, Tösen från Stormyrtorpet, 1917. [Courtesy of John Fullerton.]

den). He places his head against her breast, she cradles him and kisses his head. Then she staggers a bit and sits down on the desk chair, continuing to embrace her son as she smiles, and the shot and the film ends.

The shot maintains our involvement, shifts our attention, modifies our relation to characters, and takes us through the stages of an emotional breakthrough as carefully as any edited sequence. But four years later in his 1917 adaptation of Selma Lagerlöf's *Tösen från Stormyrtorpet* (The Girl from the Marsh Croft; French title: La Fille de la Torbière, 1917), Sjöström has accommodated a scenic breakdown for dramatic reasons. The courtroom scene in which Helga's parents have sued her former employer and seducer, Per Mårtensson, to force him to acknowledge the child he fathered, takes up only slightly more screen time than the approximately four minutes of the last shot of *Ingeborg Holm*, but consists of more than *sixty* shots (exclusive of intertitles). Courtroom sequences, because of the extent of the space involved and the importance of isolating a number of characters, as well as the inherent need for reaction shots, frequently stimulated scenic breakdown of some complexity in films not using intra-scene editing to any great extent (such as DeMille's 1915 *The Cheat* or Perret's 1914 *Roman d'un mousse*). But Sjöström goes far beyond these earlier films, using editing and close-ups to dramatise the key moment of this scene when Per puts his fingers on the Bible to swear that he is not the father of Helga's child, and Helga, terrified that he is condemning his soul to eternal damnation, snatches away the Bible.

This section of the courtroom sequence is broken down as follows (I begin with the eleventh shot of the sequence):

11. Medium Long Shot facing Judge's desk, with Per standing before him on the left of the frame, Helga standing on the right of the Judge, who is seated in the middle a bit towards the right.

Title: 'Does Per Mårtensson stand by his claim that he is not father to the child?'[10]

12. Close-up of Judge looking off left.

13. Medium Close-up of Per Mårtensson looking off left to Judge (a mismatch of eyelines).

Title: 'Are you prepared to swear an oath to that effect?'[11]

14. Medium Close-up of Helga as she looks right toward Per (correct eyeline match, Fig. 6), astonished he will commit perjury.

15. Close-up of Judge looking off left (same mismatch as before, Fig. 7).

Title: 'Place two fingers on the Holy Scriptures!'[12]

16. Per, framed as in shot 13, nods that he will.

17. Helga, framed as in shot 12, looks off to right toward Per, still astonished by his lie.

18. Medium Shot as in shot 11 of Judge's desk shot from the front, with Per standing on left, Helga on the right, the Judge in middle (Fig. 8). Per hands him an affidavit which the Judge reads.

Figs. 7 (top left), 8 (top right), 9 (bottom left) & 10 (bottom right). Frame enlargement, Tösen från Stormyrtorpet, 1917. [Courtesy of John Fullerton.]

19. Close-up of Judge's hand pushing the Bible forward (Fig. 9), opening and pointing to it. This is a truly dramatic close-up of an action and an object, balancing the facial close-ups which dominate the scene.

20. Medium Shot of Per, Helga and Judge framed as before as Judge points.

Title: Helga knows that there is no sin as terrible as perjury. There is no mercy or forgiveness for them. The gates of the abyss open up when the perjurer's name is mentioned.[13]

21. Return to the Medium Shot as in 20.

22. Close-up of Helga looking even more alarmed (the shot crosses the axis, i.e. reversing the orientation of the previous shot filmed from the front of the desk in order to show Helga's face clearly). She looks around her.

23. Medium Shot from a new camera position showing Per walking forward to the desk from right. The Judge appears in the lower right corner of the shot, barely visible. The only reason for this new camera position is precisely to emphasise Per's swearing on the Bible, the act which so disturbs Helga and which is the dramatic high point of the scene.

24. Close-up of Per's two fingers laid on the Bible. Again a dramatic close-up of the key action.

25. Close-up of Helga looking down towards right, horrified. (Proper eyeline match and a reaction shot which could mark shot 24 as her point of view.)

26. Medium Shot including desk (as in 23) as Per stands, his fingers placed on the Bible.

27. Close-up of Judge, as he speaks, administering the oath,

Title: 'I, Per Mårtensson swear and testify …'[14]

28. Long Shot framing Helga, Per, Judge and spectators in background, but from a

Figs. 11 (top), 12 (middle) & 13 (bottom). Frame enlargement, Tösen från Stormyrtorpet, 1917. [Courtesy of John Fullerton.]

Helga from a new angle as Helga stares up at Per on right.

32. Close-up of Judge (eyeline mismatched).

33. Medium Shot from a new camera position of Helga as she snatches the Bible away.

Title: 'He mustn't be allowed to swear the oath!'[15]

34. Long Shot from behind desk (as in shot 28) showing all the characters. Spectators and court officials jump up in reaction to Helga's action.

35. Medium Long Shot: spectators seated further back in the court react, looking off right.

36. Close-up of Judge calling for order looking left.

37. Medium Long Shot from behind the desk (as in shot 28 and 34) as consternation continues, Helga holding the Bible to her breast, speaking to Judge.

Title: 'He mustn't be allowed to swear falsely!'[16]

38. Close-up of Helga from a new camera position, crying out, shaking her head, and looking off left, clutching the Bible (Fig. 10).

39. Close-up of Judge looking off right (Fig. 11, proper eyeline match).

40. Medium Close-up from a new angle of Helga looking off left (at Judge) holding the Bible (Fig. 12).

41. Medium Long Shot with Judge seated on left, Helga standing on right clutching the Bible, other men (court officials or bystanders) standing watching her (Fig. 13). An angle not previously shown.

Title: 'He is the father of my child, but I don't want him to swear falsely! I want to drop the case!'[17]

new angle, shot from behind desk to the right as Per swears. This new angle further articulates the dramatic moment and allows the following eyelines in the close-ups to match with this shot.

29. Close-up of Helga's anguish (the cut no longer crosses the axis).

30. Medium Shot (as in shot 23 and 26) as Per continues the oath.

31. Medium Shot framing both Per and

In this dynamic section of the film, Sjöström not only cuts between the different characters articulating a sort of visual dialogue between them, he supplies close-ups of the Bible to express the great importance attached to the oath, and stretches out the key action of Per taking the oath and Helga grabbing the Bible from him over many shots. Further, the editing of the sequence clearly lets us know that it is *Helga's* sequence, that we are focalised in her view point, not so much in terms of literal point-of-view shots (although it could be claimed that the close-up of the Bible is from her point of view), as by the larger number of shots devoted to her and her relative screen size compared with other characters, as well as the number of angles given to her. There are eight shots in which Helga is the only major character, six shots of the Judge only (seven if we include the close-up of his hand with the Bible), two of Per (five if we include the shot of his fingers on the Bible and the shots with the Judge in the corner of the frame). Likewise, the shots of Helga tend to be much closer than those of Per (the character the scene does not empathise with), while the Judge (whose change of heart about Helga marks the end of the scene) also is shown in close-up. Perhaps most importantly, there are four different angles given to the shots isolating Helga in this sequence calibrating her movement from astonishment to action to shame. Indeed, the last fourteen shots of the section cut between ten different camera angles, creating a truly dynamic rhythm as opposed to the predictable pattern of alternation that dominates the beginning of the sequence.

Sjöström is somewhat challenged in maintaining matching eyelines, since his master shot is initially from the front of the Judge's desk, while the close-ups of Per and Helga are taken from behind the desk (as it were) and cross the axis. Per and Helga's eyelines match, but looks between them and the Judge, who is filmed from the front, do not. However, Sjöström seems aware of this problem, and, towards the end of the section, supplies another master shot, shot from an angle behind the desk. This allows most of the following eyelines to match, and works quite dramatically to articulate the turning-point of the drama as Per makes his false oath. One could read this change in orientation as intentional, and therefore less an error than a dramatic device. Whatever Sjöström's intentions were,

this second master shot shows he was not unaware of the previous matching problem and either did not care much about it or, as I believe, decided to wait for this point to correct it, for dramatic reasons.

Ben Brewster and Lea Jacobs' analysis of the turning point in Sjöström's *Ingmarssönerna* (1919) shows a similar breakdown into carefully managed shots at a dramatic turning point. Contrasting the sequence to Bauer's *Kord' Parizha* (King of Paris, 1917) in which (like *Ingeborg Holm*) the movement of the actors articulate the drama, the authors point out: 'not only do the actors express little with their faces and bodies in *Ingmarssönerna*, but all the important dramatic transitions in the scene are distributed across a large number of shots and titles, the repetition and variation of which account for the structure of the scene as a whole'.[18] Their final comparison to Griffith makes an essential contrast however: 'In so far as Sjöström's reduced style depends upon a high cutting rate, it is closer to Griffith than to Bauer. On the other hand, Griffith's films often provide the spectator with 'telling' facial expressions and poses, a point highlighted by the editing and use of titles.'[19]

Sjöström's films of the later 1910s do more than simply blend work within the single shot with American cutting. They create a cinema that blends revelation with opacity, a cinema which cues the viewer to focus on a particular character at a key moment through closer framing and editing, but whose use of acting and plot structure also maintains an element of mystery about motivation, and a complex, often undefined, interiority. Like all great directors, but especially those who come from the pictorial tradition of silent cinema, Sjöström never allows the breakdown into individual shots to become a simple processing of scenic space by dramatic needs, as if shots were indifferent pieces of a predetermined jigsaw. Instead, the space of individual shots maintains a certain independence. Even as shots are related to other shots, they are not simply equivalent parts of a homogenous whole. Each shot in its framing expresses the characters within them. Thus in the trial sequence from *Tösen från Stormyrtorpet*, the shots of Helga are arranged dynamically: she is shot from a number of angles, all of which

*Figs. 14 & 15.
Frame
enlargement,*
Mästerman, *1920.
[Courtesy of John
Fullerton.]*

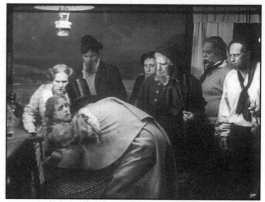

express both her anguish and her determination. In comparison, the shots of Per remain prosaic, while those of the Judge are nearly unvaried in their close-up framing. Helga is given not simply a dramatic importance, but her emotions regulate her portrayal. It is the dialectic between revelatory shots and editing schemes, and those which limit our knowledge of motivations that makes *Mästerman* such a subtle and exciting film.

Mästerman: scenic breakdown, the look of others, and the economy of desire

Sjöström's performances, in *Mästerman* as in his other films, not only provide brilliant characterisations, but define the basic style of the film, from the dynamic energy of *Berg-Ejvind* and *Terje Vigen* (1917), to the cringing guilt of David Holm in *Körkarlen*. Samuel Eneman in *Mästerman* relates more closely to Ingmar in *Ingmarssönerna*, a character with a seemingly simple exterior, almost appearing a bit simple-minded, confused about his own motivations, but ultimately discovering dimensions of desire within himself not previously recognised. Although the brilliance of Sjöström's performance in *Mästerman* has not been universally recognised,[20] I find it to be possibly his finest silent performance, deliberately muted and ambiguous. As a character, Samuel Eneman, known by the townspeople as 'Mästerman', possesses two hidden aspects. The first involves his relation to the people of the town. Supremely alienated, Eneman not only does not care about his bad reputation (embodied in the pejorative nick name, Masterman), he seems

determined to maintain or even exaggerate it, delighted to appear to care only for money. But it is not as though Mästerman's bad reputation hides a heart of gold. Eneman remains a mystery to himself as well. His love of possessions, his miserly hoarding, all involve a repression and displacement of desire within him, so that there is not only a side to Mästerman the townspeople do not suspect, but one that he himself does not fully understand. Bergman and Sjöström avoid the *Silas Marner* story that seems to be implied by this material. Eneman's character is not explained by an earlier disappointment. Simply and beautifully, it is not explained at all. And although Eneman undergoes a transformation, it is not a sentimental opening up to humanity through the innocence of a child. Instead, the transformation follows the devious paths of desire and deceit, of substitution and displacement, and ultimately renunciation.

The scene in Mother Boman's Tavern 'The Cape of Good Hope' (Goda Hoppsudden) after Eneman has rescued Tora from toughs who tried to rob or rape her, demonstrates both the ambiguity of the character and Sjöström's unique style in breaking down a scene, carving up space with the off-screen looks of characters in order to articulate both private and public drama.

1. A Long Shot of the interior of the tavern as Eneman enters from door on left carrying Tora. The camera pans to the right, revealing men seated at tables as he carries her into the background towards her mother's bar (Fig. 14).

Figs. 16 & 17.
Frame
enlargement,
Mästerman, 1920.
[Courtesy of John
Fullerton.]

2. Medium Long Shot framing Eneman with Tora in his arms on the right, Mother Boman at bar on left, sailors standing in background. A bearded sailor brings forward a chair on which Eneman places Tora (Fig. 15). As her mother bends over her, the bearded sailor leans towards Eneman and speaks.

Title: 'I knew you were a blood sucker, but not that you were one of those who can't leave young girls alone.'[21]

3. Medium Shot. Cut in along the axis from the previous shot; the framing now shows Eneman in foreground on right as the bearded sailor on right speaks to him (Fig. 16).

4. Medium shot of Tora and her mother, as Tora grabs Eneman's arm (he is mainly out of the frame) and speaks to the off-screen sailor, pointing her finger, denying his accusation (Fig. 17). This is the left side of shot 2, but also shot from a lower height.

5. Medium Shot of Eneman and sailors as in shot 3, Tora's hand at frame left holding Eneman's arm, Eneman and the sailors look off at her towards the left.

6. Medium Shot of Tora and Mother as in shot 4. Tora continues to speak off to right.

7. Medium Shot as in 3 and 5, framing Eneman and the sailors who look back at Eneman. The bearded sailor pats him on the back and turns away. Eneman shows no reaction.

8. Tora framed as in 4 and 6. She rubs her ankle, apparently hurt in the scuffle; her mother passes behind her to the left.

9. Medium Shot of bar. Mother Boman enters from right (smooth match on action and direction). She reaches under the bar and brings up a bottle which she starts to pour into a glass.

10. Medium Long Shot of bar, slightly different framing than in shot 2, from a higher angle looking down on Tora in her chair, as she rubs her ankle with Eneman standing slightly to the right of her, staring at her foot, the sailors in the background talking among themselves (Fig. 18). Tora takes off her sock.

11. Mother Boman at the bar, as in shot 9, pouring a glass; she looks off right (Fig. 19).

12. Medium Shot of Eneman bending a bit and looking down, sailors behind him (Fig. 20, matches eyeline from Mother Boman).

13. Medium Close-up from slightly high angle of Tora's bare leg, very white against the dark wood of the bar, as she rubs her ankle (Fig. 21); roughly matching Eneman's eyeline.

14. Medium Shot of Eneman as in shot 12; he straightens up a bit, but still stares downward.

15. Mother Boman looking off right. She crosses to right with glass in hand.

16. Medium Long Shot, similar to shot 2, but not angled down as sharply (Tora's

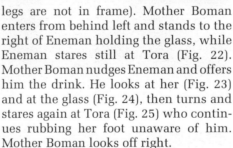

legs are not in frame). Mother Boman enters from behind left and stands to the right of Eneman holding the glass, while Eneman stares still at Tora (Fig. 22). Mother Boman nudges Eneman and offers him the drink. He looks at her (Fig. 23) and at the glass (Fig. 24), then turns and stares again at Tora (Fig. 25) who continues rubbing her foot unaware of him. Mother Boman looks off right.

17. Medium Shot of three sailors looking off left. One turns and speaks to the others then looks off left again.

18. Medium Long Shot as in shot 16, as Eneman continues to stare at Tora; Mother Boman exits with glass to right.

19. Medium Shot of sailors as in shot 17, as Mother Boman enters from left and speaks to them, looking back over her shoulder to left.

Title: 'What shall I do? He hasn't got the

sense to say thank you and he won't leave.'[22]

20. Return to Mother Boman and sailors as in shot 19.

21. Medium Shot of Eneman framed closer and from a slightly different angle so Tora does not appear in frame. He stares down to left (at Tora off-screen).

22. Mother Boman and sailors (as in 19 and 20). One sailor puts his arm on her shoulder and speaks.

Title: 'Give him five crowns. Reward! That's what he's waiting for, the blood sucker!'[23]

23. Return to Boman and sailors as in shot 22. The sailors laugh and nudge Boman toward Eneman. She exits reluctantly to the left.

24. Medium Long Shot of Eneman and Tora, similar to shot 18, but slightly to left

Figs. 22 (top left), 23 (top right), 24 (middle left), 25 (middle right), 26 (bottom left) & 27 (bottom right). Frame enlargement, Mästerman, 1920. [Courtesy of John Fullerton.]

(showing the bar) and perhaps a bit closer. Mother Boman passes from right to left in background, picks up her purse and crosses over to right of Eneman, the camera panning slightly to the right with her as she offers him some coins from the purse (Fig. 26). He continues to stare at Tora who remains unaware of him, looking down at her foot. When Eneman does

not react, Boman looks off right at the sailors.

25. Medium Close-up of the sailors laughing and nodding, looking off left.

26. Return to Boman, Tora, and Eneman as in shot 24, Eneman still gazing at Tora. Boman nudges him with the hand holding

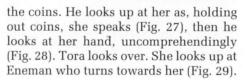

the coins. He looks up at her as, holding out coins, she speaks (Fig. 27), then he looks at her hand, uncomprehendingly (Fig. 28). Tora looks over. She looks up at Eneman who turns towards her (Fig. 29).

27. Medium Close-up as in shot 25; the sailors laugh (Fig. 30).

28. Medium Close-up from a new angle of Boman standing on the right, her hand out-stretched, and Eneman standing on the left as he looks angrily off right towards the sailors (Fig. 31). An underlit background to this shot isolates the pair.

29. Medium Close-up of sailors as they suddenly stop laughing and look away.

30. Medium Close-up of Eneman and Boman as in shot 28. He slowly looks down at her hand (Fig. 32).

31. Medium Shot of Tora looking over to the right (Fig. 33).

32. Eneman and Boman, as in shot 30, as he takes the coins from her hand (Fig. 34), looks at the coins (Fig. 35), then at her (Fig. 36).

Title: 'Bad payment for such a pretty girl. But I suppose that is all you can afford and a little is better than nothing.'[24]

33. Medium Long Shot of Tora, Eneman and Boman, both women regarding him as he speaks. He looks briefly at Tora, then turns and looks around him, then starts to leave.

34. Long Shot of bar as Eneman walks towards camera, sailors watching after him, as he moves to left, then coming after him, laughing, as he exits frame left.

35. Medium Long Shot of exterior door of tavern, low key lighting with directional highlight from doorway as Eneman exits. He closes the door, stands on the stairs, pauses, and looks at the coins in hand

Figs. 32 (top left), 33 (top right), 34 (bottom left) & 35 (bottom right). Frame enlargement, Mästerman, 1920. [Courtesy of John Fullerton.]

(Fig. 37). He brings out a purse from the pocket of his greatcoat. Then he looks off right.

36. Medium Shot of sailors inside bar laughing.

Title: 'Mästerman, the most abominable man of the port! He charged her for helping her girl!'[25]

37. Return to sailors as in shot 36, laughing.

38. Medium Long Shot of Eneman listening. He looks at his hand.

39. Close-up of Eneman's chest and hands holding coins and purse (Fig. 38), filmed from front (i.e. not from his point of view). He closes the purse, replaces it in his coat pocket, and draws a handkerchief from the other pocket in which he places the coins (Fig. 39).

40. Long Shot of tavern exterior, Eneman at top of stairs by door. He ties up handkerchief and walks down stairs. Fade out.

This sequence establishes what we could call the film's economy of desire: setting up the series of exchanges on which the film will be based, their displaced relation to Mästerman's slow discovery of his own desire, and his complex relation to how others perceive him. Like the sequence in *Tösen från Stormyrtorpet*, the scene is carefully broken down to isolate a variety of characters, and their actions and reactions. Dealing with a simpler space and orientation, Sjöström manages to maintain screen direction and eyelines matches throughout. Three characters receive shots in which they appear as the only main character: Tora, Eneman and Mother Boman, clearly the key characters of the scene. Tora is framed alone in only one shot (two if we include the shot of her leg); Mother Boman in three; and Eneman in six (seven, if we include the close-up of his hand). Three of Eneman's shots alone take place after he leaves the bar and stands alone on the stairs, and most of these are

Figs. 36 (top left), 37 (top right), 38 (bottom left) & 39 (bottom right). Frame enlargement, Mästerman, 1920. [Courtesy of John Fullerton.]

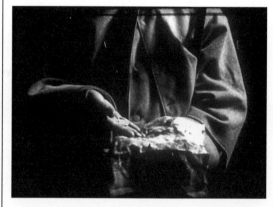

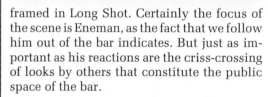

framed in Long Shot. Certainly the focus of the scene is Eneman, as the fact that we follow him out of the bar indicates. But just as important as his reactions are the criss-crossing of looks by others that constitute the public space of the bar.

This is clearest in the centre of the scene, shots 10 through 16, which surround the closest framed shot inside the tavern, shot 13 of Tora's leg. Several single character shots are intercut, and a character's look off-screen directs most of the cuts. In shot 10 we see Eneman staring down at Tora who has taken off her sock (Fig. 18); in shot 11 Mother Boman looks off and notices his stare (Fig. 19). In shot 12 Eneman bends down and directs his gaze out of the frame toward Tora (Fig. 20). Shot 13 shows the object of his attention (Fig. 21), while shot 14 returns to him staring, and shot 15 returns to Mother Boman watching him watching. Shot 13 of Tora's leg stands as an almost emblematic voyeuristic shot, embodying the male gaze. But while Tora's bare leg is bracketed by shots of Eneman's stare, his

stare itself is bracketed by Mother Boman's observation of him. Boman crosses to the right where she joins the sailors who are also watching Mästerman with complete mockery. But it is not until nearly the end of the sequence (shot 26) that Eneman will actually turn his gaze from Tora, and become aware that others are watching him (Fig. 27). Sjöström has not only organised this sequence around the relays of looks, but also differentiates between the meaning of these looks, from Eneman's wide-eyed fascination with Tora's leg (more on this later), to Mother Boman's suspicious bewilderment, to the sailors' outright mockery (Fig. 30). Sjöström stages the drama of a character becoming absorbed in his own fascinated gaze, then discovering his absurdity in the eyes of others.

We have long known that the classical narrative cinema builds both space and stories out of the off-screen glances of characters. The central place of the male gaze in this logic of looking and display has been revealed by a generation of feminist analyses of film sequences. But unfortunately the dynamic range of looks within the narrative cinema has never been explored. Here, at the foundation of the classical system, Sjöström offers a profound treatment of the varying looks of characters and the dramas that develop from them. Eneman/Mästerman's situation in this scene recalls the famous description of visual involvement offered by Jean-Paul Sartre in *Being and Nothingness* imagining a viewer absorbed in the act of looking through a keyhole: 'a pure mode of losing myself in the world, of causing myself to be drunk in by things as ink is by a blotter'.[26] But if this wholly absorbed viewer becomes aware of someone else watching, the whole orientation to the world and the self changes: the fact of being seen by another becomes the foundation of one's sense of self. It would seem that Eneman acts this process out before us, as Sjöström uses his breakdown of space through glances to reveal Eneman's alienated being.

As much as the play of glances, this sequence builds itself on a series of exchanges offered. Mother Boman first offers Eneman a drink as acknowledgement of his rescue of her daughter (Fig. 22). However, absorbed in his visual delight at Tora's ankle, he doesn't seem to understand and does not take it. The sailors then tell Boman to offer money, and she offers the coins in the exact same way she offered the drink (compare shots 16 and 26), nudging Eneman out of his absorption in watching her daughter. Why does this offer claim his attention (Fig. 28), compared with his lack of reaction to the drink? The sailors, Mother Boman, and possibly Tora are convinced they know why: because of his greedy love of money. He is willing to be paid for his services, indeed expects it. Sjöström does not explicitly answer the question but a careful observation of the cutting supplies an answer (with a bit of help from Sartre), I believe.

Sjöström's reaction to this second nudge at first mirrors his reaction to the earlier nudge and offer of the drink. He stares at it as if not recognising what Mother Boman is holding. Part of the unique, nearly absurd quality of Eneman's reaction as he stares at Tora comes from its bold-faced quality. This is not a surreptitious lustful glance, but an explicit stare carried over some sixteen shots.

Sjöström blends male lust here with a childish curiosity and fascination. One senses that Eneman has not looked at a woman for years and has almost forgotten how they are made. Although this fascination could undoubtedly be interpreted psychoanalytically, I believe its odd quality lies precisely in its rather regressive attitude, like an adolescent boy staring at a naked woman for the first time. And like a child's curiosity, it so thoroughly absorbs Eneman that he becomes unaware of anything else. Clearly his isolated mode of living, his alienation from the town, has made such forgetfulness possible. Is it the familiarity with coins that recalls him to himself?

I don't think so. As with the offer of the drink, Eneman turns his gaze away from Mother Boman's hand back to Tora. But Tora, apparently intrigued by her mother's offer, has now looked up (Fig. 29). In contrast to the previous offer, when Eneman turned to look again at Tora and she remained unaware of his gaze, she is now looking back at him, apparently curious to see what he will do. In the next shot the sailors watching to the right laugh, and Eneman turns from Tora to them, looking off angrily (Fig. 31). Eneman realises he is caught in the gaze of others, observed, rather than simply given over to his absorption in watching Tora, unobserved. The sailors, and possibly Tora, expect a certain behaviour from him, and it is with consummate alienation that he performs exactly as they expect him to. He will act out his role of Mästerman, the bloodsucking miser, for the audience of others for whom he has contempt. Just before he takes the money from Boman, Sjöström supplies the one shot devoted exclusively to Tora other than the close-up of her leg, as she turns to watch the exchange (Fig. 33). Thus he decides to alienate her as well. This duplicity, deceiving even himself about the nature of his relation to others (asserting an independence through deceiving them while actually conforming to their own hateful view of him), shows the depth of characterisation and interiority Sjöström creates for his characters through the breakdown into shots. One thinks of Kierkegaard's description of his own experience, written about the same time as the period in which the film takes place: 'What reconciled me with my fate and with my

suffering was that I, the so unhappy so much tortured prisoner, had this unlimited freedom of being able to deceive, so that I was allowed to be absolutely alone with my pain'.[27]

Eneman takes the money, counts it, and declares it a small payment for such a pretty girl, but 'a little is better than nothing'. Eneman seems to accept his characterisation as Mästerman, someone who would 'charge for helping a girl'. But his choice of words subtly turn the exchange back on the one who offers it. It is Mother Boman who believes these coins are a worthy offering for the safety of her child. Cast back into the role that others have placed him in, Mästerman exits. Alone, however, we see him contemplate his payment. The close-up of the coins in his hands (Fig. 38) stands as the only close-up in the sequence other than the shot of Tora's legs. Does this visual similarity replay the exchange: these coins = the girl? But something other than fair exchange is operating here. The image of Tora's legs is Eneman's image, the image of his desire. The coins are all he comes away with. Less than an economy of exchange, the coins represent a displacement of desire. The otherwise inexplicable action enacted in these close-ups becomes clear. Eneman begins to place the coins into his purse, transaction completed. However, the laughter in the bar interrupts him. Alone, outside the sight of the others, he now does something else. The coins that replace Tora are removed from circulation. Wrapped in a handkerchief (Fig. 39) they become a token of her and of his deferred desire.

This scene which ends in the exchange of coins for Tora takes place between two other scenes of exchanges, or series of exchanges. The first appears in the opening scenes in Mästerman's pawn shop. Here we see his avarice, his desire to take from people objects they need and exchange them for a small amount of money. He takes boots from a man (leaving him in his hole-filled stockings) and refuses to return a ring to a woman who has missed her payment deadline. He follows the motto he states in the tavern, 'a little is better than nothing'. A young girl wants to pawn her family's caged birds, and although Mästerman at first refuses, he then agrees, to the girl's delight. What motivates this softening? Are

we being told he has a hidden heart of gold? This is clearly contradicted by his previous and subsequent behaviour with customers. Another factor makes him behave untypically. This is a pretty girl, on the verge of adolescence, and rather than a hidden kindness we are seeing a glimmer of a repressed eroticism acting on Eneman, a foreshadowing of his reaction to Tora's leg. The effect of the girl's explanation that these birds sing prettily if put in the sun, and also lay eggs, hints that some stirring of Eros is working here. Finally, it is important that the girl does offer him a little *something*, so that Eneman does not feel cheated, left outside the economy of exchange. The extra bit of money he gives after the girl kisses his hand in thankfulness supports this limited economy of Eros, offering a little bit for a little bit.

The key act of exchange in the film, however, the essence of the plot, is Tora coming and offering herself for money to cover her sailor lover Knut's theft and gambling debts. Knut represents the reverse image of Mästerman: young, handsome, active, he contrasts physically with Eneman's ageing gait and often inert features. He shows the proverbial 'sailor on leave' attitude towards money. He gives gifts (the medallion necklace to Tora), pays for feasts of food and wine, gambles, and ultimately steals from his future mother-in-law, Mother Boman. Rather than Knut approaching the pawnbroker, he sends Tora (or is it her idea? There is an interesting ellipsis here between Knut spying on Mother Boman at the cash box and Tora's visit to Eneman – another example of the gaps Sjöström and Bergman leave in explaining motivation). Tora enters the pawn shop and asks for a loan of 500 riksdollars. Mästerman makes it clear he gives no money without a pledge. Tora says he helped her once before (in fact, Eneman had already approached her to return the coins from her mother, saying 'I don't want money for helping you', apparently taking her out of the economy of exchange). But Mästerman does not budge.

Tora begins to take off the medallion Knut gave her, but Mästerman offers a different exchange, telling her, 'You have got a pledge. Your self.'[28] Tora reacts in alarm, but Eneman reassures her, saying that what he needs is a

maid, and that she can in effect indenture herself in his service until her fiancé can repay the loan. Reluctantly, Tora agrees, and Mästerman slowly counts out the bills. As she leaves, Eneman rushes to the window to watch her as she gives the bills to Knut. Is Eneman honest here? Is Knut? Is Tora? Rather than practicing overt duplicity, Eneman is diverting his desire into an economy of exchange he understands and can control, gaining a new power over this woman that is expressed not only in her servitude, but in his immediate ability to keep his eye on her. He delivers the actual pawn ticket to her drunken lover the next morning, and as Mästerman leaves the bar, Tora follows behind him. Sjöström shows a close-up of the pawn ticket in Knut's hands, then cuts to one of several shots using the depth of the frame of a Long Shot as Tora follows behind Mästerman, small figures at the far end of the meadow, as if she is departing from Knut's life. Tora, of course, is caught in a masculine system of exchange, a pledge between two men, that for the moment she can only obey, but which she will try to figure out how to subvert.

Sjöström expresses the ambiguous and unstable nature of Eneman's deal in the first shots within the pawn shop after Tora's arrival. The intertitle states the uncomfortable facts of Tora's reification: 'There were many strange things in Mästerman's treasure chamber, but pawn number 1313 was the first of its kind'.[29] The next shot fades in on Mästerman's stronghold, the room where he keeps all his pledges. Tora stands stiffly and forlornly among the heaps of chests and luggage, as if he really intended to store her there. The room brightens with light from the left, and Sjöström cuts to show Eneman opening a window, letting light and air into the room. Cutting back to Tora, she seems animated by the change and looks at the strange place to which she has been brought. She turns and sees the skeleton leaning against the back wall. Turning back, she brushes against a suit of clothes, complete with shoes attached to the trouser legs, hanging from the ceiling. She reacts in terror and has to grasp the trouser legs to make sure there is no man inside. Both these objects – the man with no flesh, the clothes with no body – work as images for Mästerman's alienated and re-

pressed existence. Eneman crosses to her and with pride begins to point things out to her like a showman in a private museum. As he shows her the jewellery strewn on the table, she begins to cry, which infuriates him and he orders her to get to work, departing angrily, locking the door of the storeroom before he leaves.

Mästerman's 'treasure chamber', his storage room for pawned pledges, provides the central symbolic space of this film. As much as Sjöström's subtle but complex editing, the changes in the lighting, setting and composition in this room chart its central drama and significance. Jean Mitry contrasted Swedish cinema which he saw as devoted to nature, sunlight, and clarity with the German cinema, which he associated with enclosed and tortuous interior spaces, and Expressionism. But he also claimed that ultimately the two cinemas converge, because the Swedish landscapes seemed to impose actions on characters as much as the Expressionist sets did.[30] Such an insight typifies both the too broad generalisations as well as the penetrating insights of the first generation of comparative historians. Not all Swedish films gloried in expansive landscapes; likewise we need to resist describing a film like *Mästerman* as Expressionist, even though the treasure chamber operates as an enclosed and repressive space that initially imprisons its characters. But Mitry's description of the significance that setting played in developing character in Swedish silent cinema absolutely holds here. Such beautifully worked out visual symbiosis between character and setting remains within the realm of the Naturalist school, so uniquely developed in Scandinavia. The treasure chamber is initially Mästerman's world, the visual expression of his character, because it is the environment he has created for himself. Depositing Tora within it will cause it to transform utterly, like a chemical reaction. The drama between these characters takes on palpable form in the visual appearance of the storage room.

Mästerman begins in the treasure chamber, although we do not immediately recognise our location. No scene is more visually inventive than the opening of *Mästerman*, due to its dramatic use of lighting and symbolic use

Figs. 40 & 41.
Frame
enlargement,
Mästerman, *1920.*
[Courtesy of John
Fullerton.]

of space and objects in introducing its main character. The first shot shows Mästerman kindling a lamp and illuminating his face against a sea of darkness (Fig. 40). We are given a face but no locale in which to place it. Is he on board a ship at midnight, or crossing a dark forest? The lamp illuminates him taking out a key. The following shot shows him, lamp in hand and still shrouded in darkness, approaching a door which he unlocks and enters, his lantern beam casting highlights and shadows around a cavernous space. The next shows him, lamp still in hand, bending over a table that appears covered with jewellery, some of which he examines. Are we exploring a pirate's hoard of hidden treasure in a secret cave? Mästerman casts his lantern beam around and the space is explored, but rendered no less mysterious by the light moving around the room. In a beautifully conceived point-of-view shot, the dancing light reveals a series of incongruous things which make identifying our surroundings nearly impossible: top hats, violins, boots, candle sticks, and other objects which the moving shadows render entirely unfamiliar (Fig. 41).

The intertitle gives us an explanation: 'In his treasure chamber, where the shutters were always locked, many a strange thing was hidden'.[31] Although this explains the sort of place we are in, the shots that follow continue to accent the incongruous jumble of objects, the irrationality of this space, due to both its disorder and its exoticism. The next shot shows a stuffed crocodile hanging among old clothes, a hat apparently dangling from one leg. Mästerman's lantern moves on and the

beam catches (in the next shot) a shelf housing a model ship, a stuffed bird, a religious figurine, and a grotesque carved monkey. After intertitles tell of the stories told about Mästerman – that he had been a ship's captain and, perhaps, a pirate, made journeys around the world, and possibly sold children to the Turks – Sjöström ends this opening sequence with a rich emblematic shot. Mästerman stands next to a skeleton with a pile of weapons before it. He turns the skeleton's jaw and regards the skull (Fig. 42). Then he pulls from the pile of swords and other objects a large doll. Placing her before the skeleton, he manipulates her arms and turns her head. The shot fades and the first scene ends.

It ends without ever giving us a clear view of this dark and mysterious space. We understand it as a chaos, heaped with contradictory things, many of them threatening or grotesque. We associate its darkness and mysterious nature with Mästerman about whom so many strange tales are told. This room is dark and locked because it holds his treasure, but also because in some way that treasure is a secret, mysterious thing, hidden from all others. These are the items he has stripped from their owners when in dire need. They represent their dead desires, their lost delights which Mästerman has locked away from them. But rather than feasting upon them, he has entombed them – and himself with them. Like these imprisoned objects, Mästerman himself embodies the curtailment of desire. Mästerman playing with the doll sketches the complexity of Sjöström's portrayal. He picks up the doll immediately after the title has said, 'God knows if he hadn't sold

Figs 42 & 43. Frame enlargement, Mästerman, 1920. [Courtesy of John Fullerton.]

little children to the Turk as well!'[32] Placing it in front of the death's head, Mästerman seems to act out that darkest rumour about himself. But we also sense the irony of the title and soon realise we are watching the rather silly action of an old man playing with a doll. The regressive, child-like aspect of Eneman is introduced here, but Sjöström avoids sentimentality. The presence of the skeleton, like a *memento mori*, stresses his age and morality, and stands as an emblem of his alienated life-denying self. His play is awkward because, unlike a child, he lacks the ability to make an object come to life, although that may be his unacknowledged desire. He seems partly to be testing his pledge, seeing if its joints work. Ultimately the image is an anticipation of the scene of Tora in this same storeroom as 'pledge 1313' (Fig. 43). His manipulation of the doll mirrors his relation with Tora, whom he will also try to keep and control. But as his playing with the doll contradicts the infamous description of him as a slaver, this sequence also shows the repressed desire within Eneman, his deepest secret, hidden even from himself.

By introducing Tora into his storeroom Eneman has set in motion a force which will destroy it. But *Mästerman* is not *The Blue Angel*, and Eneman is a more complex figure than Prof. Emanuel Rath. It would seem Eneman dimly knows he needs to be delivered from his storeroom where he keeps his desires locked up. The transformation of this space, as Tora cleans and re-arranges it, from the dark mysterious cavern of the opening to a much more ordinary storeroom (and ultimately to a cosy parlour) is initiated by

Eneman himself. Eneman opens the shutter ('always locked') as soon as Tora arrives, letting the light into his secret room. Although he immediately locks Tora inside, he is not simply a passive dupe like Rath, an older man whom awakening desire will destroy because, in fact, he possesses no self other than his petty tyranny in the school room. Eneman's conflict is more interior and opaque, as he undergoes the transformation that awakened desire brings.

Tora sets to work transforming the treasure chamber immediately. Although the door is locked, the shutters are open and the room is filled with light. She discovers, hanging from the ceiling, the caged birds that Eneman took from the young girl. She unwraps the cage (Fig. 44) and places it in the window (Fig. 45, the young girl had told Eneman, 'Pelle sings beautifully – you only have to put him in the sun').[33] The images of Eneman's secret desires are united, the doll, the young girl and her birds, Tora. Tora recognises the birds as fellow prisoners, but has less awareness of the transformation she is causing. The space of the storeroom is cleared, and turned into an almost domestic interior. When Eneman returns and sees Tora sitting at the window sewing with the birds near by, he does not seem surprised at all, but leans in through the window to observe the homely scene. As he enters the treasure room, he already seems a bit transformed by his new environment. The two of them together, shot from outside through the window, strike up a new bargain, as Eneman tells her that if she sees anything she needs in the storeroom she should feel

free to take it. Framed by the window Tora shakes the old man's hand (Fig. 46).

The second half of the film still revolves around the exchange of Tora for the pledge, but a new series of contracts appear. Unlike the masculine exchange between Mästerman and Knut, these are bargains struck between Eneman and Tora. Instead of being specified by a pawn ticket, these bargains are verbal agreements and fraught with ambiguity as Tora subverts Eneman's intentions with her own interpretations. The first is Eneman's agreement she may take what she needs from the storehouse. Tora interprets this as the beginning of a new economic regime which she initiates in the following scene when an old woman comes to pawn her ragged shawl. Mästerman pulls it from her and the woman weeps, exposed. Tora enters from preparing dinner, and hears the story. In a shot which shows Sjöström's continued mastery of deep space and layered composition, Tora enters the storeroom. The storeroom lies dimly lit in

the foreground of the shot, the pawn shop seen in the background through its open door, as Mästerman and the woman stand watching. To the right of the door in the storeroom stands Mästerman's skeleton. Tora rushes into the storeroom and opens a large chest. Searching through piles of shawls, she selects one (Fig. 47), rushes back into the pawn shop, and places it on the woman's shoulders. Mästerman is astounded, but Tora responds that he said she could have whatever she needed and that she needs this shawl. Mästerman responds that that was not what he meant. Tora responds that it was what *she* meant. The women curtsies to him, Tora laughs, and Mästerman is furious. When Tora calls him into dinner, he hits his head on the door lintel, so much is his lost mastery and memory of his own house.

At dinner Tora arranges her next ambiguous bargain. Telling Eneman he would never find a wife with his bad reputation, she ambiguously tells him she would go to church with

Figs. 48 & 49.
Frame
enlargement,
Mästerman, 1920.
[Courtesy of John
Fullerton.]

him if he would simply give her a free hand. Eneman is so excited by what he takes to be a marriage bargain that he rushes from the room to his office, pauses, rushes back, and agrees (another beautifully awkward moment in his performance). Tora says she hopes he means the same things she does, but Eneman asks for no further clarification. The tables have turned, and Tora is taking advantage of Eneman's desire in order to strike a bargain he misinterprets. But Eneman seems reluctant to clarify the situation, as if believing that ultimately he can control the ambiguity to his own ends. Duped he undoubtedly is, but his part in the misunderstanding indicates a large degree of self-deception.

Tora's 'free hand' given her by Eneman involves emptying out the treasure chamber, giving freely of Mästerman's hoard to each supplicant, according to their needs (Fig. 48). We see the villagers arriving at the pawn shop and leaving like kids at Christmas, their arms laden with items from the storeroom, including the doll of the opening scene. When Mästerman objects, Tora reminds him of the promised visit to church, and he relents. Next, as the intertitle states, the pawn shop is turned into a charity organisation as the people flood in, every pawn ticket is redeemed without payment, every want satisfied. Through the crowd of people we see the carved monkey, crocodile, statuette, and even the skeleton of the opening scenes being carried out in triumph (Fig. 49). Before long Tora has totally emptied the storeroom, and it appears washed with light, clear and empty as she and a worker hang new curtains and wall paper, turning it into a parlour (Fig. 50).

Mästerman turns on the interference between two economies. First, the legal patriarchal exchange between Knut and Eneman of Tora for money, represented by the pawn ticket. Then, the ambiguous verbal agreements between Eneman and Tora. The masculine economy is one of debt and need, the feminine regime one of expenditure, festival, and the fulfilling not only of needs, but wants. The masculine economy hoards things in darkness, while Tora's regime opens the storeroom and disperses its goods to all comers. But the film is more than a simple story of a miser and dirty old man being done out of his dirty deals. This is a tale of the transformations caused by desire, and Sjöström (and Bergman) make this very clear. Mästerman's dirty deal and Tora's subversion of it allow the drama of transformation to come forward. That Mästerman is transformed by Tora's new economy forms the content of the first image after he gives her a free hand, as we see Tora dressing Eneman in new clothes, abandoning his old-fashioned greatcoat and top hat. The final moment of the destruction of his acquired wealth comes as a tramp enters the now empty storeroom. Loath to let him leave empty-handed, Tora searches the empty chests and cupboards until she finds Mästerman's old greatcoat, top hat and boots. She gives them laughing, the tramp takes them, bowing.

This process of exchange has ritual rather than economic significance. The tramp parades in Mästerman's old clothes before the louts at the local tavern yard. They set him on a table as they cheer the 'new old Mästerman'. Passing by, Eneman encounters this

mockery of his old self and becomes furious. When the tramp refuses to give up the clothes, Eneman finds he has to pay to get them back (Fig. 51). He rushes home in fury, but faces Tora surrounded by the sunlight and flowers she has brought into his house (Fig. 52). Sjöström's performance here, moving from fury to being dumbfounded by his own desire as he looks at Tora, borders on potential tragedy. He is undone by his vision of her, his anger deflating, as he nearly collapses onto a chair, holding his heap of old clothes in his lap. Even Tora is moved to pity as she crosses to him and strokes his brow. He tosses his old clothes (and any pretence to his former authority) on the floor, and as he takes Tora's hand pronounces her 'a dangerous pledge'.[34] This phrase, the title of Bergman's original short story, captures the true nature of the exchange taking place here, opening an old man to the play of desire, clearing out his secret hoard, and destroying his former identity. Truly a dangerous process. What will be left?

Eneman learns that Tora means something different than he does by 'going to church together' when he overhears her conversation with her mother. Sjöström/Bergman, however, do not let him rest within the scenario of being duped. The narrative economy will be resolved as the pledges and bargains move towards fulfilment and redemption. As Knut is about to arrive to repay the loan, Tora agrees to accompany Eneman to church. But the fulfilment of her promise, even according to her own literal meaning, continues to trouble the deal between Mästerman and Knut. Knut, hearing rumours of their wedding and seeing

the couple going to church arm in arm, is all too ready to believe he has lost Tora to Mästerman.

Having been duped by his deal with Tora, Mästerman decides to use deceit and the town rumours to bend his still unredeemed pledge with Knut to his advantage. Meeting with Knut in a tavern, he refuses to take the money the drunken sailor throws in his face, but offers instead to pay him for the pawn ticket. He lies and tells Knut he plans to marry Tora, and that she has sent him to get the pawn ticket back. Knut makes another deal, that they draw cards for Tora. Mästerman wins and leaves with Tora's pawn ticket in hand. Mästerman now feels he has laid claim to Tora through his own manipulation of the exchange with Knut. He arrives in her bedroom and awakens her by raising the window shade to the morning sun. As he hands her the pawn ticket and tells her the truth that he received it from Knut and the lie that Knut did not consider it worth anything anymore, he settles by the window and watches the caged birds. The deal between men resolved, even if dishonestly, he surrounds himself with a scenography of his desire under his control, Tora in her bed, the birds in their cage.

As the intertitle says 'there is sun in his room and sun in his heart'[35] as he stands in his new clothes before his mirror the morning his marriage banns with Tora are to be published. He bows before his bright image in the mirror (Fig. 53), perhaps dimly aware of Tora's role in this transformation. We cannot help but notice the contrast this shot at the beginning of the film's fifth and last reel poses to the

Figs. 52 & 53.
Frame
enlargement,
Mästerman, 1920.
[Courtesy of John
Fullerton.]

dark, mysterious, and sinister image which introduced him at the beginning of the first reel. He then examines the last (and the newest) of his precious objects, the necklace that is to be Tora's wedding present. Tellingly, he models it on himself in the mirror, pleased with his image.

Sjöström converts Mästerman's walk to pick up his bride into a bitter comic ritual, as Knut's sailor friends play a series of practical jokes (most importantly bedecking the back of Mästerman's coat with pawn tickets) and form a comic procession behind him (rhythmically edited with mordant wit). As Mästerman gives Tora his gift, Mother Boman discovers the pawn tickets attached to him, undercutting the effect (or redefining the nature) of the gift. When Tora defends Mästerman from the taunts of the sailors, she learns of his lie to Knut, that she sent him to buy back the ticket. The bargains now are collapsing as Tora, while admitting she must marry Mästerman because the banns have been published, tears off his necklace and brings out the medallion Knut had given her which she has kept inside her blouse. She vows she will never wear any jewels but this medallion. Mästerman rips it from her neck and grinds it with his heel. With this violence against contrary pledges of love and ownership, Mästerman's scheme has floundered. A sailor hands him the wedding bouquet, saying it now serves as flowers for his grave. If Eneman, sometimes unconsciously, sometimes deviously, has been trying to revive himself through his late-kindled desire, to bring himself back to life, resurrected from the dark tomb of his treasure chamber, here his resurrection meets its

check, his wedding becomes imaged as his funeral, as all the sailors pile flowers before him. He looks at the flowers, bends to pick up the necklace, and Sjöström frames him in Long Shot, the heap of flowers piled before him (Fig. 54).

The wedding day arrives and Sjöström continues the bitter-sweet atmosphere of this parody of a community ritual, worthy of John Ford. The bride and her mother arrive. The villagers await the bride groom. Knut on his boat hears the wedding bells, dresses, and takes the row-boat to shore. The delay makes the crowd anxious, the minister upset, the deacons angry: where is the bridegroom? As the crowd moves down the road to see if they can see Mästerman, the newly-arrived Knut exchanges shy glances with Tora. Mästerman is sighted, a tiny figure in the distance. As he approaches, he is revealed wearing his old greatcoat and now rather battered top hat (Fig. 55). If this film is about transformation, what does this return to the older identity mean?

Sjöström handles the tone of this final scene with the carefully edited looks of characters, deep composition of long shots, and meaningful use of objects that has marked all the key scenes of the film. Mästerman's appearance in the old clothes causes many in the crowd to think he is crazy (Swedish: 'inte klok', without any wits),[36] coming dressed to his wedding like this. But Mästerman responds to the Minster that he is not crazy but wise (Swedish: 'klok'), the word which previously indicated his shrewd business sense, his ability to make bargains and deals, but which now means something else. He is wise

*Figs. 54 (top left),
55 (top right), 56
(bottom left) & 57
(bottom right).
Frame
enlargement,
Mästerman, 1920.
[Courtesy of John
Fullerton.]*

enough, he says, to turn down this marriage.[37] In explanation he directs the Minster to look at the church gate (Fig. 56). There, perfectly framed in the centre of a symmetrical Long Shot composition, stand Tora in her bridal dress and Knut, forming an archetypal image of a bridal couple (Fig. 57). In this image, Mästerman recognises his own place as being outside the frame, which holds a picture complete in itself.

Eneman does enter the picture, however, to say farewell. He brings Tora one last gift. Reminding her of her vow never to wear any jewels but Knut's medallion, Eneman admits, 'you usually stick to your promises, Tora – in your own way that is'.[38] He has had the medallion he smashed repaired, and the precious wedding necklace he bought for her now serves as its chain. The gift, shown in close-up, combines two pledges of love, Knut's and his own, but it no longer seals Mästerman's bargain with her or with Knut. A true gift from him, it involves no obligation. As Tora takes

it, Eneman takes her face in his hand, the most intimate gesture he has made to her, and looks steadily into her face (Fig. 58). Sjöström cuts away to the crowd watching (Fig. 59). As with the scene in Mother Boman's tavern, Eneman's gaze at Tora is caught in the gaze of others. Again he seems unaware of them, so absorbed is he in Tora's lovely face. But both gazes are very different than before. No longer looking at Tora's ankle over her shoulder, he now gazes into her eyes. And instead of laughing mockery, the crowd watches quietly, almost reverently. Eneman slowly removes his hand, turns, and walks off, the crowd parting for him and watching him as he leaves.

Tora opens the medallion and finds a piece of paper – the pawn ticket. The young couple laugh (Fig. 60) and Eneman from a distance observes them (Fig. 61) and smiles (Fig. 62). He puts on his old hat, turns, and walks off, far down the road, out of the film (Fig. 63). If I have claimed this film is about a man transformed by desire, how can it end this way,

Figs. 58 (top left), 59 (top right), 60 (middle left), 61 (middle right), 62 (bottom left) & 63 (bottom right). Frame enlargement, Mästerman, 1920. [Courtesy of John Fullerton.]

with him walking away from all he loves, dressed in the same old clothes? The transformation cannot be doubted. This closing shot diametrically reverses the first shot. Instead of darkness, the bright sunlight; instead of a mysterious enclosed space, the extensive landscape. Instead of a sinister shadowy presence the subject of nasty rumours, a man whom we have come to know, seen change,

and who in some ways has opened himself to us and yet remained mysterious in another way, his deepest feelings held within. Instead of a man with a hoard of objects, we see one who has been divested of everything he owns, exchanging it all at first for his heart's desire and now willing to give that up as well.

If *Mästerman* recalls another film (and mas-

terpieces always echo each other) its most perfect companion I believe would be a film also made in Sweden the same year, Carl Theodor Dreyer's first masterpiece, *Prästänkan* (The Parson's Widow; French title: La Quatrième Alliance de Dame Marguerite, 1920). Like that film, *Mästerman* involves a series of deceptions, a romance that ranges between generations, and a final avowal of desire. But the greatest resonance between the two films comes in their resolutions, as the Parson's widow and Eneman both realise they need to make way for young love. Eneman's realisation is, perhaps, the harder of the two, because he must release the object of his desire precisely because of everything he has learned about desire and its difference from bargains and pledges. Like Kierkegaard and his Regina, he releases his beloved because he believes in love. And is it really the same old clothes he wears? As Eneman walks off, his coat and hat, and carefree gait recall the figure of the tramp who wore them briefly more than the former tyrant that Tora tamed and in some sense destroyed – Tora the dangerous pledge whose redemption has somehow become his own. We remember the cheer the drinkers gave to the tramp in these clothes: 'Hurrah for the new old Mästerman'. But now no one is there to cheer, except for us cinema viewers, the final gazers on the scene.

Acknowledgements

I would like to thank my good friend Jan Olsson for asking me to write this essay, making it possible to do so, and for making Stockholm into my second city; Bo Florin for first screening the film for me, and to my wife Deborah for her wonderful insights into this film.

Notes

1. Bengt Forslund, *Victor Sjöström: His Life and His Work*, trans. Peter Cowie, Anna-Maija Martinnen and Christer Frunck (New York: Zoetrope, 1988), 110.

2. Kristin Thompson and David Bordwell, *Film History: An Introduction* (New York: McGraw-Hill, 1994), 65–69. One must acknowledge the recent scholarship on early Swedish film centred around Stockholm University and the work of Jan Olsson, John Fullerton, Bo Florin, Astrid Söderbergh Widding, and many others, and regret that little of this has been translated.

3. Ibid., 67.

4. Jean Mitry *Histoire du Cinéma* (Paris: Editions Universitaires, 1967) I, 370–428. Georges Sadoul, *Histoire Générale du Cinéma* (Paris: Denoël, 1948), II: *Les Pionniers du Cinéma 1897–1909*, 141–154.

5. Yuri Tsivian, 'Two Stylists of the Teens: Franz Hofer and Yevgenii Bauer', in Thomas Elsaesser (ed.), *A Second Life: German Cinema's First Decades* (Amsterdam: Amsterdam University Press, 1996), 264–276.

6. See Ben Brewster and Lea Jacobs, *Theatre to Cinema: Stage Pictorialism and the Early Feature Film* (Oxford: Oxford University Press, 1997), 111.

7. Tsivian, 'Two Stylists of the Teens', 270–271.

8. Although almost certainly shot in a single take, it is interrupted by one title (at least in the English-language version) and by the insert of the son's photograph of his mother, so it could be described as consisting of five or six shots. However, the action take place in one single framing with no cut to another space, other than the insert of the photograph.

9. Editors' note: The screenplay indicates that an outdoor scene, now missing from extant prints, may have been inserted into the shot series at this point, see typewritten screenplay, *Ingeborg Holm*, scene 81, pages 38–39, Swedish Film Institute Library, Stockholm. This may explain the small alteration in camera set-up between the first and second shot in the shot series.

10. The intertitle reads: 'Vidhåller Per Mårtensson sitt påstående att ej vara far till barnet?'

11. The intertitle reads: 'Är ni beredd att avlägga ed därpå?'

12. The intertitle reads: 'Lägg två fingrar på den heliga skrift!'

13. The intertitle reads: Helga vet, att det inte finns någon synd så förfärlig som mened. Det finns ingen nåd eller tillgift för den. Avgrundens portar öppna sig själva, då menedarens namn nämnes.

14. The intertitle reads: 'Jag Per Mårtensson svär och betygar . . .'

15. The intertitle reads: 'Han får inte gå eden!'

16. The intertitle reads: 'Han får inte svära falskt!'

17. The intertitle reads: 'Han är far till barnet, men jag vill inte, att han skall svära falskt! Jag vill lägga ned rättegången!'

18. Brewster and Jacobs, *Theatre to Cinema*, 136.

19. Ibid., 136.

20. See the dismissing remarks in Forslund, *Victor Sjöström*, 106.

21. The intertitle reads: 'Nog visste jag att du är en blodsugare, men inte att du är en sådun, som inte kan lämna unga flickor i fred!'

22. The intertitle reads: 'Vad skall jag göra? Inte tar han någon täring till tacka, och inte vill han gå.'

23. The intertitle reads: 'Stick åt honom fem riksdaler i hittelön! Det är det, han väntar på, blodsugarn!'

24. The intertitle reads: 'Dåligt betalt för en så vacker flicka, men Mutter tör inte ha råd till mer, och något är bättre än intet.'

25. The intertitle reads: 'Mästerman, hamnens rikaste karl, tog betalt för att han hjälpte flickan!'

26. Jean-Paul Sartre, *Being and Nothingness*, trans. Hazel Barnes (New York: Washington Square Press, 1966), 348.

27. Søren Kierkegaard, *The Point of View for My Work as an Author: A Report to History*, trans. Walter Lowrie (New York: Harper Torchbooks, 1962), 79.

28. The intertitle reads: 'En pant har du ju. Du har dig själv.'

29. The intertitle reads: Många underliga ting funnos i Mästermans skattkammare, men panten n:o 1313 varden första i sittslag.

30. Mitry, *Histoire du Cinéma*, I, 317–318.

31. The intertitle reads: I hans skattkammare, var fönster luckor ständigt voro tillskruvade, gömdes mång underlig ting.

32. The intertitle (in part) reads: ... Gud vet, om han inte sålde små barn till hund-turken också!

33. The intertitle (in part) reads: '... och Pelle sjunger så vackert, bara Mäster ställer honom i solen!'

34. The intertitle (in part) reads: '... en farlig pant.'

35. The intertitle (in part) reads: ... sol var det i hans kammare, sol var det i hans hjärta.

36. The intertitle (in part) reads: 'Karln är inte klok!'

37. The intertitle (in full) reads: 'Visst är jag väl klok prosten. Jag är så klok, att jag säger nej i brudstolen, och till det tör jag väl vara fin nog, som jag går och står.'

38. The intertitle (in part) reads: '... Och du brukar ju hålla dina löften, du Tora – fast på ditt sätt förstås.'

Spearhead in a Blind Alley: Viking Eggeling's *Diagonal Symphony*

Gösta Werner

Döbelnsgatan 1, 111 40 Stockholm, Sweden

For over seventy years a great many myths have circulated concerning Viking Eggeling and his only film, *Diagonal Symphony*, which was given its first public screening in Berlin on 3 May 1925. Viking Eggeling, a Swedish artist, left Sweden in 1897 at the age of seventeen. He came into early contact with European conceptions of art such as Futurism and Dadaism, and later the French and German *avant-garde* movements in film. At the beginning of the 1920s he temporarily left painting to produce a film in Berlin, which has often been called the first abstract film.

The film, *Diagonal Symphony*, was a silent one. Over the years it has received increasing international interest, and today prints of the film are included in many film archives all over the world. Several attempts at interpreting the film and Eggeling's intentions have been made, but no one has proposed any approach other than theoretical points of view on abstract art and patterns of rhythmic movement, 'a score of abstract forms'.

All these former researchers have concentrated on the visual effects of the film. No one has approached the musical problem which I, as a film researcher, and my friend, Bengt Edlund as a musicologist, suspect has been hidden in the film. We have established that the film is constructed as a classical sonata, and that the stream of images is organised as visual analogies to the compositional principles of musical form.

Very few, if any, earlier film historians have realised that the *Diagonal Symphony* could be related to the musical theories of the 1910s and the beginning of the 1920s, and that the film was the first (and only) experiment at realising these ideas in practice. Eggeling's film was a spearhead towards the future, but in the years to come no one showed any interest in his ideas. Obstinate and summoning all his strength, Eggeling threw his spear into a blind alley.

The background

From the very first films, movement was the obvious key to understanding the new medium. Moving pictures could be realised in different ways, but the earliest artists and film theorists tried to find the possibilities of using the moving medium's characteristics for absolute, independent, artistic purposes.

The first ones who paved the way for such ideas were two Italians, Ricciotto Canudo and Filippo Tommaso Marinetti. Canudo was a

film theorist and Marinetti the leader of the Italian school of Futurism. The futurist painters tried to find strong, convincing and absolute visual expressions for movement itself, for a strong, predominant rhythm. Independent of each other and in their separate ways both Canudo and Marinetti maintained the excellent possibilities that film displayed for making movement central to the spectator's experience of the medium.

Their ideas, however, were transformed by the French *avant-garde* movement and its young film enthusiasts, among others René Clair, his brother Henri Chomette, Germaine Dulac, who called the film 'the music of eyes', Louis Delluc, Jean Epstein and Abel Gance, who enthusiastically exclaimed, 'The days of the image are here!'. And so the French *avant-garde* was soon established.

Now the time was ripe for more tangible thoughts concerning the roles and possibilities of not only the image but also the music. Canudo had maintained that 'our whole intellectual, aesthetic and religious life strives to become music'. The French *cinéastes* already perceived a way of developing film: the role of music in film should not only support the continuous, dynamic stream of images; music should to the same great extent serve as a pattern for the film as a whole.

With his film *La Roue* (The Wheel, 1923), Abel Gance and the young composer Arthur Honegger tried to realise these intentions, and afterwards Abel Gance enthusiastically exclaimed, 'The film, that is the music of light!'

And now, first Canudo, then the French *cinéastes* proclaimed that the languages of film and music were more related to each other than any other language. They have the same dramatic and dynamic construction, and they are both ruled by the laws of musical composition. The music is the elementary thing; it is more important than the images, and should govern the whole narrative pattern. A film, constructed throughout according to the rules of music, will be a 'pure film'. But this was a theoretical belief; it could not be proved in practice simply because no one knew how to do it.

At the same time other young, European *cinéastes* worked on other experiments of a similar kind. Joris Ivens, Walther Ruttmann, László Moholy-Nagy, Alberto Cavalcanti, Oskar Fischinger and Hans Richter tried with various results to reach 'the absolute film', as it was now termed. The only one who went the whole way was Viking Eggeling, a rather unknown Swedish painter, working on a film in Berlin, *Diagonal Symphony*.

The rise of the film

Viking Eggeling was born on 21 October 1880 in the Southern Swedish university city of Lund. His father was a German who had left Germany in about 1848 and moved to Sweden. There he had married a Swedish woman, worked as a music teacher, and opened a music shop in Lund. When Viking was nine years old, his mother died. When he was fifteen, his father died. Two years later he left Lund to travel about Europe. He was now making his first drawings and sketching, and painted in a cubist and expressionistic manner.

Eggeling encountered Futurism and Dadaism. Hans Richter made him interested in film and he moved with Richter to Germany. There he made drawings for an abstract film. In the summer of 1923 he met the young Erna Niemeyer, who had been studying at the Bauhaus in Weimar. He succeeded in borrowing a table for trick filmmaking and together they started work on *Diagonal Symphony*.

The film was produced in two versions or in two stages. The first one was finished in autumn 1924 and was shown privately in Berlin on 4 November 1924. Eggeling had been expecting a lot from this showing, but it passed without any attention. By this time the old and, for Eggeling, once so important and fruitful relationship with Hans Richter had finally broken down.

Eggeling and Erna Niemeyer decided to revise and/or extend this first version of the film. But in January 1925 she left him. Some years later she married Hans Richter, for a short time only. Then she moved to Paris where she later married the French poet Philippe Soupault. Alone, and in bad health and poor conditions, Eggeling was left to complete the film. It was shown to the public on 3 May 1925 in a matinée programme arranged by the

artist's circle, Novembergruppe in Berlin. The film programme was titled 'The absolute film', and apart from *Diagonal Symphony*, included René Clair's *Entr'acte* and other short films by Walther Ruttmann, Hans Richter and Fernand Léger.

When *Diagonal Symphony* at last reached the public on 3 May 1925, Eggeling was seriously ill and could not attend. He did not recover, and two weeks later he died on 19 May 1925. As before, his film received little or no attention. Very few film critics mentioned the film, and those who did, wrote in the reviews only about the film's visual form and design. The most exhaustive analysis of the film was published by a critic who had not seen the film in its second version but only in its first version.

Hans Richter, who once must have been aware of Eggeling's intentions in the film, has written much about the time with Eggeling, but never a single word on *Diagonal Symphony*. Nor has Erna Niemeyer, who for a long time was Eggeling's close friend and collaborator on the film, ever told anything about Eggeling's ideas for the film.

We, who have made this new analysis, think that the key to the film lies in its musical structure.

The musical structure

The title, *Diagonal Symphony*, was taken to provide a clue to the course of its visual content. The term 'symphony' refers to an orchestral work in four, contrasting movements. No such separate, self-contained portions can be found in the film, however. On the other hand, the musical form upon which the first movements in symphonies, sonatas, string quartets etc. are usually built, 'sonata form', seemed to be a promising candidate for the generative principle of the visual process.

Diagonal Symphony starts with an 'exposition' in which several episodes establish the various pictorial themes or motifs, and in which the dialectical opposition between the determined first and weaker second theme, basic to sonata form, is replicated by means of angular and rounded shapes. Then follows a 'development' characterised by complex,

multi-motivic pictures undergoing several changes simultaneously, a kind of visual polyphony. The material of the exposition reappears in condensed form as a 'recapitulation', and finally there is a fairly extended section with further metamorphoses of complex pictures, corresponding to the 'coda', the (optional) closing part of the sonata scheme.

Not only the formal process at large, but also the details of the film turned out to be ingeniously organised according to musical patterns. Sequences of gradual enlargement or reduction of pictorial size strongly suggest effects, respectively, of increasing and decreasing dynamic level. All pictures shown are certainly diagonal, but this background uniformity of orientation is used in a varied manner throughout the film to highlight an alternation between pictures emanating from or leaning towards the right or left side, a procedure that reminds us of the way in which music, especially classical music, gains coherence by means of complementary or contrasting symmetries.

The restoration of the film

Diagonal Symphony was shot with single-frame exposure. From the beginning all designs were drawn in black on a white background. All changes were made with a white plate, which was continuously passed over the design until it appeared and respectively disappeared. All designs were drawn with a compass and ruler.

When the film was developed, the white had become black, and the exposed film was in fact a negative. This negative remained *unchanged* as the 'original print' of the film. As far as I know, neither the original material nor the earliest prints have survived. The print we used for our work is estimated as the sixth generation of the original material of the film.

Our analysis of the musical structure of *Diagonal Symphony* indicated that a number of frames were missing from the surviving film material. What has been cut out from the original material and never put back, is of course definitely missing. This was also proved by the fact that some of the missing frames from the film were reproduced in

publications where *Diagonal Symphony* was reviewed.

Before the official opening of the film in Berlin in May 1925, it was approved by the German film censorship on 21 April 1925 with its length stated as 149 metres. This length is equivalent to 7,748 (± 26) frames, and with a projection speed of 18 frames per second means a running time of 7 minutes and 10 seconds.

Either in practice or in theory the film could be restored to this original length or quality. But our work in establishing missing frames has, as a theoretical result, given a length of 7,609 frames and a projection time of 7 minutes and 3 seconds. To that can be added three occasions where, in all probability, it is likely that 84 other frames are missing. With this supplementary material the film would be 7,693 frames with a projection time of 7 minutes and 7 seconds. The difference from the original version of the film is then 55 (± 26) frames or approximately 3 seconds.

The musical analysis of *Diagonal Symphony* has indicated that the film is a sonata. Was the sonata planned to be the first movement of a symphony which gave the film its title?

Acknowledgement

A detailed report of the restoration work on *Diagonal Symphony* is published in Gösta Werner/Bengt Edlund, *Viking Eggeling Diagonalsymfonin: Spjutspets i återvändsgränd* (1997). With English and German summaries and a CD-ROM with the restored film. Novapress, Box 1114, S-221 04 Lund, Sweden.

Snow-White: The Aesthetic and Narrative Use of Snow in Swedish Silent Film

Marina Dahlquist

Department of Cinema Studies, Stockholm University, 105 21 Stockholm, Sweden

Saturday, 15 June 1929. We are woken at 7 a.m. by the steward with the news that we have *met the ice.*

Shouts of joy! Everybody eagerly gets up.

Sjöberg-Lindblom and Dahlqvist-Westerberg embark on board the *Maud*, where the shooting of the film started shortly. The ice-floes are floating, blue, green, white, the ocean and the sky seem enchanted, everything is unreal …

Monday, 17 June 1929 … By and by we force the ice, and the ships pass as smoothly as cats between the treacherous floes with their dangerous bottoms underwater …

Monday, 1 July … The ice has changed character. The floes have become connected wholes as big as Ladugårdsgärde … The sensation of the wasteland, its colours and grandiosity, were unforgettable and never before experienced.

Tuesday, 2 July … Suddenly a report of 'bear on the ice' … After one hour we spot it – the king, slowly shambling over the waste of ice. He goes into the water! We put out a boat that is dragged over the ice.

Djurberg by the bow, Dahlqvist in the stern. They go out – after an enormous struggle they get a lasso round the neck of the old, grey bear and hold him, hour after hour, while our ships force the ice, millimetre by millimetre, at times by means of dynamite. Then we come loose and hasten to the bear. Three boats are finally put out, after tremendous difficulties we loosen the snare, and he swims towards the waste of ice. The boats with the cameras follow. He dives under an ice-floe, gets up on the ice, and dies after three shots …

Tuesday, 16 July … We are filled with manly pride and a pleasant feeling of having bravely overcome suffering, when we hear our guests' unconcealed amazement and admiration for us, as we have been tossed on the raging sea in this egg-shell; and in this Spartan and uncomfortable way we have braved dangers and put up with hardship for a whole month …[1]

This is an excerpt from the director Alf Sjöberg's diary during the production of the Arctic drama *Den Starkaste* (Strongest, 1929). The production was described as an expedition not only by the crew but by the contemporary press as well.[2] It is a drama that concerns the battle between two men, but also between man and nature. It is vital to conquer the rival and get the better of nature to win the reward – the woman – and to avoid death. Both in the film's narrative and in the description of its production, the Arctic conditions of the extreme North test man. Physical strength is expressed as an ideal as well as self-discipline, endurance and skill.

A national landscape

Snow is a recurrent phenomenon in Swedish silent film during the 1910s and 1920s. It is not solely Swedish, but snow, ice and cold winters are important elements in a number of films during this period, creating an image of a specific Nordic landscape which is of great importance for an aesthetics closely linked to the narrative. In the American film *Lucky Star* (Frank Borzage, 1929), for example, the snow could just as well be any kind of natural phenomenon – it is only an obstruction to surmount – while in Swedish films it is often linked to a specific national landscape. The interrelation between man and nature, and the confrontation with the sometimes extreme Northern conditions become an important part of the construction of the national Swedish cinema (Fig. 1). As a contemporary review of *Den Starkaste* claimed:

> Qualities as strong, rugged, and manly signify this new Swedish film. All that is sugary and sentimental is practically banned from the script. We are shown men who fight for their livelihood under harsh conditions, men who struggle with the forces of nature in the Arctic Ocean's majestic, but also desolate, region, fraught with danger. 'Den Starkaste' is primarily a film about men and their tussle, with each other; the woman has a voice in the matter only as a stimulus, a motive in the struggle that is both figuratively and literally fought out by the two marksmen …[3]

At times the scenery is linked to an idea of a typical Swedish national character, something that becomes evident in the first part

Fig. 1. Production still, Den Starkaste, *1929. [Courtesy of the Stills Archive, Swedish Film Institute. Polar bear hunting.]*

(of two) of John W. Brunius' *Karl XII* (Charles XII, 1925), for example. As the king is described in a programme: 'The young hero … comes from a barren and austere land, an outpost of civilisation at the border of the dominion of wintry darkness. He is the king over a people whose living conditions are courage and hardship, uprightness and helpfulness.'[4] In this film there are several scenes where the fearlessness and the heroism of the Swedes is associated with snow, as in the early scene when Lasse is hunting a bear;[5] but perhaps it is most evident in the Battle of Narva. The Russians are threatening, the winter is imminent, and many inhabitants want to surrender since they do not believe the king and his troops will arrive in time. However, the governor's answer to their request is: 'There is no choice. A Swede never gives up!'[6] His statement shows a sense of duty of which the Russian czar is not capable, as is shown when he deserts his men before the battle. When the Swedes, headed by their king, arrive at 'the enemy defences, a snowstorm broke that lashed the faces of the Muscovites'.[7] At times the blizzard seems to take over the image, like the Swedes take over the battle. The snow appears to be their element rather than the Russians', and in spite of the oppo-

nent's overwhelming superiority in numbers, the battle becomes an easy victory. The duration of the snowstorm is however very brief, and next morning the sun is shining and the snow completely gone.[8]

Even in the film's last scene with its funeral procession, when Karl XII is carried back to Sweden over the snowy mountains of Norway, the Swedish king is surrounded by Nordic wintry scenery. The scene is staged to evoke Gustaf Cederström's well-known painting *Karl XII:s likfärd* (Bringing Home the Body of King Karl XII of Sweden, 1883–84, Nationalmuseum, Stockholm). Even though the painting, as the film, is historically correct in the details of the uniforms etc., the setting is a fabrication since Karl XII was never carried over the vast expanses of snow on an open bier.[9] The dead Swedish hero is thereby portrayed as mourned by his people in the most Nordic of landscapes.

Karl XII was an explicit attempt to awaken patriotic feelings in Sweden during a period when spending on the armed forces was cut. The initiative for making the film came from the military, and a new production company, AB Historisk film, was created for this purpose.[10] For a few years in the mid-1920s a new historical and spectacular patriotic genre became popular. The idea to remind the Swedish people of the moral demands of their history, via the film medium, was conceived in the beginning of the 1920s in military and nationalistic circles. The life of Karl XII seemed very suitable to portray the central qualities of this genre: devotedness, bravery and loyalty.[11] The last major project of the genre was *Gustaf Wasa* (1928), a winter saga with the king's famous skiing tour, also directed by Brunius.[12] The critics' opinion about the patriotism in *Karl XII* differed; it was both criticised as chauvinistic and as propaganda for the military,[13] and praised as a national epic that had eminent educational importance for the nation's youth.[14] The film was revived in November 1940 during the time when most of Europe was at war. Even a shortened version with music and sound effects was released in November 1933.

According to Richard Dyer, the idea of the excellence of white people can be seen as a heritage from the Romantics' admiration for

remote, cold and 'pure' places, and the virtues that it brings such as clean air, a harsh climate and terrain, closeness to God, and 'the presence of the whitest thing on earth, snow'.[15] Physically impressive and morally upright, white characters were thought to be formed by battles with the elements, white women and men with an affinity for the surrounding whiteness. Such notions can still be found during the twentieth century in the cold North forming the identity of white settlers in Canada, as well as in the German *Bergfilm* (mountain film) of the 1920s and 1930s.[16] In Swedish films, however, there are generally no explicit racial references. The Sami people who take part in quite a few films are actually the people who are portrayed as closest to the harsh climate and snow.[17] In several films they even rescue the 'Swedes' from the white death, as in Victor Sjöström's *Högfjällets dotter* (Daughter of the High Mountain, 1914), Mauritz Stiller's *Gunnar Hedes saga* (Gunnar Hede's Saga, 1923), Gustaf Molander's *Hjärtats triumf* (The Triumph of the Heart, 1929), and his sound film *Dollar* (1938).

John Fullerton finds that the cinema of attractions continued to be developed in the late 1910s where spectacular landscape played a part. Scenes of natural landscape from different provinces in Sweden, often from the north typical of the fjell, river and mountainous landscapes create majestic settings, serving as both documentation and as a dramatic element.[18] To a certain extent the winter landscapes were given an exotic and picturesque character. In a review of Lau Lauritzen's comedy at a winter-sports resort, *Kärlek och björnjakt* (Love and Bear-Hunt, 1920), the film's potential for export is noted since 'a film farce with snow is seldom made by the Americans'.[19] In this film, as well as in other comedies such as *Flickorna i Åre* (Girls from Åre, 1920), also by Lauritzen, and Gustaf Molander's *Charlotte Löwensköld* (1930), the snowscape becomes a playground. The snow is not linked to cold and hunger, for it is not regarded as a threat, but to romance and recreational activities such as skiing, sledging and sleigh rides. The landscape functions as an attraction, but according to Bo Florin, is given a new and increased importance as an independent actor in the narrative as it inter-

acts with characters.[20] The central role of the northern landscape (often linked to national culture) as an expressive element in Swedish films during the 'golden age' recurs in critical writing on Swedish film.[21] Nature becomes a part of the narrative, thereby creating a background and a framework that is integrated with the characters. As Fullerton points out, the snow and ice in Victor Sjöström's *Berg-Ejvind och hans hustru* (The Outlaw and His Wife, 1918), are closely linked to the narrative. The effect is similar to that of the sea in Sjöström's earlier film *Terje Vigen* (A Man There Was, 1917), where the sea is not merely a symbol, but integrated in the narrative. The sea both creates and unites the community of Grimstad. The sea is the basis of the community's economy and geographical location, but also an instrument for the community's protection and a potential danger. In *Berg-Ejvind och hans hustru* snow serves as protection from the law, but eventually causes the death of the two main characters. The snow both separates them from the others and links them to each other: 'Again we have the same paradoxical, schematic duality of joy and community/desolation and isolation, though here the paradox is further developed with instances of joy in desolation/isolation and desolation in community'.[22]

Both Sjöström and Stiller were great dramaturgs of nature. The elements and the weather create intensity with an often troubled nature that participates in the terrestrial drama. This becomes obvious in Stiller's *Herr Arnes pengar* (Sir Arne's Treasure, 1919) with its intense atmosphere of Nordic winter where the ice literally keeps the unjust captured. During a bitter winter, the worst within living memory, the sea is frozen in Marstrand. The ships are ice-bound, and there is no promise of open water, especially not for the ship that is going to take Sir Arne's and his household's murderers back to Scotland. Only when the captain is informed of who he has on board and hands them over to the people, are the icy fetters that hold the ship imprisoned broken, and all the gates of the sea are opened wide. The cold, dark and severe people are kept imprisoned by the equally severe ice and winter. Not until justice is secured does the ice loosen its grip.

Opaque and simplified images

The snowscape is an important element in many narratives where characters are linked to the cold climate and the whiteness of the snow. This whiteness also affects the aesthetics of the image as the landscape and the background are erased by a blanket of snow. The snowy landscape is an empty space, it is an aesthetics of the void, opposed to the ontology of the filled and registered space of André Bazin. The landscape is empty, since it is a landscape with hardly any inhabitants, and a void since the snow itself erases the details and forms of the landscape, a space from which life seems to be removed.[23] The snow functions as a means to change the character of the background (and at times the foreground as well), to make it blank and obscure, or even more accentuated. The snow, thereby, becomes an expressive means in film.

Film historians commonly assume that cinematic techniques during the 1910s developed in order to achieve greater clarity and expressivity, especially in Scandinavia, Italy and the USA. Unlike these historians, Kristin Thompson tries to distinguish between clarity and expressivity, and examines the rise of expressivity in film as a goal in itself.[24] She assumes that many of the techniques of early cinema that were to become universal (such as cut-ins, parallel editing, eyeline matches, and shot/reverse shots) were introduced in order to assure narrative clarity. Around 1912, many filmmakers were able to tell stories clearly with the help of these techniques, and some directors started to explore the expressive possibilities of the medium. Thompson sees oblique or indistinct views of action as one example of expressivity. Unlike those films which strive to make objects, characters, gestures, and other aspects of the *mise-en-scène* more clearly visible, some films use these devices to make the action less visible or even disorienting through the use of new techniques or through using old ones in new ways.[25]

An example of a deceptively simple shot staged in a conventional way is the sequence in Victor Sjöström's *Ingeborg Holm* (1913) where Ingeborg's son leaves with his new foster-mother. The action is staged in depth,

in one take without any cut-ins, and with Ingeborg's back turned towards the camera most of the time. Not only is her face hidden, but her body is also hidden as she hides in the doorway to make the boy believe that she has left him behind.[26] The clarity of the staging was no longer as important as it would have been even a few years earlier when everything would have been clearly visible. As in this example, the house, the door and the gate, as well as the face of the character, would have been seen straight-on, turned towards the spectator. During the 1910s, however, expressivity became more important, and sometimes even worked against clarity. This example indicates that filmmakers realised that to heighten suspense in a scene, the explicit depiction of emotion could be just as effective and, at times, even more intense if withheld. The exploration of expressivity is, according to Thompson, the basis of the avant-garde cinema in Germany, France and the Soviet Union during the 1920s.[27]

One can find a similar use of expressive means in a snowscape which creates an indefinable

and uncertain sense of space like that of darkness in low-key Lasky lighting. Snow has a masking effect similar to the iris or an unlit background since the image seems to be over-exposed. Snow covers the landscape like a carpet, it is a landscape without distinct form. All the elements – the water, the land and the air merge into one. It gets difficult to orient oneself, it is a landscape in disguise. By the use of expressive means a very vague and fugitive image is created. The indistinct and burned-out background focuses our attention on the characters in the foreground at the same time as they appear as silhouettes. The expressive means of stark backlit silhouettes, usually shot against a daylight exterior or a large window, became widely used during the 1910s. In many striking films of the period, as for example in Benjamin Christensen's *Det Hemmelighedsfulde X* (The Mysterious X, 1913) and *Hævnens Nat* (Blind Justice, 1916) or Cecil B. DeMille's *The Cheat* (1915), startling contrasts in lighting accentuate the emotional impact of a scene.[28] Silhouetted figures are made obscure and more anonymous when their features and facial expressions become dark. It is an image in which characters are placed in a foreground that is no longer clearly visible. Also in images of the snowy landscape we see dark figures set against a light background. As with silhouette images, the background becomes very light and the figures very dark as the contrast between light and darkness, whiteness and blackness, is emphasised. Thereby light and darkness may be used to disguise figures, mask characters and their position in space, and sometimes even transform space itself. The characters as well as the image become obscure in settings that become both deep and indistinct.

According to David Bordwell, directors during the 1910s strove for sharp focus on all planes. But continuity editing employing close-ups posed problems for this aesthetic since it was difficult to maintain focus. The close-up isolates the object in space, not only through framing, but also through a relatively shallow depth of field.[29] The viewer's attention was thereby controlled as the foreground was emphasised and the distracting backgrounds were masked off by throwing them out of focus or by creating an effect like that of the iris. Both methods keep the spectator's attention from straying to background areas. In *Herr Arnes pengar* the contrast between light and darkness in the very snowy scenery, as well as the alternating use of the black and white iris, create an effect of emphasis as well as an almost invisible masking that corresponds with the background. The use of a black iris is more accentuated, but the use of a white iris, at times very hazy, like falling snow, impedes our view (Fig. 2). The distinction between the white iris and the diegetic snow becomes vague. Through the use of selective focus, a play and interaction between different planes of the image can be achieved, creating what Bordwell terms a laminated space, as in for example *The New Babylon* (Grigori Kozintsev and Leonid Trauberg, 1929) where rain blurs the figures in the background while the figures in the foreground remain in sharp focus. It shows that staging can be structured in depth even when foreground focus is localised. By the mid-1920s some American cinematographers also explored a hazy style for all planes of the image, creating glamorised stars and lyrical landscapes.[30]

Snow either covers and masks the ground, or masks the whole image by its movement as it falls. It hides the landscape and/or the action in it. In both cases snow conceals the content of the image and makes it blurred. Despite their varied opinions about the patriotic value of *Karl XII,* critics were most enthusiastic about the battle scenes, especially the movement and rhythm of the cutting in the Battle of Narva.[31] The snowstorm, as well as the dust from the gunpowder, are central to the feeling of movement in the scene. The way in which our view is blocked helps create the sense of order and disorder that one critic expected of battle scenes.[32] The snowstorm seems to overtake the image where the diffuse and dark silhouettes of soldiers move in the dust and snow which disguises both the background that is completely blocked, and the foreground in front of the soldiers. There are no clear planes in the image at all (Fig. 3).

But the snow not only disguises the landscape, it can also make it more open, distinct and simplified. At the opening of the second

Fig. 3. Frame enlargement, Karl XII, 1925. The Battle of Narva.

part of the film, when the Russians withdraw to the forest from a snow-clad field, Karl XII exclaims: 'Let them run to their recesses! A Swede wants open fields and an open battle!'.[33] Snow accentuates the open landscape and promotes visibility while at the same time the snow thrown up by the horses makes the landscape less distinct. A wintry landscape is a land defined by absence where a person is exposed and where there are no places in which to hide. The similarities to a desert, a seemingly opposite type of landscape and climate, is striking. As Jane Tompkins points out in her analysis of the Western, the desert makes the human figure seem dominant against the blankness of the background. The figure becomes emphasised, in an image based on the contrasts between the figure and the surrounding, not only between the dark figure against a light background, but also between the vertical figure against a horizon-

tal landscape. The blankness extends the view as far as the eye can see, and everything and everyone is visible and accessible to the characters. The horseman in the desert can freely move across the terrain. In this unlimited, virgin space the possibilities are infinite (Fig. 4).[34]

In *Med Sven Hedin i österled* (Going East with Sven Hedin, Svensk Filmindustri, 1928), we follow Hedin's expedition through the interior of Asia, a journey full of hardship through a barren landscape. This land is very similar to that of the snowy landscape. Two members of the expedition even ski in the desert (Fig.5), and all the tracks made by a camel thief are covered by the whirling sand. The similarities between the two apparently very different climates become obvious when the expedition is first stricken by a sand storm, and later, when the wind has abated, they are overwhelmed by a snow-storm. The images are conspicuously similar. Both the sand and the snow render the view obscure, snow being only lighter in tone. In spite of that, the snow means an end to the shortage of water, it creates the *tour de force* of the expedition (and provides the film's dramatic climax) as the snow leads to a shortage of food and severe cold. Many of the camels die, and Hedin has to stay behind due to sickness.

Snow also functions as a source of light that clarifies the surrounding. In the dark Nordic winter nights, the ground and the back-

ground, rather than the sky, become the source of light. In the calm and quiet winter nights the landscape itself is the light, the ground is radiant against the dark sky. It is a light from which one cannot escape, not even at night, since snow diminishes the concealing power of darkness. At the beginning of Christensen's Danish film *Hævnens Nat,* an escaped convict vainly chases shadows in a moonlit and snow-covered park on New Year's Eve. It is almost impossible to hide in the exposing landscape where everything is lit and is as discernible as during the day; even the man's tracks are fully visible. The snow that reveals tracks can, however, also hide them. A flurry of snow covers the pursued man's tracks, and convinces his pursuers that he is not in the area. In this scene snow not only creates a light from which it is difficult to hide, but a sound as well: 'The crunching snow seemed to cut through the night air like gunfire. He sought the shadows as he ran.' The intertitles connected with the snowy scenes are illustrated with dark trees with white outlines against a jet-black background. The snow emphasises the man's exposed and hopeless situation. The night scenes, lit by snow, become realistic since there is no visible lighting.

Den Starkaste, on the other hand, is set above the Arctic circle during the summer where the sun is up twenty-four hours a day. The light summer sky does not create any contrast to the white landscape of snow and ice, but looks the same, everything is light. Here the two Nordic lights, that of summer night and that of snow, co-exist. Form is simplified as the characters stand out as dark figures against the constantly light, unchanging landscape. The weather is clear all the time, except in the scene in which Gustaf, together with some other members of the crew, are surprised by fog when they are out on a small boat among the ice-floes and can no longer see their ship. The scene is most dangerous for the male hero who collapses on the ice and almost gets killed. He stays in control only as long as the surrounding landscape is fully visible. The ice and fog dissolve visibility. The ice cannot, however, conceal anything since there is nothing underneath it except the ocean. It is a landscape that hardly exists, a landscape

that is constantly changing. One gets the impression that the elements themselves emanate light, an effect similar to what Fabrice Revault d'Allonnes describes as typical of modern lighting. For Revault d'Allonnes, modern light seems to emit from the objects themselves, and characters and things can exist as equals, in contrast to the theatrical light of classical film where symbolic illumination, in keeping with the drama, is projected onto characters and objects. A light that emanates also reflects certain ideas of the period, and demonstrates the power of nature over characters.[35]

Snow as narrative climax

Snow elucidates the physical presence of characters with a masked and erased white background, and the Nordic light of night and winter. Thereby, snow often creates a narrative climax as well as a specific imagery. Freezing nights in the snow often underscore important narrative situations where a person's (or a creature's) vulnerability becomes accentuated. This theme recurs in Stiller's *Gösta Berlings saga* (The Story of Gösta Berling, 1924) where there are several night scenes in the Värmland winter. In the film's first exterior night scene, Gösta Berling, a recently defrocked priest, finds a small wounded bird in the snow when he wanders along the road. He picks the bird up and puts it inside his jacket to give it warmth (he himself is very poorly dressed), and takes it with him. The scene shows the bird's, as well as Berling's, exposed nature and vulnerability.

The snowscape works as a melodramatic space for climactic scenes in a number of films. Quite often there is only one scene with snow, a scene that is central to the narrative as, for example, in the fight between the two rivals in Ivar Johansson's *Rågens rike* (Land of Rye, 1929), or where Marit is found in a snow-drift by her future husband in Stiller's *Johan* (Troubled Water, 1921).[36] In *Berg-Ejvind och hans hustru* snow is an important element in several of the film's central scenes. The film's plot starts and ends with devastating winter nights. Berg-Ejvind's life as an outlaw arises from his theft of a sheep to save his starving family during a hard winter. As

Florin points out, the scenes with winter and snow stand out in sharp contrast to the happier summer days at Halla's farm and the early years in the mountains.[37] The combination of snow and cold is a metaphor for extreme distress (Fig. 6) as an intertitle at the end of the film makes clear: 'It was a winter night so terrible, that the roots of the grass were trembling with anguish under the snow ...'.[38] The snow-storm has lasted for seven days and Berg-Ejvind and his wife are starving. Halla leaves their cabin without closing the door since she no longer needs its warmth. Berg-Ejvind discovers her tracks and follows them to find her lying in the snow, waiting to die. They are united in a last embrace while the snow whirls into their home, covering the floor as the wind blows out the fire in the hearth. The film's very last image shows a bright dawn, after the snow-storm, as if Berg-Ejvind and his wife have dissolved into the celestial light.

In the Nordic winter landscape women are usually portrayed as quite helpless. They do not seem to be able to grow out of the element in the way that men do. Those who are exposed to the freezing elements usually collapse in the first snow-drift, and are completely dependent upon someone passing by to save them. The women succumb to the snow and the cold, while men survive; for them it becomes a challenge. After the dramatic scene on Ekeby in *Gösta Berlings saga*

Fig. 5. Production still, Med Sven Hedin i österled, *1928. [Courtesy of the Stills Archive, Swedish Film Institute. Members of the expedition skiing in the sand.]*

which results in Marianne's father furiously leaving her behind, Marianne runs all the way home in pursuit of her parent's sleigh in the cold and snowy night, only to discover that her father has locked her out. She then collapses in a snow-drift where Gösta Berling finds her and takes her home (he saves her again later in the film from the fire). 'Poor is the bride of Gösta Berling – in the snow-drift he found her... .'[39] During this eventful night, even the major's wife at Ekeby is driven from her home. But she is a shining exception to the cliché of weak women. She does not fall into the snow in despair, but wanders day and night in the cold winter to ask her mother to remove a curse from her. Not only a person's vulnerability may be shown in this setting, but also a character's strength, as in the example above. In the portrayal of the major's wife the winter night scenes are central.[40]

A snowy landscape is like the desert in the Western, a *tabula rasa* where a certain kind of person (almost always a male) can be in control of himself as well as the external world

through his physical and psychological strength,[41] despite the constant presence of such physical challenges as hunger, pain and death. Snow is a symbol of freedom and of the opportunity of conquest, but at the same time one can never master nature. It is the one thing that is larger than man, the ultimate challenge. The Western, according to Tompkins, is an escape from modern society, a negation of its comforts, and a code of asceticism. It is a hostile environment, that of death. Death is a central phenomenon in the landscape of the Western, a landscape where nothing lives: 'To go west, as far as you can go, west of everything, is to die'.[42] The desert is the landscape of an always-present death which is one of the genre's most essential features. Even the landscape of snow and ice can be a space of death. As in the Western, it is a death by beauty, of an almost spiritual transcendence under the power of nature. The Arctic landscape is a land defined by absence: of trees, vegetation, houses, shelter or comfort. It is a negation of any sign of civilisation, nature is immense and transcendent. In a recent paper, Ioulia Fokina compares the diaries of two Polar explorers, Fridtjof Nansen (from Norway) and the Russian, Eduard Toll, and shows that they both compare the vast space of the Arctic with death.[43] Nansen finds that: 'To be in the North means to be before the cold grave of nature. There are all the enemies of life here: frost, ice, and night. ... The mystery of life disappears in this endless space.'[44] In *Herr Arnes pengar* there are three scenes that link death with the vast expanse of the frozen sea: firstly, the tracks from the sleigh in which Sir Arne's murderers escape, that end abruptly at the edge of a hole in the ice, so making the pursuers believe that the murderers had found their grave; secondly, when Elsalill's dead foster-sister follows Sir Archie over the ice, and finally, the funeral procession at the end, when the women of the town come to the ice-bound ship in a procession to bear home the body of Elsalill. Even though these three scenes are linked to death, and in a film where a number of murders are committed, nobody actually dies on the ice (with the exception of the horse that pulls the sleigh).

The colour white can be a symbol for good,

and the spiritually pure; whiteness can also bring about death.[45] The image of death is, according to Dyer, central to Christianity. It is an image of a transcendent dissolution in light, blank or immaterial, or even an intimation of nothingness.[46] Light from within merges into the celestial, just as white figures merge with the snow. In Gustaf Molander's *Förseglade läppar* (Sealed Lips, 1927), a disabled woman takes her life when she realises that her husband is in love with another woman. She sits in her wheelchair on the terrace and freezes to death in the first snow of the year. This scene stands out in the film since it is the only one that contains snow or even cold weather. The scene actually has two other references to snow and death, one (to which she does not pay any attention) is the polar bearskin that is placed on the floor just inside the door to the terrace, the other is Guy de Maupassant's novel *Le Colporteur*, which she reads and which gives her the idea to commit suicide in the snow.

White death is, however, a purifying death where the victim usually is a woman. According to Gaston Bachelard, water is the element of the truly female death. Water is the true element of a beautiful and peaceful death, or a masochistic suicide such as Ophelia's. Clear water is also purifying in a moral sense; one enters water to be renewed.[47] Clean white snow also seems to be able to purify the moral burden of protagonists. Towards the end of D.W. Griffith's *Way Down East* (1920), the heroine, Anna, is physically purified by the cold and the ice. She does not obtain complete redress when the truth of her situation is revealed, but her physical purification is necessary. Linda Williams points out that the melodramatic scene, which starts with the naming of the villain, is the heroine's only divergence from silence, her only action. Anna then runs out into the snow-storm in a suicidal gesture. The last-minute rescue from the icy river is necessary to recognise her innocence and virtue. Williams finds that her sexual guilt remains after the nomination of the villain. According to the patriarchal laws of society she is still guilty, but the icy river makes redress possible since the natural elements take the place of the villain.[48] It is the cold river that endangers her. Anna's ordeal occurs in three stages: first, a snow-storm, second, the river with its ice blocks, and finally, the waterfall. The journey towards death both emphasises her helplessness and the rescue at the very last moment. Even in the final scene in *Berg-Ejvind och hans hustru*, the two protagonists are purified and forgiven, not by man, but by God when they commit suicide in the snow-storm. As they are covered by snow, seemingly becoming one with the whiteness, the film's penultimate intertitle makes clear that 'Death gave them forgive-ness ...'.

Notes

1. Quotation from Alf Sjöberg's diary from the production of *Den Starkaste*. Undated source from Svenska Filminstitutets bibliotek, Stockholm. Unless otherwise stated the translations are made by the author. Ladugårdsgärde, a large open land in Stockholm, and former military training ground.

    '*Lörd. den 15/6– 29*. Vi väckas kl. 7 av stewarten med nyheten att vi *möta isen*.

    Stort jubel! Alla upp med iver.

    Sjöberg–Lindblom och Dahlqvist-Westerberg embarkerar ombord på Maud, där genast filmningen igångsättes. Isflaken flyta, blå, gröna, vita, havet och himlen verka förtrollande, det hela är overkligt ...

    Månd. den 17/6 – 29 ... Snart forcera vi isen och skutorna gå smidiga som kattor mellan de förrädiska flaken med farliga undervattensbottnar ...

    Månd. 1/7 ... Isen har förändrat karaktär. Flaken bli sammanhängande och stora som Ladugårdsgärde ... Sensationen av ödemark, färger och storvulenhet var oförglömmelig och aldrig förr erfaren.

    Tisd. 2/7 ... Plötsligt kommer rapporten om 'björn på isen' ... Efter en timme se vi den – konungen, långsamt lufsa fram över floran. Han går i vattnet! Vi sätter ut en båt, som släpas över isen. Djurberg i fören, Dahlqvist i aktern. De gå ut – få efter oerhörda vedermödor en lasso om Gammel-Grålas hals och hålla honom, timme efter timme, medan våra skutor forcera isen, millimeter för millimeter, ibland med hjälp av dynamit. Så kommer vi loss och ilar till nallen. Tre båtar sättas äntligen ut,

efter en massa besvär lossa vi snaran och han simmar mot floran. Båtarna med kameror efter. Han dyker under isflak, kommer upp på floran och dör efter tre skott …

Tisd. 16/7 … En behaglig känsla av tappert övervunna lidanden och manligt högmod fyller vår barm, när vi höra våra gästers ohöljda förvåning och beundran över att vi på detta äggskal gungat över vreda hav och i denna spartanska obekvämlighet trotsat faror och funnit oss i umbäranden under en hel månad …'

2. For example, in *Social-Demokraten* (22 May 1929).

3. *Dagens Nyheter* (29 October 1929): 'Det är starka, kärva, manliga tag i denna nya svenska film. Det sliskiga, sentimentala är så gott som bannlyst i manuskriptet. Man har att göra med människor som kämpa för sin utkomst under hårda förhållanden, män som få brottas med naturens krafter i ishavets majestätiska, men också ödsliga och farofyllda trakter. 'Den Starkaste' är först och främst en film om män och deras nappatag. Med varandra; kvinnan har sitt ord med i laget endast som en sporre, en drivfjäder i den kamp som både bildlikt och rent bokstavligt utkämpas mellan de båda mästerskyttarna …'

4. Festschrift by Hjalmar Bergman and H. E. Uddgren 1925: 'Den unge hjälten … kommer från ett kargt och kärvt land, civilisationens utpost vid gränsen till det vintriga mörkrets välde. Han är konung över ett folk, vars livsbetingelser äro mod och möda, redbarhet och hjälpsamhet.'

5. The bear-hunt is a recurrent theme in Swedish films, showing the dangers of the milieu, and the courage and strength of the protagonist. According to Brunius, the early collaboration with the German directors Lupu Pick and Henrik Galeen were not only broken due to economic reasons, but also because the scene of the bear-hunt was regarded as un-Swedish, since it did not express a notion of danger as the Swedish people would have liked, see *Filmjournalen* (no. 1, 1925). Even though the scene was remade in Sweden, it was criticised for showing a bear that was so tame that the audience felt sorry for it. 'XX', *Göteborgs Morgonpost* (31 January 1925). In Lau Lauritzen's comedy *Kärlek och björnjakt* (Love and Bear-Hunt, 1920) this theme was used for a comical scene. In the film, Greta, a young woman, is impressed by Glob bragging about his courage at bear-hunts. His rival decides, with the help of a friend, to reveal Glob by dressing up in bearskins and chasing him.

6. The intertitle reads: 'Här finnes intet val. En svensk ger sig aldrig!'

7. The intertitle reads: 'de fientliga skansarna, bröt en snöstorm lös som piskade moskoviten i synen …'

8. Later in the film, the army is finally overcome by the insuperable difficulties that confronted them in the heart of Russia – cold, hunger, and the vast expanse of land. The cold climate had now become their enemy.

9. For an account of the historical background, see *Nationalmuseum Stockholm* (Höganäs: Bokförlaget Bra Böcker, 1984), 47–52.

10. Lars Åhlander (ed.), *Svensk filmografi*, II, (Stockholm: Svenska Filminstitutet, 1982), 242–243.

11. The film's producer, Herman Rasch saw in the life of Karl XII an emblem of determination and firm Nordic strength, see interview with Rasch, 'L', uncatalogued article, Svenska Filminstitutets bibliotek.

12. *Svensk filmografi*, II, 15–16. The critics were especially enthusiastic about the skiing tour to the Norwegian border and the genuine Swedish landscape represented in the film, see, for example, Arthur Nordén, *Stockholms-Tidningen* (6 March 1928), *Svenska Dagbladet* (6 March 1928), and 'Hake' in *Aftonbladet* (6 March 1928). The series of patriotic and historical films also includes Rudolf Anthoni's *Carl XII:s kurir* (Courier of Charles XII, 1924), Elis Ellis' *Två konungar* (Two Kings, 1925), and *Fänrik Ståls sägner* (Tales of Ensign Steel, 1926).

13. For example, *Arbetaren* (3 February 1925), 'Bes', *Folkets Dagblad Politiken* (3 February 1925), 'D', *Göteborgs Handels- och Sjöfartstidning/Göteborgstidningen* (31 January 1925), and 'Es Ån', *Göteborgs-Posten* (31 January 1925).

14. For example, see *Stockholms-Tidningen* (3 February 1925), and 'J. Hbg.', *Kvällstidningen* (January 1925).

15. Richard Dyer, *White* (London, New York: Routledge, 1997), 21.

16. Ibid.

17. Several films were made about the Sami people that describe their culture and way of life, as in *Lappbilder* (Svensk Kinematograf, 1906), *En resa i midnattssolens land* (Svenska Biografteatern, 1908), *Med svenska lappar på vårflyttning* (Pathé Frères, 1915), *Där norrskenet flammar* (dir. Ragnar

Westfelt, 1923), *I fjällfolkets land* (dir. Erik Bergström, 1923), and the sequel by the same director *Med ackja och ren i Inka Läntas vinterland* (1926). Even fiction films were made such as *Lappens brud eller dramat i vildmarken* (dir. John Bergqvist, 1913), and *Kultur och natur* (dir. Ivar Berthel, 1919).

18. John Fullerton, *The Development of a System of Representation in Swedish Film 1912–1920*, Doctoral Dissertation, Department of Film Studies, University of East Anglia, May 1994, 302.

19. '[T]y en filmfars med snö servera amerikanerna mera sällan', *Aftonbladet* (31 Augusti 1920). Even Lauritzen's *Flickorna i Åre*, another comedy, also made in the skiing resort of Åre in the same year, received similar comments. A critic noted that the snow-covered landscape is how he/she would wish to present Sweden abroad, see 'AL', *Stockholms-Tidningen* (7 December 1920).

20. Bo Florin, *Den nationella stilen. Studier i den svenska filmens guldålder* (Stockholm: Aura förlag, 1997), 199–200.

21. For a detailed analysis of the norms of style during the Swedish 'golden age', see Florin.

22. John Fullerton, 'The First Swedish Film Masterpiece: Terje Vigen', *Focus on Film* no. 20 (Spring 1975): 54.

23. For an analysis of the aesthetics of the void in film, see José Moure, *Vers une esthétique du vide au cinéma* (Paris: Éditions L'Harmattan, 1997).

24. Kristin Thompson, 'The International Exploration of Cinematic Expressivity', in Karel Dibbets and Bert Hogenkamp (eds.), *Film and the First World War* (Amsterdam: Amsterdam University Press, 1995), 65–85.

25. Ibid. 65–69.

26. Ibid. 67.

27. Ibid. 83.

28. Ibid. 76.

29. David Bordwell, *On the History of Film Style* (Cambridge, Mass., London: Harvard University Press, 1997), 201–204.

30. Ibid. 204–205. For a discussion of lens diffusion of a selected area of the frame in French films, see Barry Salt, *Film Style and Technology: History and Analysis* (London: Starword, 1992), 161.

31. For example, see 'Marfa', *Dagens Nyheter* (3 February 1925), 'D', *Göteborgs Handels- och Sjöfarts-tidning / Göteborgstidningen* (31 January 1925), and *Stockholms-Tidningen* (3 February 1925).

32. 'XX', *Göteborgs Morgonpost* (31 January 1925). The effect of falling snow is similar to the Swedish artist Nils Kreuger's way of covering the surface of his paintings with thousands of dots, as in *Aprilväder* (April Weather, 1907), where big snowflakes cover the painting rendering the subject obscure. Such effects were common in Swedish painting during the 1880s as painters such as Kreuger and Carl Larsson created a feeling of participation for the observer, of 'being inside' the motif, by raising, or at times even completely omitting, the horizon. Even in Bruno Liljefors' work, the ground often covers the whole painting, see Lindgren, Lyberg, Sandström and Wahlberg, *Svensk konsthistoria* (Lund: Bokförlaget Signum, 1993), 374–391.

33. The intertitle reads: 'Låt dem löpa till sina skrymslen! Öppet fält och öppen strid vill svensken hava!'

34. Jane Tompkins, *West of Everything: The Inner Life of Westerns* (New York, Oxford: Oxford University Press, 1992), 74–75. For an analysis of the emptiness of the scenery in the Western film, see Moure, 34–35. As the life of Berg-Ejvind and Halla in the mountains is described in *Röda Kvarns Film-Nyheter*: 'For five years they both lived happily together as outlaws. It is true that man hunted them as animals and life was harsh among the colourless gorges of the desert and the everlasting ice, but they were masters of the land as far as they could see, and their love was the sun in their lives.' 'I fem år levde de båda lyckligt tillsammans i fredlösheten. Visserligen voro de jagade som djur av människorna, och livet var hårt bland klippöknens färglösa klyftor och eviga is, men de voro landets härskare så långt de kunde se, och kärleken var solen i deras liv.'

35. Fabrice Revault d'Allonnes, *La lumière au cinéma* (Paris: Editions Cahiers de cinéma, 1991), 18, 39, 47.

36. In *Johan* snow also exists in the scene that follows where Marit's link to Johan is emphasised as she is now his wife.

37. Florin, 82.

38. The intertitle reads: 'Det var en vinternatt så fruktansvärd, att gräsrötterna skälvde av ångest under snön . . .'

39. The intertitle reads: 'Fattig är Gösta Berlings brud – i snödrifvan hittade han henne …'

40. The first time we meet her, when she hits a man who is whipping a horse, she finds Berling at night in the smithy about to take his life, and at the end of the film she sets Ekeby on fire. In Selma Lagerlöf's novel she even finds Berling unconscious in the snow and saves him. Another exceptional example where a woman can survive by herself in a snowy landscape and actually save someone else is *The Ends of Earth* (Vitagraph, 1911). In this film a man leaves his wife to go North to the snowy wilderness. After six months the wife sets off after him and finds him totally helpless in the snow with a broken leg. The modern urban woman actually saves her husband from certain death.

41. Cf. Tompkins, 70.

42. Ibid. 24.

43. Ioulia Fokina, 'Man and nature in Russian and Norwegian culture', paper presented at Nordiskt samehistoriskt symposium, 1998, Kautokeino, 17–18 November 1998.

44. The silent polar night creates an eternal space where a man's death means nothing, Toll wrote in his diary, during 1900–02, on an expedition, equipped by the Academy of Sciences, to research the Taimyr peninsula in search of the legendary land of Sunnikov. Toll also pays attention to the lifelessness of the Arctic landscape, and sees travel to the North as a journey to the country of Death.

45. For discussion of the ambiguity of white and black, see Revault d'Allonnes, 91–95.

46. Dyer, 207.

47. Gaston Bachelard, *L'eau et les rêves* (Paris: Libraire José Corti, 1942).

48. Linda Williams, unpublished paper, 'Melodrama Revised', delivered at the Department of Cinema Studies, Stockholm University, November 1995, 48–56.

Victor Goes West: Notes on the Critical Reception of Sjöström's Hollywood Films, 1923–1930

Bo Florin

Department of Cinema Studies, Stockholm University, 105 21 Stockholm, Sweden

By the time of his departure for Hollywood in 1923, Victor Sjöström had gained a solid reputation in Sweden as the most important and influential director during the period that has been characterised as the 'golden age' of Swedish cinema, 1917–23. He was challenged only by Stiller who, however, never reached the same level of fame of his colleague. The fact that Sjöström was hired by Metro-Goldwyn-Mayer has, therefore, been generally seen both as a logical consequence of his competence and as an irreparable loss for Swedish national cinema. As critics and, to some extent, later historians thought, the decline in national production that took place in the mid-1920s has frequently been explained by Sjöström's and, later, Stiller's move to Hollywood.[1] After their departure, there only remained:

> ... in relation to cinema, both yesterday and today, certain equally untalented gentlemen who later, when it had become necessary to tighten one's belt, and Stiller and Sjöström had already lifted their wings in an inspired flight over the Atlantic, simply but not painlessly demonstrated on what miserable foundations Sweden's much-vaunted film art was built.[2]

The example of Sjöström underlines the importance of the press as a cultural institution, active in the ongoing process of interpreting individual films as well as the cinema institution itself. Thus, the press contributes to the regulation of cinema, both of production in the past and of our historical understanding of its development. Criticism, in Sabine Hake's words, 'was a weapon in the struggle for cultural dominance, it was a product of modern consumer culture, it was a form of political and intellectual resistance'.[3] In studying this particular aspect of film reception, my approach is also close to that of Janet Staiger in *Interpreting Films*: I treat the notions which, implicitly or explicitly, figure in the press, as 'significant historical *reading strategies*'.[4] I am interested not only in what they say about Sjöström, but also in the hypotheses and conclusions – if any – that they permit concerning the intersection of the film cultures in Sweden and America in the 1920s.

So far, there are relatively few contributions to the history of silent film criticism in Sweden. A dissertation by Elisabeth Liljedahl offers a broad survey of the field, but presents little in-depth analysis.[5] Several essays by Jan Olsson (one offering a more general account of criticism in the daily newspapers of the period, another more specifically concentrating on the development of Swedish censorship) provide important contributions to the history of the ways in which cinema was conceptualised. On the specific subject of Sjöström in Hollywood, Bengt Forslund's biographically-oriented dissertation on the director mentions the reviews of the different US films, but does not discuss them systematically.

Thus, the purpose of this essay is twofold: to discuss the critical reception in Sweden of Sjöström's American productions on one hand, and to sum up the discourse in the US press concerning Sjöström on the other, with particular emphasis on his role as a European director. I will proceed through a close reading of press reviews, with special focus on the question of Europe versus Hollywood. The question of a Swedish national film culture or, more generally, a European film culture and its relation to (inter)national American cinema, is to be found at the heart of the debate of the period. Thus, through this analysis, I also hope to offer a contribution to the history of the critical reception of cinema in the 1920s, focusing on the relation between a relatively small European film country and the production giant in the west.

Background

Sjöström's unique position in Sweden, as well as the general idea of a 'golden age' in Swedish cinema, are clearly expressed in Swedish newspapers and film journals in the period preceding the director's departure for Hollywood. In the discussion of Swedish cinema – which is often identified with Sjöström/Stiller – in relation to Hollywood, a recurrent theme is the competition between quality and quantity. A typical example of this line of argument is to be found in an article in the magazine *Filmen* from 1919:

> When things have got back into the old

groove again in the world, we will have reason to hope that Swedish films *with Swedish trade marks* shall go round half the world or the whole world. According to the press, there are plans to increase our production so that, even quantitatively, we will become fairly 'American'. As long as there is no legislation disadvantageous to the cinema, there is a real opportunity for us to become the most distinguished film nation in Europe.[6]

The critic apparently seems to acknowledge the dominant position of American cinema, the argument being that Swedish cinema is already 'American' from the point of view of quality, if not of quantity. A critic in *Filmjournalen* the following year, however, turned out to be more sceptical towards the Americans. At the same time, with remarkable self-assurance, he expresses the same certainty about the unique quality of Swedish cinema as his *Filmen* colleague:

> The Swedish contribution to the film season that has now come to an end has as strikingly as before claimed the old truth that our Nordic film art clearly defends its position, even compared with the big, leading American nation and its quantitatively overwhelming production which, however, is not always qualitatively that impressive. … And after having established this fact, the question has to be posed: will our own film art be able to keep its position as at least number 2 in the world?[7]

While these cited examples discuss the position of Swedish cinema in general, most of the reviews focus on Sjöström's films in particular, sometimes together with Stiller's. Either it is in a positive manner, as in the comparison of a new Stiller film doomed as superficial with earlier masterpieces by both directors, or negatively, as in a review of Sjöström's *Karin Ingmarsdotter* (1920) by 'Damsel' (Siri Thorngren-Olin) who had had enough of peasantry:

> Victor Sjöström's latest film, Karin Ingmarsdotter, treads faithfully in the footsteps of its predecessor – this should be said both by way of praise and by way of blame. One will find the same solidness

as well in structure as in execution, with the same pleasure as in the previous film. One will gaze at all the beautiful pictures that are unfolding, pictures of both external and internal beauty; one will be caught by the true Swedish tone that is permeating the entire performance. But does it not taste a bit of stagnation with this Ingmarssonian trot in the beaten track, and will not the viewer, less so the faithful native than the foreign one, be easily overfed by the thoroughness that lets realism expand to the extent that there will hardly be space left for imagination?[8]

This review is representative of a certain tendency in the Swedish press of the period, where critics suppose that the decline in Swedish cinema is the result of the dissatisfaction of the audience towards the Swedish model of filmmaking, which in turn had to do with its insufficient internationalisation. The other main tendency, on the contrary, claimed that the cause was to be found precisely in the superficiality that attended internationalisation. 'Quelqu'une' (Märta Lindqvist) in the national daily newspaper *Svenska Dagbladet* thus wrote:

> It is with a certain sadness that one notes in 'Gunnar Hedes saga' [*The Blizzard*, 1923] that Swedish film seems to be far removed from the old, distinguished traditions. In this film, there is little of the spiritual strength, the culture, and the artistic purposefulness that made masterpieces out of 'Stormyrtösen', 'Ingmarssönerna', 'Herr Arnes pengar', and 'Körkarlen'.[9] Instead, there are troublesome tendencies, feelers thrown out in order to satisfy banal foreign taste. It would be more than regrettable if practical–economical reasons should bring about a diminishment of the strict artistic principles that have brought Swedish cinema to an exceptional position in the international film market.[10]

The contradiction in the argument is worth noting. On one hand, the critic is reproachful of the wish 'to satisfy banal foreign taste', but on the other hand, she praises the 'strict artistic principles' just because they have brought international fame to Swedish cinema; obviously, foreign taste should not always be accused of banality. But 'Quelqu'une' was right to some extent in so far as Stiller's film was well received in the US, a fact that was discussed in a later issue of *Filmjournalen*.[11]

Swedish voices

There were obviously several quite contradictory positions concerning the subject of Hollywood versus Sweden in Swedish film journalism during the 'golden age'. With the new generation of critics that replaced the old ones at the time of Sjöström's and Stiller's departure for Hollywood, one might expect a change in attitude.[12] In trying to investigate Swedish perspectives on Sjöström's American productions, I have chosen one main example: reviews from *Filmjournalen*. This journal started in 1919 and was the most influential of the specialist Swedish film journals. As a rule, its reviews were quite extensive, and were written by several different reviewers with one critic, the writer Sven Stolpe (sometimes also using the signature 'Spes'), dominating the scene. This makes it possible to follow both changes and variations in the attitude towards Sjöström's foreign career, most notably in its relation to American cinema. Even though the selection of material is limited, it nevertheless seems sensible to suppose that these reviews reflected general opinions expressed in Sweden on the subject of Sjöström in Hollywood. The representative role assigned to this journal on the subject is confirmed by the comparison of the reviews to those published in daily newspapers as well as other film journals.[13] On a few occasions, however, I will also refer to other press commentaries.

At first, Sjöström's stay in Hollywood was obviously expected to last for only a short time. Critics noted that he was leaving, but only for a year – after which it was supposed that he would undoubtedly continue his work in Sweden.[14] One critic rejoiced in the general importance of Sjöström's journey for Swedish film production, firstly, because Sjöström would bring back fresh impulses and new knowledge from Hollywood, and secondly, because his departure for the States meant that the significance of Swedish film had been duly acknowledged by the whole world.[15]

This argument is perfectly in line with the articles cited above, discussing the international role of Swedish cinema and assigning it a specific national quality which only seemed to await recognition. The audience present at the release of *Name the Man* in Stockholm also sent a telegram to the director, certifying that if Sjöström would continue as he had begun he could be assured of its gratitude. 'Continue the way you have begun, faithful to your own specificity and your traditions, and you may always be assured of the gratefulness of your native country regarding your artistry, your enthusiasm, and above all, the depth and authenticity of your feelings that bring fame to Sweden over there.'[16]

In 1924, *Filmjournalen* also took up the theme of the 'progress of Swedish film in America', a progress which to a large extent was attributed to Victor Sjöström's accomplishments. The article mentions the success of *The Girl from the Marsh Croft* and *The Stroke of Midnight*, and it claims the success of *Name the Man* in the US (which is not all that evident from American reviews). On the subject of the American reception of *Name the Man*, it is striking that despite the ambivalent or negative reactions in the US, Swedish critics generally noted with satisfaction and a great deal of national pride that the film had been well received. 'Far from having been suffocated by gigantic American production, Victor Sjöström's honesty and authenticity still dominate, and his skills have won fame at the cost of many aspects that hitherto had been praised, although only for a short while.'[17] Apart from Sjöström's films, the *Filmjournalen* article also points to the breakthrough in the US of Stiller's *Gunnar Hedes saga*. 'One was not able to understand how a small distant country like Sweden could have made such accomplishments – that this small nation could surpass *America* in film production. How do they manage to do it?'[18]

Under the headline 'Victor Sjöström's American film', 'Csd' (Ragnar Cederstrand) in *Filmjournalen* went on to discuss *Name the Man* (1924), as if the film might be his only production in the United States. In this article, the ambivalence towards Hollywood that is so clearly expressed in the press commentaries during the 'golden' years returns forcefully. The argument, somewhat contradictory, seems first to suggest that the film is a disappointment, but then goes on to praise both its character portrayal and its particular 'Sjöströmian' quality. It is as though expectations had been higher just because of the American context, but then again, the anticipated 'Hollywoodness' that might have been present in the film turns out to be absent from the finished film: 'The first impression of "Name the Man" is, it must be mentioned, not quite as overwhelming as one might have expected. The film lacks neither brilliance nor technical virtuosity, but the mixture of American and Swedish is confusing.' According to the critic, this confusion has to do with Sjöström's ambition to create a human drama based on character development and not only a narrative where certain events unfold. He concludes: 'To us, "Name the Man" is only a new and highly interesting Sjöström film – "only" here understood as: only the best is good enough!'[19]

Unlike the evaluation of the director's first film in Hollywood as typical of Sjöström as well as Swedish in many ways, Sven Stolpe discovers a clear American influence in Sjöström's next film, *He Who Gets Slapped* (1924), particularly with its more marked emphasis on dramatic action. The ambivalence, though, is still present:

> 'He Who Gets Slapped' is a strong dramatic piece, rich with intensely captivating scenes. Some might be considered as too 'American' – in any case, they would have been unthinkable in Sjöström's Swedish films. We think of such a horrible scene as the one where the lion dashes into the small room and before the eyes of the dying clown tears his two enemies to pieces! Still, the boundary between the sensational and the tasteless is never crossed.[20]

Thus, on one hand, the action scenes are praised for their dramatic intensity; on the other hand there is an implicit argument that precisely these same 'American' qualities might diminish the value of the film. Writing on *Confessions of a Queen* (1925), 'Spes' explicitly develops this argument:

> The great problem for Victor Sjöström

during his stay in Hollywood – may it soon come to an end – has been to avoid being transformed into Seastrom. So far, he has been successful. In spite of great difficulties, which have to be kept in mind by anyone who picks up a pen in order to evaluate his American productions, Sjöström has remained European. The rustling dollar bills have not made him give up the invaluable cultural tradition which places the European one step higher than the American. On the other hand, Sjöström has learned a great deal from the yankees. His art is still essential, it has remained serious and kept its human truth, but he has sharpened his eye and become more light-handed.[21]

The Swedish film critics' general ambiguity towards Hollywood has rarely been expressed more directly or in a more concise way than in this article. As in the review of *Name the Man* as well as in numerous reviews of his films from the Swedish period, the quality of the human drama is here pointed out as Sjöström's distinctive mark. According to the critics, then, the threat of the US context seems to be that this specific emphasis might be lost. It is also striking that the comments on this particular point disappear from *Filmjournalen* reviews after *Confessions of a Queen*. We will return to the issue of human drama in the discussion of American reviews where it is mentioned as well.

At the same time, it is clear from the review that American know-how is much admired – even the most European-minded critic obviously feels obliged to admit the superiority of Hollywood narration in these respects. Still, European quality seems to be something that has to be preserved at all costs in an environment full of risks. The two different contexts of film production are often contrasted with one another in this way: European qualities or projects have to be cunningly implemented and/or energetically defended in the US. This strange mixture of admiration and contempt recurs in the reviews.

The critic concludes that *Confessions of a Queen* is a minor film. 'But why shouldn't a great artist also on some occasions be allowed to rest? In any case, the film is incomparably superior to the standard productions that the dollar country spreads over the world: if it doesn't move, at least it entertains and diverts.' This duality between the great artist on one hand and the gigantic Hollywood machinery for mass productions where he is put to work on the other hand, appears as a favourite figure in the rhetoric of several critics.[22]

In discussing *The Tower of Lies* (1925), 'Spes' especially mentions the triumph that it meant to Sjöström to bring Swedish Nobel prize-winner Selma Lagerlöf's *Kejsaren av Portugallien* to the screen in Hollywood, having made no less than four films from her books in Sweden. 'Spes' then goes on to complain about the 'compulsory concession to the demands of American producers' – a happy end to the sad story. However, he notes that the Swedish version lacked this 'superfluous ending'.[23] Yuri Tsivian has pointed out that Russian pre-Revolutionary cinema usually contained two endings, a tragic version for Russian distribution and a happy end for export.[24] This Russian preference for tragic endings seems to a certain extent to have been shared by Swedes; at least they too strive for fidelity with regard to the final tragedies in literary sources. In an interview, Stiller relates how a British company wished for an alternative, happy end to *Herr Arnes pengar*, a request, however, that the director refused.[25]

The shortcoming of Sjöström's as to the ending of *The Tower of Lies* also has to be related to the scrupulous respect that was generally paid to Selma Lagerlöf's original plot outlines in the context of Swedish production. The author was offered rights, if not to the final cut, at least to a kind of veto as to the shape of the manuscript. Stiller, however, on a couple of occasions, ignored the explicit requests of Lagerlöf, while Sjöström in Sweden always remained faithful to her authorial vision. It might be relevant to keep this background in mind when reading the review of *The Scarlet Letter* (1927) under the headline, 'A brilliant renaissance for "our own" Victor Sjöström'. According to this critic, there was a need for renewal after several quite similar American productions where no room was left for anything specifically Swedish. Still, it is the particular national quality that remains the focus of interest:

So far, Victor Sjöström [sic] American

productions have been strongly influenced by the yankee context: after the artistically weak 'Name the Man' followed the cosmopolitan 'He Who Gets Slapped' and then 'The Tower of Lies' which, in spite of the Selma Lagerlöf literary original, was a quite blurred Swedish-American mixture without Sjöström's narrative force. What makes 'the scarlet letter' [sic] all the more convincing is that Sjöström here has recovered, getting back to his old, Swedish self. On seeing this film, 'Vem dömer?'[*Mortal Clay*, 1922] comes to mind with which 'The Scarlet Letter' has much in common … This film seems more Swedish than American, which is meant as a way of recommending it. It is Swedish in the particular sense that was true of our films during the halcyon days …[26]

The explicit comparison to Sjöström's Swedish films, which had so far been absent from the commentaries on his Hollywood productions, comes back once again in the review of *The Wind* (1928) by 'M.W.': 'There is a striking resemblance between this mystic of no man's land and the mystic developed by Selma Lagerlöf in "Körkarlen" – secret forces are at work through supernatural impulses that poor earthly creatures are not able to penetrate.'[27] The introduction to the film in the advertising programme of the Stockholm cinema, China, also made the same comparison: 'its story about loving and struggling men is told with a fury, an absorbing intensity that brings Sjöström's Swedish masterpieces to mind'.[28] It is striking that this film presents the clearest divergences between Swedish and American reviews. Whereas the Swedish critics seemed to be even more enthusiastic than usual, their American colleagues on the contrary were quite negative; whereas Swedes saw the film as 'national' in its imagery of nature, Americans tended, as we shall see, to judge this symbolic quality as being too obvious.

As to *The Divine Woman* (1928), the *Filmjournalen* critic characterised the film as 'Greta Garbo's latest film'. Still, the reviewer – 'T.V.' – opens with the statement that Garbo's career, 'over there in the great dollar country', has raised a lot of questions, and that her earlier films had scarcely been convincing. In a somewhat contradictory manner, the critic then goes on to argue that in this particular case, the fact that Garbo had been working with two fellow citizens was important. Still, the main reason for the success that he points to 'is the strange hothouse temperature of California that has made this little woman from the southern [part of Stockholm] flourish with such lovely fragrance …'.[29]

It is not until the end of the review that Sjöström is mentioned at all, but then, as in the review of *The Scarlet Letter*, he is characterised as 'our own' Victor Sjöström. What is particularly striking is that such 'possessive' traits on the part of reviewers do not appear until quite late in the director's American career. It is as though the need to remind the audience of his Swedishness became more urgent as time passed by, to recapture him, as it were. But there is also a vein of national pride in these comments: a Swedish national director has made a great international success, and through him as well as through Garbo, Sweden has been put on Hollywood's map.

The next Sjöström film, *Masks of the Devil* (1928), was never reviewed in the proper sense of the word in *Filmjournalen*. Instead a short story containing a summary of the film's plot with some quotation from its dialogue was published with rich illustration.[30] The same mode of presentation was also used by the journal in the case of his last Hollywood production, *A Lady to Love* (1930).[31] It is both tempting and quite plausible to draw the conclusion that this choice was the result of an aesthetic evaluation of the films as being inferior to previous productions. Still, Sjöström remained a national symbol abroad, which made it difficult to pass public judgment concerning the quality of his films. Particularly noteworthy also is the relative lack of direct judgments as to the quality of Sjöström's work in Hollywood. In the rhetoric of the texts two alternative and partly contradictory readings are offered, and the conclusion often seems to be somewhere in between: even though there are obvious problems with these films, Sjöström remains true to himself and to good old Swedish traditions. Despite the generational change in the film press noted above and the shift of critical paradigm that the new generation inaugurated, these critics' arguments remained much the same as those during the 'golden age'. What, then, might be said of Sjöström's work by the critical institution in the country where he had arrived?

Reception in the US press

In discussing the American reception of 'Mr Seastrom's' work, I use examples from different newspapers and journals: *The New York Times, Motion Picture News, Exceptional Photoplays, Photoplay, Variety,* but privilege *The New York Times.* This choice might seem surprising, considering Richard Koszarski's claim that the newspaper in question 'was never very interested in motion pictures and gave them extremely low priority throughout the silent period'.[32] However, the dominance of one critic – Mordaunt Hall – is interesting to compare with Sven Stolpe's dominance in *Filmjournalen,* while the broadened perspective which several other contributors bring to the debate assures that a sufficiently wide perspective is presented.

Not surprisingly, the main difference between the American and the Swedish reviews seems to lie in their respective perspectives: while the Swedes compare 'their' director to his new context, critics in the United States evaluate the newcomer in the light of his international contribution to American national cinema. In a couple of articles in *Photoplay* under headings such as 'The Foreign Legion in Hollywood' and, adopting the same military trope, 'The Swedish Invasion', Metro-Goldwyn-Mayer's strategy of bringing European directors to Hollywood is discussed. The 're-discovery of America by the Norsemen' is one aspect that is discussed, another being the threat this might pose American talent. In an article published in July 1926 it is claimed that the foreigners 'are playing their own game together against American producer, director and actor alike', and that Americans have become foreigners in the Scandinavian colony.[33]

As to Sjöström's films, the reception they were accorded varied from the outset: *Name the Man* was enthusiastically received in *Variety,*

while the *New York Times* critic was more sceptical. Both mentioned the fact that the director was foreign, 'Fred.', observing more generally in *Variety*: 'However much depends on the story, and the cast, it is the direction that is going to go a long way toward carrying it to success. It is another proof that the foreign directors when given American casts and American co-operation in production can come pretty near topping all of the regular run of American directors with the exception of a few in the matter of detail.'[34] As to the *New York Times* critic, he also brings up the economic aspect – one of the clearest differences between American and Swedish systems of production – which was often mentioned by Swedish critics as well. This review seems to suggest that the director had difficulties in adapting to the new production context:

> Those familiar with the film work of Victor Seastrom, the noted Swedish director, know and admire his penchant for strong dramatic subjects ... Mr Seastrom's first production to be made in America is 'Name the Man,' an adaptation of Sir Hall Caine's novel 'The Master of Man' ... 'Name the Man' is therefore a Manxman's narrative of his native heath – the Isle of Man – produced by a Swede in America, and, although it is a dramatic story, it is doubtful whether Mr. Seastrom is at his best under the burden of such a combination. Where Mr. Seastrom ignored monetary appeal, the producers of this picture have obviously insisted on a production that would be a strong box-office attraction, both in the title and the theme. It does not seem to us that this director saw eye to eye with his story in certain incidents, and occasionally where he had an original idea he has dwelt on it at such length that the effect is frequently diminished and occasionally spoiled.[35]

As we have seen, the director's preference for 'strong dramatic subjects' mentioned in the review also recurred in the Swedish press, as Sven Stolpe's review of *He Who Gets Slapped,* cited above indicates. However, Swedish comments tended to stress the importance of these subjects which seemed even to conceal the faults of the films. It is as though the director was able to extract dramatic qualities

even from mediocre stories. In the US, the critics make a clearer distinction between the story on one hand and the director's contribution on the other. A good example of this distinction may be found one year later, as the same characteristic trait is pointed out by Mordaunt Hall in *The New York Times* when discussing *Confessions of a Queen*: 'It is hardly the story suited to Mr Seastrom, whose real forte is in the picturing of heavy dramatic subjects.'[36] In the case of his second American film, Seastrom had worked on the manuscript with Carey Wilson (the only script on which Seastrom worked in Hollywood), a fact that isn't mentioned in the reviews. However, by hinting at the way in which Hollywood provided a finished script without regard to the director's special skills, the critic touched on one of the most central aspects of the difference between the Swedish method of production (with directorial control from script stage to editing) and that of the American system, largely based on a division of labour.[37]

Before *Confessions of a Queen*, however, Seastrom had also directed *He Who Gets Slapped*, a production which turned out to be quite successful in America and was generally well received by the critics. The *Photoplay* critic contrasted the film to the previous failure:

> When Victor Seastrom presented his version of Hall Caine's 'Name the Man' we were disappointed. He failed to rise much above the level of a fourth rate novel. But this adaption of Leonid Andreyev's 'He Who Gets Slapped' is a superb thing – and it lifts Seastrom to the very front rank of directors.[38]

Mordaunt Hall in *The New York Times* was equally enthusiastic about the production: 'Mr Seastrom has directed this dramatic story with all the genius of a Chaplin or a Lubitsch, and he has accomplished more than they have in their respective works'.[39] The comparison with Lubitsch, which also occurred elsewhere (in this case also with Griffith), is particularly interesting as Lubitsch had also come from Europe; still, in the comparison, he is discussed as an American director.[40] As we shall see, there is a similar tendency in the reviews of Seastrom's later films of the Hollywood period; apparently, the imported workers be-

came naturalised relatively quickly by the motion picture industry. But Seastrom's work was not only compared with other great names of film history, but also with his own accomplishments in other films. A quote from the review in *Exceptional Photoplays* shows that the critic was particularly sensitive to Seastrom's capacity for low-key effects: 'The picture is full of typical Seastrom effects. He is a master of light and shade and knows how to get the most out of his groupings without using huge mobs.'[41] Here again, the critic apparently establishes a contrast, albeit implicit, between Hollywood and the small-scale mode of production with which the director was used to working.

In *The New York Times'* review of *The Scarlet Letter*, Mordaunt Hall also made reference to the director's previous films: ' "The Scarlet Letter" was directed by Victor Seastrom, an earnest Swedish director who gained no little fame through his production "The Stroke of Midnight", a picture which has never been exhibited publicly in this country. Mr Seastrom also made the film version of "He Who Gets Slapped".'[42] In this review, however, it is striking that the reason for mentioning these earlier films seems less the comparison this allows, than the fact that the director needs to be reintroduced in the American context where he had been praised in most spectacular terms only two years earlier.

The cause of this decline is to be found in 1925 – a year before *The Scarlet Letter* – with Seastrom's direction of *The Tower of Lies*. Once again, the American critics turned out to be more ambivalent in their reception of the film. Mordaunt Hall, as usual, comments in *The New York Times*, but this time quite sceptically:

> As this Swedish narrative is told, it is more of a short story or a sketch than a photodrama ... Ian Keith, as the successful wooer, is never in need of a haircut or shave. He looks as if he had stepped from a Hollywood ballroom floor to the farm fields of Sweden.[43]

Still, Hall gives some credit to the director: '... in certain stretches the hand of Victor Seastrom, the artist, is revealed'.[44] In *Photoplay* on the other hand, the critic 'A. S.' opens

with the following statement: 'If the director had been as concerned with telling the story as he was with thinking up symbolic scenes, this would have been a great picture. As it is, Victor Seastrom was so busy being artistic that he forgot to be human.'[45] This is, to my knowledge, the first time that a new theme appears in the reviews, where Seastrom is accused of being a formalist at the cost of precisely those human, dramatic or psychological qualities that formerly had been praised, not least in his Swedish productions. As we shall see, this theme reappears as may be observed in several reviews of *The Wind*. But the scepticism these two critics display was not shared by the reviewer in *Exceptional Photoplays* who, on the contrary, insists on the particular low-key qualities of Seastrom's work, probably more typical of Swedish cinema than of Hollywood: 'For this picture is different. It is an attempt to tell a story largely through the powers of suggestion and calls upon the audience to use its imagination instead of anticipating the obvious.'[46] The reception of *The Wind*, however, was unanimously critical. Interestingly enough, in one review, Seastrom has become American; he is mentioned among 'our' directors, sharing their problematic qualities, and he is criticised for having forgotten his special Scandinavian touch. The obviousness with which he is now accused turns out to be the same characteristic of Hollywood cinema – which has been named an excessively obvious cinema – that he was previously said to have avoided in *The Tower of Lies*:

> The film shows one bad tendency of our directors and scenarists, its atmospheric chord is twanged too often. In the present case in their anxiety to make the wind felt and heard (and sound synchronisation will only make matters worse), they have blown the bellows and shoveled the sand over-long and with too much energy. It is surprising that Victor Seastrom, noted in his Scandinavian days for his eerie touch and delicate hintings, should so far have lost sight of the art of suggestion in a story made exclusively to his hand as to have, so to speak, piled it on until the illusion is well nigh buried under and winnowed away. What might have become imagina-

tive cinema has been made obvious movie, no matter what excellent movie it may be.[47]

Mordaunt Hall in *The New York Times* is even more sharp in his comments on the film. Seastrom this time is accused of having overworked the film, the result thus becoming too obvious:

> Victor Seastrom hammers home his points until one longs for just a suggestion of subtlety. The villain's sinister smile appears to last until his dying breath. Mr Seastrom's wind is like some of the vocal effects in sound pictures, for nobody can deny its power, but it comes in strict continuity, with seldom the impression of a gust. And instead of getting along with the story, Mr. Seastrom makes his production very tedious by constantly calling attention to the result of the wind. If it were realistic, it would all be very well, but it isn't. Sand and dust are discovered on the bread, on the dishes, on the sheets, and wherever Letty (Miss Gish), a spiritual young Virginian, turns.[48]

In *The New York Times* review of *The Divine Woman*, Seastrom is once again noted as a Swede, together with his leading actors. The text appears as somewhat contradictory, at first emphasising the importance of the Swedes to the finished film, but then immediately going on to point out the director's complete lack of artistic ability:

> Sweden is responsible for most of this production, for besides the usually fascinating Miss Garbo, who hails from the land of Northern Lights, there are her compatriots, the leading man, Lars Hanson, and the director, Victor Seastrom. It is to be assumed that the lethargy of this production is due to Mr Seastrom, who has good ideas, but when it comes to putting them in motion he does it so that in this instance the effect is hopelessly artless. Hence, although the decorations, costumes and properties are exactly what one could hope for, the characters seem to have no more depth than the shadows that meet the eye.[49]

Here again, human qualities and psychological character portrayal are perceived to have

failed. This stands in sharp contrast to the reviews of his Swedish or his early American productions where character portrayal is emphasised as one of the main qualities of the films. This negative tendency continued in the reviews of Seastrom's next film, *The Masks of the Devil*, where the critic is overtly contemptuous:

> The characters in this production, which was directed by Victor Seastrom, dangle rather than live, and yet their weird conduct is not uninteresting ... Blossoms and the sunshine invariably accompany a love-lorn scene in motion pictures, and so they are not neglected here, and Mr Seastrom elicits a little comedy from a sudden thunderstorm. Then, after having made use of the rain, he tops it off with a further outburst from Old Sol and smiles from his people.[50]

Seastrom's last Hollywood film, *A Lady to Love*, is treated with the same coldness. Here, too, character portrayal is dismissed by *The New York Times*, albeit ' ... with at least one performance, that of Edward G. Robinson, arising out of the mist of only fair direction, and a striving by the other players toward realism that just misses being excellent'.[51] According to the *Telegraph* critic, there is also a tendency in this film to overdo the direction, something of which Seastrom was accused by critics reviewing *The Wind*. 'Unfortunately, however, Mr Victor Seastrom has directed the piece with a great deal more patience than imagination. He has put into it every word, every gesture, every shading; nothing has been left undone. On the contrary, almost everything has been overdone, with the frequent result that the picture becomes tiresome.'[52] This severe judgment is all the more striking as it is contrasted, in positive terms, with the grand theme of the film, its good story, and the equally good cast.

With the exception of *The Divine Woman*, the perspective of reviewers of the director's later American films seems to have changed. Whereas in the earlier films the director was often pointed out as a foreigner in Hollywood (for better and for worse), he is now treated as if he were American, i.e. as part of the system. The emphasis is altered: instead of discussing the particular Seastrom qualities,

with more or less explicit references to his Swedish background, the critics now undertake a general evaluation of his directorial know-how, noting, in particular, his shortcomings.

Returning to Europe

Relatively few commentaries in the American or Swedish press greeted Seastrom as he returned to being Sjöström in Sweden. On the occasion of his comeback to Swedish production with *Markurells i Wadköping* (1931), however, Sven Stolpe wrote in *Filmjournalen* that the event was remarkable from several points of view:

> This is the last time that we meet a work of Hjalmar Bergman's on the screen, and it is the first time after his American sojourn that Victor Sjöström appears in a Swedish film as director and actor ... Much has been said and written on the loss that Sjöström's American engagement made on Swedish cinema. Now that he is finally back and even appears as an actor in a talkie, he is to be welcomed both with emotion and emphasis. In truth – we needed him![53]

The Swedish discourse on Sjöström's return to Sweden thus seems to choose the path of recognising his greatness and, as it were, regards his comeback as an achievement for national cinema. This mode of interpretation efficiently covers the possibility that his reason for leaving Hollywood may quite simply have arisen from the failure of the last films that he directed in the US.[54]

What is most striking in this connection is the way in which European traditions are contrasted with American technological competence, an aspect which is both admired and despised. But the worst problem of all, according to the critics, seems to be the dollars, the difference in economic conditions that attends a comparison of the Hollywood system with the small national cinemas of Europe. Thus, implicit to these reviews and articles is a warning that European directors in Hollywood have to take care so as to avoid being too influenced by their new context. The promises Hollywood seems to offer might impress them on a superficial level, but at the

same time, the critics obviously claim that it remains a dangerous threat to a director's independence and their particular, national genius.

An article by Frank Tilley in the British journal *Kinematograph Weekly*, which received much attention in Sweden, is also particularly interesting from this point of view. The article was paraphrased in *Filmnyheter* under the headline 'Victor Sjöström the renewer of American cinema', but also quoted almost *in extenso* in *Svenska Dagbladet*.[55] Tilley claims that Sjöström's departure for Hollywood was one of the most important events in the history of cinema as he had helped create 'a new spirit', a film culture existing in Sweden but remarkably absent from America. He then goes on to brand American cinema as false and pretentious, and admonishes Sjöström for becoming too American. Removed from Swedish traditions, he might without noticing be too influenced by his new environment, and this would be 'the worst crime, the biggest vandalism ever committed' by Hollywood, which, according to the author, is already guilty of numerous similar crimes.[56] An article from the following issue of *Filmnyheter* discusses 'Victor Sjöström's responsibility towards his new mission', and quotes Sjöström who claims that 'at home, we have no idea of the vastness of the abyss separating European art from American – NB, I say this without any implicit critique. The whole thing is a matter of opinion and taste.'[57]

The process of contrasting Europe with America is, of course, not limited to the Swedish press. The British example referred to above indicates that in widening the perspective to other European countries, many similarities between the different European national cinemas in their attitudes towards Hollywood are revealed. However, not all shared the views of the critical establishment. Sabine Hake gives an account of the opposite point of view towards American film in European film criticism when she discusses the particular case of Herbert Ihering. Obviously, there was no general agreement in Europe on the superiority of European national cinemas and on the need to reject Hollywood cinema. In Hake's words: 'Ihering warned against the imitation of American methods but, at the

same time, defended Americanisation as a necessary part of the filmic condition'.[58] But towards the end of the 1920s, Ihering changed his opinion in favour of a more critical judgment wherein Hollywood cinema was now seen as 'a form of cultural imperialism'.[59] Still, he characterised German cinema as being nationalistic and not genuinely national (i.e. authentic) in its expression. According to Thomas J. Saunders, however, there was a more general shift in attitudes towards film cultures in Germany during the first half of the 1920s. At first, American cinema was held in high esteem, but gradually, German national cinema won recognition as being superior to Hollywood, with arguments similar to those used in the Swedish press.[60] In France, the whole debate is summarised by Emile Vuillermoz:

> The French cinema is about to perish. Its demise is no more than a matter of months … French filmmakers then either will have to become Americanised under the guidance of the American film companies [harbingers of a regularised aesthetic] or else disappear.

> That is distressing. All hope of raising the intellectual level of the cinema seems more and more chimerical. American technique has reached an unmistakable state where its commercial quality enjoys a level of competition we can only envy. But the artistic value of their production is no longer improving.[61]

If, thus, European critics to a large extent – although not without noteworthy exceptions – remained sceptical towards Hollywood, it is clear from the choice of reviews cited above that the discourse surrounding the Europeans and, in particular, the Scandinavians in America was equally ambivalent. From the invasion of the 'Norsemen' to admiration for their special skills and traditions; from mentioning Seastrom as a foreigner to his complete incorporation as a Hollywood director, the scope is wide. Some particular points, however, might be noted. The contrast or even competition between two different cinema cultures remains at the very centre of discussion. That the European colony is considered a threat to American talent indicates a certain

cultural complexity which corresponds well with the arrogance sometimes expressed in European articles. References to the great Scandinavian days of the Swedish director also point in this direction.

On the other hand, many critics seem just as convinced of the superiority of the Hollywood system. This is clear from the above-cited expression 'Sweden is responsible for most of this production' which seems more to indicate a liability than an accomplishment. Likewise, it is expressed in the opinion that foreigners may become very successful through their collaboration with American actors and producers, and by the comparison between the newcomers and American directors, be they native-born or naturalised. The tendency to incorporate foreigners in the system is quite clear, which in Seastrom's case is followed by a rejection of his directorial abilities. His original contract in Hollywood stated that he would be granted the right to approve the final script version and to choose the actors, the assistant director, and the cinematographer as well as supervise the editing.[62] However, these exceptional conditions of work seem to have been quickly reduced in direct proportion to the degree that the director became Americanised. As an American director amongst others, he no longer held any particular interest for the critics.

What seems to be the main argument for critics discussing European filmmakers, and more specifically Sjöström in Hollywood, then, is 'the case for quality', where specific cinema cultures are generally evaluated according to different qualitative criteria. To Swedish critics, quality seems to be the moral characteristic of a film, designating its seriousness of purpose, i.e. the earnest search for a truthful, artistic rendering of life – Sjöström's celebrated human qualities – together with a certain ideological emphasis, where dollars in particular are of low value. To American critics, on the contrary, quality is largely synonymous with technical know-how, even though the purpose may be the same, i.e. character portrayal characterised by skilfulness and depth.

In the conceptualisation of cinema which attends Sjöström's American productions, political questions – the distinction between art and commercialism, films produced by a small national cinema industry compared with technically advanced Hollywood productions – are generally central. The discourse formation in Sweden and America thus reveals a gap concerning two different cinema cultures that remains to be analysed in the case of Sjöström, both from a stylistic point of view and from the more general perspective of reception studies.

Notes

1. See *Filmjournalen* 6, 22 (1924): 435, G. Charensol, *Panorama du cinéma* (Paris: Éditions Kra, 1930), Forsyth Hardy, *Scandinavian Film* (London: The Falcon Press, 1952).
2. *Film och Scen* 1, 1 (3 October 1927): 10.
3. Sabine Hake, *The Cinema's Third Machine: Writing on Film in Germany 1907–1933* (Lincoln, London: University of Nebraska Press, 1993), xi.
4. Janet Staiger, *Interpreting Films: Studies in the Historical Reception of American Cinema* (Princeton: Princeton University Press, 1992), 95.
5. Elisabeth Liljedahl, *Stumfilmen i Sverige – kritik och debatt, Hur samtiden värderade den nya konstarten* (Stockholm: Proprius, 1975); Jan Olsson (ed.), *I offentlighetens ljus, Stumfilmens affischer, kritiker, stjärnor och musik,* (Stockholm/Stehag: Symposion bokförlag, 1990); Jan Olsson, 'Svart på vitt: film, makt och censur', *Aura. Filmvetenskaplig tidskrift* 1, 1 (1995): 14–46; Bengt Forslund, *Victor Sjöström, hans liv och verk* (Stockholm, Bonniers, 1980).
6. 'Filmens nationella uppgifter', *Filmen* 3 (1919): 1.
7. 'Inför sommarens inspelningsoffensiv', *Filmjournalen* 2, 7 (1920): 210.
8. *Stockholms Dagblad*, 3 February 1920.
9. The English-language titles for these films are, respectively, The Girl from the Marsh Croft, 1917; Ingmar's Sons, 1919; Sir Arne's Treasure, 1919; The Stroke of Midnight, 1921.
10. *Svenska Dagbladet*, 2 January 1923.
11. *Filmjournalen* 6, 15 (1924).

12. Jan Olsson also notes this change in *I offentlighetens ljus*, 272.
13. This key role of *Filmjournalen* is confirmed both by Jan Olsson in his study of the press in the era of silent cinema, see Jan Olsson, *I offentlighetens ljus*, 272, and my analysis of the press reception of the films of the Swedish 'golden age' in Bo Florin, *Den nationella stilen, Studier i den svenska filmens guldålder*, Doctoral Dissertation, (Stockholm: Aura förlag, 1997), 31–66. Olsson also mentions the 'monopoly' of *Filmjournalen* which had became an imperative for a whole new generation characterised by the ideals of the Hollywood dream factory.
14. *Filmnyheter* 34 (1923): 5.
15. *Filmnyheter* 2 (1923): 2.
16. *Filmnyheter* 9 (1924): 1.
17. *Filmnyheter* 8 (1924): 4.
18. *Filmjournalen* 6, 15 (1924).
19. *Filmjournalen* 6, 7 (1924): 122.
20. *Filmjournalen* 7, 23–24 (1925): 394.
21. *Filmjournalen* 8, 1 (1926): 8.
22. See, for example, *Filmnyheter* 2 (1923).
23. *Filmjournalen* 8, 16 (1926): 505.
24. Yuri Tsivian, 'Some Preparatory Remarks on Russian Cinema', in Paolo Cherchi Usai and Yuri Tsivian (eds.), *Silent Witnesses: Russian Films 1908–1919* (Pordenone: Edizione Biblioteca dell'Immagine, and London: BFI, 1989), 24, 26.
25. *Filmnyheter* 6 (1920): 6.
26. *Filmjournalen* 9, 2 (1927): 42–43.
27. *Filmjournalen* 10, 20–22 (1928): 14.
28. *China Filmnytt* (October 1928).
29. *Filmjournalen* 10, 5 (1928): 18.
30. *Filmjournalen* 11, 10 (1929): 20–24, 29.
31. *Filmjournalen* 12, 14 (1930): 18–21, 25.
32. Richard Koszarski, *An Evening's Entertainment: The Age of the Silent Feature Picture, 1915–1928* (Berkeley, Los Angeles, London: University of California Press, 1990), in particular chapter 7, 'Watching the Screen', 191.
33. *Photoplay* (February 1926, July 1926).
34. *Variety*, 17 January 1924.
35. *The New York Times*, 24 March 1924.
36. *The New York Times*, 20 June 1925.
37. An analysis of this change is made by the author in 'From Sjöström to Seastrom' in a forthcoming issue of *Film History*.
38. *Photoplay* (January 1925).
39. *The New York Times*, 10 November 1924.
40. *Svenska Dagbladet*, 20 February 1923.
41. *Exceptional Photoplays* 5, 5 (October-November 1924).
42. *The New York Times*, 10 August 1926
43. *The New York Times*, 28 September 1925.
44. Ibid.
45. *Photoplay* (November 1925).
46. *Exceptional Photoplays* 6, 4 (November 1924).
47. *Film*, The National Board of Review Magazine (December 1928).
48. *The New York Times*, 5 November 1928.
49. *The New York Times*, 16 January 1928.
50. *The New York Times*, 26 November 1928.
51. *The New York Times*, 1 March 1930.
52. *Telegraph*, 3 February 1930.
53. *Filmjournalen* 13, 3 (1931): 4.
54. In his dissertation on Sjöström, Bengt Forslund discusses the various reasons for Sjöström's return

to Sweden. While Forslund mentions the restrictions of the Hollywood system which, according to Forslund, became oppressive after *The Wind* (see Bengt Forslund, *Victor Sjöström*, 269), he does not consider the more general issue of failure in Sjöström's Hollywood career.

55. *Filmnyheter* 9 (1923); *Svenska Dagbladet*, 20 February 1923.
56. Ibid.
57. Filmnyheter 10 (1923).
58. Sabine Hake, *The Cinema's Third Machine*, 116 ff.
59. Ibid., 119.
60. Thomas J. Saunders, *Hollywood in Berlin: American Cinema and Weimar Germany* (Berkeley, Los Angeles, London: University of California Press, 1994), 120 f.
61. Emile Vuillermoz, 'Before the Screen: Aesthetic' [1927], in Richard Abel (ed.), *French Film Theory and Criticism, 1907–1939*, I, *1907–1929* (Princeton: Princeton University Press, 1993), 225.
62. Contract signed 25 January 1923, preserved at the Swedish Film Institute, Stockholm, also quoted in Bengt Forslund, *Victor Sjöström*, 191.

Industrial Greta: Some Thoughts on an Industrial Film

Mats Björkin

Department of Cinema Studies, Stockholm University, 105 21 Stockholm, Sweden

Film's ability to document events and objects for its time and for the future in a comprehensible, truthful and immediate way, is now well-known to everybody. It is not necessary, therefore, to discuss cinema's importance for advertising and the archive.

In these words the Tullberg Film company, Sweden's leading industrial film production company during the 1920s, presented itself to its customers.[1] According to Tullberg, the company specialised in the production of advertising and archival films. They not only wanted to produce good films to promote companies, organisations, or Sweden as a nation; they wanted to produce films so good that they could survive as valuable archival documents. This strategy was not a serious concern for history or the nation's cultural heritage – it was business. Swedish industry and the Swedish government realised how useful films could be for promotional purposes.

The history of Swedish industrial film has yet to be written. This essay poses some questions that are important for research on the subject of early industrial films. I concentrate mainly on one company, Tullberg Film, not because they were first, but because their production policy during the 1920s was central to establishing industrial film as a well-known category.

Tullberg Film produced different sorts of films and was very keen on characterising them appropriately: industrial films, business films, educational films, home films, family films.[2] The manager of Tullberg Film, Ragnar Ring, also used another typology, not based on subject, but on the purpose of their films. This typology made it possible for Tullberg to argue that their films were more elaborate than those of their competitors. The first category used by Tullberg was 'industrial films'; relatively inexpensive films promoting an industry, which may include images and explanations of processes, not in order to document processes as such, but to show the technological sophistication of the company. According to Ragnar Ring in 1923, these films had limited importance in advertising and propaganda.[3] The second category was 'advertising films'. These were, according to Ring, more complicated to make in that they were short and had to be more sophisticated to impress the audience.[4] The third category was 'propaganda films', which were longer and had to be both informative and entertain-

ing.[5] This was the kind of film by which Tullberg became most famous, and these were the films Tullberg used to expose its own expertise. The fourth category was 'technical films'. A technical film described, explained and/or analysed technical processes. The most pertinent feature of the filmic image was its evidentiary status, though technical films were, according to Ring, the most cinematic. In order to present an industrial process, any cinematic means could be employed.[6] Technical films did not have to be about industrial or technological subjects. For Ring, a tourist film was, and had to be, a technical film. Ragnar Ring's categories are somewhat confusing, but his emphasis on narrative and visual construction and their elaboration is important to an understanding of the films made by him and the Tullberg film company.

Exactly how many films Tullberg produced is not known. Ring mentions in 1928 that he had made 300–400 films. I have so far only found notices for approximately two hundred films, of which about one hundred still exist. It is difficult, though, to decide how to count the films. Some of the films are made in different versions or, rather, remade a couple of times. A large number of the Tullberg films were also made for foreign audiences, and sometimes re-edited for screenings in different countries. It was not only a question of intertitles in different languages; they even re-edited the images. These problems concern the definition of individual films.

Another kind of film Tullberg produced was the long compilation film made for special occasions, for example, industrial or tourist expositions, or for special enterprises such as the Swedish battleship *HMS Fylgia*'s promotional voyages around the world. Only one of these films exists today, in an incomplete print at the Swedish Television Archive: *Sverige och svenska industrier* (Sweden and Swedish Industries), probably made in 1921 or 1922. The film is almost identical with *Tokiofilmen* (The Tokyo Film, 1922) made for the industrial exposition in Tokyo in 1922.

This five-part compilation film is presented with intertitles in English and Chinese. Each part begins with a very young Greta Gustafsson (Garbo) in front of a map of Sweden showing where in Sweden the following sequences take place. The first intertitle explains what the film is about: 'This series of motion pictures was made for the Swedish Government by Hasse W. Tullberg of Stockholm, for the purpose of spreading information about Sweden in the Far East'.[7]

The film begins in Stockholm, showing the City Hall (still under construction in 1922), the House of the Nobility, the Royal Dramatic Theatre, the Bank of Sweden, the Royal Palace, and the changing of the guard at the Royal Palace. The Stockholm Fire Brigade is then used to show different parts of the city. Then comes a section on the foundations of economic growth: The Royal Technical University of Stockholm, interior of a Swedish Commercial College, a modern Swedish Primary School, and the Free Port of Stockholm. Traditional city views and images of street life are put together to present Stockholm as a modern city with a reliable infrastructure and, most important, with an advanced educational system in the service of trade and industry.

Many of the opening shots were used in other films for different purposes, and put together here to establish the main argument: the economic growth and strength of Sweden and Swedish industry. At the same time a second and a third argument are presented: the economic power of the company is based on the nation's cultural and industrial traditions, and the basis for both development and tradition is the wealth of Swedish nature. All set in a beautiful landscape.

The transition from the establishing sequence of Stockholm to the first industry considered in the film is, therefore, secured via a ride through the landscape. From the harbour, the camera films from a boat to a town just outside Stockholm where the first industrial footage is presented: 'Instrument Aktiebolaget Navigator, makers of the Navigator Log, the principal automatic ship's log in the world'. This sequence shows the manufacture and assembly of the logs. The Navigator sequence does not give any close analysis of the production process, only a brief overview of assemblage and an indication of how advanced the Navigator technology was. The first part of the film ends with the export of the logs: 'A great number of large steamships

belonging to various countries have been fitted with Navigator Logs'.

If we read the Stockholm sequence and the Navigator sequence as the first impression a foreign audience will have of Sweden and Swedish industry, two things seem to be particularly important. First, Sweden should be seen as a highly developed country when it comes to infrastructure, education, trade and high-tech industry. Second, this high level of industrialisation is not only of local or regional importance in Northern Europe; the widespread use of Navigator logs is an example of the international importance of Swedish industry. Cinematically these sequences are very simple. They are, of course, valuable as documents of certain environments and interiors, but not much more than what could have been revealed by a photograph.

In part two Greta guides us to Gothenburg: 'The second largest city in Sweden is Gothenburg which is the largest export harbour'. Even Gothenburg is introduced through international trade. So far, part 1 and the first scenes in part 2 have concentrated on a collection of films with the purpose of showing and telling (via the written word). After the harbour, the film presents the second industrial sequence concerning the SKF Company (Volvo started as a part of the SKF company): 'The largest industrial establishment in Gothenburg is the Swedish Ball Bearing Co. (S.K.F. Co)'.

According to Tullberg's categories the footage from SKF could be seen as an industrial film, although there are many close views of the production process for manufacturing ball bearings. The film shows: the staff of workmen; workmen leaving the factory(!); interiors of different parts of the factory; automatic cold pressing of small balls; ball polishing, and how races, balls, and retainers are assembled.

The film then goes on to a short demonstration: 'The S.K.F. bearings are manufactured in many different sizes and are applied to all kind of machinery, trucks etc.' 'With a plain bearing of 70 mm. shaft diameter, 16 kilos coal brickettes are required per week to overcome the friction between the journal and the bearing.' 'To overcome the friction in an S.K.F.

ball bearing of corresponding size and for the same period are required only ... 2.4 kilos.' 'The S.K.F. bearing is self-aligning.' The SKF sequence only shows the wide range of ball bearings that the company produces. There are no detailed descriptions of the process, but for the close study of how ball bearings are assembled. This short scene not only presents the different parts (race, balls and retainer); it also demonstrates how the ball bearings were assembled by hand. The SKF sequence uses cinematic means (medium shots, close-ups and texts) in a more elaborate and analytic way to demonstrate an industrial process.

On the one hand it is possible to argue that the importance of the film as a document of a specific industrial process is the same in both the SKF and Navigator sequences. On the other hand, if we develop Ragnar Ring's categorisation and distinguish technical from industrial films by the different mode of analysis of a certain process, the SKF sequence can be seen in a different light. In using a technical sequence, mixed with many industrial sequences, Tullberg also privileges a specific process. Does this mean that the manual assembly of the ball bearing is especially important? When Ragnar Ring gave technical films a specific value as (historical) evidence, the filmic representation of the manual assembly of ball bearings is not only a document of a worker's skills. The film documents an argument that proposes that the strength of Swedish industry consists of the combination of high technology and skilled labour of such importance that it has to be recorded and saved for future posterity. If so, use of technical sequences in industrial compilation films ('propaganda films' in Tullberg's terminology) emphasises certain processes or products in order to present how important they were for Swedish industry. Maybe the technical sequences were also supposed to indicate that by using a modern technology such as cinema, the processes and products should be regarded as even more modern and advanced.

The film continues with images from the harbour of Malmö. Part two ends with scenic shots from a fishing village on the West Coast of Sweden, and some snowy winter scenes.

Part three begins with more snowy scenes, from the locks of Göta Canal to the state power plant in Trollhättan. The following intertitle explains that the General Swedish Electric Co, ASEA, makes the 175,000-horsepower electric generators. By this short journey the film has reached the most important part of Swedish industry at the time – electricity. The following scenes show different production units at the ASEA plants. The intertitles present all 'important' facts, in order to emphasise ASEA's strength: 'Allmaenna Svenska Elektriska A.B. (known by its initials as A.S.E.A.), Head Office and works for small motors, Vaesteraas [Västerås], Sweden. Delivered over 200.000 machines with a total capacity of about 7.000.000 horse power.' 'View showing interior of factory for large machines.' '24.000 kva alternator.' 'One of the workshops in A.S.E.A's factory for small motors.' 'Transformer factory.' 'Switchboard Department.' 'Electric locomotive 2.100 horsepower, constructed by A.S.E.A. for the Swedish Government Railways Ore transportation trains.'

The strong emphasis on 'industrial' sequences continues. Central to the treatment of ASEA is the promotion of international trade in transformers and other power plant equipment. It is also worth noting that the emphasis on transportation is maintained, from the Navigator logs and SKF ball bearings to ASEA's electric locomotives. Heavy Swedish industry was not to be regarded as conservative or provincial.

The film leaves ASEA, and begins to explain where the ASEA motors and transformers are used: 'The Saltsjoe [Saltsjö] Railway Stockholm 1.500 volt DC.' 'Some power stations with A.S.E.A. installations.' 'Sidney, Canada, capacity 4.000 kva.' 'Bullerforsen, Sweden, capacity 22.000 kva.' 'Rjukanfos, Norway, capacity 113.000 kva.' 'The Swedish government Power Station at Trollhaettan [Trollhättan]. Capacity 175.000 kva.'

The ASEA episode ends with the symbol of the company, a swastika. Some market scenes from Stockholm replace the heavy industry, but the film soon continues with the Swedish iron industry. Greta helps us to locate the most important companies. As in all Tullberg films of iron industries, these images really exploit the dramatic nature of the industrial process, while the intertitles explain what we see: 'Swedish iron is famous all over the world for its fine quality'. Map showing the location of iron mines and deposits. 'The S.K.F. Hofors Steel and Iron works in Central Sweden. Established in the 17th century.' 'The ore and the lime stone used for the iron manufacturing are obtained from the company's own mines.' 'A blast hole being bored 1230 feet under ground.' 'The blast furnace being charged.' 'Pig iron being tapped from the blast furnace.' 'Pig iron and waste steel are converted into steel in the Martin furnaces.' '– and cut into billets.' 'The ingot being rolled.' 'Steelwire being rolled.'

The iron sequence is the most analytic and visually elaborate sequence of the film. This is close to what Ring meant by 'technical film'. These close studies of mining and the iron industry were one of Tullberg's many specialities,[8] perhaps not surprising if we bear in mind how dramatic these processes were: hot, glowing iron, fire and smoke, huge industrial spaces etc.

Part four concentrates on the production of weapons, especially the Bofors company. In this episode the uses of the products are even more emphasised than in the ASEA episode of the film. In the Bofors film, Tullberg clearly shows what Ragnar Ring meant by propaganda. Here, descriptions of processes are combined with spectacular examples and images of the armed forces: 'Aktiebolaget Bofors (Bofors, Ltd). Founded in 1646, makers of guns.' 'The Bofors Ordnance and Steelworks make guns as a speciality.' 'Pressing of the gun casting.' 'Turning and boring.' 'The guns are hardened in this turret.' 'Grooving of the guns.' 'Mounting of the guns.' 'Manufacturing of shells.' 'Manufacturing and inspection of fuses.' 'A.B. Bofors Nobelkrut, Bofors, Sweden (The Nobel Gunpowder Works, Ltd). Makers of gunpowder.' 'Nobel gunpowder consists mainly of nitroglycerine and guncotton.' 'Manufacture of nitroglycerine and guncotton.' 'Manufacture of guncotton.' 'Mixing of nitroglycerine and guncotton.' 'Nobel gunpowder are moulded into tubes.' 'Swedish soldiers in the barracks and on the manoeuver fields.' 'The Commanding-general.'

The first Bofors films were made soon after

the end of the First World War. Sweden had stayed neutral during the War (and has argued for neutrality ever since). At the same time, the weapon industry has been well-integrated and a financially important part of Swedish industry during the twentieth century. In this film, the Bofors sequence (almost the entire fourth part of the film) has been placed after trade and infrastructure, mechanical technology, and basic iron and steel industry footage, all necessary foundations for the weapon industry.

After the basic ingredients of a modern industrial society, part four ends with a short film in a rural setting, a Swedish farm during harvest: 'The girls on the farm can both bind the grain by hand and drive harvesting machines'. ' "Grandfather" takes a hand in the work.' Tradition and modernisation go hand in hand in Tullberg's Sweden.

The fifth part of the film concentrates on another of Sweden's most important industries in the 1920s, the wood and timber industry. Again, Greta shows on the map where the economically most important forests, and the major sawmills and lumber factories are located. As in the other films, the texts explain what we see and give some background detail: 'Norrland, the Northern section of Sweden, is the center of the timber industry'. 'In spring, when the ice has melted, the logs are floated in "timber frames" in brooks and rivers down to the large sawmills on the coast.' 'Sawmills of a large lumber company.' 'The logs arrive at the sawmill and are measured branded and warped into the saw sheds.' 'The timber is sawn up into boards and deals.' 'The boards are cut in proper lengths and loaded for shipment.' 'Swedish spruce wood is converted into paper for the newspapers of many countries at the paper mills of the Holmens Bruk & Fabriks A.B., Hallstavik, Sweden.' 'Chemical woodpulp is produced by boiling the wood in various chemical solutions with the object of separat-ing the fibres.' 'Mechanical woodpulp is produced by grinding the wood into fine fibres.' 'Paperpulp is obtained by mixing the chemical and mechanical woodpulp.' 'The paper machines convert the paperpulp into newsprint.'

The film ends at Gripsholm Castle where a slow tracking shot stops in front of two Russian cannons. A very symbolic end, at a royal castle with cannons as trophies of past military victories. The message is clear: Swedish industry will continue that tradition, only this time we will sell the weapons, not use them.

Sverige and svenska industrier is only one example out of almost one hundred films produced by Tullberg Film that survive in archives in Sweden. Most of them can be found at the Swedish Film Institute and the Swedish Television Archive,[9] although some prints can be found at local archives around Sweden. The archival situation for industrial films is highly problematic. Like other early non-fiction films, these films have been neglected by archives and researchers, although their importance for historians and for film scholars cannot be overemphasised. Visually they are often quite compelling, especially films shot in steel works and mines. The ride in the Fagersta mine is one of the must beautiful scenes in Swedish films from the 1920s.

Sverige och svenska industrier may give a good picture of how Sweden and Swedish industry wanted to be seen in the 1920s: a peaceful country where tradition and modernisation go hand in hand with an industry that claims international importance. On the other hand, the film can be seen as a 'propaganda film' for a nation and an industry ready to make money from a Europe in ruins and a colonial world facing many more wars. Therefore, Tullberg Film was particularly far-sighted in using the young Greta Gustafsson, soon to be Greta Garbo, to promote the products you need for modern warfare.

Notes

1. *Tullberg Film* (Stockholm: Hasse W. Tullbergs förlag, 1923), 5.
2. The difference between home films and family films is not evident in their catalogues.
3. R. [Ragnar] L. [Lasse] Ring, *Kallprat om film* (Stockholm: Tullberg Films Förlag, 1928), 26.
4. Ibid., 27.

5. Ibid., 27.

6. Ibid., 30.

7. The intertitles cited in this essay are quoted as they appear in the film, including the anglicisation of Swedish names.

8. For example: *Fagersta Bruk* (1925), *Fagerstafilmen* (1925), *Kättingtillverkning vid Ljusne Woxna AB* (1925).

9. Many of the prints at the Swedish Film Institute cannot be viewed as they currently exist only as negatives.

Index

Page references in **Bold type** *refer to illustrations appearing in the text.*